New
Aldeburgh
Anthology

The *New Aldeburgh Anthology* takes its inspiration from Ronald Blythe's classic *Aldeburgh Anthology* of 1972, which summoned the spirit of Aldeburgh and the coast of east Suffolk in words and images that resonate still. This collection brings the story up to date, combining new voices, with old, those of writers and musicians with poets and artists, of historians with naturalists, architects and ecologists, and the people of Suffolk.

As with the original edition, Britten and Pears' Aldeburgh Festival and its descendant, Aldeburgh Music, lies at its heart. Much has changed, but Aldeburgh Music still owes its unique appeal to the inspiration of its founders, as well as to their strong sense of place. Here their legacy is considered by many musicians and writers. Aldeburgh and its surroundings are about so much more than music, so poets, writers and artists who have all been inspired by its bright yet haunting landscape contribute.

The very frontiers of east Suffolk are on the move, too, its coastline responding to the vagaries of climate change and traditional ways of life, of farming and fishing giving way to new. The long history of encroachment and defence stretches from the Viking incursions at Snape and Sutton Hoo to the secret airfields and bunkers of the Cold War.

Amongst its many debut contributions, the New Anthology contains some classic articles from the original by George Crabbe, E.M. Forster, W.H. Auden and of course Ronald Blythe himself. The result is a book that will appeal to those already drawn back to Aldeburgh year after year for its music and arts, but also to all who care for the landscape, the sea and the unique character and the life of the Suffolk Coast.

ARIANE BANKES has worked in publishing for many years and now combines running a small arts festival with freelance writing and reviewing. She first attended the Aldeburgh Festival as a Hesse Student in 1974 and has returned regularly ever since.

JONATHAN REEKIE became Chief Executive of Aldeburgh Music in 1997. Prior to that he worked for Musica nel Chiostro, Batignano, Glyndebourne, and the Almeida Theatre.

Aldeburgh Music
Snape Maltings Concert Hall
Saxmundham
Suffolk IP17 1SP
www.aldeburgh.co.uk

Cover photograph: Peter Silk

New Aldeburgh Anthology

Compiled by
Ariane Bankes and
Jonathan Reekie

Foreword by
Ronald Blythe

Aldeburgh Music
The Boydell Press

First published 2009
The Boydell Press, Woodbridge
Reprinted in paperback 2010
ISBN 978-1-84383-588-2

*For Honor and Rosie, growing up in Suffolk,
and in memory of Celia*

The Boydell Press is an imprint of Boydell & Brewer Ltd
PO Box 9, Woodbridge, Suffolk IP12 3DF, UK
and of Boydell & Brewer Inc.
668 Mt Hope Avenue, Rochester, NY 14620, USA
website: www.boydellandbrewer.com

A catalogue record for this book is available
from the British Library

This publication is printed on acid-free paper
Printed in Great Britain by
CPI Antony Rowe, Chippenham, Wiltshire

Contents

6
Where Have You Come From?
VISITORS

7
Water Married to Stone
THE HUMAN LANDSCAPE

8
Beneath the Dazzling Sky
LAND, RIVER AND MARSH

List of Plates

BILL BRANDT

Foreword
Ronald Blythe

This wonderful book could not have – in their wildest hopes for the future – been imagined by the three young men who, just after the war, determined to cease wandering and to settle for a music festival on the Suffolk coast. Neither they nor Aldeburgh itself could have foreseen what would flow from this decision, nor would they have given any thought to it. For them the excitement was in the present. The very austerity of both the time and the place suited what they had to do. In 1948 the shingle was still littered with concrete blocks and barbed wire, the vast river of herring was vanishing, the industrial enterprises of the Garrett brothers were failing and the local accommodation for Festival audiences verged on the severe. There is no more accurate account of those early days than Imogen Holst's Diary.

And yet, what happened! The historic severity of this coast inspired a distinctive type of creativity which can now, via these vivid contributions, be seen not as a 'school' but as something which does not exist elsewhere. Thus this second *Aldeburgh Anthology* has the dual quality of being both an absorbing read and an important addition to our understanding of the arts – and music in particular – during the late twentieth century. They have thrived in a sharp climate. But then they always have, as anyone can see when they look up at the medieval oak and flint churches or into the stern couplets of George Crabbe. One of the most engaging things about these many writers, musicians, artists and photographers is the way in which Aldeburgh has 'got them'. Although they show every kind of response to it, the little town and its surrounding countryside seem to hold them in its grip. Just as they did its genius-interpreter Benjamin Britten. I would meet him on the marshes in the cold afternoons, not very wrapped up, walking lightly, the wind tearing at him, the sea sullen and Aldeburgh itself white in the near distance. It was etiquette not to see him, to walk on. To be 'working', as he was working at that moment. Many of these contributors are in their various way working walkers in that unique territory.

To give the necessary balance to so many gifted incomers, the *New Aldeburgh Anthology* allows Suffolk to speak for itself and in all kinds of voices. Local historians and fishermen, natives and 'foreigners' all put their oar in, so to speak, adding to the vigour of the selection. Almost everything said and done is cinematic to some degree, the East Coast weather dominating music, writing, painting, sailing, thought. All this atmosphere blows through the book and is present even where it isn't mentioned. It makes for clear statements. What should not astonish the reader, but which nevertheless does, is the variety of the contents. If nothing else, they remind the reader of the broad vision of 'Aldeburgh' from its early days to the present, and how it has always striven to include every talent.

Unlike most arts festivals, the Aldeburgh Festival doesn't fit into distinctive periods. Even the earthquake move from the Jubilee Hall to Snape Maltings now has a seamless feeling to it, the original spirit of the enterprise travelling with it. It was Garrett Anderson who built the Hall and his father-in-law who built the Maltings, so it could have been an inevitable progression. Devastation followed that move, then a brilliant renewal as music, marshland and architecture coalesce. Even after many visits, it is always exciting to arrive at Snape, to glimpse Iken through the reed-beds and, for myself, to have glimpsed the old maltsters raking the barley. And then, nearly as historic and phantom, to see Ben, Peter and Imo in their brick opera box. This is why the *New Anthology* is so pleasurable – and now and then so sad – because it is a series of evocations. A memory map, as Marina Warner would have called it.

It also shows writers, composers and artists quietly working away in the East Anglian villages and towns much as they ever did, and emerging now and then for festivities, and especially for Aldeburgh. The festival has always created a sense of 'belonging' and a mart, a place in which to shed for a day or two the isolation which the work demands. The region may now be filled with motorways, commuters, restaurants and all the movement of ordinary 21st-century life, and more or less emptied of the traditional workers, whether on the farm or on the boats, yet it retains its beauty. And never before, as many of these contributions witness, has there been such a passionate interest in its birds and plants, or such a knowledge of its peerless churches, or such care taken of its inherited treasures.

Had the *New Anthology* consisted of a score or two contributors I would have praised them by name. But it is no slight affair. The first and the latest 'Aldeburgh' people have their say in it, and what they tell us should last for ages to come. Ariane Bankes and Jonathan Reekie have been generous editors and a more satisfyingly representative crowd of East Anglian apologists it would be hard to find. For me there were so many old friends, so many new names, so much I knew backwards, so much I learned anew. And throughout it all there drifted the music, the witty lectures, the gossip, the bitter wind, the familiar voices saying, 'Come in.' And one sees the expansion, so that Aldeburgh in these pages is at Blythburgh, Orford, Framlingham, and everywhere in the world. Each one of us in different ways is a carrier of what we have heard.

What lingers with me is *Curlew River*, going to the Slaughden fair with Peggy Somerville, sleeping on a camp bed in the Moot Hall to guard the Millets on show there, and working alongside Imo at her father's desk. Other readers will have their own lists.

Introduction

The *New Aldeburgh Anthology* was inspired by Ronald Blythe's classic *Aldeburgh Anthology* of 1972, which so evocatively captured the essence of the Aldeburgh Festival and its setting in the landscape, culture and history of the Suffolk coast. Our own book began life when we were both (separately) approached by different publishers about a history of the Aldeburgh Festival. Whilst unquestionably a rich subject, we suggested that a project with broader appeal would be a new *Aldeburgh Anthology*, keeping to the spirit of the original but bringing the story right into the twenty-first century, encompassing all that is happening in and around Aldeburgh today.

It seemed particularly timely, as the original was compiled to raise money at a key moment in the history of what was then called the Snape Maltings Foundation. In 2009, as this book is published, Aldeburgh Music will undergo its biggest expansion for a generation. A major capital development creating new rehearsal and performance spaces at Snape Maltings will reinforce the Suffolk coast as one of the world's great centres for nurturing musical and artistic talent – a project that Britten and Pears were dreaming of back in 1972. This new initiative and the resulting growth in artistic and educational activity require finance, so the royalties from this book will go towards its support.

We were motivated, too, by the fact that the original *Anthology* is long out of print and second-hand copies much sought after, so it seemed a good idea to put together a new selection that weaves together classic pieces from the original with new commissions, the best of Aldeburgh Festival programme books since 1972 and numerous other writings with a Suffolk connection. A letter seeking Ronald Blythe's blessing was met with typically enthusiastic and generous endorsement, including anecdotes about the first *Anthology* that underlined what a rich range of possibilities there was.

In fact, that is precisely where our headaches began. How were we to define such a book, and how to limit it? Our premise, in theory, was simple: to gather together the best we could find – essays, fiction, reminiscences, poems, photographs, illustrations – by locals, visitors, artists and experts, and to supplement these with a range of new writings. Without setting out to be exhaustive or comprehensive, we have tried to capture the unique spirit of Aldeburgh and the Suffolk coast (roughly east of the A12 between the Rivers Deben to the south and the Waveney to the north). We wanted to give a sense of how Aldeburgh and its surroundings have evolved over the course of history, and in particular since the last Anthology was published. Benjamin Britten and Peter Pears and their legacy would provide the backbone, because – before non-musicians put this book back on the shelf – it is undeniable that their lives and work were inextricably bound up with Suffolk and the local community. The colourful threads of local and natural history, architecture, the visual arts, land and sea, ecology and economy all contribute to that elusive 'genius of place' that still defines Aldeburgh Music and its Festival and makes it so unique, and we have attempted to distil this between hard covers in both words and imagery. We hope thereby to have created something that appeals not just to music lovers but to lovers of Suffolk and all it represents.

The eight sections – opening with the sea and moving through Aldeburgh, its Festival and the lives of its inhabitants into the surrounding built and natural landscape – are loose groupings (to say the least) and some subjects intentionally crop up in more than one section. So much has been published on Britten and his music that we have largely turned our attention to pieces of a more human or personal nature and about his Suffolk roots.

Much like planning a festival, we have followed our own interests and inclinations in making our selection in the hope that if we have enjoyed an essay, memoir, image or poem, then our readers might, too. We hope we have created a book that can be read cover to cover or dipped into, with a mixture of the familiar, the rediscovered and the new – just like the Aldeburgh Festival itself, in fact.

Ariane Bankes and Jonathan Reekie

Snape Maltings with the new Britten Studio in 2009 (Photograph by Jeremy Young)

The Sea

George Crabbe

Turn to the watery world! – but who to thee
(a wonder yet unview'd) shall paint – the Sea?
Various and vast, sublime in all its forms,
When lull'd by Zephyrs, or when rous'd by Storms,
Its colours changing, when from clouds and Sun
Shades after shades upon the surface run;
Embrown'd and horrid now, and now serene,
In limpid blue, and evanescent green;
And oft the foggy banks on ocean lie,
Lift the fair sail, and cheat th'experienc'd Eye.

From *The Borough*, 1810

Glitter
waves

'Glitter of waves
And glitter of sunlight
Bid us rejoice
And lift our hearts on high.'

Ellen Orford in *Peter Grimes*
Act 2

The Suffolk Sea

Julian Tennyson

Yes, in Suffolk we are at odds with nature: we are pitted against that most cruel and impassive of enemies, the sea.

Oh, so slowly does it beleaguer us! Could you see it in summer, drawling up the beach, brushing the shingle with coquettish lips, so gentle, so harmless, so indolent, you would scoff at the idea of evil lurking in that serene and imperturbable bosom. But come to it in winter, when the same innocent sluggard is grey and cold, when the great white waves come driving in to crash and snarl against the shore, when the fishermen stand helpless on the beach beside their little boats and the wildfowl chatter uneasily in the safety of the rivers and the marshes – come back to Suffolk then, and see how dreadful is the change from meekness to ferocity. Edward FitzGerald once said: 'There is no sea like the Aldeburgh sea. It *talks* to me.' I've no doubt that there were times when it roared at him, too.

The devastation known as coast erosion has been going on for hundreds of years. I believe that a disaster was first recorded in the time of Edward the Confessor. That is one of the terrors of it: it is as slow, as fraught with the tortures of suspense as is the dragging inevitability of a cancer. Awful to think that a thousand years ago our ancestors struggled against it, succumbed to it, just as today we struggle and just as we succumb. Those hardy Suffolk men, were they not driven from their homes, did not their towns and villages crumble about them and go crashing down into the gluttonous waves – towns and villages that have never been rebuilt? What could they do? They fought, they cursed, they strained their brawny shoulders to the breach, but what could they do? They could only retreat and watch their dear creations torn into ugly, shapeless lumps of brick and stone, half buried beneath the sea. And what can we do? Nothing, it seems. We are as impotent as they.

As a continuous encroachment it is hardly noticeable. For fifty years, perhaps, the North Sea will appear as innocuous as a lily-pond in summer, and the scare of erosion will die away until an irresponsible generation has forgotten it altogether. And then it will come again, suddenly, furiously, with the sea storming up the shore – and there will be nothing to stop it.

Erosion came last year – and it came as a veritable flood. In February I went to Minsmere marshes: they didn't exist. In their place was a huge lake that lapped about the edges of the woods on Westleton heath, two feet of salt water which killed every living thing that could not get out of its way – trees, fish and thousands of rats. It did not stay for long; the sluice was opened and it went gracefully back, leaving a surface of sand and shingle on the marshes and a gaping breach in the sea wall to be repaired by a gang of workmen. The poor sea wall – what a pitiful defence!

A house gradually destroyed by the sea at Slaughden

I went to Aldeburgh, where the sea washed over the High Street, obliterated the road to Slaughden Quay, and put the last touches to the destruction of that lonely red-brick house on the shore in a dark corner of which Bob the fisherman used to boast that he was born. I saw the lake that covered the town marshes teeming with flocks of widgeon, and heard the worthies cursing because the shooting season had closed less than a week before – their homes and their land might be in peril, but to those sturdy sportsmen wildfowling came first. At the far end of the marsh the sea and the river struggled to reach each other: a few inches of river wall kept them apart. Had they once come together, God knows what would have happened. The wall held at Aldeburgh, but not at Iken. I went to Iken in August, intending to walk over the lovely marsh stretching up to Snape Bridge; I found it a brown, filthy, stagnant, stinking swamp, a muddy morass of leering, oily pools, at the back of which sprawled the ancient trees on the edge of the wood, gaunt and misshapen and hideously naked. Why, I wondered, had the good people of Iken not let the water out, chased it out, forced it out? I found that I wronged them. They had chased it out. And every time they chased it out it came rushing in again through a hopeless gap in the wall, until they gave up in despair and waited for the fury to subside. Then they set about repairing the breach, and they were still doing it in the middle of the following winter. For a hundred yards inland at this point the ground was strewn with grotesque, rock-like lumps of mud which the force of the tide had torn up from the bed of the river and hurled through the breach. From end to end the poor marsh looked like a battlefield after some annihilating bombardment.

Thus it was all down the coast. Southwold, I was told, though I did not see it, was a perfect island, stranded by the flooding of the Blyth behind and below it and the onslaught of the sea above.

From *Suffolk Scene*, 1939, reprinted by Alastair Press, 1987

Ramsholt to Shingle Street: a sea voyage with interludes
Richard Barber

We park the bikes behind the trees next to the dinghy park. It is almost sacrilege to have to lock them, for this is Ramsholt at nine on a Sunday morning, as quiet a place as you could hope to find. We row out to the mooring, where our clinker-built yawl *Kathleen May* lies, one of the very few boats on the river to have a varnished hull. She is really a stranger from Devon, built for us in Salcombe thirty or more years ago; but these are the only waters she has ever sailed.

We are bound for Shingle Street, a voyage down the Deben and out to sea that will be punctuated by churches. Ramsholt is the first and simplest of these, its round tower and simple nave just below the ridge of the hill perfectly aligned for a view of the river through the clear glass of the windows if the sermon proves too dull. Until fifty years ago, a row of decrepit cottages climbed the hill towards the church, but these were demolished, and the church is bereft of the dwellings which once huddled round it. This was always a backwater: a century after the Norman Conquest it still had a Saxon priest, Edric. When his daughter was sick, Edric prayed to that most English of martyrs, St Thomas Becket; his daughter recovered with the saint's aid, and it was declared a miracle. On another occasion, a girl in the village benefitted from one of the saint's *jocula*, little jokes rather than full miracles: she had been given a cheese to put away for safekeeping, and had forgotten where it was. They searched high and low for it until her brother suggested a prayer to St Thomas, who 'has worked innumerable miracles'. The saint obliged by appearing in a dream and reminding her that it was in an old iron pot; the story was duly related to Edric, who took the family to Canterbury, 'where almost everyone who heard the story burst out laughing', delighted at the idea of the great saint taking an interest in such a humble matter. [1]

Ramsholt Church stands clear and proud above the river. Churches were often the seamarks for passing sailors, as a sixteenth-century chart shows: Bawdsey and Alderton are marked, as well as Hollesley. Today only Hollesley's fine tower is clearly visible from the sea. Alderton probably tried to emulate it, but the church there is set low, and the tower and its sea mark were very high. In the early nineteenth century it was already ruinous, and much of the rest collapsed during Sunday service, sparing the parishioners, but killing a cow which was grazing in the churchyard beneath. About the same time, at Bawdsey, a great beacon was lit on the tower to celebrate George III's recovery from

1. The original is in *Materials for the History of Thomas Becket*, ed. J.C. Robertson, ii 153-5; London 1876. It has never been translated.

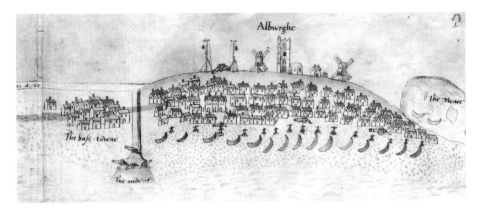

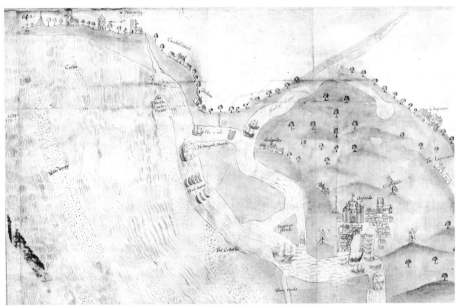

Aldeburgh and Orford, from an Elizabethan chart of the Suffolk coast by an unknown surveyor, *c.*1590
(BL MS Cotton Augustus I i 64)

madness. It burnt well, and destroyed the wooden superstructure, leaving the original four-square Norman base.

It is a perfect sailing breeze, a westerly which means we can slip downriver against the tide. Between the river wall and the water, a pristine snow-white egret eyes disdainfully a nearby seal which is rolling with abandon in the mud; and the distinctive smell of the saltings hangs in the air. It is one of those magical moments when we have the river entirely to ourselves. In the hazy sunlight of early autumn, the marshes melt into the river, and even the low sea wall barely separates the river from the land.

As we approach the river mouth, we steer to starboard of the Horse Sand, down the narrow channel on the Felixstowe side, easy for a dayboat like ours but difficult for a yacht. This was once much deeper: just to landward lies the silted harbour of the King's

Fleet, possibly the site of the vanished medieval port of Goseford, lying next to the royal manor of Walton Castle. Bawdsey itself was a thriving home to merchant ships and fishermen. The medieval kings of England had no royal navy, and the transport of troops as well as the defence of the coast depended on requisitioning ships from round the coast. When Edward III set out to enforce his claim to the French throne in 1338, Goseford provided fifteen ships, against ten from Ipswich and five from Orford. Bawdsey also supplied ships; the names of men like John of Oxney, master of the *Rose* of Bawdsey, and Edmund Paris, master of the cog *St Marie*, were duly recorded in the royal accounts.

Before the river walls were built, there were wide marshes on either side of the Horse Sand, stretching up to the edge of modern Felixstowe and across to Alderton. But the main channel was easier to navigate in medieval times. We know that in the time of Henry VIII, the charts marked Bawdsey Haven as 'too fadome deepe and a quarter lesse', in other words about ten feet deep. Edward III's cogs were boats of up to 75 feet in length, designed more for the carriage of goods rather than easy handling, much less sea-kindly creatures than the Saxon longships that had once sailed up to Sutton Hoo. We once found ourselves sailing alongside a replica of one of these longships, and the yawl, speedy enough by modern standards, was hard put to keep up.

The bar today, as we come out into the main channel, is a more formidable obstacle, and it is the best defence for the landscape along the Deben. It is shallow and shifting, and new charts are issued monthly; certainly not an entrance to attempt at night or in bad weather. There is only one marina here, at Woodbridge, unlike the River Orwell to the south, which has forests of masts in several places. We sailed in over the bar with a friend in a 47ft cutter five years ago, and had some anxious moments coming in; but the skipper, who had not been on the Deben for many years, declared that it had hardly changed since he first knew it sixty years ago. And by day it is indeed as unspoilt a stretch of water as you could hope to find in southern England. Only at night does the lowering light of Felixstowe break the illusion, and even then you can turn your back and look northward into an almost total darkness.

But this is daytime, and we slip down past the eccentricity of Bawdsey Manor, monument to the Victorian entrepreneur and stockbroker Sir Cuthbert Quilter, with its Tudor frontage towards the river and a front modelled on a whim after a French château he had seen on holiday. It stands on cliffs made of Pulhamite, one of those wonderful inventions of the Victorian age, a special cement which imitates rock.

It was here that the composer Roger Quilter lived. His opus 1 was *Four Songs of the Sea*, settings of his own poems, and dedicated to his mother. But although he seems to have loved Bawdsey Manor itself, he was uneasy with the life of a younger son in a conventional Edwardian country house and in the family stockbroking firm. He met my grandfather during his brief spell on the Stock Exchange, and they became good friends, presumably through their shared love of music: I still have my grandfather's copies of the single-sided 78s of Quilter's most famous songs, sung by their mutual friend Gervase Elwes. In 1908 he was best man at my grandparents' wedding. They used to come occasionally to Bawdsey, and sixty years later my grandmother was delighted to recognise the Bawdsey road when she came to see us just after we had moved to Suffolk. I never discovered whether she had crossed the river on the chain ferry from Felixstowe, which was the usual method of arriving by motorcar before the First World War.

Sir Cuthbert Quilter was the owner of a yacht which had once belonged to Edward

JOHN NASH

FitzGerald, who introduced The *Rubáiyât of Omar Khayyam* (or rather his paraphrase of the Persian original) to Victorian England. FitzGerald was a leading figure in Woodbridge society, and his yacht was named the *Scandal*, after the chief product of the town. His skipper was a local fisherman, 'Posh' Fletcher, a much loved character; but when he and FitzGerald set up a herring-fishing venture with a lugger called *Meum and Tuum* ('Mum Tum' to the puzzled locals) it ended in failure, and the two men parted company, though FitzGerald could still write of him as 'the Greatest Man I have known' – probably thinking more of his handling of a boat in a North Sea gale than of his ability as a businessman.

FitzGerald had distinguished predecessors in the way of pleasure sailing off this coast. Phineas Pett from Woodbridge built yachts for Charles II; Charles was a keen sailor, racing his yachts just as he raced his horses at Newmarket. He even took a hand in the yacht designs, as Samuel Pepys tells us. On a visit to Harwich in 1668, Charles and his brother and a group of courtiers enjoyed a day's voyage to Aldeburgh. And in the 1860s the *Livonia*, which was the Royal Harwich Yacht Club's challenger for the America's Cup in 1871, sailed in these waters.

Today business is much more in evidence: to seaward the skyline is marked by a file of container ships making their way into Felixstowe. Small yachts cross the dredged seaway as quickly as they can, with a sharp lookout for these monsters. Inshore, the fishing boats from Felixstowe Ferry ply their business with nets and lobster pots; we see our neighbour at the Ramsholt moorings with a fishing party on board. This is the *Will Laud*, named after the smuggler hero of Richard Cobbold's Suffolk novel *The History of Margaret Catchpole*. And we dodge our way through the racing dinghies from Felixstowe Ferry; these are not as numerous as they were twenty years ago, but there are far more small yachts around.

As we slip through the inshore channel by the Manor – always a heartstopping moment as the tide tries with all its might to sweep us back into the river – the artificial Pulhamite cliffs come into view, followed by the radar mast and the real sandy cliffs where the missiles used to be stationed, reminding us of Bawdsey Manor's latterday fame as the place where radar was developed. The sailing directions on the sixteenth-century chart tell us that from Bawdsey to Hollesley is 'hyghe clyffe and no londing', which is only partly true: the high cliffs peter out after a mile or so, and give way to a line of three Martello Towers and a long shingle bank. A fourth tower was overwhelmed by the sea in 1906, and a similar fate threatens its neighbour today. Behind the shingle bank, we can make out Bawdsey on the hill which was once an 'eye' or island, and Alderton to the north of it.

Hidden by the bank are the marshes, said to have been drained by Dutch engineers in the eighteenth century. Before that they were of little use, and even dangerous, as Thomas Fuller tells us in *The Worthies of England*, published in 1662. He records that Giles Fletcher, a poet in the early seventeenth century, was appointed rector of Alderton. He was not appreciated by his parishioners; they were 'clownish and low-parted (having nothing but their shoes high about them)', and their treatment of him, combined with the bad air of the marshes (for which the high shoes were needed) 'disposed him to melancholy, and hastened his dissolution' at the early age of twenty-five. An eighteenth-century rector was evidently better suited to this unhealthy dim-witted parish: his epitaph, still to be seen in the church, records that 'he was not distinguished for his learning, nor for his industry; but he was, what is more, a truly honest man'; and he survived to the ripe old age of seventy-eight.

Today the marshes are rich farmland, and the sea air is clean: moss, that litmus test of the atmosphere, grows easily and abundantly. By now the breeze has brought us past the hidden marshes and the row of Martello Towers to Shingle Street and the entrance to the Alde. If the Deben bar is difficult, the Alde entrance is a shape-shifter, moving forever to and fro, though the channel is usually deeper. One of the best early estate surveys was done at Orford in 1604 by the draughtsman John Norden, whose maps are still familiar as decorative pictures. We can trace the changes from then on through a series of charts, including that dedicated to Samuel Pepys Esquire, MP for Harwich and Secretary to the Admiralty, by Greville Collins. Our methods are a bit more modern: a laser-printed update diagram and a GPS bring us safely into the Alde and an anchorage on the shingle bank, to await the turn of the tide which will take us back home.

Shingle Street

Tim Miller

Shingle Street … the name conjures up the whistling wind, the crash of the waves, a trickling sound as pebbles are drawn down by the retreating water, the sun rising above the horizon, the cry of seabirds. The small lane from Hollesley turns sharply around the fields until it reaches the sluice. As you cross the bridge and go over the marsh, you enter a different country. It is a powerful, enchanted place, where the sky meets the sea. Standing on the shore, you feel that there is nothing but sea between you and the North Pole.

My love affair with Shingle Street began when I was a boy growing up in Suffolk after the war. My father had bought a long, low redbrick house with the romantic name of the German Ocean Mansion. It stood at the water's edge with some old huts where Eric Andrews, coastguard and fisherman, kept his nets and lobster pots. Nearby Miss Pritchard Carr handed out trays with a pot of tea, a scone and an iced cake from the window of a coastguard cottage, the start of a celebrated career as a caterer. In those days of rationing she produced wonderful birthday cakes, to the delight of my friends.

In *The Rings of Saturn*, an account of walking along the Suffolk coast in 1992, W.G. Sebald allowed his imagination full rein: 'The most abandoned spot in the entire region, Shingle Street, which now consists of just one wretched row of humble houses and cottages and where I have never encountered a single human being.' Not surprisingly the inhabitants failed to appreciate this gothick description of their homes but in his flight of fancy Sebald captures the feeling of solitude, of a haunting spirit on the stony beach between Orford Haven and Deben Head. As the light fades over the marsh and is reflected

JOHN NASH

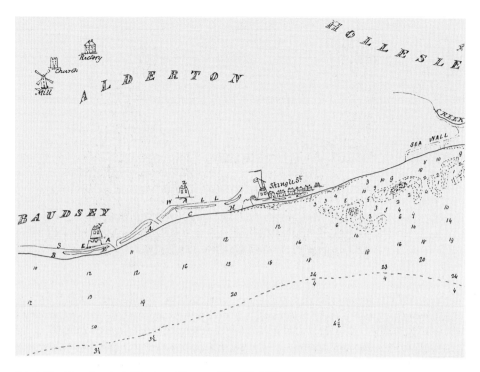

Shingle Street from the chart of Lieutenant Chapman Wise RN, 1838

on the sea, there are evenings when M.R. James' ghost story 'Oh, Whistle, and I'll Come to You, My Lad' suddenly springs to mind and makes me shiver and hurry home.

The beach indeed has its ghosts and has known tragedies. In 1914 five coastguards stationed there were drowned in the mouth of the river close to the shore and within sight of their homes when their cutter capsized in rough weather and a boiling tide. Only one body was recovered, but two men survived by struggling to a shingle bank. To this day it remains a treacherous estuary with boats running aground on the shifting shingle bar. In 1975 Trinity House, the ancient corporation responsible for safeguarding navigation, placed the Orford Haven Buoy with its bell in the mouth of the river. 'Safe in Abraham's Bosom,' the old sailors used to say when they had entered the Ore and made the anchorage on the landward side of Havergate Island.

Today Shingle Street is a small settlement of twenty-five dwellings stretching from The Beacons, where the Ore flows into the sea, to The Battery, originally built to guard Martello Tower AA. The coastguard station is built into the row of white cottages where the men and their families lived. They look out onto the shallow curve of Hollesley Bay, marked to the north by the Orford Light and to the south by Martello Tower W at East Lane. Between them you see the fo'csles of ships hull down below the horizon and the ferries from Harwich making the dogleg round the Shipwash Bank. The Bay is the only anchorage on this part of the coast, where Nelson was forced to shelter from a storm and lost three prize ships returning from the Battle of Copenhagen in 1801.

The Street is made up of a mix of the old wooden fishermens' cottages, Victorian villas for sea bathing, 1950s houses built in compensation for war damage and two or three

Shingle Street
residents of the
1930s

more modern constructions. The most significant piece of architecture is Beach House, which John Penn designed as his home. He had been brought up in the neighbouring village of Bawdsey and in the 1960s built a series of Suffolk villas, of which Beach House was his favourite. He was one of many artists, painters, writers, designers and carvers to find inspiration at Shingle Street. Describing it, he said: 'The light transforms everything. Whatever it touches is ringed with fire.'

Shingle Street proper may have come into existence with the building of Martello Tower AA in about 1808. As Norman Scarfe, former Shingle Street resident and Suffolk's distinguished historian, commented, this was three years after the battle of Trafalgar demonstrated that there was no further risk of French invasion! But this had been Bonaparte's consuming passion. 'The Channel is but a ditch,' he boasted, 'and anyone may cross it who has the courage.' And so the massive quatrefoil Martello CC was built south of Aldeburgh at Slaughden and from there the East Coast towers stretched down to Tower A at St Osyth Stone in Essex. The cost was enormous and the towers deeply unpopular with the public who had to pay for them. They were nicknamed Pitt's Pork Pies.

Some have been demolished and others washed away but a line of four towers stretches along the marsh from Shingle Street to East Lane. Their fortifications of batteries, ditches and moats are shown in detail on the conveyance of September 1899 from Her Majesty's Principal Secretary of State for the War Department to my great-grandfather, who was busy enlarging his estate and his home at Bawdsey Manor. The 24-pounder guns and the howitzers with which they were armed never saw action. They had turned out to be colossal white elephants and in 1823 William Cobbett wrote: 'Here has been the squandering! Here has been the pauper making! To think that I should be destined to behold these monuments of Pitt!' Despite Cobbett's disapproval, they still stand, squat and sturdy, the Bomb Proof Towers with up to half a million bricks in each.

In 1844 White's *Directory of Suffolk* referred to 'the hamlet of Shingle Street on the fine beach of Hollesley Bay, where the Life Boat Inn and several houses were erected in 1810 for the accommodation of sea bathers.' No mention was made in this genteel description of the smuggling that was the staple industry, nor of the terrible battles fought between the excise men and the local free traders. The story of Margaret Catchpole, the Suffolk girl who loved the smuggler Will Laud, recounts a bloody encounter at Shingle Street. It was a brutal trade. Informers could be knocked on the head and thrown into the lime kilns at Slaughden, and the name of Dumb Boy Cottage near the Sluice is a grim memento of the fate of those who blabbed.

Reminders of the trade are everywhere. When I was a boy a pit inland from the beach was known as Lanthorn Dip, where the kegs were stored after landing until the carts came to collect them. Nearby at Alderton an underground passage runs from a vault in the church to the ancient farmhouse beside the graveyard and in the other direction to the pub. Smuggling was widespread along the Suffolk Coast. It continues today with different cargos.

Napoleon's flat-bottomed boats never reached Hollesley Bay but the fear of invasion was rekindled in 1939. The inhabitants of Shingle Street were evacuated, the beach was mined, jagged teeth projected from the shore to hole embarcation craft, and only soldiers and coastguards remained. It was long believed that a war-time photograph showed Barnes Wallis, inventor of the Dam Busters' bouncing bomb, standing on the beach with police and coastguards and, although there is no evidence that he ever came, a bomb was tested and successfully demolished the Life Boat Inn and the surrounding houses in March 1943.

The poet Alun Lewis was stationed here as a young soldier guarding the beach and wrote

From Orford Ness to Shingle Street
The grey disturbance spreads
Washing the icy seas on Deben Head.

Cock pheasants scratch the frozen fields,
Gulls lift thin horny legs and step
Fastidiously among the rusted mines . . .

Did something extraordinary happen on that beach? Nothing is known for certain but for years rumours have persisted that a submarine landed a small invasion force, that the sea was set on fire, that burnt bodies of German soldiers wearing British uniform were buried in Staverton Thicks at dead of night, that the intended quarry had been Watson Watt and his radar research team at Bawdsey Manor. Or had a defence exercise gone horribly wrong?

Speculation was fuelled when the Ministry of Home Security File HO 207/1175 on Shingle Street was classified under an extended 75-year embargo. Such was the press interest in The Mystery that the Home Secretary declassified the file, but little was revealed. Two Shingle Street coastguards well known to me, Harold Maskell and Ron Harris, lived on well into their nineties but if they knew what happened, they never revealed it. A woman who as a girl had lived at Church Farm across the marsh recalled bodies being laid out in a certain room, but many bodies were washed up in the War.

Perhaps the secret of Shingle Street is that nothing extraordinary occurred.

Or did it? Despite the lack of hard evidence, it is just possible that some kind of attempted invasion was made. An eyewitness account from a member of the Home Guard

Above: The beach and Coastguard Cottages in 1968
Right: Fisherman in the 1930s

stationed at Aldeburgh in August 1940 states that a red alert was declared late in that month and every available man was dug in behind a wall facing the Aldeburgh marshes. 'It was a clear dark evening about 9pm when the heavens appeared to open up south of Orford lighthouse in the Shingle Street area. We heard a tremendous amount of gunfire and explosions. The night sky was lit up with a red glow. Sporadic gunfire went on for several hours. We received word that a German landing had taken place.'

Shingle Street today is quiet. Children are born, the old eventually depart, often at a great age. Residents meet together for a bonfire on 5th November, for the carol service in the coastguard wash house at Christmas, and to celebrate birthdays and local events. Visitors come to fish, to walk their dogs, to watch birds, to write or paint or simply to enjoy the silence. It is a peaceful place, the only threat coming from the encroaching sea.

Little has changed from my first memories of Shingle Street over sixty years ago. In summer the beach is covered with the Great Horned Poppy, the giant shapes of Sea Kale, which in the half-light resemble a flock of sheep, the purple flowers of the Sea Pea, drifts of Bladder Campion. I still look for cornelians and find the occasional small lump of amber among pieces of bone and fragments of wormeaten ships' timbers. Once the waves deposited a long churchwarden clay pipe with a shell impression on the bowl, unbroken inside its thick wrapping of seaweed. Life is controlled and measured by the Sea. Each day the ebb pours with great force across the bar as white horses mark the shingle banks. At night I go to sleep with the bell buoy sounding in the mouth of the river and the wink of the Orford Light on the point of the Ness.

Dawn on the East Coast

Alun Lewis

From Orford Ness to Shingle Street
The grey disturbance spreads
Washing the icy seas on Deben Head.

Cock pheasants scratch the frozen fields,
Gulls lift their horny legs and step
Fastidiously among the rusted mines.

The soldier leaning on the sandbagged wall
Hears in the combers' curling rush and crash
His simple self-centred monotonous wish;

And time is a froth of such transparency
His drowning eyes see what they wish to see;
A girl laying his table with a white cloth.

*

The light assails him from a flank,
Two carbons touching in his brain
Crumple the cellophane lanterns of his dream.

And then the day, grown feminine and kind
Stoops with the gulfing motion of the tide
And pours his ashes in a tiny urn.

From Orford Ness to Shingle Street
The grey disturbance lifts its head
And one by one, reluctantly,
The living come back slowly from the dead.

Glitter of Waves: imagery and music

Colin Matthews

'Dawn', the first of Britten's four *Sea Interludes* from *Peter Grimes*, has become so closely associated with the unique shore line of Aldeburgh that you could almost be forgiven for not knowing which came first: did that coast inspire the magical dawn opening, or did the music summon the sea into being? But a more serious question could be, What is it about that music that conjures up a feeling of landscape and place? Is there anything particular about its language or technique that can be defined or analysed?

A prosaic response might be that if Britten had called it, say, 'Midday in Venice' there would be no particular difficulty in finding appropriate images to match: the abstract nature of music means that the mind is easily led towards associations, whether they are appropriate or inappropriate. Britten's essentially practical, somewhat objective approach to composing means that he hardly ever resorted to simple 'tone-painting' – the evocation of a specific object or place by means of sound (the vivid pictures of, for instance, Richard Strauss's *Alpine Symphony* are far removed from Britten's world). Apart from *Grimes*, almost the only works that contain explicit imagery are the early *Canadian Carnival*, and the much later *Death in Venice* (and there, only the barcarolle-like music that evokes the rowing of the gondolier).

There is, of course, a difference between music that conjures up an atmosphere of place, and music that is deliberately pictorial. The representation in music of something specific, such as a bird or an animal, goes back a long way, to the stylised bird calls in Vivaldi's *Four Seasons* and Beethoven's quail, nightingale and cuckoo and imitation of a storm in the *Pastoral Symphony*, and reaches forward to the sheep in Strauss's *Don Quixote* and Messiaen's innumerable birds (Respighi's gramophone recording of a nightingale in *The Pines of Rome* hardly counts!). The *Pastoral Symphony* is perhaps the first instance of an impression of place, even if it is nothing more precise than 'the countryside' (Beethoven's bird calls appear in the context of the stylised representation of a rippling brook). One of the earliest explicit representations of a particular place is *Fingal's Cave* – although in fact Mendelssohn notated the main theme of the piece before he was inspired to write the Overture by a visit to the Hebrides.

Opera, of course, is as likely to evoke place as any other medium. 'At the bottom of the Rhine', says the first stage direction in Wagner's *Das Rheingold*, at the head of the remarkable Prelude, and the same opera contains the first ever 'scenic interludes', depicting the descent into and ascent from the underground world of the Nibelungs (the use of 18 anvils in the score gives a reasonably clear picture of what it is the Nibelungs do under the earth). These interludes are at the same time a contrivance to allow the scenery to be changed; and the same is true of the *Sea Interludes* – Britten had actually to extend the 'Storm' interlude when the producer Eric Crozier asked for more time in order to change the set between the scenes in Act I of *Grimes*. (I recall a production of *Albert Herring* at Snape where one of the longest interludes in opera was insufficient to effect the transformation into Mrs Herring's greengrocery shop.) The *Sea Interludes* themselves do not advance the plot – apart from the depiction of the storm, they remain largely abstract pictures. However the final interlude – not included in the concert version – is a more graphic representation of the fog, the man-hunt, and Grimes's state of mind; while the Passacaglia, like Berg's great D minor interlude in *Wozzeck*, allows the composer himself to step into the frame and express his feelings directly.

Although all four are called 'Sea Interludes', only the first specifically evokes the sea itself: Britten annotated the draft libretto 'Everyday. Grey. Seascape' at that point. The others – 'Sunday Morning', 'Moonlight', and 'Storm' – have, if taken out of their operatic context, no inescapable association with the sea. But if we try to forget the link with Aldeburgh, difficult though that may be (the visual tie is almost as unavoidable as the identification between specific music and TV commercials that the advertising industry works so hard to impose), is there anything that can be pinned down as, to put it crudely, 'sea music'?

The 'Dawn' interlude has three elements: a long, tranquil, high line for violins and flutes – the grace-notes suggest the call of gulls, the melody itself perhaps evokes an open sky, early morning. Then there is a scurrying figure for clarinets, harp and violas, with the plash of a cymbal behind it – the gentle rise and fall of waves breaking on the shingle? Thirdly, a solemn brass chorale-like sequence of chords: the sea as elemental, a force of nature, perhaps. The imagery, though, is essentially objective – if the dawn incorporates a sunrise, it's a very understated one. The brass rise to a crescendo, but then fall, and the music fades back to its beginning (compare Strauss's epic sunrises in *Also Sprach Zarathustra* and the *Alpine Symphony*). The three ideas are mostly kept separate from each other, a simple block construction rather than a conventional musical development.

This is very different from what is perhaps the most famous of 'sea pictures', Debussy's *La Mer*, where the interaction between themes and textures is extraordinarily fluid. Yet there are undoubted similarities: the long-limbed, not quite tranquil theme of the third movement of *La Mer*, the harp figuration and especially the pervasive soft roll of the cymbal, and the brass 'chorale' that ends both first and third movements. It is the treatment, and the sound world, that is so unlike. The more sensuous, impressionistic nature of Debussy's music makes it more immediately evocative of the sea – but, again, which came first? Is there anything really sea-like about the music, or is it because it has become so associated with the sea that we read more into it than is really there? If Debussy had called it simply by its subtitle, *Three Symphonic Sketches*, would we have any idea of what the work is 'about'? Perhaps we would be tempted to agree with the implicit criticism of Erik Satie, who, when asked what he thought of the first movement, 'From dawn to midday on the sea', replied, 'I especially liked the bit between half past ten and quarter to eleven'.

This is, of course, a circular argument. It's neither possible nor advisable to ignore – as deconstructionist theories would have us do – the composer's intention. Holst's *Egdon Heath* (played in the same 1997 Festival for which this essay was originally written) is a case in point. Here is a specific location (even though Thomas Hardy's Egdon Heath has its roots in fiction as much as in reality), but the music is essentially abstract, as it has to be: there are no musical rules for depicting a landscape, after all. But Holst appends a quotation from *The Return of the Native* –

A place perfectly accordant with man's nature – neither ghastly, hateful, nor ugly: neither commonplace, unmeaning, nor tame; but, like man, slighted and enduring; and withal singularly colossal and mysterious in its swarthy monotony.

– and thereby tells us what he is trying to portray. Consequently we can hardly help but hear in the piece something of the unchanging mystery and loneliness of the landscape. It is probably the strangest, and most elusive, piece that Holst ever wrote – for which reason we almost need to know what the work is 'about' in order to help our musical understanding of it; at the least the extra awareness helps us towards understanding the nature of the music.

So the answer to whether there is anything in the *Grimes Interludes* intrinsically of the sea, and of the locality in which Britten (and Peter Grimes) lived, is both yes and no. Britten, it goes without saying, intended to portray a sea-dominated landscape, but in a sense it is up to us to read what we will into the music: for instance, what I suggested might be the cry of a gull could just as easily be the call of a bird of prey over a moorland; but the fact that Britten has called it a seascape pushes us in the 'right' direction. The important point is that musically it does not matter at all what kind of bird it is, or whether it is a bird at all: if it did not have inherent musical interest no amount of verbal explanation would help. Our knowledge of Aldeburgh and the Suffolk landscape may colour our approach to Britten's music; but the music has no need of that knowledge in order to make its incomparable effect.

Reprinted from the Festival programme book, 1997

Longshore Drift: a radio-poem

Katrina Porteous

When I visited Aldeburgh as writer-in-residence to its Poetry Festival in October and November 2002, the Suffolk coast was new to me. Its physical geography surprised me, its stony shores unexpectedly bleaker and more exposed than the sandy beaches of Northumberland. In the four weeks I spent there, however, I soon found many similarities to home – particularly in the crisis facing the longshore fishermen. Dwindling fish stocks, low prices due to imported and farmed fish, and crippling quotas and regulations designed to prevent over-fishing by much larger boats meant that the longshoremen were finding it increasingly difficult to make a living. When I wrote this poem seven boats fished from the beach at Aldeburgh. Two years later, only three were left.

The Suffolk longshoremen fish according to season: that November, they were using long lines to catch cod, trammel nets for sole and sea bass, pots for crabs, and drift nets for herring. As in Northumberland, the longshoremen's small-scale, traditional methods are generally more sustainable than those of bigger boats. Whether they fish from clinker-

JAMES DODDS

1 **Fisherman at Aldeburgh** 2 **Summer Wave at Slaughden**
(preceding page) *(above)*
Jeremy Young Maggi Hambling, 2007–8

3 **Bunker and Wave** (top)
4 **East Lane** (bottom)
Simon Read

5 **James Cable** *(right)*
H.H. Finch, 1922
© Aldeburgh Museum Trust

6 **The James Edward** *(below)*
John Craske
Bought from Craske by Valentine
Ackland in 1927

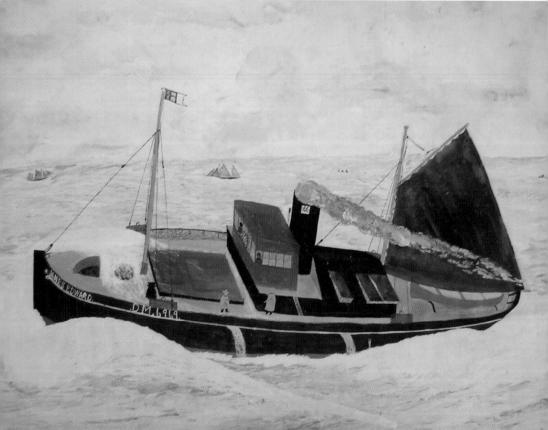

JAMES DODDS

built wooden boats or modern fibreglass vessels, their fishing days and the weight of gear that they carry are restricted by the boat's length, usually between 20 and 26 feet. Even with modern navigational aids, the men are extremely reliant upon traditional knowledge. They work with the sea, not against it, and their lives depend upon their respect for it.

Although it was late in the year, I was fortunate to go fishing off Sizewell and Aldeburgh. I was fascinated to see long lining and drift netting at close quarters. Once staples of fishing in Northumberland, these methods have long since vanished from the North East coast, where small-boat fishermen now largely rely upon crabs and lobsters. Small-scale drift netting and long lining are much less damaging to fish stocks than trawling and seine-netting: fish trapped in a trawl, if under-size or over-quota, are thrown back dead; but those hooked on a long line are still alive. This made me all the more aware of the value of the longshoremen's skills and knowledge. As I crunched along the Suffolk beaches, I reflected on the mutability of that coast. I looked out towards the lost city of Dunwich, once one of England's biggest ports, now almost entirely sunk beneath the sea. I thought of the decline of the longshoremen's way of life, handed down for generations, now vanishing before our eyes. I have tried in this poem to capture a glimpse of what we are losing.

Longshore Drift was written for radio. It is made up of a number of 'voices', based upon interviews recorded with the fishermen I met in the Aldeburgh area. The men speak of 'a dozen an' two', by which they mean twelve or fourteen long lines, at one time a self-imposed limit for small boats on the Suffolk coast. In the radio-poem, the fishermen's voices are heard as songs, accompanied by contrapuntal chants. In the following extracts they are indicated by italics.

Ten a.m. Dean's shed is full
Of strip-light, music and the smell
Of crab-meat, winkled from its shell.

At a bench the two men stand,
Each with a teaspoon in his hand,
Dean to the claws, Paul to the backs.

Michael's balanced on a box,
Arranging small, square, snowy blocks
Of frozen squid on rows of hooks
That barely touch: a lifetime's skill.

Passing customers who call
For newspaper parcels of cod and sole

Pause at the door, stare inside,
Consume the three men with their eyes –

Salt-steeped, weary from the sea
In boots and oilskins, they appear
More present, anchored, and alive.

A static hiss. The music stops.
Dean picks a sole out of the box,
Peels its skin off like a glove.

Gale force eight, the radio warns.
He shrugs. Four lines still to haul.

It's more than fish his callers buy.

We've always lived on the edge, boy;
Small boats, lines and nets.
We've always fished as the old men fished,
And the old men showed the sea respect;

For they'd wait for the fish in their season,
Shootin' a dozen an' two.
I'll tell you, there's just one skipper out there
And that's not you.

When a dozen an' two was your limit
Your twelve long lines might fetch
A hundred stone. Now a hundred lines
Won't land you ten. And there's the catch.

Technology's killed the fishin'.
Sea never gets no rest.
Now politics' gonna finish the job
With the law like a millstone round our necks;

And it's duck, dodge, bend like a reed;
Small boats, little gear.
If we was to land every fish we caught
They'd still be there another year.

* * *

My body's at ease on the water,
More than on the land.
I'm at home on the sea. I was born for this life.
I call myself a happy man:

Though I've slogged out me guts for nothin'
But heartache an' little pay,
And I wouldn't want to see me own boy battered
As the sea has battered me many a day.

For how can you call it a livin',
Winter with no cod,
And the boats gettin' fewer on the beach each year?
I'm the last of the line. You can call me mad,

But it's out on the boundless water
Under the endless sky,
I think of the people I meet on the land
And I know there's envy in their eyes.

For how can you call it a livin',
Bound to an office desk?
When you see that sun come up – God knows,
It's a hard haul an' little rest

When you're haulin' for home, me darlin',
When you're givin' it all you can –
But if I was to die in my sleep tonight
I'd die a happy man.

The Crabbe Apple

Roger Deakin

... at Aldeburgh, I go down to the black-tarred pine fishermen's huts on the beach to buy fish and find a living counterpart to the trees at Holme. On a radio somewhere inside a voice gives out the weather forecast and wishes everyone good fishing. I buy a pound of sprats to cook on a shovel in the fire later on. The fisherman, his tattooed forearms silver with fish scales, wraps them in newspaper. I walk north up the beach towards Thorpeness and Hambling's controversially sited giant bronze oyster shell. 'I hear those voices that will not be drowned,' she has written in bronze across the shell, quoting from *Peter Grimes*. Sure enough, quite a few voices have been raised in Aldeburgh against the siting of Hambling's sculpture in so commanding a position, and will not be drowned.

In the dunes behind the big shell there's an unobtrusive natural memorial to all the drowned fishermen of this coast, just keeping its head above the shingle, surviving against all odds. In its quiet it is more spectacular than the *Oyster*. It is an apple tree, growing miraculously out of the barren-looking pebbles in a low crown only three to four feet high but seven yards in diameter and thirty in circumference. The tree is something of an iceberg: most of it is invisible, overwhelmed by the invading dunes. It is only the topmost branches you see in leaf.

I keep puzzling about that tree, buried up to its neck in the shingle beach like a daddy. It can't quite see the sea. If it grew another ten feet, it could peep over the top of the long ridge of shingle that sweeps from Aldeburgh to Thorpeness. It grows in the shelter of a bunker, a hollow in the dunes of shingle and sand that protects it from the winds of the Ural Mountains that whip across the muddy North Sea. The sheer withering intensity of the wind must prune the budding twigs relentlessly, so the tree takes the one course of survival open to it: it creeps ever outwards, crouching low and close to the shingle, creating a pincushion of densely branched fruiting spurs. I have met people gathering apples from it in summer, a little too early and too green, so as to beat the competition and ripen them in the fruit bowl. I want to pick an apple to identify but am too late, beaten by the eager Aldeburgh scrumpers. Outside the seasons of its blossom and fruit, most people would pass by the tree, mistaking it for a scrubby goat willow like those on the marsh that backs the dunes. George Crabbe used to go there and botanise, and lick the wounds inflicted by the scornful, bullying fishermen of Aldeburgh, who, having known him as a boy, scrubbing out barrels in the town, despised him, first as a doctor and later as their curate. He seriously thought about throwing himself in the marsh, but decided instead to go to London, where he received the generous patronage of Edmund Burke and began to make his way in life.

No doubt the salt spray of winter gales must provide the tree with an anti-fungal dusting to help keep it healthy. A hundred yards inland, looking over the marshes just the other side of the road to Thorpeness, is the derelict cottage whose orchard, once much further inland, may originally have contained this tree [see 'A Halfway House', below]. As the North Sea has eroded more and more of this coast, it has edged the shingle bank further and further inland, burying the orchard and stifling all the trees but this one. Somewhere down below, where the shingle sits on the chalk, the roots are finding fresh water, perhaps from a spring. It must count as one of the hardiest apple trees in Britain, and grafts should be propagated. And even if Crabbe lived too long ago to have known this particular tree, he must surely have known the orchard. The Crabbe Apple deserves official recognition by the town.

From *Wildwood, A Journey Through Trees*, Hamish Hamilton, 2007

A Halfway House
Neil Powell

Etched into dusk, it shows we're almost there:
Those lidded windows, biscuit-stucco walls
Between the water-meadows and the sea
Signal exact abandonment. Years drift:
Spring tides engulf it, lapping at the sills;
Gulls claim an apex among missing slates,
Shout their possession from the staring rafters;
Awash all winter, yet on summer nights
The beach will grow through shingle into sand
And turn this place inland.
                              A halfway life
May teach regard for this enduring ruin,
Weathered defender of uncertain ground,
And milestone marking that consoling point
Of nearing home, or starting out again.

On Sizewell Beach

Blake Morrison

There are four beach huts, numbered 13 to 16,
each with net curtains and a lock.
Who owns them, what happened to the first twelve,
whether there are plans for further building:
there's no one here today to help with such enquiries,
the café closed up for the winter,
no cars or buses in the PAY AND DISPLAY.
The offshore rig is like a titan's diving board.
I've heard the rumours that it's warmer here
for bathing than at any other point along the coast.
Who started them? The same joker who bought
the village pub and named it the Vulcan,
'God of fire and metalwork and hammers,
deformed and buffoonish, a forger of rich thrones'?
Whoever he is, whatever he was up to,
he'd be doused today, like these men out back,
shooting at clay pigeons, the rain in their Adnams beer.
And now a movement on the shingle
that's more than the scissoring of terns:
a fishing boat's landed, three men in yellow waders
guiding it shorewards over metal-ribbed slats
which they lay in front of it like offerings
while the winch in its hut, tense and oily,
hauls at the hook in the prow, the smack with its catch
itself become a catch, though when I lift
the children up to see the lockjaws of sale and whiting
there's nothing in there but oilskin and rope.

I love this place, its going on with life
in the shadow of the slab behind it,
which you almost forget, or might take for a giant's
    Lego set,
so neat are the pipes and the chain-mail fences,
the dinky railway track running off to Leiston,

the pylons like a line of cross-country skiers,
the cooling ponds and turbine halls and reactor
   control rooms
where they prove with geigers on Open Days
   ('Adults and Children over 14 years only')
that sealed uranium is less radioactive than a watch.

One rain-glossed Saturday in April
a lad from Halesworth having passed his test
and wanting to impress his girlfriend
came here in the Ford he'd borrowed from his father
and took the corner much too fast, too green to judge
the danger or simply not seeing the child
left on the pavement by the father - no less reckless
who had crossed back to his Renault for the notebook
he'd stupidly forgotten, the one with jottings
for a poem about nuclear catastrophe,
a poem later abandoned, in place of which
he'd write of the shock of turning round
to find a car had come between him and his daughter,
an eternity of bodywork blotting out the view,
a cloud or an eclipse which hangs before the eyes
and darkens all behind them, clearing at last
to the joy of finding her still standing there,
the three of us spared that other life we dream of
where the worst has already happened and
we are made to dwell for ever on its shore.

At Dunwich

Anthony Thwaite

Fifteen churches lie here
Under the North Sea;
Forty-five years ago
The last went down the cliff.
You can see at low tide,
A mound of masonry
Chewed like a damp bun.

In the village now (if you call
Dunwich a village now,
With a handful of houses, one street
And a shack for Tizer and tea)
You can ask an old man
To show you the stuff they've found
On the beach when there's been
   a storm:

Knife-blades, buckles and rings,
Enough coins to fill an old sock,
Badges that men wore
When they'd been on pilgrimage,
Armfuls of broken pots.
People cut bread, paid cash,
Buttoned up against the cold.

Fifteen churches, and men
In thousands working at looms,
And wives brewing up stews
In great grey cooking pots
I put out a hand and pull
A sherd from the cliff's jaws,
The sand trickles, then falls.

Nettles grow on the cliffs
In clumps as high as a house.
The houses have gone away.
Stand and look at the sea
Eating the land as it walks
Steadily treading the tops
Of fifteen churches' spires.

Written in 1963

JOHN NASH

Seafood in East Anglia

Matthew Fort

In 1991 my mother rented a house at Brancaster to accommodate a party of fifteen – children, grandchildren, wives and friends – for two weeks during the summer. It was an idyllic period of bucket-and-spading, frolicking in the sea, huge lunches, easy-going dinners and trips to Wells-next-the-Sea and Aldeburgh. But most of all I remember a colossal haul of cockles and what we did with them. We deployed the entire family forces on a cockle-gathering blitz one day, and ended up with a dustbin full of them. We washed them repeatedly until clean of sand and then we cooked them in batches. For about two days we ate nothing but cockles – just warm from the pan in their juices; cockles on toast; spaghetti alle cockle (far superior to spaghetti alle vongole); cockles as a sauce for poached haddock; cockle chowder; cockle salad; cockles with bacon; one hundred ways with cockles. And it didn't seem to matter how many we ate, we never grew tired of them. I have to confess, that passion still burns brightly within me.

When you look at the great buttock-curve of East Anglia, you realise just why seafood of almost every description has played such an important part in its economy and it culinary heritage. Just think of oysters from Butley and crabs from Cromer, herrings from Yarmouth, cod from Grimsby, cockles from Leigh On Sea and Stiffkey and shrimps from Kings Lynn. There are lobsters and whelks, sea trout and turbot, mussels and monkfish, kippers and bloaters. In each case, the geographical provenance has become a guarantor of quality and character. (In retrospect, as a result of researching for this article, I rather regret not having extended our cockle-gathering to Stiffkey, not because I wished to pay homage to the rackety rector who was mauled to death by lions in Blackpool, but because we never got to taste the legendary Stewkey Blue cockle, a local variant with a distinctive blue-grey shell.)

Of course, the treasures of East Anglia's sea don't stop at the water's edge. The most obvious land-locked marine ingredient is that *ne plus ultra* of saline condiments, Maldon salt. But more recently seaside vegetables have been putting in appearances on the menus of fashionable metropolitan menus and even fishmongers' slabs. Samphire has become almost ubiquitous, and how long will it be before sea kale, sea beet and sea purslane follow suit, thanks to the proselytising efforts of chefs and writers such as Mark Hix and Thane Prince?

In our rush to proclaim the supremacy of ingredients from elsewhere, be it balsamic vinegar from Modena or lamb from Pauillac or mustard from Dijon or extra virgin olive oil from almost anywhere, we seem to have forgotten to celebrate the virtues of our own indigenous produce. Luckily there are others who will celebrate for us. A few years back, the great American chef Alice Waters was cooking lunch at Le Manoir aux Quat' Saisons using indigenous seasonal ingredients, according to her creed. I was talking to one of her American helpers afterwards, and remarked on the excellence of the crab-based first course. Where did the crabs come from, I asked. Cromer, he said. 'I wish we could get crabs as good as this in the US,' he added.

Of course, the whole business of which fish and shellfish to eat and how much to eat of them has become fraught and confused in recent years. Consumers are being battered around the head by contrary advice. On the one hand we are being advised to eat more and more fish for the sake of our health, and on the other we are being warned that if we do so, certain species will vanish for ever. In 1991, we gave no thought to the effect that our depredations might have had on the cockle population of Brancaster. It never occurred to us whether or not our haul would seriously affect the ecosystem of the beach. Sustainability was not the buzzword in the 1990s that it has become since. I wonder if we would have been so profligate now.

However, even then we knew about the demise of cod in the North Sea. The annual battle between EU quotas based on scientific projections and the practical experiences of the men and women whose communities and way of life relied on the sea, was already being waged. The trouble is that you can't count fish or even track their movements in the same way you can count cows or sheep or migrating wildebeest. This is even more the case as we now have to take into account the effects of global warning on fish movements. It leaves so much unquantified and unquantifiable. All we can be certain of are the consequences if nothing is done. The lessons of the disappearance of the herring from the North Sea and cod from the Grand Banks seemed to have been largely forgotten, or rather, are having to be learned again. That dread phrase 'the stocks are on the point of collapse' gets aired with increasing frequency and desperation. International efforts to control and police fishing fleets seem patchy at best, ineffective at worst, and are certainly open to abuse. There seems to be scarcely any of the fish that we traditionally favoured that we can eat with a clear conscience. And now, of course, further concerns are being raised about other species. We are being warned that skate, turbot, monkfish, even dogfish are under threat.

But one fish's demise is another fish's opportunity. It wasn't that long ago when the monkfish was deemed too ugly to be put out for display. This was solved by removing its head and only serving up its meaty body. And I can recall meeting an old fishmonger who said that sea bass was regarded as too common to be sold to smart restaurants. If ever a fish had a makeover in that case, it was the sea bass.

I must say that I find it curious to see pollack becoming the new fashionable fish on menus as environmentally-conscious chefs cast around for one fish they can serve their customers with a clear conscience. Pollack constitutes a really serious challenge to the creativity of a chef. In my view there are very good reasons why it has never topped the seafood popularity contest: it is utterly without interest of any kind, and none of the versions I have yet had have persuaded me to change my mind. Much better to turn to the gurnard, which is also sustainable – for the time being. (I would also like to give a quick mention in passing to the fishy glories of East Anglia's inland waters, too – pike, perch, zander and eels – at which we turn up our noses when it comes to their gastronomic merits, in spite of the fact that any of them will show a good many sea fish a clean pair of heels when it comes to flavour and texture.)

JAMES DODDS

Of course, there is a substantial difference between the scale of catches made by small on-shore boats, landing catches to satisfy the local market, and the trawlers that go out from the great ports, and whose catches have to satisfy the ever-increasing demand for fresh fish. There is a strong argument that we should treat fish as we are beginning to treat other foods – shop seasonally and locally. Admittedly that puts the inhabitants of our inland towns and cities at a disadvantage, but the fact is that neither fish nor shellfish should ever be counted as a cheap resource. We may be able to grow a chicken from egg to maturity in five weeks, or get a cow ready for the abbatoir in two years, but it takes a turbot five years before it can start making little turbots; no one really knows how long it takes a lobster to become sexually active, because it's almost impossible to tell their ages at all. The period may be shorter for haddock and cod than for the turbot, but the principle remains the same. If we take too many immature fish or shellfish out of the sea, at some point there won't be any left for us to eat.

So let us treasure Cromer crabs, Stewkey Blues, King's Lynn shrimps, Brancaster mussels, cod in Aldeburgh and Butley oysters. Let's celebrate them, savour them, and, above all, make sure there are enough for us to enjoy them all in the years to come.

Odd Times

Simon Read

The wind is southwesterly 5–6, the tide flooding, visibility good but the seastate rough. This is enough to put anyone off negotiating the entrance to the River Ore, except in dire necessity. The shingle knolls are exposed; here and there seas break over them and also over those lumps and bumps barely covered but still hidden. From the beach it is difficult to identify the right parallax relationship to discern a safe passage. From the sea it is a matter of trust that certain transits still hold good. There is no longer a pilot and out of season when there are no buoys, recourse is to known landmarks that always were used and must align in strict order: church tower between coastguard cottage and bungalow, high chimney to beacon. Navigating this is a heart-in-your-mouth experience where the force of the incoming tide is so strong that it is easy to be pushed off course and there is little room for error.

Once, when there was malting at Snape and the Alde/Ore River was busy with commercial shipping from steamers and barges to colliers and smacks, there was a need for a pilot based at Shingle Street to help negotiate the intricacies of the tidal bar and the lower reaches. If the tide was flooding and a ship appeared in the offing flying the signal flag 'G', it was his duty to turn out. Any other time he could go fishing, but never when the conditions were ideal because that was when he could expect to be busy piloting. His free times were those odd times that he was not standing by, which were not always the best times. Because of this, when he had a new boat built, he named it *Odd Times*. The memory of this is enshrined at Felixstowe Ferry at the entrance to the River Deben in the ferryboats *Odd Times* and *Late Times*.

A brisk northeasterly storm changes everything. The fickle sea can scoop out shingle, wash right up to the doorstep and neatly put it all back again with an ornamental lagoon the next winter. Shingle Street is a precarious toehold on a shingle ridge thrown up and left behind by the tide; although its original denizens managed to wrest a living from the sea at the front door and the marsh at the back, this was set to change during the course of the twentieth century.

The Second World War was a catalyst: the village was declared off limits and a military exercise zone; what was left of it afterwards succumbed to other sensibilities that rejoice in extreme weather from a secure vantage point above the tideline. As it is for many who live close to the sea and below the 5-metre contour, the threat has now become more explicit; uncluttered clear bright skies and the battened-down-hatch cosiness of winter are accompanied by uncertainty over whether storm-driven seas will let the place survive. If this threat were to become imminent, would there be the will or the means available to do anything about it? It would be tough convincing any authority to vouchsafe the future for such a tiny settlement in such a shifty place.

Look anywhere along the immediate coast or within the river; it is all on the move. Has it ever been otherwise? Maybe not, but perhaps an appreciation of this is subject to the rate at which it happens measured against a lifespan. Conditions shift incrementally and then suddenly changes happen that have been centuries in the making, precipitated by heaven knows what – by a sudden event like a storm, or insidiously, as the unpredictable consequence of well-meaning defence work here or a dredged channel there. Who knows? It is a chaotic environment where there are so many influences that it is impossible to attribute cause or blame. Since the time that the Moot Hall migrated from the centre of Aldeburgh to its seaward edge, not a great deal has changed – or so it seems. I am unsure whether the profile of the beach has become steeper or not, but for now it appears to be in equilibrium. And this is in spite of stark evidence that it has not always been thus, nor would it likely be in the future if improvements to the defences immediately to the north at Thorpeness have the knock-on effect of disrupting the movement of sediment southwards.

The Environment Agency, which has the unenviable task of coming up with workable defence strategies for a mobile coastline, is hard put to decide what to protect and what to let go in the sure knowledge that whatever it does, it will be wrong. It is an absolute certainty that once you start meddling with a coastal regime, you are committing to a continued interference. The responsibility for defence will never be free from dilemma; improving protection for the front at Southwold will affect the natural processes of erosion and deposition of sediment that its neighbours rely upon to survive. If, as a consequence, the low land at Walberswick were deemed a hopeless case and allowed to retreat, Southwold would in due course become a hard point on the coast and eventually an artificial Ness for the sea to outflank. To pick and choose is a dangerous game and one

that nobody wants to embark upon: identify a shoreline that at first sight is a justifiable candidate for letting go and pretty soon you have eroded your way all the way to the next hard spot – and so it goes on.

During the 1980s substantial work was carried out on the seaward side of Slaughden. This was seen as vital, not just for the sake of making sure that the River Alde continues to debouch as the River Ore at Shingle Street, but also as a backstop for Aldeburgh itself. Walk along the shingle ridge to where the northern end of Lantern Marsh has been allowed to flood and it becomes clear that beneath the shingle is a colossal amount of granite, forming a core to the graded beach in front. A new groyne system was put in place to retain the shingle and it is telling that where the groynes have stopped, an embayment is beginning to establish. Periodically the beach has to be replenished with more shingle as a check on the excessive loss of material from the foreshore. The implication of this is that these recent works that stop south of the Martello Tower at Slaughden have induced sediment starvation.

Orfordness Lighthouse happens to be at the southern end of this developing bay and is rapidly losing its own foreshore. Anyone who has read the history of the lights on Orfordness knows that they have a habit of falling into the sea; the current light was originally one of a pair that together formed a transit to clear the Whiting Bank. Eventually the Low Lighthouse became unstable and was demolished in 1889, leaving behind the High Lighthouse roughly in the form that we have it today. Look at maps and charts of the Ness and it is clear that it has been very mobile over the centuries; better still, look at aerial photographs and wave upon wave of shingle can be seen successively built up over the centuries and leached away by the tide. So, small surprise should the magnificent red and white tower we have now [see plate 20] also succumb; this time however its loss might be in part due to those well-intentioned works further north.

In the nicest possible way the Environment Agency would like to renounce the ad-hockery of previous times and embrace sustainability, but of course this is easier said than done. It is after all only the logistics arm of what government and the people desire, and right now government policy and public perception seem particularly out of step. The extreme alternative advocated by Natural England, the agency that advises government on the natural environment, could be interpreted as a 'year zero' solution giving preference to landscape integrity over social need, which, if consistently applied, would be breathtakingly irresponsible.

I am torn on these issues. Believing strongly in the importance of empowerment and the right of self-determination for communities, I applaud the quixotic approach of the landowners of Bawdsey and Alderton in committing personal resources to shore up East Lane and the ingenious creation of a huge sacrificial revetment to shield the crumbling cliff at Easton Bavents. But I wonder whether individual cases such as these are, in the long term, diversions from the urgent need to establish a constituency that has an informed grasp of the implications of climate change, or conversely whether they are an essential preliminary to forcing the debate. Intellectually, it is intriguing to speculate what would happen were the controlling hand lifted and events allowed to take their course. Were the River Alde to break through at Slaughden, what would happen to the rest of the river and whatever would become of Shingle Street, where we started out? For the very first time in its history, it could become stable – and just imagine the pilotage for the new Aldeburgh Haven.

Aldeburgh Storm

George Crabbe

View now the Winter-storm! ...
All where the eye delights, yet dreads to roam,
The breaking billows cast the flying foam
Upon the billows rising – all the deep
Is restless change; the waves so swell'd and steep,
Breaking and sinking, and the sunken swells,
Nor one, one moment, in its station dwells:
But nearer land you may the billows trace,
As if contending in their watery chase;
May watch the mightiest till the shoal they reach,
Then break and hurry to their utmost stretch;
Curl'd as they come, they strike with furious force,
And then re-flowing, take their grating course,
Raking the rounded flints, which ages past
Roll'd by their rage, and shall to ages last.

Far off, the Petrel in the troubled way
Swims with her brood, or flutters in the spray;
She rises often, often drops again,
And sports at ease on the tempestuous main.

High o'er the restless deep, above the reach
Of gunner's hope, vast flights of Wild-ducks stretch;
Far as the eye can glance on either side,
In a broad space and level line they glide;
All in their wedge-like figures from the north,
Day after day, flight after flight, go forth.

In-shore their passage tribes of Sea-gulls urge,
And drop for prey within the sweeping surge;
Oft in the rough opposing blast they fly
Far back, then turn, and all their force apply,
While to the storm they give their weak complaining cry;
Or clap the sleek white pinion to the breast,
And in the restless ocean dip for rest.

From *The Borough*, 1810

Peter Grimes

George Crabbe

Alas! for Peter, not a helping hand,
So was he hated, could he now command;
Alone he row'd his boat, alone he cast
His nets beside, or made his anchor fast;
To hold a rope or hear a curse was none –
He toil'd and rail'd; he groan'd and swore alone.

Thus by himself compell'd to live each day,
To wait for certain hours the tide's delay;
At the same time the same dull views to see,
The bounding marsh-bank and the blighted tree;
The water only, when the tides were high,
When low, the mud half-cover'd and half-dry;
The sun-burnt tar that blisters on the planks,
And bank-side stakes in their uneven ranks;
Heaps of entangled weeds that slowly float,
As the tide rolls by the impeded boat.

From *The Borough*, 1810

The Borough

'Describe the Borough – though our idle tribe
May love description, can we so describe,
That you fairly streets and buildings trace
And all that gives distinction to a place?'

George Crabbe, *The Borough*, 1810

News from Aldeburgh

Elizabeth Sweeting

King Edward VI (1547–53)
[We] bare to its inhabitants there singular love.

William Camden (1551–1623)
The corn throughout the kingdom, having been blighted by an unfavourable season in 1555, the inhabitants of this part, about the autumn, were supplied by a crop of pease, which, in a very extraordinary manner, sprung up among the bare rocks, without any earth among them. More sensible people suppose them to have been thrown there by some wreck, which takes off from the wonder. [This is the first reference to Aldeburgh's famous plant *Lathyrus maritimus* or Sea Pea. The only other places where it is found in any quantity is at Dungeness and at Chesil Beach in Dorset.]

Robert Reyce in The Breviary of Suffolk *(1618)*
In the English voyage to Portugall (1589) under those two famous generals Sr. Francis Drake and Sr. John Norrys Knights ... in the first squadron were the Susan of Aldborough ... in the 3rd Squadron was the pelican of 180 tunne ... in the 4e Squadron was the Grehound of Aldborough of 180 tunne.

From Queen Elizabeth I Justices' Report
There is yearly adventured by the inhabitants so many fishers and fisher boats for herring fishing which carry in them 800 mariners ... There is also yearly adventured by the said inhabitants 300 mariners for the sprat fare ... Also there is manned every year by the inhabitants aforesaid 14 ships and crayers small vessels into Iceland and the North Seas having in them 40 mariners at the least.

From an Elizabethan petition
The town of Aldeburgh doth stand low and is not defended from the rage and violence of the sea but by certain loose shells or shingle wrought up with the violence of the sea which lieth up as a beach between the town and the sea, which when by contrary winds is in any place wrought out then the houses adjourning thereunto are with the violence and rage of the sea overthrown. [The petition asks that jetties should be erected 'along the east of that town southerly in places most needful, the cost of which would amount to £700 or £800 which sum the inhabitants are unable to expend'.]

James Dodds, Aldeburgh Beach

The Reverend George Crabbe in the Life *of his father, the poet*

George Crabbe, the Poet ... was born at Aldborough on the Christmas Eve of 1754. Aldborough (or as it is more correctly written, Aldeburgh) was in those days a poor and wretched place, with nothing of the elegance and gaiety which have since sprung up about it, in consequence of the resort of watering parties. The town lies between a low hill or cliff, on which only the old church and a few better houses were then situated, and the beach of the German Ocean. It consisted of two parallel and unpaved streets, running between mean and scrambling houses, the abodes of seafaring men, pilots and fishers. The range of houses nearest the sea had suffered so much from repeated invasions of the waves, that only a few scattered tenements appeared erect among the desolation. I have often heard my father describe a tremendous spring-tide of, I think, the 1st of January, 1779, when eleven houses were at once demolished; and he saw the breakers dash over the roofs, curl round the walls, and crush all to ruin.

Aldborough Described (1819)

The shores of Aldborough have, of late years, become in a peculiar manner, the constant resort of rank and fortune, of opulence and respectability ... Recreational amusements are innocently enjoyed; and the society of Aldborough is gay without profligacy, and pleasurable without mingling in debauchery ... There are several excellent machines stationed on the beach which may be used at all times with perfect safety ... These machines form a kind of close caravan, having a door and small flights of steps behind by which the bather descends to the water, as well as an awning or a pendent covering of canvas by which he is concealed from view ... The machines which are used by ladies have, in general, what is called a *cradle* attached to them, which enables the fair bather to plunge into the ocean without risk, fear, or danger.

Aldeburgh High Street, 1953

Thomas Carlyle (1795–1881)
... a beautiful little sea town, one of the best bathing places I have ever seen ... If you have yet gone nowhere, you should think of Aldeburgh.

Edward FitzGerald (1809–83)
I was ruthlessly ducked into the Wave that came like a devouring monster under the awning of the Bathing Machine – a Machine whose Inside I hate to this day.

There is no sea like the Aldeburgh sea – it *talks* to me.

Grant Allen (c. 1890)
It is a place in which nothing commands one's love. And yet everybody who has once been there still would go; he knows not why, he asks not wherefore. The whole borough, like the chameleon of natural history, lives on air. ... It exhilerates the heart of man (and woman) like the best Sillery.

Virginia Woolf in The Common Reader *(1925)*
... that miserable, dull sea village.

The Earl of Harewood (June 1953)
The distance between the fifth and sixth Aldeburgh Festivals is to be measured not so much in terms of twelve calendar months as of one flood night, 31 January 1953 ... The loss of life was fortunately not as great as that suffered in some other towns, but the damage to property and means of livelihood was very extensive, so that it is, I think, no exaggeration to say that not a single person who lives or works on the sea front or in the High Street is ... back to normal.

Aldeburgh Resurgent

Lamorna Good

or *How a Frowning Coast was transformed into Youth Renewed
by the Benevolence of a Nobleman*

On 14 September 1799 King George III wrote from Weymouth to his Lord Chamberlain: 'On Thursday I received the Marquis of Salisbury's letter. I desire he will remain at Aldborough, though the Parliament meets the 24th, as a continuation of sea bathing is recommended to him...'

In fact, the First Marquess was staying on in Aldeburgh in order to lay the foundations of a small estate he was to build up over twenty-five years. On 12 September he had bought The Bowling Green, which abutted the grounds of The Casino, a cottage with stables and coach house in Church Walk. The Lord of the Manor of Aldeburgh, Leveson Vernon, had reluctantly sold him The Casino in 1798 – reluctantly, because Mr Vernon was anxious to see which way the property market might move should the new fashion for sea bathing reach Aldeburgh and bring prosperity back to the town.

For in the latter part of the eighteenth century Aldeburgh was in the financial doldrums; a decline in the fishing and ship-building industries had brought unemployment and the Borough itself was running out of money. The sand roads and clay cottages were at the mercy of the encroaching sea (eleven houses swept away in one storm in 1779), and parish assistance was granted only to those willing to bear a badge of red cloth with 'PA' on it. With the high taxes on imports, smuggling had become a way of life for many people. Aldeburgh had not only its own Customs House but also a detachment of the Norfolk Regiment, commanded by Lord Orford. After little success, Lord Orford observed that 'the clergy, lawyers and doctors of the area were all smugglers and that in Aldeburgh itself, every inhabitant was a smuggler except the parson'.

In 1783, the poet George Crabbe published *The Village*, in which he contrasted poor, corrupt present-day Aldeburgh with an arcadian past; nymphs were now prostitutes and swains, smugglers. Of the inhabitants he wrote:

Here joyless roam a wild amphibious race
With sullen wo' display'd in every face
Who far from civil arts and social fly,
And scowl at strangers with suspicious eye.

What could have brought such a fashionable couple as the Marquess and Marchioness of

Salisbury to downtrodden Aldeburgh? Born in 1748, James Cecil, later Earl and then Marquess of Salisbury, became a dutiful servant of the crown, loyal to the King and to the Tory party. He married in 1774 a beautiful, high-spirited Irish girl, Lady Emily Mary Wills. In the 1780s Lady Salisbury became a famous and ambitious political hostess for the Tories, and a leader of society and fashion to rival the Duchess of Devonshire. She was also a favourite of the Prince of Wales, a relationship depicted in a cartoon by Gillray, published in 1752, which shows an angry Marquess, a disconsolate, discarded mistress (Mary Robinson), and the Prince clasping the hand of Lady Salisbury while declaiming his love for her. Only thirteen years after marriage did the Marchioness give birth to the first of her four children, Georgiana.

In 1793, when Lord Salisbury suffered ill health and was forced to give up hunting at Hatfield, sea bathing was no doubt recommended. Where to go? A connection with Aldeburgh existed through the Court of St James, where the Lord of the Manor of Aldeburgh was a Gentleman Pensioner and his sister a Maid of Honour to the Queen. There may of course have been other reasons for Lord Salisbury to prefer an unfashionable seaside town.

The journey from Hertfordshire to Aldeburgh could take two days in 1801; there are many bills in the archives at Hatfield House for turnpikes and post horses, with stops at Hertford, Hockall, Dunmow, Colchester, Copdock and Woodbridge. Between 1798 and 1809 the Marquess bought nine pieces of land or houses in Aldeburgh. By 1809 he had changed the Casino cottage into a pretty, white-painted Regency villa, an image of which hangs at Hatfield House today. Overlooking the sea, the Casino had a Drawing Room, Dining Room, Billiard Room, Reading Room, Study, and servants' quarters. Verandas with trellised pilasters and gothic arches ran around the house; red and green screens painted with sea views were added later, no doubt to give shelter from the north-east wind. Two cannons on the lawn faced the sea – for Aldeburgh was perceived as a probable invasion target for Napoleon's forces. Around Christmas in 1803 gunfire was heard out at sea, so the guns at Fort Green were fired and the drums on the quay beat the alarm.

At the Casino, furniture was brought down from London. An upholsterer's bill in 1801 included: 10 back chairs, 10 cushions, 4 large elbow chairs, mahogany card tables, fine satinwood tambour writing desk, carved girandoles with ornaments, etc., totalling £359. Lord Salisbury appointed Mr Thomas Sparkes as his agent – was this George Crabbe's brother-in-law? Local builders were employed to build and glaze, to maintain and paint; colours used included Prussian blue, Verdigrease (sic), green, salmon, stone, chocolate and vermilion. Some workmen were employed for nine months of the year, running up large bills. In 1808 the Marquess spent at least £638 on builders; in today's terms that would amount to around £33,000. Labour seems relatively inexpensive (for seven days' work, one man was charged at £1.6/-) but materials were costly; every item is detailed on the bills, so we know, for instance, that 3,296 3/4-inch nails cost £68.13.4d. Around the house the land was ploughed and harrowed by two men and four horses (one day, 15/-) and planted with privets, laburnums, elms, poplars, jasmines and potatoes, bought from the nursery at Melton. A chicken coop and game house, a children's play house and a pew in the church, a pleasure boat painted blue and white and a bathing machine and house are mentioned in the bills – the last being secured by the builders only for the Marquess later to receive a bill from four local men for 'saveing the Materials of the House standing on the beach £1.1.0.'

The Casino, Alborough, 1809

The Marquess was not just a summer visitor. He ceased to be Lord Chamberlain in 1804 and began to spend longer periods in Aldeburgh. In September 1811 he wrote to the Prime Minister about the incompetence of the burgesses of the Borough, fearing that the Charter might be dissolved. (The Prime Minister wrote back telling him not to worry.) In November 1811, as Colonel of the Hertfordshire Militia, Lord Salisbury gave a ball and supper at the Ipswich garrison. In October, he came down to shoot and to go to the Saxmundham Ball. In the spring, he often enjoyed himself at The White Hart; one dinner for fourteen gentleman at 3/- each is accompanied by 21 bottles red Port at £5.15.6d, 9 bottles of sherry at £21.18.6d, punch, porter, tea, tobacco, nuts and oranges. A curious item added at the bottom of this particular bill reads '*to bringing Young Lion ashore 7/11d*'.

We know that by 1810 the Marquess was running two substantial houses; the Casino had been renamed The Great Cassino and further down Church Walk lay The Little Cassino. While 'casino' can mean a small house as well as a gambling den, Cassino was indeed a game of chance, the Great Cassino being the ten of diamonds and the Little Cassino the two of spades. Lady Salisbury was a renowned gambler; at Hatfield House she is said to have started regular Sunday morning card games and concerts which proved so popular that eventually the Vicar himself attended. In Aldeburgh, there were bills for cards and counters and lottery tickets. She was also famous for driving her coach at a furious pace and there are Aldeburgh bills for repairs, refurbishment and the repainting of the Salisbury arms on a phaeton.

The Great and Little Cassinos were some 150 yards apart but linked by a passage. In August 1810 Lady Salisbury received a letter from an outraged Mrs Isabella Strode, refuting allegations of '*the impropriety of mine and my daughters' conduct with regard to his Lordship...*' and in particular of her daughters visiting Lord Salisbury by the covered way. Although Mrs Strode was a member of the Court, being the Housekeeper at St James' Palace, we know that she also lived in Aldeburgh, as the Marquess paid not only her bills for coal and building work but also her local taxes. Thus, in 1810, on the same piece of paper, the Marquess is billed for 51 windows at his house and for 15 windows at Mrs Strode's.

The Marquess was celebrated for his hospitality in Aldeburgh. October bills show pineapples being sent down from London at a cost of five guineas, with china sugar boxes, lobsters and barrels of fresh native oysters bought locally. From Ipswich, a man came to set up illuminations, including 196 transparent lamps. An automusicon was installed and around 1814 the Marquess and Marchioness gave 'a splendid ball and supper' at the 'elegant Casino ... the Conservatory was ornamented with a brilliant transparency, exhibiting a striking likeness of Field Marshall the Marquis of Wellington ... the ball was opened at half past ten ... and supper, which consisted of every delicacy of the season, was served up at 1 o'clock ... the dance was kept up with spirit till 6 o'clock, when its indefatigable votaries concluded their exertions by tracing the graceful mazes of the Boulanger.'

A 'portable ballroom' was included in the sale of the Great Cassino and its contents in 1824. The First Marquess of Salisbury had died in 1823; his obituary in *The Gentleman's Magazine* said that the Cassino 'was his romantic and favourite residence' and that Aldeburgh had been 'enlivened by his constant hospitalities'. He had 'gained the general esteem and affection of the inhabitants'. The poor had also 'liberally participated in the bounties' and during the previous hard winter, the 'beneficent hand' of Lord Salisbury had supplied them with food and clothing.

The change brought about in Aldeburgh's fortune by the beneficial presence of the first Marquess of Salisbury and the rich noblemen who followed him to the Suffolk seaside was not lost on the ageing poet George Crabbe, who on a visit in 1823 wrote:

> Thus once again, my native place, I come
> Thee to salute – my earliest, latest home:
> Much are we alter'd both, but I behold
> In thee a youth renew'd – whilst I am old.

Quotations from papers at Hatfield House by kind permission of the Seventh Marquess of Salisbury.

BILL BRANDT

Victorian Aldeburgh

Norman Scarfe

Carlyle recommended Aldeburgh to his wife in August 1855. 'A mile of fine shingly beach, with patches of smooth sand every here and there; clear water shelving rapidly, deep at all hours; beach solitary beyond wont, whole town rather solitary ... Never saw a place more promising.' Mrs Carlyle's experiences of the seaside included 'falling among bugs' at Ryde, and at Ramsgate smells of 'spoiled shrimps complicated with cesspool'. She didn't come to Aldeburgh. Her husband had been driven over for the day from Woodbridge by Edward FitzGerald. It was a Victorian Sunday. The sight of the egregious pair in Fitz's gig was too much for the churchgoers, whose expressions of sanctimonious horror added appreciably to everyone's enjoyment.

Edward Clodd, a fifteen-year-old Aldeburgh boy, was presumably at that time on his way to the Union Baptist Chapel. It wasn't the sight of FitzGerald and Carlyle in a gig, but the arguments of Jowett, Huxley and Tylor in the '60s and '70s that freed him and enabled him to write his Darwinian best-seller, *The Story of Creation*. At twenty-one he wrote (anonymously) the *Guide to Aldeburgh* (1861), the most informative guidebook ever devoted to the town. Back in '55, he and the other boys used to crowd into the Reading Room to hear the Vicar, dull Mr Dowler, read the Crimean news in *The Times* from its famous war correspondent, W. H. Russell. One September morning that year Newson Garrett's children were all at breakfast at Alde House up on Church Hill when their great, blond, blue-eyed father strode into the room with a newspaper in his hand and the words: 'Heads up and shoulders down; Sebastopol is taken.'

Newson Garrett bought up a corn-merchant's business, with trading vessels and premises at Snape Bridge, and came to live in Aldeburgh in 1840. His elder brother Richard carried on and vastly expanded their family iron works at Leiston. Another brother, Balls Garrett, was equally successful with the Medway Iron Works at Maidstone. It was a dynamic family and Newson quickly became the leading businessman in Aldeburgh, from about 1850 until his death in 1893. He transmitted his remarkable energy to some of his own children, notably Elizabeth and Millicent. Millicent Garrett Fawcett's *What I Remember* provides perhaps the freshest first-hand observation of life in Aldeburgh in the early Victorian years.

She remembered walking along the Crag Path ('we always resisted with vehemence any Cockney attempt to call it The Esplanade, The Parade or any such name') when still young enough to be holding her father's hand (she would have been six or seven) and listening 'with all my ears' to his arguments as he tried to persuade the leaders among the beachmen (the fishermen, as distinct from the merchant-seamen) to volunteer for the Navy in the

Crimean War. One good independent beachman repeatedly declared that he was as ready as any man to sacrifice himself for his country, 'But volunteer, sir, I will not.' Young Millicent Garrett had an accurate ear for Suffolk speech, and a child's innocent eye for politics. When the Tsar died she thought the war would stop at once. The 'giant liar' of Tennyson's *Maud* was dead. There could be no reason to fight any more. 'Grown-ups never seemed to see the things that were so obvious, to a child.' One of the good results of the war was the spread of the Turkish bath. Garrett had one built at Alde House, and a groom was heard grumbling: 'Master is buildin' hisself a sweatin' house: if he'd rub the hosses down he wouldn't want no sweatin' house.'

The little seaside town of these years is formally described in White's *Directories* of 1844 and 1855. Its numbers grew from 1,500 to 2,400, almost to its present size, during the Victorian age. In '44 about forty vessels belonged to the port on the river, averaging about 60 tons, and employing about 150 men. No less than 200 licensed fishing-boats brought into the beach in summer soles and lobsters 'in great abundance', and in the autumn herring and sprats to be dried and salted for Holland, London, and other markets. Watson's General Telegraphic Station on the terrace above the town reported to London by post all vessels observed off shore.

A national school, built by subscription in 1839, was attended by about sixty boys and fifty girls in 1844. A charitable society for the relief of the poor was founded in '43. A wharf at Slaughden, given by a Wentworth Lord Strafford years ago, produced about £50 for the schooling of poor children. There were three private 'Academies' and a circulating library. Among tradespeople seven shoemakers were named, seven tailors and drapers, fourteen 'fishermen and smack-owners', twelve master mariners, four pilots, nineteen lodging-house keepers and two hairdressers. Garrett's name appears among the six coal and corn merchants and the two shipping agents in 1844. His personality may be detected in many of the changes recorded in 1855.

His is the largest personal entry in 1855: 'merchant, maltster, agent to Lloyd's and Harvey & Hudson's Bank and Royal Insurance Co.; receiver of droits of Admiralty, vice-consul for Norway and Sweden; supervisor of pilots etc.' Since '44 the four pilots had increased to seventeen 'under the superintendence of Mr N. Garrett, the agent to Lloyd's'. There is a reference to the proposal of 1851 to force a channel 15ft deep at low water through the spit from sea to river, to make Aldeburgh a great harbour of refuge, 'which it is estimated would cost only about £60,000'. 'On the beach is an excellent Life Boat, built in 1855; and a Coast Guard Station with Manby and Dennett's apparatus for saving the lives of the shipwrecked ... After the Moot Hall had been long disused, the Corporation determined in 1853 to have it completely renovated ... Gas Works are about to be erected by a company of shareholders.'

These changes registered in the 1855 Aldeburgh *Directory* are intelligible only in terms of Garrett's impulsive energy. And much of the remaining detail of that directory is given life and meaning only through his family's records. How dull, for instance, this entry: 'Metcalf, Hy. Percy, gent.' – until Millicent tells how he was a shipbuilder from the Tyne, who built ships at Snape for her father, and whose passion for music transformed the social life of Aldeburgh in a quite prophetic way, bringing Bach, Mozart and Handel. 'He was less enthusiastic about Beethoven ... I can hear now my sister Agnes singing Spohr's *Who calls the Hunter to the Wood?* with the piano accompaniment in Mrs Metcalf's rather inadequate hands – Mr M. playing the horn obligato and taking the horn from his lips from time to time to say to his wife quite good-naturedly, "What a fool you are, my dear".' It reminded Mrs James of 'her naughty days' when she used to go to the opera. Mrs James, grandmother of M.R. James, was a sugar-planter's widow, reduced in fortune since the emancipation of the slaves. She lived at Wyndham House, a portion of which (again anticipating the future) she set apart for use as a public elementary school. Mary Reeder, listed under 'Milliners, etc.', had a lively recollection of the Napoleonic wars. Her father and four other Aldeburgh sailors were taken prisoners about 1798. The wives of the others gave them up, 'but my mother, she say, "Noo, I will niver put on black for Joe Reeder not till I know he's dead, not if I can afford it iver soo".' She lived to be about a hundred, and to have a municipal vote when in 1870 it was given to women rate-payers.

Newson Garrett's connection with the improved coastguard and lifeboat service was not confined to mere commercial interest. One terrible day, 2 November 1855, seventeen ships were driven ashore and broken up on the shoals off Aldeburgh. He received the thanks of the R.N.L.I. for his help in the 'rescue through the surf of nine out of the eleven of the crew of the Swedish brig *Vesta* ... near Orford Low Lighthouse'. George Cable, father of the famous lifeboat coxswain James [see p.64 and plate 5], lost his life in the surf relieving Garrett at the end of the human chain.

The Reading Room was an improvement of 1850, a decent, single-storey building with three tall windows. (It was converted into the Jubilee Hall – at Garrett's instigation – to mark the fiftieth year of the Victorian age.) It began as a reading, lecture and concert room for visitors and members of the Aldeburgh Literary Institution and Public Library, with more than a thousand volumes in 1855. Joseph Buck, the printer and stationer, was Secretary. In '61 he printed Clodd's guidebook. In '65, he was printing a number of lampoons and broadsheets directed against Garrett, two of which are reproduced here.

Clodd's *Guide* describes the establishment of the new grammar school in Crespigny House under the Rev. Wm Tate, MA. He describes the original bedsteads in the Martello Tower, constructed to hold four men. He enumerates the different kinds of fishing-boat, and the two separate parties of boatmen with yawls of 'assorted sizes', ranging from the 'bad weather boat' to the rowing 'gig'. These parties were the Up Towners and the Down Towners, whose spirit of rivalry 'exists in greater intensity among the small boys'. He brings out the colour: the promenade is 'newly cragged and therefore brightly orange in the sun'. He suggests the names of the visiting couples, the men's very fashionably inspired by the Victorian court: he thinks of the wonderful North Sea sunrise, before 'the Julias and Floras with their Fredericks and Adolphuses have begun lounging on the shingle to read *The Woman in White* together'.

The railway came on to Aldeburgh from Leiston in 1860, and Wilkie Collins came about the same time. (He owed his Christian name to the friendship of Sir David Wilkie with his father, the painter William Collins, whose popular line in sea-side scenes was illustrated in a Festival Exhibition.) In 1862, his novel *No Name*, with its skilful verbal sketches of the Aldeburgh sea-front, appeared and went into several editions [see p.241]. In the spring of that year, FitzGerald was over in Aldeburgh again 'to have a Toss on the Sea and a Smoke with the Sailors. We have Grog and Pipes in a little Tavern Kitchen,' he wrote to his friend Stephen Spring Rice, 'and sometimes in a sort of Net-house where (on a Saturday Night) we sing songs too. One of the Songs is *The Pride of Aldboro*, and I gain Applause in *Pretty Peg of Derby*-O! The childishness and Sea Language of these People pleases me.'

ADVICE GRATIS before ten in the morning (and after.) *B. Feb fr*

Let the Cobbler keep to his ball of wax and lapstone.

Let the Tailor keep to his goose.

And let the limb of the law, residing not 100 miles from the Town Hall at Aldeburgh, keep to the Bankruptcy Court, settling accounts in *full* (with a small dividend.)

Who threatened Mr. Smith, the carter, 3 times with a summons for driving his cart on the crag path, or public foot and carriage road? *Roxburgh.*
Who summoned the poor afflicted Mr. Swaby for driving his carriage on the said road? *Roxburgh.*
Who threatened Lady Franklin (the much to be pitied widow) with a summons for having a hired carriage on this said road? *Roxburgh.*
Who ordered Mr. Hele's carriage off another public foot and carriage way? *Roxburgh.*

FAIRPLAY.

J. BUCK, P -TER BLYTHBURGH St., HIGH STREET, ALDEBURGH, SUFFOLK.

QUESTION. *Feb fr*

Is it lawful under the Highway Act, for one man to cart on, and deliver from a public foot path, in the High Street, Aldeburgh, Seven one-horse loads of Salt, about Six Tons, without name or address on his carts?

I say that it is not lawful, and I will prove that at the Town Hall.

A poor man dares not draw a Truck, or wheel a Barrow on the same path.

I will keep a sharp look out for Mr. Garrett's Salt carts, and when I leave for Twickenham, I will leave on duty an *Experienced Detective*, in plain clothes.

Justice for the poor man with his wheelbarrow.

Richard Pratt.

J. BUCK, PRINTER, ALDEBURGH.

In 1865 the Crag Path was the scene of encounters more harrowing than anything Miss Trotwood ever inflicted upon the donkey-boys in her neighbourhood. Millicent Garrett candidly owned that her father's temperament was not only sanguine, generous, daring, impulsive and impatient: she was afraid she must add 'quarrelsome'. In 1865, he came to the conclusion that nobody but himself had the right to take quadrupeds or carriages on Crag Path. He personally barred the way of an unfortunate visitor, a Lloyd's underwriter called Thomas Greenwood, who was taking his invalid wife for her customary donkey-ride on the path. When Greenwood enquired as to Garrett's authority he was told 'Mr Garrett was corporation and magistrates and everything else'. Dragged before Garrett's brother magistrates, Greenwood unwisely expressed himself 'satisfied that if it had been the interest of your worships to prevent invalid ladies from riding on the path you would not have left so delicate a duty to be performed by any irresponsible tradesman'. He was fined five shillings with costs, and warned that next time the 'full penalty would be inflicted'.

Richard Pratt was the next victim, but although the draft conviction of Pratt is still among the papers of John Wood, then clerk to the Aldeburgh justices, it appears from the best of the series of lampoons printed by Buck that Richard Pratt got off. It is a long doggerel ballad, entitled *A Curious Sort of Tail* [see p.89]. Garrett was one of the two magistrates who, in 1868, committed a boy of thirteen to Ipswich gaol for stealing 'three pounds weight of lead of the value of sixpence'. The Chairman of the Aldeburgh bench was Nicholas Fenwick Hele, a Scottish surgeon. His *Notes and Jottings about Aldeburgh* appeared in 1870, its chief interest bird-life.

In the '70s new National Schools were built by subscription and were soon attended by 550 children. The old school building of 1859 was turned into a coffee-house by the Church of England Temperance Society and, after a number of vicissitudes, for a while became the Festival Club and Gallery. The younger generation of Garretts – and others – were coming into their own [see p.86]. A strong critic of their father, writing in the *Suffolk Mercury*, admitted that Elizabeth and Millicent 'almost alone, have raised the whole platform (of feminism) to the level of respectability'. Elizabeth had taken the diploma of the Society of Apothecaries and the medical degree of the University of Paris. Millicent had married the blind Henry Fawcett, later Postmaster-General in Gladstone's unhappy second Administration, and launched the lectures that led to the founding of Newnham College at Cambridge. Garrett had sometimes had misgivings, had feared that his encouragement of his daughters in their careers would, as he put it, 'kill' their devoted but old-fashioned mother. But they had his determination. One of the best moments in his life must have been the burst of applause in the Senate House at Cambridge when he heard the announcement that Millicent's daughter had been placed 'above Senior Wrangler'.

Garrett's disagreeable outbreaks on the Crag Path in the '60s may have been expressions of his inner embarrassment at quitting the Conservative Party ('casting the traditions of his family and his own professions to the wind'), and developing into a full-blown Liberal at about the time when 'the blind professor became enamoured of his accomplished daughter Millicent'. Aldeburgh Corporation's shortcomings were exposed at the time of the Municipal Reform Act in 1855, but it remained unreformed; perhaps because it had lately lost its rights as a Parliamentary borough, which had been the chief cause of its municipal corruption. Garrett quickly secured entry to the Corporation and was for years the dominant member.

In these circumstances he obtained a long lease (150 years) of thirty-five acres of Corporation land, formed a company consisting solely of members of his family, covenanted to plant 10,000 trees and expend a minimum of £5,000 on building private residences. This 'Park Estate', was not much built on during his lifetime, but the Corporation was reformed (1885), and many people hoped Garrett would retire from public life. On the contrary, he picked a team of eleven and contested vigorously for the government of Aldeburgh. (A leading opponent, Mr Roxburgh, had been involved in the Crag Path affair.) The Grand Old Man's team was soundly beaten, and he himself came fourth in the poll. Nevertheless, he was elected first mayor of the borough. He was rightly in the chair at the Jubilee dinner, after so long a local 'reign' of his own. In 1889 he became the first representative of Aldeburgh on the County Council, from which he resigned in 1892, less than a year before his death.

In its last years Victorian Aldeburgh lived up to its reputation. The tenth edition of Black's *Guide to the Watering-places of England* said 'The principal charm is that it is retired and quiet'. According to Millicent Garrett the Aldeburgh gentry made no impression on the lives of the townspeople: on the Terrace, the Thellussons and the Adairs owned houses that still bear their names, and at the north end of the town the Vernons had an interesting Italian villa, now gone. In the '70s a Thellusson did try to promote a pier, but it quickly failed. The visitors who came for retirement and quiet were not interested in the possibilities of expansion or development. A photograph exists from perhaps the early Edwardian reign showing two young men riding donkeys on the Crag Path outside the Brudenell Hotel! That terrace was designed and built by Garrett himself, but already he belonged to the past. Uninhibited enjoyment appears on the faces of the bystanders. Occasional controversies stirred in the press as to the desirability of bicycling on Crag Path, or the proposed systems of sewerage and water supply.

But periodically, in the winter, when most of the visitors were away, the quiet was broken by the elements, and the town became one in its peril and distress. The storm of December 1897, the year of the Diamond Jubilee, is best remembered because it shortened Orford Ness. It was the occasion of remarkable heroism by Cable and his crew, who launched the lifeboat in the fiercest sea anyone remembered. This is how the storm gathered. It is a fine descriptive report from a local newspaper:

> The fishermen were busy with the sprat and cod lines and certainly Saturday looked more like the opening of a successful fishing. Several tons of fish were landed and the fishermen, eager to continue, floated for a night's drift of sprats, and had barely

James Dodds, Young and Old

got above the town to their different stations when the gale sprung up, and a general run homeward was hurriedly made. It was a weird scene, men and women rushing about the coast-line with lanterns, eager to render what assistance they could. The major part of the lifeboat crew being afloat, one by one, after hauling their fleet of nets, managed to reach their stations, and great anxiety was felt as the others did not turn up so quickly. A party of men rushed away to leeward, and one by one the castaways reached the shore, until the last one was secured nearly two miles from Aldeburgh. All night long the sailors were on the move, hauling up boats and securing the general litter of a coast-line during the fishing season. Just before daybreak it became apparent that the gale brought up a cruel tide.

How those lanterns conjure up the storm in *Peter Grimes*! In that black December gale, Victorian Aldeburgh was at one again with Crabbe's Borough.

Reprinted from *Aldeburgh Anthology*, 1972

Disaster to the *Aldeburgh*

James Cable

On December 7, 1899, our life-boat [the *Aldeburgh*] was called out to a vessel in distress on the Sunk light. I was suffering from influenza at the time, but when I heard the rockets fired I got up and went. I got into my oilskins and was just having my lifebelt strapped on when my doctor came and forbade me to go. The second cox was also on the sick list, so the boat was in charge of the bowman. We got the boat away from the shore by the haul-off warps, then they set the sails. The gale was blowing dead on shore and they were trying to get over the sandbank. A very big sea caught the boat broadside on, and to our horror, we saw that she was turning over. Everybody ran to where the boat was only a hundred yards from the shore. Twelve of the men were thrown clear of the boat, but six others were underneath it. There were plenty of people waiting to help the twelve men ashore. One of them was very ill at the time, and died soon after. The boat came on shore bottom upwards and it was impossible to lift her. I got on to the bottom and tried to hack through with an axe, but after the planks there were air cases and decks to get through, and I could not do it. We had about two hundred helpers trying to lift the boat with long poles, but it was not until the tide went down hours after that my men were able to crawl under the boat, and we knew that the six poor fellows must be dead. That was a very sad day for Aldeburgh and will never be forgotten. A large sum of money was subscribed for the widows and orphans, and a large marble monument was erected. There was also a cross at the head of each grave, and a tablet of copper hung in the church.

The boat had been altered three years previously, having decks put into her and self-acting valves, and we all agreed that she was never so good as before. After this, she was broken up by the orders of the Life-boat Institution. As for me, I got wet through twice that day, and most of my friends thought I should die of cold; but my wife had plenty of hot water and mustard ready for me, and in a few days I was quite well.

Our next life-boat was the *Mark Lane*, similar to the lost *Aldeburgh*. I was afraid after the accident that we should have some trouble in getting a crew; but I was wrong. Several of them were young men who had not been out before, one of them being my own second son. There was a big gale and a heavy sea on the shore and banks. Trying to cross the bank we went head first into a huge wave which knocked the boat astern. The iron tiller that I was steering by knocked me over the side. But I had one hand on the tiller and with the other I got hold of the mizzen backstay, and called to the man standing on the other side of the tiller to put the helm over. In this way I was pulled into the boat again, and our service was carried out without further mishaps.

Another time we saved a German crew and vessel, for which I received through the

Coxswain James Cable

German Consul a silver watch, containing the Emperor's photograph and an inscription. The second cox and the bowman also received watches, and the crew a sum of money.

In the summer of 1914, we had our new life-boat, the *City of Winchester*, at that time the largest sailing life-boat in England. It weighed about eighteen tons with all on board, and was very strongly built of oak. The designer had consulted us a great deal about it. I went to London and put my views about self-acting valves to Professor Algar and Mr Watson. When I had explained my preference for holes fitted with plugs they agreed with me. We had a grand day in Aldeburgh when the boat was christened by the Marquis of Winchester.

In 1906, when the Dunwich and Thorpe Ness Stations were abolished, we had another similar, but smaller boat. Both these boats have been very successful. The Coxswain-Superintendant takes out whichever boat he considers most suitable for the distance and the weather. The smaller one is much quicker to launch, but in a heavy gale the men put most faith in the larger boat. Boat No.2 is named the *Edward G. Dresden*.

I will not weary the reader by detailing all the rescues these two boats were responsible for. Often we had salvage jobs to do, but always our first work was to save life. Though there was often considerable danger and always much discomfort, I never knew there to be any trouble in getting a crew together. On a dark night, in a snowstorm, in fog, in a gale, the rocket signal would bring forth numbers of men from their beds, dressing as they

Surveying damage on Crag Path after the 1937 storm

came, their women carrying their clothes for them. Often on a long job they suffered from cold and hunger, glad to drink hot soup out of their sou'westers (thus freeing the oil to mingle with the soup), glad to eat raw potatoes.

Twice we were greeted by drunken crew, and once threatened by the captain's revolver. Once when we reached the scene of a wreck we were distressed to find a boat bottom upwards, but no trace of the crew except some caps and such personal belongings floating about.

Sometimes, having set out to do one rescue, we would find others in our course. Once we rescued three ships during one absence from home. It was on one such occasion that I arrived home to find a reporter from the *Daily Telegraph* waiting for me. I told him to wait a bit longer until I had had a few hours sleep!

I have told you sufficient to indicate the need to vary our methods according to each case. Sometimes one way, sometimes another would bring off the rescue. Once we had to cut a two and a half inch cable chain with a small hacksaw. It took two hours.

Many times during the war we were called to ships that had been struck by mines or torpedoes. One time I met two soldiers carrying a body on a stretcher. They said he had died from drowning. I asked if they had tried artificial respiration, and they replied that they knew nothing of it. My companion thought he had seen an eyelid flicker, so we stripped the man and set to work. A hospital nurse came along, and she was a great help. After about forty-five minutes we could see a little life in him. Then he was taken to the Martello Tower where the coastguards were, and with the help of a fire and warm sandbags was soon breathing normally.

From *A Lifeboatman's Days: The History of James Cable, ex-coxswain of the Aldeburgh Lifeboat, Told by Himself*, no date; see also plate 5.

Owlbarrow

Kathleen Hale

My next book was *Orlando's Seaside Holiday*. The Navy had left Douglas [her husband] with a passion for the sea, and we went to Aldeburgh for a sailing holiday. The trip was a great success, imbuing the boys with a permanent love of sailing: they have always owned some sort of boat ever since. For myself, I hated sailing, for there was never a moment in which to contemplate the river scenery, water-plants, fish, and herons. I spent my time cowering in the bilges to avoid being knocked senseless by the swinging blows of the boom.

Aldeburgh (Owlbarrow in the book) is the background for *Orlando's Seaside Holiday*. When we arrived just as the sun was setting, we were entranced by the steep descent before us leading down to the tiled roofs of the lovely old town, with the unlimitable expanse of the sea at our feet [see plate 7]. We came armed with two dozen of our own hens' eggs for our landlady (food rationing was still gripping us by the throat). I loved the 'fantaisie' villas on the seafront, and found these bizarre constructions of red brick, white stone, turrets, and battlements, which looked as though they had been built of nursery bricks, much more amusing to draw than the elegant Georgian houses. When I produced *Orlando's Seaside Holiday* I had to alter the fantastical architecture of the little seaside villa which I had drawn meticulously as the home of bad-tempered Mr Curmudgeon. The editor at *Country Life* warned me that I could be sued for libel, because the association with such a gloomy character might deter a potential purchaser for the villa. It was the first time that I knew that you could slander a house!

Like many writers for children, I was reliving my own childhood in this book, trying to convey the magical impact that seaside holidays had on me as a child. I did a drawing of the lifeboat and the famous decrepit old ship (now defunct) beached above the tide which is where Orlando and his family spent their holiday. I decorated one of the pages with glass fishing floats, each one encased in an openwork net of coarse twine, which I had found abandoned on a beach. (I still have them. One had a hairline crack and was awash with seawater inside, which has evaporated over the years; the glass is now crazed and white as though frosted.)

Eric appears as Mr Cattermole on the beach flying a kite; I have substituted sand for the Aldeburgh pebbles. The dachshund Daisy was a personal friend of mine, a dog belonging to Cedric Morris's sister Nancy. Many other things in the illustrations were from life, including our old-fashioned bath at Rabley with its fancy feet, and the canvas-covered wooden trunk with a domed lid which I had bought in Etaples all those years ago.

From *A Slender Reputation*, Frederick Warne, 1994

Aldeburgh Literary Clerihews

Craig Brown

George Crabbe
Found Aldeburgh very drab
But I doubt he'd have had more fun
At Juan-les-Pins.

Edward Clodd
Said, 'isn't life odd?
I've been ever so slack
Yet I've still earned a plaque!'

Edward FitzGerald
Was a literary herald:
I'd give my right arm
To have written *The Rubáiyât of Omar Khayyam*.

M.R. James
Adored outdoor games
Like 'Who Can Find the Dead Dog
In the Thick Blanket of Fog?'

Barbara Vine
Says, 'Wooh! I feel fine!
A headless corpse has just been
Found in my dustbin.'

George Crabbe commemorated the people of Aldeburgh 'with sullen woe displayed in every face' in his poem *The Borough*. *Edward Clodd* lived at Strafford House, which now bears a plaque in his memory. *Edward FitzGerald* declared himself happiest 'going in my little Boat round the Coast to Aldbro', with some Bottled Porter and some Bread and Cheese'. *M.R. James*, the celebrated writer of ghost stories, lived at Wyndham House, Aldeburgh. Ruth Rendell, aka *Barbara Vine*, had a house on Crag Path. Her Vine novel *No Night is too Long* is set in Aldeburgh.

An Aldeburgh Boyhood

Jon Canter

Some children grow up in a happy home. I grew up in two. Our London house was in Notting Hill, just off Kensington Church Street, giving me splendid access to all the museums and concert halls London has to offer. Then, most weekends and every summer, my mother, father, sister and I motored eighty-six miles north-east of London, to our Cecil Lay house, High Ridge, in Aldeburgh, on the Suffolk coast. High Ridge was high above the town, overlooking the tennis courts, twixt[1] the marshes and the sea. To call High Ridge our 'second home' gives the wrong impression. In my mind, High Ridge was as much my home as 12 Kensington Walk. You could say it was my 'first equal' home.

It was in Aldeburgh that I learned to ride a bike, sail, play tennis and swim. It was here that I saw my first stained-glass window; here that I played my first hand of bridge; here that I learned to love the music of Benjamin Britten and the ghost stories of M.R. James; here that I had my first holiday job, helping the greengrocer's man deliver boxes of fruit and veg.

There were so many other like-minded souls from so many other good families. They too had houses in Priors Hill Road, Park Road, The Terrace or (best of all) Crag Path – which, despite its prosaic name, is the jewel of Aldeburgh. Crag Path is a seaside promenade lined with marvellous eccentric private residences, as opposed to the cheap hotels, bingo halls and souvenir shops that disfigure the seafront of most English seaside towns. Crag Path has been called a relic of the nineteen-fifties, as if that were not a compliment.

On a typical August day, in any year from the mid-sixties to the mid-seventies, I would leave High Ridge in the morning and not return till dusk, hungry as a hog for the ham and chutney and boiled potatoes and frozen peas and apple crumble that would be waiting for me on the sideboard, my ice-cream as tepid as my ham.

'What have you been up to?' my mother would ask.

And always I would give the same reply: 'Having fun!'

'Very good!' she'd say.

My partners in fun were the younger generation of these Aldeburgh house-owning families: the Holts, the Pilkingtons, the Thodays, the Moxon-Smiths, the Cattos, the Farquharsons, the Hamilton-Woods. The back doors of their houses were always open. It

---

1. Yes, a winsome and 'writerly' word. But appropriate in this context.

was true then and it is true today. Of how many places can that be said? Where in London can a back door be left unlocked, without being removed from its hinges?

After supper it was time for a bath in which to soothe my battered knees. Knees, in those days, took a most terrible battering. They were always muddy and often grazed. Then I'd stare in the mirror to see what other damage the day had brought. A bump on the head from a flying apple. An elbow bruise, acquired in some rough-and-tumble game. Or a pain in the stomach, from a punch by Pilkington, largest and most vicious of my Aldeburgh contemporaries.

Do not tell me, please, that my childhood was unhappy because Pilkington punched me. Pilkington punched Martin Thoday. Pilkington punched Stephen Catto. Pilkington punched Damian Hawes and Jeremy Hamilton-Wood. (Once, when they were standing side by side, he punched them simultaneously, with a double-fisted jab I've never seen elsewhere, not even in a film.) His punches were invisible badges of honour, forced on members of my boyhood club. Had I not been punched by Pilkington, I'd have been unhappy.

❊ ❊ ❊

Every Christmas, on the eve of Christmas Eve, my parents invited the tradesmen of Aldeburgh to High Ridge for a drink. Year after year they came – Mr and Mrs Martin the greengrocers, Nancy and Jim our appointed newsagents, Jack the coalman, Bert the gardener, Dudley who tinkered with my father's cars, Rita who nursed my maternal grandmother through her terminal years, Terry the handyman, Eric the builder, Billy who 'did' the boiler, Margaret the treasure who cleaned High Ridge for more than twenty-five years. The butcher was there, as was the baker. Had my parents patronised a candlestick-maker, he would have been there too.

My father moved from guest to guest, spending the same short time with each. Handing round the snacks, gripping the bowl as tightly as Oliver Twist, I could sense the esteem in which my father was held. My father knew how to talk to a greengrocer – not with oily charm but with benevolence. As Bert the gardener said to me, taking a fistful of crisps in his black-fingernailed hand: 'Your father's a good man, boy. Never makes me feel like a criminal.'

Indeed. My father made everyone feel they weren't criminals. Even criminals. They recognised, as did everyone else, that he sought and found in them a common humanity.

'Call me Michael,' he said, hoping his guests wouldn't call him anything.

He didn't want to watch them struggling for the right form of address. Mrs Martin, who took pills 'for her nerves', called him 'Your Worship' – then, sensing she'd made a mistake, over-compensated with 'Sir Judge'.

'Give Mrs Martin a crisp!' said my father, helping an awkward moment on its way. I stepped up with the bowl. Mrs Martin looked anxiously into it and selected the only remaining crisp.

My mother, meanwhile, was in the kitchen, where no guest ventured. My mother was the daughter of the Lord-Lieutenant of Gloucestershire. It was she, not my father, who'd inherited High Ridge, built as a seaside bolt-hole by her grandparents in the late nineteenth century. But at Christmas, when my maternal grandmother – Granny P – came to stay, my mother wasn't the hostess in her own house. On the eve of Christmas Eve, she remained out of sight. Her mission was to sit with Granny P in the kitchen, keeping her away from the guests. They wouldn't have known how to respond to my grandmother's senility. They'd have been embarrassed and unhelpfully polite, unlike my mother.

I entered the kitchen to refill the crisp bowl.

'Do you know what the doctor wants to do with me now?' asked Granny P. 'He wants to send me to see a psychiatrist.'

'Do shut your cakehole, ma,' said my mother.

'Do you know what a psychiatrist is?' asked my grandmother.

'Yes,' I said. But it didn't stop her telling me.

'A nosy Jew.'

'Bring on those crisps, Robert!' called my father, from the door.

My father was a delicate man with pronounced cheekbones and swept-back silver hair. He looked exactly as a judge should. In 2003, on Andros, Mike Bell told me my father looked 'like an actor playing a judge', as if the old man's dignity and probity had to be feigned. My father's integrity was as shiny as an apple's – therefore, it had to be skin deep. It is a typically contemporary presumption. Bad apples are presumed to be the rule. We hear 'judge' or 'policeman' and what do we see? We see perverts, not upholders and enforcers of the law. We see the judge in – where else? – a brothel, paying a sadist to beat him up. Is he not aware that the sadist's a policeman who'd – of course! – beat him up for free?

The eve of Christmas Eve invitation said: 'Drinks. 6 to 7p.m.' Sure enough, the guests arrived at six on the dot. By ten to seven, they'd all gone. Their main aim, in attending the party, was to leave and be seen to leave at the correct time. No one wished to overstep the mark. They could see the mark approaching on the clock on the wall and accordingly understepped it. They'd been invited for a drink and a drink was what they had. They knew their place.

It's seen as bad that such as Bert knew their place. But how bad was it to know one's place, when one's place was in a dignified Suffolk coastal town where everyone knew their place? That gave one a sense of security, continuity, rightness and order. The Queen was in Buckingham Palace. My father was in High Ridge. Bert was in the garden. Amen.

Extract from *A Short Gentleman* by Jon Canter, Jonathan Cape, 2008

Night Fishing

Herbert Lomas

They sit on the shoreline
under a green umbrella, wielding quidsworth
of equipment and catching a few whiting.

At the eye clinic, behind me, a lady said,
'She's so much older than him, you know.
She won't leave him alone. He's had to
take up night fishing.' But no: they munch
a sandwich under the wind, share it
with their dog and stare at the silver
the moon's unrolling to their feet,
feeling how the world was before it was
so well-organised and understood,
and in the dawn a red ball rises
swiftly out of the sea
and disappears inside a cloud like a god.

BILL BRANDT

The Aldeburgh Band

Kevin Crossley-Holland

Somehow a mouth-organist
has got into the flue
of the gas stove in the Baptist Chapel.

Every minute or two
she draws a plaintive chord
that dies as the north-easterly
roars in the stack
and the blue flames leap.

But it's in the gazebo
painted star-white,
all the benches wet with mist and fret,
that I recognise what's happened:

when the timpanist plays hide-and-seek
and beats his tiresome tom-tom
in whichever cubicle I'm not,

I soon see or, rather, hear,
the whole ragged band
is billeted piecemeal
around Aldeburgh.

So, for instance, the fat man
with the alpenhorn
has found his way into the massive
stone head of the sea-god –
Aegir, president of the flint-grey waves
– and he keeps bellowing in my ear
every time I pass him.

There's a pretty lutanist
behind that lattice window
on Crag Path;
whenever she leans out,
she runs her light fingers
along the modillion.

And the contralto with the treacly voice:
there's no escaping her!
She's always under sail, beating
up and down the windy High Street,
decked in globs of amber.

But where's the maestro
– some say magician?
Is he locked in the foundation
or under the long-eared eaves, still
tuning in?
The Aldeburgh Band:
did he have a hand in this?
Those who tell don't know.
Those who know don't tell.

Darkness comes in to land and I walk
along the beach
past the very last silent fisherman
with his lantern
and ghostly-green umbrella.
Crunchcrunch under my feet. Crunchcrunch.

Down to the water's edge
and still the music's everywhere:
all the strings night-bathing
and phosphorescent,
playing glissando;

the stray with the cor anglais,
lonely as a whimbrel
over dark water;

and far away,
far under the glagolitic ocean,
the now-legendary player
of the tubular bells.

On receiving the Freedom of the Borough of Aldeburgh
Benjamin Britten

Britten accepted the Freedom of the Borough of Aldeburgh with a speech on 22 October 1962, for which this is his draft.

Your Worship, ladies and gentlemen –

It may seem an odd way of saying 'thank you' for the great honour paid to me this evening, if I start by saying that I'm afraid I rather *distrust honours*. In the arts, at least – it is so often the wrong person who gets them, or for the wrong reason. It is the dull, the respectable, the one who *kow-tows*, who *sucks up*, the members of that favourite name today – the Establishment. You know what I mean (conveniently forgetting for the moment honoured names like Sir Peter Paul *Rubens*, *Lord* Tennyson, *Chevalier* Gluck) – think of Schubert, unwanted; Mozart, a pauper's grave; Van Gogh mad like Blake; Wilfred Owen killed at the age of 25 – how far honours were from *these* great names and hundreds like them. The trouble really is that the people who hand out honours usually know so little about the artists. They take a famous name, and that's that. Why is it then that I am unexpectedly proud and touched this evening? After all, I shall not be able to write *H.F.A.B.A.* (Honorary Freeman of the Ancient Borough of Aldeburgh) after my name; and I am very clearly made to understand that I cannot (as the result of being a free man) park my car on the wrong side of the High Street without lights, and I gather I must continue to pay 24 shillings in the pound! No, I am proud because this honour comes from people who *know* me – many of whom have known me for quite a long time too, because, although I didn't have the luck to be born here in Aldeburgh, I have in fact lived all my life within 30 miles of it.[1] As I understand it, this honour is not given because of a *reputation*, because of a chance acquaintance, it is – dare I say it? – because you really do know me, and accept me as one of yourselves, *as a useful part of the Borough* – and this is, I think, the highest possible compliment for an artist. I believe, you see, that an artist should be part of his community, should work for it, with it, and be used *by* it. Over the last 100 years this has become rarer and rarer, and the artist and community have both suffered as a result.

The *artist* has suffered in many cases, because, without an audience, or with only a specialised one – without, therefore, a direct contact with his public – his work tends to

---

1. Discounting his time at the Royal College of Music in London and as a young professional in the capital, and then his years in America.

become 'Ivory tower', 'hole in the corner', without focus. This has made a great deal of modern work *obscure* and *impractical* – *only* useable by highly skilled performers, and only understandable by the most erudite. Don't please think that I am against *all* new and strange ideas – far from it (new ideas have a way of seeming odd and surprising when heard for the first time). But I am against *experiment* for *experiment's sake*; *originality* at all costs. It's necessary to say this because there are audiences who are not discriminating about it: they think that everything new is good, that if it is *shocking* it must be important. There is all the difference in the world between Picasso, the great humble artist, or Henry Moore – and tachist daubers; between Stravinsky – and electronic experimenters.

On the other hand, the *Public* has also suffered from this divorce. It has stopped using the serious artist for occasional or commissioned work, as hundreds of monstrous public monuments, acres of hideous stained-glass windows, nasty cheap music in the theatre or cinema, bare [*sic*] witness. *None* of this would have been *necessary* if the public and the artist could have got together – with an open mind on both sides.

It is this gulf between the public and the serious artist which has helped to encourage a deep-seated philistinism about the arts, which there is – I hate to admit it – in so many English people. It was not always so. In the glorious 16th Century, for instance, it was considered an *essential* part of *good social behaviour* to be able to sing a part in a complicated madrigal; and in the waiting rooms of the 17th Century there were not glossy periodicals, but a lute to be strummed on to while away the time. It is difficult to see *that* being popular in the 20th Century,! but we are making progress; we are getting back to thinking of the arts as *important* again, not something just silly, or suspect, or even wicked. And here I think I can blow *Aldeburgh's own small trumpet*. It is a considerable achievement, in this small Borough in England, that we run year after year a first-class Festival of the Arts, and we make a huge success of it. And when I say 'we' I mean 'we'. This Festival couldn't be the work of just one, two or three people, or a board or a council – it must be the corporate effort of a whole town.!! *And if I may say so what a nice town it is!* Festival visitors are always charmed by it, by its old buildings, *though like me they are nervous about how its new developments will look in 50 years time.* But Everyone is charmed by its lovely position between sea and river, and the *beach* with the fishing boats and *Life-boat*, the fine *hotels*, the *golf course*, wonderful *river* for sailing, the *birds*, the *countryside*, our *magnificent churches, and of course the shops too!* I have a very choosy friend from abroad who regularly *re-stocks* her wardrobe here, and buys most of her Christmas presents too, I believe.[2] All these excellent qualities are the result of the hard work, the imagination and friendship of everyone in the town.

If you have chosen to *honour* me as a *symbol* I am deeply grateful, but I can't help feeling that it is *all* of us, all of *you* who deserve it. So, in the name of *all* of us, all of *you*, I want to say a heart-felt 'thank you' for this touching, very special, and very treasured honour, which I have received this evening.

2. Probably Princess Margaret of Hesse

Britten in Aldeburgh High Street, 1949 (Photo by Kurt Hutton/Picture Post/Getty Images)

Rooted

here

'I am native, rooted here.'

Grimes in *Peter Grimes*
Act 1, Scene 1

George Crabbe: the poet and the man

E.M. Forster

This is the article which Benjamin Britten read while he was living in America and which drew him back to his native Suffolk in 1942.

To talk about Crabbe is to talk about England. He never left our shores and he only once ventured to cross the border into Scotland. He did not even go to London much, but lived in villages and small country towns. He was a clergyman of the English Church. His Christian name was George, the name of our national saint. More than that, his father was called George, and so was his grandfather, and he christened his eldest son George, and his grandson was called George also. Five generations of George Crabbes!

Our particular George Crabbe was born (in the year 1754) at Aldeburgh, on the coast of Suffolk. It is a bleak little place: not beautiful. It huddles round a flint-towered church and sprawls down to the North Sea - and what a wallop the sea makes as it pounds at the shingle! Nearby is a quay, at the side of an estuary, and here the scenery becomes melancholy and flat; expanses of mud, saltish commons, the marsh-birds crying. Crabbe heard that sound and saw that melancholy, and they got into his verse. He worked as an unhappy little boy on the quay, rolling barrels about and storing them in a warehouse, under orders from his father. He hated it. His mother had died; his father was cross. Now and then he got hold of a book, or looked at some prints, or chatted with a local worthy, but it was a hard life and they were in narrow circumstances. He grew up among poor people, and he has been called their poet. But he did not like the poor. When he started writing, it was the fashion to pretend that they were happy shepherds and shepherdesses, who were always dancing, or anyhow had hearts of gold. But Crabbe knew the local almshouses and the hospital and the prison, and the sort of people who drift into them; he read, in the parish registers, the deaths of the unsuccessful, the marriages of the incompetent, and the births of the illegitimate. Though he notes occasional heroism, his general verdict on the working classes is unfavourable. And when he comes to the richer and more respectable inmates of the borough who can veil their defects behind money, he remains sardonic, and sees them as poor people who haven't been found out.

He escaped from Aldeburgh as soon as he could. His fortunes improved, he took orders, married well, and ended his life in a comfortable West Country parsonage. He did well for himself, in fact. Yet he never escaped from Aldeburgh in the spirit, and it was the making of him as a poet. Even when he is writing of other things, there steals again and again into his verse the sea, the estuary, the flat Suffolk coast, and local meannesses, and an odour of brine and dirt - tempered occasionally with the scent of flowers. So remember

Aldeburgh when you read this rather odd poet, for he belongs to the grim little place, and through it to England. And remember that though he is an Englishman, he is not a John Bull, and that though he is a clergyman, he is by no means an 'old dear'.

His poems are easily described, and are easy to read. They are stories in rhymed couplets, and their subject is local scenes and people. One story will be about the almshouses, another about the Vicar, another about inns. A famous one is *Peter Grimes*: he was a savage fisherman who murdered his apprentices and was haunted by their ghosts; there was an actual original for Grimes. Another - a charming one - tells of a happy visit which a little boy once paid to a country mansion, and how the kind housekeeper showed him round the picture gallery, and gave him a lovely dinner in the servants' hall; Crabbe had himself been that humble little boy. He is not brilliant or cultivated, witty or townified. He is provincial; and I am using provincial as a word of high praise.

How good are these stories in verse? I will quote some extracts so that you can decide. Crabbe is a peculiar writer: some people like him, others don't, and find him dull and even unpleasant. I like him and read him again and again; and his tartness, his acid humour, his honesty, his feeling for certain English types and certain kinds of English scenery, do appeal to me very much. On their account I excuse the absence in him of a warm heart, a vivid imagination and a grand style: for he has none of those great gifts.

The first extract is from *Peter Grimes*. It shows how Crabbe looks at scenery, and how subtly he links the scene with the soul of the observer. The criminal Grimes is already suspected of murdering his apprentices, and no one will go fishing with him in his boat. He rows out alone into the estuary, and waits there – waits for what?

> When tides were neap, and, in the sultry day,
> Through the tall bounding mud-banks made their way ...
> There anchoring, Peter chose from man to hide,
> There hang his head, and view the lazy tide
> In its hot, slimy channel slowly glide;
> Where the small eels that left the deeper way
> For the warm shore, within the shallows play;
> Where gaping mussels, left upon the mud,
> Slope their slow passage to the fallen flood.

How quiet this writing is: you might say how dreary. Yet how sure is its touch; and how vivid that estuary near Aldeburgh.

> Here dull and hopeless he'd lie down and trace
> How sidelong crabs had scrawl'd their crooked race;
> Or sadly listen to the tuneless cry
> Of fishing gull or clanging golden-eye;
> What time the sea-birds to the marsh would come,
> And the loud bittern, from the bull-rush home,
> Gave from the salt-ditch side the bellowing boom:
> He nursed the feelings these dull scenes produce,
> And loved to stop beside the opening sluice.

Not great poetry, by any means; but it convinces me that Crabbe and Peter Grimes and myself do stop beside an opening sluice, and that we are looking at an actual English tideway, and not at some vague vast imaginary waterfall, which crashes from nowhere to nowhere.

My next quotation is a lighter one. It comes from his rather malicious poem about the Vicar of the Parish 'whose constant care was no man to offend'. He begins with a sympathetic description of Aldeburgh Church, and its lichen-encrusted tower, and now he turns, with less sympathy, to the church's recent incumbent. Listen to his cruel account of the Vicar's one and only love affair. He had been attracted to a young lady who lived with her mother; he called on them constantly, smiling all the time, but never saying what he was after; with the inevitable result that the damsel got tired of her 'tortoise', and gave her hand to a more ardent suitor. Thus ended the Vicar's sole excursion into the realm of passion.

> 'I am escaped', he said, when none pursued;
> When none attack'd him, 'I am unsubdued';
> 'Oh pleasing pangs of love!' he sang again,
> Cold to the joy, and stranger to the pain.
> Ev'n in his age would he address the young,
> 'I too have felt these fires, and they are strong';
> But from the time he left his favourite maid,
> To ancient females his devoirs were paid:
> And still they miss him after Morning-prayer ...

He was always 'cheerful and in season gay', he gave the ladies presents of flowers from his garden with mottoes attached; he was fond of fishing, he organised charades, he valued friendship, but was not prepared to risk anything for it. One thing did upset him, and that was innovation; if the Vicar discerned anything new, on either the theological or the social horizon, he grew hot – it was the only time he did get hot.

> Habit with him was all the test of truth:
> 'It must be right: I've done it from my youth'.
> Questions he answer'd in as brief a way,
> 'It must be wrong – it was of yesterday'.
> Though mild benevolence our Priest possess'd,
> 'Twas but by wishes or by words express'd:
> Circles in water, as they wider flow,
> The less conspicuous in their progress grow;
> And when at last they touch upon the shore,
> Distinction ceases, and they're view'd no more.
> His love, like that last circle, all embraced,
> But with effect that never could be traced.

The Vicar's fault is weakness, and the analysis and censure of weakness is a speciality of Crabbe's. His characters postpone marriage until passion has died; perhaps this was his own case, and why he was so bitter about it. Or they marry, and passion dies because they are too trivial to sustain it. Or they drift into vice, and do even that too late, so that they are too old to relish the lustiness of sin. Or like the Vicar they keep to the straight path because vice is more arduous than virtue. To all of them, and to their weaknesses, Crabbe extends a little pity, a little contempt, a little cynicism, and a much larger portion of reproof. The bitterness of his early experiences has eaten into his soul, and he does not love the human race, though he does not denounce it, nor despair of its ultimate redemption.

But we must get back to the Vicar, who is awaiting his final epitaph in some anxiety.

Now rests our Vicar. They who knew him best,
Proclaim his life t'have been entirely rest; ...
The rich approved, – of them in awe he stood;
The poor admired, – they all believed him good;
The old and serious of his habits spoke;
The frank and youthful loved his pleasant joke;
Mothers approved a safe contented guest,
And daughters one who back'd each small request: ...
No trifles fail'd his yielding mind to please,
And all his passions sank in early ease;
Nor one so old has left this world of sin,
More like the being that he enter'd in.

For the Vicar has died as a child, who retains his innocence because he has never gained any experience.

Well, the above quotations from *Peter Grimes* and from *The Vicar*, one about scenery, the other about character, should be enough for you to find out whether you have any taste for the story-poems of George Crabbe. Do not expect too much. He is not one of our great poets. But he is unusual, he is sincere, and he is entirely of this country. There is one other merit attaching to him. The George Crabbe who was his son wrote his life, and it is one of the best biographies in our language, and gives a wonderful picture of provincial England at the close of the eighteenth century and the beginning of the nineteenth. Even if you are not attracted as much as I am by Crabbe's poetry, you may like to get hold of his life, and read how the poor little boy who rolled barrels on the quay at Aldeburgh made good.

83

Suffolk Smugglers: a rum lot and a rough lot, too

Julian Tennyson

The Blyth once ran into the sea at Dunwich, but its mouth is now four miles to the northward, just above Walberswick. So complex are the workings of the sea that the Alde, which once ran out at Slaughden, behaved in precisely the opposite way; it turned southward and joined up with Orford's river, the Ore. And so for centuries these two have made one river running alongside the coast; but the sea, instead of leaving them as they are, is now trying to reclaim them for its own. The whole river is in jeopardy; each year the seaward side of the entrance moves a little farther back, and at Slaughden, too, the sea is eating through the shingle, as if it were trying to open once more the ancient mouth of the Alde. Heaven help the Alde and the Ore – it seems that no one else can.

Sea and river are separated by a strip of land which in some places is barely a couple of hundred yards wide. It is strange country, this, sand and shingle and stiff, spiky grass; a stretch more desolate and austere I have never found on the whole English coast. Man never goes there unless he must, for the fearful loneliness and the dull, deadening roar of the sea are too much even for the strongest nerves. In spring this place is a nesting-ground for thousands of birds, and their dismal wailing makes it seem more of a wilderness than ever.

And yet it has had its uses in the past. It was ideal for one thing – smuggling. There were probably more 'bad cargoes' landed here than anywhere else in Suffolk, and that is saying a good deal, for this coast, with its rivers and creeks and long, lonely stretches, was a smugglers' paradise from end to end.

They were a rum lot, the smugglers, a rum lot and a rough lot, too. If I were to rake up old stories, humorous and tragic, and to launch out into the ways and means and whereabouts of those hardy fellows who thought in terms of contraband, this book would run to two volumes. It is a limitless subject, and before you can appreciate the details of it you need some working knowledge of the coast; besides, all kinds of smuggling tales have been told already by people more competent than I am. Best of all is Richard Cobbold's classic story of Margaret Catchpole. This book was my bible when I was young; I read it at least twice a year, and the tears I shed over poor Margaret's two trials, Will Laud's fearful battles up and down the coast and his death at the supreme moment of Margaret's life, would well-nigh have flooded the river Alde. I read it again last year, and I must say that it wears extraordinarily well.

Cobbold brings in every detail of Suffolk smuggling: the famous cave at Bawdsey, the sinister, unscrupulous man who worked the smugglers like marionettes and made great fortunes from them, the way the 'crops' were run in and the thousand ruses used to disperse them. Above all, he tells you something of the Preventive Servicemen, whose lives were even more dangerous and desperate than those of the smugglers. No wonder half of them were dismissed for drunkenness or for lending a hand in the very traffic they were meant to destroy; for lying buried in the sand for a day and half a night, while the wind turned your blood to ice, a smuggler's bullet through your heart or a smuggler's club across your skull was not a very tempting reward.

Yes, the smugglers were a rum lot. In character they were very like the old-time poachers; in fact, many of them were poachers when necessity kept them on land for any length of time. And, like the poacher, their success depended upon two essential virtues – wits and courage. The coward and the fool soon came to an inglorious end in the sea or on the gibbet or at the feet of their enemies.

I believe that at the 'Jolly Sailor' at Orford there is one of the original handbills offering £50 reward for the capture of Margaret Catchpole after she had escaped from Ipswich gaol in March, 1800. It was only a few miles away, on Sudbourne Beach, that she was taken, while she and Will Laud were waiting for the boat which was to carry them to safety and happiness in Holland. Laud, in his last desperate stand, was shot dead by Edward Barry, the Coastguard officer, brother of the man whom Margaret was eventually to marry after her transportation to Australia. And on this same stretch of coast Laud's villainous henchman, John Luff, received his last wound in a shocking affray while he and his gang were trying to land a large cargo; it was in the shepherd's cottage on Havergate island [...] that 'at last, with one wild scream, his spirit, like an affrighted bird, fled away'.

Not one hundredth of our smuggling stories are told in *Margaret Catchpole*, but the best of them have found their way into papers and books at one time or another. They deal mostly with the hiding of cargoes. There was, for instance, that load of liquor at Coldfair Green which brought destruction upon its owners. It was left for some while deep in the ground under a rubbish heap, and the smugglers were so impatient when they came to get it out that two of them were suffocated by the foul air. Sometimes cargoes were hidden in ingenious ways in the boats themselves, sometimes in cottages and churches, while I have heard that one good lady kept a constant store of silk and spirits under the floor of the Meeting House at Leiston. In Rishangles church there was a hold under the pulpit, at Westhall there was one in the roof, and at Theberton (where the sixteen men of the German Zeppelin which was brought down in June, 1917, are buried) there was another under the altar.

The smuggler's prowess was on the wane a hundred years ago, and when in 1856 the old Preventive Service was reorganised as the Admiralty Coastguard, it very soon petered out altogether; and now the Coastguard itself is a travesty of its own name, for telephone, wireless and lifeboat station have well-nigh put it out of business. I suppose that in these days we can look back on smuggling as grand and romantic, for it has become as famous in legend as Arthur's Round Table or the Crusades; but it must really have been a brutal and desperate job, and the Suffolk shores are better off without it.

From *Suffolk Scene*, 1939, reprinted by Alastair Press, 1987

The Redoubtable Garrett Sisters

Jan Dalley

When Newson Garrett brought his young family from London to settle in Aldeburgh, in 1841, it was a homecoming. Nearby in Leiston, Newson's family had made agricultural machinery for three generations; now the age of twenty-nine he could buy a corn and coal merchant's business at Snape Bridge, one of the hundreds of small tidal ports on the east coast of England.

Four little children arrived with their mother Louisa: six-year-old Louisa (known as Louie), Elizabeth, born a year later in 1836, and two boys – Newson and Edmund, aged two and one. The family moved into Uplands House, opposite the church in Aldeburgh, but within ten years Newson built a far more imposing home to accommodate his growing family, which eventually numbered ten children. Alde House, with its stables and outhouses, kitchen garden and ice house, was a testament to industry and prosperity, and by the mid-1850s Newson's business had expanded so much that he was building the Maltings at Snape Bridge. He and his brother Richard, whose works at Leiston had prospered in parallel, were two of the most powerful men in the area.

Newson had had very little education, but he sent his boys to well-known schools and his girls to a boarding school in Blackheath where they made invaluable contacts. Louie married the brother of a schoolfriend, James Smith, in 1857, and it was in James and Louie's London house in 1860 that Elizabeth met Elizabeth Blackwell, a young woman who had qualified as a doctor in America, and found her vocation. At first, Newson ranted: the idea of a woman doctor was 'disgusting'. Her mother took to fits of violent weeping. It was nothing to the opposition Elizabeth was to meet over the next decade, as applications to august institutions all over the land brought one rebuff after another.

Undaunted, Elizabeth started as an untrained nurse in the Middlesex Hospital, to prove she had the stomach for the horrors of medical treatment before antibiotics or antiseptics. She took her instruction where she could get it: private teaching, classes in anatomy in London, St Andrews and Edinburgh, sometimes the chance to sit in on surgical procedures. But high-Victorian prudishness meant that her very presence was deemed 'indecent', 'repugnant' – at the Middlesex, the male students petitioned the Governors that 'the promiscuous assemblage of the sexes' in anatomy classes was 'an outrage on our natural instincts'.

In those days, to call a woman 'strong-minded' was highly derogatory, but Elizabeth had a strong-minded ally – her father Newson. After the initial opposition, he had joined battle, and later in life Elizabeth attributed her success to 'the extra amount of daring which I have as a family endowment'. Newson would turn up in the wards where the small and rather girlish Elizabeth was working; he threatened legal action against the institutions that turned her down; he paid for expensive private lessons with top medical figures. Five years into her haphazard training, Elizabeth discovered a loophole in the rules of the Society of Apothecaries – when they tried to bar her, Newson rattled his lawyers at them and in 1865 they were forced to allow Elizabeth to take their examinations. (They immediately amended their constitution, to stop any other woman doing the same.)

From then on, the Victorian prudishness that had worked against Elizabeth acted to her advantage – many women wanted to be treated by someone of their own sex. Now properly entered on the *Medical Register*, she could establish her own consulting rooms as well as working for the creation of the New Hospital For Women and later a medical school for women (where her own daughter was to qualify). In 1870 she learnt French in order to take an MD at the University of Paris – the first woman to do so.

By now, Elizabeth was internationally famous. But she wanted to challenge another taboo, and to show that marriage, motherhood and domestic happiness were not ruled out by success in the world. In Skelton Anderson, who worked for the Orient Steamship Company, she had the luck to meet a very unusual man, who after their marriage in 1871 proudly supported his wife's advancing career, and did so through 36 years of rock-solid (if very unconventional) marriage and the birth of their three children. Margaret, the middle child, died young of meningitis, and perhaps because of that, Elizabeth was a surprisingly anxious mother to the eldest, another Louisa, and her brother Alan.

Louie Smith had died in 1867: now it was Elizabeth and Skelton Anderson who provided the London base for the younger members of the family. Millicent, born in 1847, was the prettiest and probably the cleverest of the lot, and certainly had the family's 'extra amount of daring'. She had left school at only fifteen, but soon an introduction to the libertarian thinker John Stuart Mill, the great advocate of women's rights, set her path both intellectually and personally. Through Mill, Millicent met a young Liberal MP named Henry Fawcett, who was also a Cambridge don, even though he had been blinded in an accident. At nineteen, Millicent agreed to marry Fawcett, despite some opposition: 'I have been rather heavily jumped on by dear old Lizzie,' she wrote cheerfully (it is unclear whether she knew that Fawcett had also proposed to dear old Lizzie some years earlier). Millicent threw herself into the job of being Fawcett's guide, reader and notetaker – a role that took her into places otherwise closed to women, even into Gladstone's cabinet meetings.

It seems to have been a very affectionate marriage (they had one daughter, Philippa) and a partnership that brought Millicent intellectual and social satisfactions. Fawcett became Professor of Political Economy at Cambridge just as the movement for the education of women was starting: Elizabeth's old schoolfriend Emily Davies was beginning the campaign for the foundation of Girton College, Millicent herself was working towards the founding of Newnham College, and before long her elder sister Alice was writing from India that 'Millie's fame as a terrible little radical has spread to the Cambridge men here'.

The terrible little radical was encouraged by her remarkable husband to write her books on women's education and in her work for women's suffrage. At twenty, she joined the newly formed London National Society for Women's Suffrage, and became a prominent public speaker. After Henry Fawcett's death in 1884, the young widow made this political battle her life's work.

The passionate fight for women's voting rights united the family (one large rally saw at least a dozen Garrett sisters, in-laws, cousins, children), but divided its most prominent sisters. Millicent believed in peaceful methods – she was a suffragist rather than one of the Pankhurst 'suffragettes' – and became the president of the law-abiding National Union of Women's Suffrage Societies, while Elizabeth sided with her more militant daughter Louisa (who once spent six weeks in Holloway for smashing windows).

There were other differences between these powerful sisters. Millicent's belief in individual freedom led her to some strange opinions – to Elizabeth's bafflement and fury she opposed the movement for compulsory smallpox vaccination that was one of her sister's most dearly-held projects. But they supported each other, too: when Elizabeth took part in the Suffragettes' attempt to storm the House of Commons in 1908, Millicent, although she disapproved of the violent action, quietly arranged with the Home Secretary that Elizabeth should escape the truncheon-beatings that were a regular occurrence.

Elizabeth and Skelton returned to Aldeburgh and there were many happy years when Alde House was filled with children and grandchildren and a life of travel, writing, and work. Skelton became the town's Mayor after Newson's death in 1893, and with Elizabeth's help vigorously set about seeing to roads, drains and building plans – they understood that the once busy port had to find itself a new life in attracting visitors. After Skelton's death in 1907, Elizabeth herself was eligible to stand for election (local government laws made this possible) and – no doubt attracted by scoring another 'first' – she became Britain's first female mayor in 1908.

But some of her suffrage activities were too much for the small community. After she invited the notorious Emmeline Pankhurst to stay at Alde House, there were complaints from her fellow aldermen, and in 1910 a local hotelkeeper was elected Mayor in her place.

Elizabeth died in 1917, at Alde House, but despite all her achievements and her international reknown there was no recognition from her country. Militancy was never forgiven.

Millicent, by contrast, was made a Dame in 1924, her law-abiding tactics rewarded. In 1918 the enfranchisement of women over thirty had crowned a life of campaigning, and Milllicent spent her old age with her sister Agnes, the redoubtable old pair becoming inveterate travellers. While they were on a trip to Jerusalem in 1928 a telegram arrived that, according to a friend writing home, made 'the two dear octogenarians so happy that they joined hands and danced around the room'. It was the news of the 1928 Bill that gave the vote to women over twenty-one, on the same terms as men. The following year, 1929, Millicent died at the age of eighty-four.

There is much to say about the next generations of this remarkable family, but it is the daughter of Elizabeth and Millicent's brother Sam, the eighth of Newson's brood, who brings the Aldeburgh story full circle. Margery Garrett, who became a prominent social campaigner under her married name, Margery Spring Rice, lived near Aldeburgh and was a devoted music-lover: in 1948, just over a century after her grandfather Newson had sailed into the town with his young brood, she helped in the organisation of the first Aldeburgh Festival [see p.189].

A Curious Sort of Tail

Giles Scroggins

The powerful influence Newson Garrett wielded, both as Justice of the Peace, councillor and later mayor, caused some resentment. He wished to limit the use of the Crag Path to those on foot, and on two occasions, some twenty years apart, he prosecuted those who defied him [see p.61].

Joseph Buck, schoolmaster, printer and publisher of Aldeburgh magazines, printed a Cockney doggerel poem about the first case, said to be by one Francis Francis of Ipswich, editor of *The Field*, sheltering behind the name Giles Scroggins, a fictional character from *Punch*.

A newcomer, Richard Pratt, finding his way barred by posts put up by Garrett, dug them up, and found himself up before the bench. The tables were turned when the defendant's barrister addressed the magistrates:

Come list to me, ye gentles all,
And ye shall quickly hear
A very strange proceeding, which
But lately did occur.

All in the town of Aldeburgh
Down by the Suffolk shore
A gent named G—t flourished
For twenty year and more –

Which had a many ships and boats
And coals and coke likewise
And the profession of J.P.
Also did exercise.

Afore that town there was a beach
And on that beach was laid
A gravel walk, most pleasin', which
Was called the Promenade.

And there the little childering
Did play up many a game,

And nuss'ry maids, and missuses
Did occupy the same.

Our bold and haffable J.P.
thereon did often stalk
'Eld up his 'ead & boldly said
"I'm cock of this 'ere walk.!

No carriage on this path shall come
In any sort of weather!
No cart, nor barrow, nor no chair,
Nor nothin' whatsomdever."

But "cock-a-doodle" sometimes do
Get out of his account
And reckon cock-a-doodle do
When cock-a-doodle don't.

One Richard Pratt did come that way
For 'ealth to be a waiter,
His house were "Independent" named
Which likewise was his nature.

His carriage was a phaeyton
And varnished o'er splendacious,
His 'osses stepped tremendious
And snorted most owdacious.

And all along that Promenade
Them 'osses pranced and tore
As no-one never seed two 'osses
Do the like afore.

All out of bounce to that J.P.
Which when he saw the same,
Bust out in such a horful way
As I could scarcely name.

He ses, ses he, "What's this I see?
A phaeyton and a pair!!!"
A-foamin' at the mouth was 'e
And a-tearin' of 'is 'air.

"You musn't come on this 'ere walk,
In a chay and pair," ses 'e.
"But 'ere I ham," ses Richard Pratt
"And 'ere I means to be."

"You'll summonsed be & have to pay
If so you do persist!"
"And what's the Hodds?" says
     Richard Pratt
"There's money in my fist."

Then 'omeward to his carpingter
Our J.P. did betake him
And ordered 'im to fix three posts
As strong as 'e could make 'em.

When Richard Pratt goes out next day
He stops and ses, "I'm blowed
If that J.P. aint been and put
Three posts across the road.

I've got the will to 'ave 'em down
And 'tis well known, they say,
That wheresomdever there's a will
There always is a way.

There's no way here, so one we'll make
With a shovel & a pick."
So 'e works away at them there posts
And makes 'em cut their stick!

A Bobby in a bran new 'at
Then came to him next day
And 'anded him a paper which
This message did convey:

"Victoria of Westminster
The presence doth bespeak
Of that there wicked Richard Pratt
Afore her blessed Beak!"

So Richard couldn't 'elp 'isself
But was obliged to go
Afore the bench, with feelings of
No end of grief & woe!

He couldn't prove no alley bi
So things looked precious queer,
The beaks was all agreed to make
Poor Richard pay – most dear.

When up there rose a lawyer bold –
From Brentford town was 'e
And 'ow 'e flummoxed them 'ere beaks
Was wonderful to see.

He pitched into 'em right and left
Till they was in a fix
"Here's on to you," 'e ses, ses 'e,
Like 'alf a thousand bricks.

"Now do your worst, or do your best,
We'll meet you face to face!"
But they couldn't do no worst, and was
Obliged to adjourn the case.

And when the case come on agin,
The burthing of their song
Was "Richard Pratt wos werry right:
J.P. wos werry wrong."

Fitz and the Sea

Frank Hussey

Edward FitzGerald was born at Bredfield House in Suffolk on 31 March 1809. His now demolished birthplace stood within two miles of the Deben estuary. The Napoleonic threat was then much in evidence: Trafalgar was fresh in the mind and the period is marked by the many Martello Towers along the Suffolk and Essex coastline. FitzGerald described Bredfield and this first link with the sea vividly in a letter of 20 October 1839 to Bernard Barton, the Woodbridge poet:

From the road before the lawn, people used plainly to see the topmasts of the men-of-war lying in Hollesley bay during the war. I like the idea of this: the old English house holding up its enquiring chimneys and weathercocks (there is a great physiognomy of weathercocks) towards the far-off sea, and the ships upon it.

Writing of the Lowestoft fishermen Fitz declared: 'They are obstinate Fellows with wonderful Shoulders: won't take one out in one of their Yachts for a Sovereign though they will give one a ride when they go out to get nothing at all.' *In another letter from that port in 1859:* 'This place of course is dull enough: but here's the Old Sea (a dirty Dutch one to be sure) and Sands, and Sailors, a very fine Race of Men, far superior to those in Regent Street.'

Some of Edward Fitzgerald's thoughts concerning the sea and the Suffolk coast appear in a letter of 6 September 1860 to Mrs Charles Allen. In it Fitz adapted some of Crabbe's lines from Fragment written at Midnight. 'I have had to stay with me the two sons of my poor Friend killed last year ... I took them to our Seaside; not a beautiful coast like yours – no Rocks, no Sands, and Yew Trees – but yet liked because remembered by me as long as I can remember. Anyhow, there are Ships, Boats, and Sailors: and the Boys were well pleased with that. The place we went to *is called Aldborough: spelt* Aldeburgh: and is the Birth place of the poet Crabbe, who also has *Daguerreotyped* much of the Character of the Place in his poems. You send me some Lines about the Sea: what if I return you four of his:

Still as I gaze upon the Sea I find
It waves an Image of my restless mind:
Here Thought on Thought: there Wave on Wave succeeds.
Their Produce – idle Thought and idle Weeds!'

The whole atmosphere of Fitz's sailing at the time comes out in a letter of 22 May 1861 to Edward Byles Cowell: 'My chief Amusement in Life is Boating, on River and Sea. The

Country about here is a Cemetery of so many of my oldest Friends: and the petty race of Squires who have succeeded only use the Earth for an Investment ... and make the old Country of my Youth hideous to me in my Decline. There are fewer Birds to be heard, as fewer Trees for them to resort to. So I get to the Water: where Friends are not buried nor Pathways stopt up: but all is, as the Poets say, as Creation's Dawn beheld. I am happiest going in my little Boat round the Coast to Aldbro', with some Bottled Porter and some Bread and Cheese, and some good rough Soul who works the Boat and chews his Tobacco in peace. An Aldbro' Sailor talking of my Boat said – "She go like a Wiolin, she do!" What a pretty Conceit, is it not? As the Bow slides over the Strings in a liquid Tune. Another man was talking yesterday of a great Storm: "and in a moment, all as calm as a Clock".

Again to Cowell, in 1862, he wrote of his new boat Scandal: 'I am now a good [deal] about in a new Boat I have built, and thought ... I would take Dante and Homer with me ... I took Dante by way of slow Digestion; not having looked at him for some years: but I am glad to find I relish him as much as ever: he atones with the Sea: as you know does the Odyssey – these are the Men!'

To George Crabbe, son of the poet, he wrote in October 1863: 'I only returned yesterday from my Ship: in which I have been puddling about to Brightlingsea, Alboro' etc. I have somehow got to like living in it very much: with all its Cold and Discomfort. ... I was wishing for you in my Boat only yesterday, that you might have told me how or where to get a better Fireplace, or Stove; so as to burn Coke, not Coal, which spoils my sails with Smoke: and also such a Stove as would warm both Cabin and Forecastle.'

And in a letter to Charles Keene addressed from The White Lion, he described the Aldbro' he knew so well: 'No Sun, no Ship, a perpetual drizzle, and to me the melancholy of another Aldbro' of years gone by. Out of that window there 'le petit' Churchyard sketched Thorpe headland under an angry Sunset of Oct. 55 which heralded a memorable Gale that washed up a poor Woman with a Babe in her arms: and old Mitford had them buried with an inscribed Stone in the old Churchyard peopled with dead 'Mariners': and inscription and Stone are now gone. Yesterday I got out in a Boat, drizzly as it was: but today there is too much Sea to put off. I am to be home by the week's end, if not before. The melancholy of Slaughden last night, with the same Sloops sticking sidelong in the mud as sixty years ago! And I the venerable Remembrancer!'

Edward Clodd described Edward FitzGerald not long before his death: 'One June morning many years ago there approached a tall, sea-bronzed man wrapped in a big cloak, with a slow gait and wearing a slough hat kept with a handkerchief tied under the chin. "Don't you know who that is coming along?" said the fellow townsman with whom I was walking, adding "That's FitzGerald, he has written some poetry. You know they say he is ..." and my friend tapped finger on forehead. I remember him as hobnobbing with the beachmen, among whom he had his favourites, recipients of his bounty in boats and gear – everybody knew Old Fitz by sight and many called him Dotty.'

Extracted from *Old Fitz* by Frank Hussey, Boydell Press, 1974

The Other Side of the Alde

Kenneth Clark

I spent the first fifteen years of my life from 1903 to 1918 across the river from Aldeburgh in a house called Sudbourne Hall. It was one of Wyatt's characteristic East Anglian jobs, large and square, red brick outside, pseudo-Adam inside, and has now been pulled down, all but the stables, which were probably the best part. It had belonged to Sir Richard Wallace, but the only signs of his taste were a few French mantelpieces and a number of bottles of peach brandy. My father had bought it because of the shooting; the estate stretched from Snape to Gedgrave and from Butley to Orford, and provided three months' sport as good, I believe, as any in England. My parents arrived from Scotland in time for the first of October, when pheasant shooting begins, and left for Monte Carlo on about the tenth of January, when all but the wiliest of old birds had been polished off. I remained there alone for the greater part of the year.

Edwardian shooting parties were conducted with ceremony. The keepers and loaders wore bowler hats (most of the guns brought their own loaders), and an army of beaters wore specially designed smocks with red lapels. They plunged through the wintry woods shouting 'hi, hi, hi,' and beating the trees with their sticks. At 10.30, after colossal breakfasts, the guns left for the district where the beats were to take place, in a fleet of archaic cars. Then came the dreadful moment when they drew lots – little silver spillikins – for their stands, and if by ill-luck some famous shot found himself at the end of the line, with some duffer in the centre, the day's troubles would begin. At lunchtime they were joined by the ladies in enormous hats with veils, and the whole party would then repair to thatched pavilions in the woods which had been specially constructed, one in each district, to contain a lunch party of fourteen. Striped awnings were stretched round the walls, and from brass-bound hay-boxes there appeared a magnificent meal. How they ate! Local oysters and liver paté, steak and kidney pudding, cold turkey and ham, treacle tart, double Cottenham cheese, and always, to fill in the corners (as was often said with satisfaction), a slice of plum cake. The guns also drank as much as they dared (which was a good deal) but they sometimes had to forgo that second glass of Kümmel, because on the afternoon beats the ladies would be at their sides, and they would be more than ever anxious to show their skill.

No one, of course, could have been invited who was not a fair shot; but this was a highly competitive sport, and throughout England shots were graded, like seeded lawn-tennis players, with Lord Ripon and the Prince of Wales at the summit. It sometimes happened that a famous performer had an off day. Then his chagrin knew no bounds. The lady at his side would withdraw, and he would return silently to the house, not to be seen again till dinner. Indeed, if things had gone really badly he would refuse to come down to dinner, and a tray would be taken up to his room.

The last stand took place when it was already growing dark, and a flash could be seen from the barrels of the guns. Then the whole party would return and, I suppose, queue up for baths: because although there were twenty-five bedrooms at Sudbourne I remember only about four bathrooms. The ladies changed into tea-gowns and the gentlemen into smoking suits. I presume that the ladies drank tea, but I do not remember it, because my attention was always occupied by the gentlemen in the billiard room. The click of billiard balls is music to my ears, and on these occasions it was accompanied by the splash and crash of soda syphons ceaselessly diluting enormous tumblers of whisky. However, before the game was over I was sent upstairs to eat my prunes and junket. Then, safely in bed, came my favourite moment of the day. The ladies had changed again into dresses of splendour and elaboration, and by some means I had persuaded them that they must parade in my bedroom, in order that I might give a prize to the one I thought most effective. I now see that it was kind of them to humour me in this way; but at the time I thought I was conferring a favour on them, and took my judgements very seriously.

The guests usually dispersed on Saturday, to avoid the tedium of Sunday; and my father then turned to the other Sudbourne speciality, his prize animals. They were Suffolk Punches, red poll cattle and 'large black' pigs. All three won prizes at every show, and my cellar is still encumbered by silver cups, and vast ebony stands, which I have not the heart to get rid of. We visited the Suffolk Punches on Sunday morning (my parents never went to church). Their stables were dispersed about the park, each one ringed with beech trees, and these dear animals, vast, gentle, perfectly proportioned, would emerge like folk dancers and do a few steps for us. Then they would go to my father for their reward – a minute peppermint, of the kind called 'curiously strong', which made them sneeze, but seemed to give them pleasure. I think that Suffolk Punches provided my earliest experience of sculptural beauty. The memory of their full, compact shapes and silky brown surfaces, which I recover every time I open a conker, may still underlie my artistic judgements. I was also fond of the 'large blacks', and thus learnt early that *il bello é il caratteristico*. Their consistent ugliness, and eager acceptance of every kindness shown them, won my heart; and when a prize sow produced a fortunate litter the most promising piglet was called by my name. Alas, he became too famous, and during my first year at school his portrait appeared on the front of the *Daily Graphic* with the caption 'Sudbourne K: the biggest boar in the Show'.

My days were all pleasure. Most children suffer from boredom, but I do not remember a dull moment at Sudbourne. I loved the Suffolk country, the heaths and sandpits, the great oaks in Sudbourne wood and the wide river at Iken. To reach these favourite spots I reluctantly mounted a pony. Horses instantly recognise that I am afraid of them, and either bolt or rub up against walls or (most humiliating of all) lie down. However, a pony was the only means of getting as far as Butley Priory or the Maltings at Snape, and these were the two romantic boundaries of my world. They were both just off the estate, so, apart from their architectural beauty, they gave me the thrill of a journey abroad.

My greatest treat was a trip to Aldeburgh. For this I was allowed to borrow a governess cart, driven by an elderly groom with Dundreary whiskers and the good Suffolk name of Pryke (I suppose that the housekeeper in *Albert Herring* was really Miss Pryke, but Miss Pike is easier to sing.) We would drive to a point opposite Slaughden where a large bell

Horses at Shingle Street

hung from a wooden gibbet. If one rang it long enough a man would row over, grumbling, and take one back. I would then walk to Aldeburgh, have tea at Reading's, and spend the rest of the afternoon on the beach looking for amber, which of course I never found, and collecting pocketsful of pebbles, which of course lost their lustre by the time I got them home. I usually ended by buying a small piece of amber in Mr Stephenson's shop.

The charm of Aldeburgh is very difficult to define, as I often find when I try to persuade an American or Italian friend to visit the Festival. I could not explain to my parents why I liked it so much, and they were slightly annoyed by my frequent requests to go there. For some reason I had got it into my head that this was a place where my wits were brighter and my senses more alert than anywhere else.

I have never lost this feeling; and when, almost forty years later, there was a reason for going there again, I felt sure that a piece of myself would be recovered. To my astonishment it had hardly changed, and I found that I, too, had changed much less than I had expected: I immediately began to look for amber, although by this time I knew quite well that I should never find it; and I brought back even larger handfuls of fast-fading stones. I found that the delicate music of the Suffolk coast, with its woods straggling into sandy commons, its lonely marshes and estuaries full of small boats, still had more charm for me than the great brass bands of natural scenery, the Alps or the Dolomites. To all this was added the fact that Benjamin Britten had settled there, and made it a centre of inspiration. Others are better qualified than I am to understand the technical mastery of Ben's music; but in so far as it takes some of its colouring from the sea, and the skies and marshes of East Suffolk, I can claim to be an initiate.

Grimes and Herring are my compatriots. To sit in Orford Church, where I had spent so many hours of my childhood dutifully awaiting some spark of divine fire, and then to receive it at last in the performance of *Noye's Fludde*, was an overwhelming experience. I heard the *Fludde* again at a rehearsal in Orford Town Hall (where at the age of twelve I had been sent by my parents to make a patriotic speech); and while the procession of Mice, Crows and Doves was being organised, I reflected on what it would have meant to me if, between the ages of nine and fifteen, such marvellous works of genius had been within reach; and I had been allowed to participate in that more enlightened world which, as I already believed, existed on the other side of the Alde. I do not complain of the rich, sporting, philistine atmosphere in which I was brought up. I can think of many other milieus - clerical, academic or military - in which I should have been far less happy. But from an early age I knew that the only society I enjoyed was the society of artists, the society of people whose minds were free, whose senses were alert, and who felt the need to communicate their joy. As things turned out I have spent the greater part of my life with such people. But to have known them as a child; to have met them simply by crossing the Alde! With what rapture would I have clanged the bell at Slaughden and waited for the reluctant ferryman.

Reprinted from *A Tribute to Benjamin Britten on his Fiftieth Birthday*, ed. Anthony Gishford, 1963

George Ewart Evans

Matthew Evans

When George Ewart Evans and his wife and four young children first came to live in Suffolk in 1948, he was unknown there. Initially, people found him very hard to place; some thought he might be a farmer or horse breeder, perhaps a gentleman scholar with private means or a classical historian with an unusual curiosity about agricultural crafts and language. His pronounced Welsh accent and his Quaker wife added to the conundrum.

In fact he was born in 1909 in a mining village in Glamorgan, South Wales, one of thirteen children, and the son of a grocer who subsequently went bankrupt as a result of the Depression and the costs of sending George to Cardiff University to read Classics. He emerged as a nascent writer in the 1930s and became a communist, emigrating to England to find employment as a teacher in Cambridgeshire, where he met his wife, Florence. He was dogged with depression, and his stint in the RAF during the war did nothing to ameliorate this. It was decided to move to Suffolk, and his wife was offered a job as headmistress of Blaxhall village school. There they moved in 1948, to a house with no electricity, sanitation or running water, where George planned to write and look after the children while Florence was sole breadwinner.

Sitting in the schoolhouse trying to write poetry and fiction, George slowly realised that under his very nose was the subject that was going to occupy him for the rest of his life. He realised that he was living in a village populated by farm workers who had lived through the virtual disappearance of the horse as the main presence on the land, and into a period of increasing mechanisation. He realised that it would be an important piece of social history to record the voices, experience, attitudes, the feelings of these people before they died and their memory was lost forever.

We can speculate about what it was that made George suddenly look around him for his inspiration. In one way, the clues were in his background and undoubtedly he had a profound sense of the past. One of the most interesting books in his library is a copy of George Crabbe's poems. Crabbe was born in Aldeburgh in 1754 and George's copy of the selected poems has in it *The Village*, which is very heavily annotated by him. Perhaps it was reading this poem again, reading heavily underlined lines such as 'Our farmers round, well pleased with constant gain, like other farmers, flourish and complain', that helped him see where his future as a writer lay. With his tape recorder he interviewed many people and David Thomson would listen to the recordings and produce them into programmes that were transmitted on the Third Programme. He also realised that by recording and transcribing he might make available a resource that could he used in book form. So it was that in 1956 he wrote to Faber and Faber, amongst other publishers, and he said the following:

> For the past eight years I have been living in the above village which is in a remote part of Suffolk; and I have been struck by the number of interesting survivals here.
>
> The old people, who have such a knowledge of the village community which is quickly passing, are dying out; and with their going much of real value is being lost. I have recorded some of the material they knew and have included it in the enclosed MS. I offer it to you as something that might be of interest.
>
> The four accompanying photographs are sent merely as suggestions for a type of illustration. They could be supplemented by photographs of the old people mentioned in the MS, and by other photographs – if desired.

Unsolicited manuscripts, then and now, arrive at Faber and go into something called the 'slush pile'. Every manuscript is looked at by a reader and commented on. The reader for the manuscript which turned out to be *Ask the Fellows Who Cut the Hay* was Jan Perkins. She wrote on the bottom of his letter, 'Mr Evans has collected stories from the oldest inhabitants of his Suffolk village which he presents against a background of old country customs and manners. If he were not so revoltingly pompous and pedantic this book might be interesting for the way of life it recaptures. As it stands it is dulled by the author's personal interpolations.' This letter, annotated by Miss Perkins, was then passed to an editor to look at the manuscript and decide whether the dread capital 'R' for rejection was appropriate or not. Morley Kennerly, an American director of Faber's, wrote on the same letter, 'This book is a joy, most readable. Nothing patronising or ye olde about it and the author's treatment just right. It will have a market over the years and will pay its way.' He also underlined the word 'revolting' in Jan Perkins' notes and said 'nothing could be further from the truth'.

Morley Kennerly was a tall, elegant American who could have stepped out of the pages of a Scott Fitzgerald novel. He was the antithesis of my father. He was married to a lady with a title, went shooting in Suffolk at the weekends and drove around in a Bentley given by Barbara Hutton as a wedding present. He and George became very close friends, with a massive, almost daily correspondence, now in the Faber archive. Morley guided my father through Faber as he wrote his books, and when he retired Peter du Sautoy took over and also became a very close friend of George's. Peter had very strong connections with Aldeburgh – he was, with Donald Mitchell and Benjamin Britten, one of the founders of Faber Music, and his widow Molly lived in Aldeburgh until a year or so ago.

Ask the Fellows Who Cut the Hay is the first of ten books by George that Faber published. He broadcast and published countless articles on the old traditions, work that was to become the backbone of a writer who can be credited with starting the oral tradition in Britain. It would take another hour to discuss the importance and the problems of oral history and the oral historians, but even the detractors of this sort of history would concede that George's contribution was original and highly significant. Growing up as a teenager, my memory is of young academics coming to sec him, as his approach clearly appealed more to the younger academics than to the established ones. [...]

George, with the new-found confidence afforded by his hearing aid and some success as a writer, clearly became more settled in himself and began to do many things. For example, he had a passion for education and spent a great deal of his spare time working for the Workers' Education Association – the WEA. He would cycle off in all weathers at all times of the year to engage and interest people less fortunate than he had been with his formal education. It was an all-embracing passion for him. In the village he became a councillor, he was the driving force behind setting up a playing field (health again) and a village hall, and he became a very well liked and respected figure in the village, as did my mother. Looking back, this was an extraordinary achievement. Suffolk people are not known as welcoming to outsiders but my father, in particular, managed to get beneath their difficult reserve and had perhaps a unique ability to gain the confidence of village people, who would talk to him openly and frankly with the recording machine between them.

It may be that people in the village realised how difficult life was for the family in the early years. I remember a plucked chicken being left on the doorstep at Christmas time. Mrs Reeve, who was the housekeeper in the school, gave us cooked food, saying it was for the children, but I think she saw a family near the breadline. A few years ago we went back to Blaxhall when a plaque commemorating our father's life was unveiled.

From the early '50s the strain of the children was diminished as we all went off to the Friends School in Saffron Walden, paid for by the Friends Education Council. I asked my parents why we were sent away to school and they were genuinely concerned that if we had grown up in Blaxhall we would have become part of that enclosed society and might not have escaped. There is an irony in that four children from that background had a private education, but that was something I never talked to my father about. He remained a communist by conviction, if not an actual party member, until his death. He made me, as a member of CND and of the Labour Party, seem extraordinarily right wing.

We moved on to Needham Market, where my mother became head of a much larger primary school and we lived in the High Street in a dark and gloomy Tudor house and my father continued to write. He was very happy to discover that the vicar of the church opposite, Rev. Hargrave-Thomas, was, joy of joys, both Welsh and a communist, and they spent a great deal of time in each other's company. After a few years in Needham Market we moved on to Helmingham, where there was a schoolhouse next to the school. This was my mother's final job.

I have told the story of George's life as objectively as I can. I sense that […] I may have given the impression of somebody who was rather self-centred and depressed. In fact, he was an extremely kind man, caring and generous, and took enormous trouble with people. This meant that when anybody came to talk to him he welcomed them into the house, whatever the circumstances. Let me give you one example. He was fanatical about rugby and the great event of the year for him was watching England play Wales. I remember settling down with him one Saturday afternoon in the 1960s and fifteen minutes into the game, somebody who he barely knew knocked on the door and wanted to have a talk with him. I would have sent the person away, but my father took him into the study, talked to him, made him tea and missed the match.

With critical if not commercial success came some settlement of his inner demons. The one thing he wanted to do was move back to Wales but my mother, when she retired from being a headmistress, having spent her entire life working to support her husband and her family, did not fancy the idea of living in Wales, so they moved to Brook in Norfolk. He said bitterly, 'Back to suburbia.'

May I leave the last word on my father to my brother-in-law, David Gentleman. David first met George when he did the drawings for his third book, *The Pattern under the Plough*, and subsequently illustrated many of his books. Not only did he do the drawings but he married my youngest sister, Susan. David says: 'George was in his mid-fifties when I first saw him, but he seemed younger: upright and vigorous, with an open and friendly manner and a clear, piercing gaze. He looked the part of a countryman, in a tweed jacket, a hat also of tweed, drill trousers, and stout brown shoes. As I grew to know him, I discovered that he was sympathetic and generous with help and encouragement. He was intelligent and shrewd; his judgements, though seldom sharply expressed, were acute and penetrating. He was humorous, balanced and rational. In conversation he was tolerant and unassertive, but it was soon clear that he held independent views with firmness and conviction.'

David goes on: 'The scope of George's work is complex and hard to define. His books might seem on the surface to be simply about subjects: the countryside, and the past. Much in them is indeed remembered: old people talking clearly and vividly about how things were, in their recurrent phrase, "at that time of day" – that is, when younger. Certainly one can enjoy the books in a spirit of nostalgia, and take pleasure in the charm of the rural subject matter. But George was too clear-headed and too objective for nostalgia, and one quickly finds out – as he did – that the lives and times he recorded were far too hard for anyone with any humanity to wish them back. Rather, he used the past as a way to understand the present.'

From a memoir privately published in 2003

DAVID GENTLEMAN

From Milkround to the Maltings
Bob and Doris Ling

Bob and Doris Ling became caretakers of the concert hall at Snape Maltings in 1971. Bob had worked as a maltster at Snape Maltings until it closed down in 1965, when the pair became gravediggers. Their friend Eric Crozier recorded their reminiscences, which Simon Loftus edited and published in 1987, and from which the following extracts are taken.

BOB: ... At the time of the fire we were living in the little bungalow I had renovated along Snape Terrace. We had a card-school with some friends and relations of ours from Leiston, and that night we were having a nice evening together, with some cherry-pies and ham and things like that, and one of the ladies looked out of the window and said: 'There's a chimney on fire down the road', and I looked and of course it was the Maltings. I wasn't working there then, so I had no connection with it.

DORIS: You were very cut-up about it, though.

BOB: I phoned the fire-brigade right away, but there had been lots of calls. We could see the flames coming out of the 'bluffers', especially the first one, the east one above the stage. We all stood watching from the terrace – there was nothing anybody could do – and before we separated one of the company said: 'You beat us tonight, Bob. We would have to flood Leiston High Street to equal that!'

DORIS: What a sight that was! All those flames – just as though the heat lifted the roof, because it seemed to be suspended in the air above the flames, and then it went down again. That was the illusion from where we were. There were crowds watching from the terrace and when they heard the snapping they thought it was whisky-bottles exploding, not realising it was the asbestos slates on the roof going bang, bang, bang!

BOB: It began about 9.30, and it was still burning at eleven o'clock or midnight.

ERIC: How was it you both went to work at the Maltings?

DORIS: We did a milk-round, and we weren't very happy...

BOB: That was when we left gravedigging. The milkman told us one day there was a job going at Hill Farm Dairy and we thought: 'What a nice job! Just putting bottles on doorsteps' – but that turned out the worst job I have ever done in my life. I would rather have carried twelve, sixteen stone of barley from six in the morning until midnight. It was terrible! […] Your hands and your clothes were filthy and the old type of van stank of sour milk – God alive! – and a little dog in one place used to bite my leg all the way up the path and all the way back and then the lady would pick it up – (falsetto) 'Oooh, you little dear! He loves you, Bob!' […] A milkman has to do everything! One old lady before us used to want her mattress turned every so often – they'll stop and do things like that! 'Will you do like the other man did - call at the shop and pick me up half a pound of marge and a pound of tea, and bring my newspaper?' Very often, after all, they live in the wilds of the country. One old lady gets the milkman here to do up her corsets or fasten her zip or something! All part of the service – 'A pot of cream and two pints of milk and my corsets done up'!

They weren't really sorry to see us go – but how it happened we went from milk to the Maltings, was, one day we were going to a funeral out Bury St Edmund's way, and my brother-in-law […] told me there was a job going at the Maltings, and next day we went down to see George Hardy, who worked for the Festival. We thought he was the managing director, with his feet up on the desk. They wanted a couple, and 'You two will do me fine,' he said. … So that was the end of the milk-round.

DORIS: We had been going to try window-cleaning next.

BOB: We went over to Aldeburgh for a chat with [General Manager] Stephen Reiss and he decided to take us on. But within three months, Stephen was over at Snape, taking off his glasses and wiping them, and saying: 'I had a terrible job. I had to sack George.' – 'Good God!', I said. – Then, 'Will you take it on, Bob?', he asked. So there we were, thrown straight into a theatre not so long after a massive fire.

DORIS: What worried me was, we didn't know a thing about it … When he was first told about the job, I said: 'It's like this, Bob – I don't want to jump into it like we did the milk round. I don't mind what it is – I love working with you – but I don't want any responsibility', because I don't like responsibility. But the next thing, there we were, and I used to be so worried because we used to have the fire-chiefs down a lot, and even now, although I laugh and carry on, I'll get Bob to go back with me at night, because if that building burned down … It isn't an expensive building and you'd get lots of insurance - but everybody loves it, we love it, it's a home for opera, and although I don't understand music, over the years the sound sends hairs up my arms.

BOB: So many people get enjoyment out of it.

DORIS: When the opera is over and the orchestra has gone and you have said: 'Goodnight! God bless you! Safe journey home!', there is this lovely building and its foyer so peaceful and quiet, and sometimes that terrifies me … I think, if I could only retire now and go up the road and know I've left it safe. […]

When I was younger and when I went out to work, I never listened to music – I was always a great reader. I loved the Brontës and things like that. When we came to the Maltings, I

BILL BRANDT

was honest about reading being my thing, not music, and they told me: 'You're doing somebody out of a job who would love to be here for the music' – but if I had loved music, I would have wanted to be there in the hall, not cleaning the place up afterwards. But I enjoy the concerts now I've been here so long.

BOB: ... When Ben had a performance at the hall, he used to pop in to see us on the way from his dressing-room, and he'd say: 'Get me a whisky, will you, Bob, so I can have a wet when I come off-stage?', and I would pop up to the bar to get him one. Other times he would say: 'Come and listen to the bittern', and we would go outside and hear the old bittern booming.

DORIS: When the Queen Mother came here we were cleaning late one night and the bittern was booming away like a foghorn. [...]

ERIC: I shall never forget Ben's funeral at Aldeburgh in 1976 and you and Bob standing by the graveside, and how you had brought rushes along to line the sides - that was lovely.

BOB: I did one like that at Newbourne with greenery, and there was General Reed at Aldringham, at River Hundred - when his wife was buried, he said to me: 'Bob, she didn't like dirt at all, but she loved flowers, so I'll have two vanloads of flowers.' I bought some netting and pegged that all round the grave and I threaded all the flowers into the net and barrowed the soil away, and there were flowers round the grave, too. For Ben's grave I got hessian and made wire pegs to fasten it against the sides, so that the plumes of the reeds stood up - the top ones were just above the top of the grave. We didn't dig Ben's grave - that was done by the Council: but luckily we knew the lad who was digging it, so I asked him to make it six inches wider all round to allow space for the reeds. Ben always told us he wanted to be buried at the Maltings. One day we were in the flat and Bill Servaes [General Manager of the Festival] was there, and Lilias and Robin Sheepshanks had brought the colonel down from the American Air Force base at Bentwaters, and Ben said: 'I want Bob and Doris to bury me, and I want to be buried in the reeds over here.' But this isn't consecrated ground, of course, and his family and everyone wanted him to be buried at Aldeburgh: so Bill Servaes thought the next best thing would be to lay some reeds in the grave. Then one night Doris and I were lying in bed talking and we thought of the idea of lining the whole grave with reeds.

Call me 'Imo'

William Servaes

William Servaes, Festival Manager from 1970–80, brilliantly summoned up Imogen Holst in his unpublished memoirs.

A couple of days after I joined [the Festival, as General Manager] I was sitting in my 'cupboard' when the telephone rang. It was Imogen Holst. As was her custom she was direct. 'Do you know what your duties are as General Manager of the Maltings Concert Hall?' she said rather grandly. There was no point in prevaricating. 'No,' I said. 'Right,' she said, 'if you can spare half-an-hour, come and see me at 10 o'clock tomorrow and I will tell you.' 'Fine,' I said, 'I'll be there.' And punctually at 10 the next day I presented myself at her front door. The house had been designed for her by Jim Cadbury-Brown and was uncompromisingly modern and entirely appropriate. It was even the same kind of creamy-porridge colour that she was. Imogen opened the door, invited me in, sat me down and, wasting no time, began.

'First,' she said, 'you must call me "Imo"; you will in the end anyhow, and we may just as well save time and start right away. Secondly, I want to apologise to you.' No doubt I looked as surprised as I felt, and she went on with considerable emotion. 'I was appalled at the way you were treated at your interview that day. It was intolerable that you had to sit gazing into the sun like that. I could hardly bear it.' This was very characteristic of Imo, who was a strange mixture of stern professional and feeling woman, sometimes seeming as if she had strayed in from some play by J.M. Barrie. To me everything about her exuded the 1920s: severe hair drawn into a bun – one felt she ought to have telephones over her ears – the way she stood ('I was a trained dancer, dear') and a kind of feyness.

The subject of her discourse was to be my role as concert manager and off we went. Imo was a marvellous teacher. If there was one thing at which she excelled, it was detail, and over the next two hours she role-played everything from the set-up of the hall, the arrival of the artists, the rehearsal and so on through to the actual concert itself and afterwards. I was a blank page and she did not forego the opportunity to write upon it.

There were a number of Don'ts:

Don't forget that the artist is probably extremely nervous, and that this may be reflected in his or her behaviour.

Don't give any discouraging information (' Such a pity so few seats have been sold', for instance).

Don't interrupt a rehearsal insensitively. If you need to do so, stand within the artist's field of view. He will stop in his own time.

From left to right: Julian Potter, Imogen Holst, Benjamin Britten and Mary Potter at an Aldeburgh Music Club night at Crag House, Aldeburgh, 1954.

Don't criticise at the time - if you have to, do it later.

If you have to go in front of a huge orchestra tuning up behind you to make an announcement, do it like this. Stand quite still in the middle of the stage and wave your arms above your head. She leapt onto a sofa to demonstrate. Soon people in the audience will notice and start to quieten down. As they do so, lower your arms slowly, timing it so that the audience is silent by the time your arms are at your side. Then say what you have to say clearly and distinctly.

But the tenor of her song really was that to invite the best performances, it is sensible to provide the best possible support for the artists and it is extraordinary how quickly a very intense relationship builds up – a dependence almost – that just as quickly evaporates at the end of a performance. Imo, who had been brought up at Thaxted in Essex, had worked with CEMA [Council for the Encouragement of Music and the Arts] during the war and then on the music staff at Dartington. She threw in her lot with Aldeburgh in the early 1950s and became Britten's amanuensis. Having had ballet lessons as a child, she felt she had been particularly helpful during the composition of *The Prince of the Pagodas* ('Dancers take off just after the beat; I could explain all that.') I asked her if she had kept a diary and she said she had started to, but had come firmly to the conclusion it was 'what comes through the sieve that matters. The important thing being what one remembers over time.' Eventually the resurgence of interest in her father's work, which incidentally made her very comfortably off, caused her to pass the job on to Rosamund Strode and spend much of her time dealing with matters arising from her father's estate. She was also expert at expressing herself on paper and wrote a number of books. She became an Artistic Director in 1956, and her interests apart from her father's work were mostly focused on early music [see p.192], folk music [see p.197], bell-ringing, country dancing and of course Britten, whom she unhesitatingly judged to be a genius, and to whom personally she was devoted. Ben viewed her with a kind of amused admiration not infrequently tinged with exasperation. She was often assigned a concert to conduct in the Festival. 'Who', Ben said, 'would not cross England to see Imo conduct?'

She was an expert on brass bands and perhaps her finest moments came when she conducted them. She was sometimes invited to Kneller Hall, the Army School of Music, and when the band came to Framlingham in 1975 she shared the rostrum with their Commanding Officer. Her attention to detail followed her even there and her dress, specially made for the occasion, was 'exactly the same colours as the Bandsmen's tunics'. The Band's response was terrific and they played like demons under her baton.

There were many sides to Imogen. She could be notably funny introducing items of music in between bouts of wine-tasting in the Jubilee Hall or drilling an audience (which included the Queen Mother) in bird calls from *Let's Make an Opera*. She could also, on occasion, be tough. One Good Friday Peter turned up at the Maltings for a rehearsal of the *St Luke Anon Passion* for two male soloists and a small choir, which is sung *a capella*. He was swathed in scarves and clearly had a cold.

'I'm very sorry,' he said, 'I'll have to cancel.' Imo didn't bat an eyelid. 'That's all right, Peter dear,' and she turned to me, 'Bill can read it.' John Shirley-Quirk, the other soloist, turned rather pale and suggested perhaps he might sing it himself. He had, after all, sung both parts before. But Imo was adamant. I was to read it and she thrust the words into my hand and packed me off to study them. 'Don't worry, dear, I'll see you through.' There is no point in describing what I felt about it, but I went. Needless to say, Peter sang.

Imo did not believe in wasting time. When Mary Potter was painting her portrait, she was 'going over the *St John Passion* in my head'. Anyone looking at the finished article will find this not difficult to believe. Also, 'If I don't happen to recognise you in the street, I'm not cutting you dead. It's only that I am going over a piece of work to myself.' A close friend of hers told me that a more likely cause was her increasingly short sight. But Imo liked to live her own legend.

While her devotion to Ben was never in question, her attitude to Peter was obviously ambivalent. On the one hand she was fiercely loyal to both of them – some say, and I think fairly, to a fault – on the other, Peter's unpredictability and dislike of any kind of confining discipline was in direct conflict with her own concept of professionalism. If Peter had enjoyed an engagement he would not infrequently, and without reference to anyone, invite those with whom he had been performing to 'come to Aldeburgh', and was often both surprised and pained (as we were) when the promise had to be honoured. On one occasion he invited an entire choir of over a hundred people to come at a time of the year when our patrons were mostly sailing or sitting on the beach with their grandchildren. True, they came without fee, but they nonetheless had to be fed and watered and in straitened circumstances, with as good as nothing to come from the box office (we sold about 100 seats). The strain on our resources was considerable.

At a meeting later Peter was contrite. 'No more choirs,' he said. Imo seized a piece of paper, wrote in block letters 'NO MORE CHOIRS' and thrust it at him. 'Now sign it,' she said. He did and, it has to be said, signed similar undertakings on other occasions. It never made any difference and while she admired him as an artist she was very wary of him as a person. Imo and I were discussing a storm that had broken about our heads and I happened to say – this, as is obvious, was some years ago – 'Well, at least Peter is a gentleman.' There was an intake of breath, a pause, and 'That,' she said, 'is a term we never used in Thaxted.'

Humphrey Jennings

Dawn Adès

'Humphrey Jennings is a film director and painter. He was with the GPO and Crown Film Units from 1934 to 1947, and is now working for Wessex Film Production. He has also painted continuously since 1930. Home ground: East Anglia. Politics: Those of William Cobbett.' (*Our Time*, December 1947) In this laconic autobiographical note Jennings sums up what mattered most to him at the time – painting and film-making – but gives only a partial picture of a ferociously active and many-sided life. Missing are his involvement with surrealism, theatre design and production, research on Elizabethan poetry and plays, the founding of Mass Observation, the epic compilation *Pandaemonium*, his own poems and a few sharp, critical essays. On top of this, his friends commented that his extraordinary vitality often spent itself in talking, a side of his creative energy lost now for good.

Jennings' 'home ground', East Anglia, figures frequently in his films and paintings. Jennings describes Minsmere in the 1948 film *Dim Little Island*; this piece of marsh on the Suffolk coast was the rehearsal place for the Dieppe landing, 'the beach mined and the trees blasted by shell-fire'. Today 'the marsh there and the surrounding woods are one of the few places where birds can nest in peace'. Much as he loved the land, marshes, heath and sea, he was most interested in the people who lived there. In his 1949 film *Family Portrait*, the figures – types really – of Farmer, Miner, Miller and Landscape Artist are seen in long-shot and then close-up. 'Above them the moving clouds. Around them the movements of the wind in the grass, on the leaves, and the face of the streams. This is East Anglia. We should suggest the brush dipping into the painting water like the leaves of the willow in the stream. For a moment it should be difficult to distinguish brush marks from reality.'[1] A Suffolk voice speaking the words of Constable contrasts with the 'scientific voice' that narrates the historical and industrial sequences. East Anglia 'offers one of the most self-contained and enduring of educations in English social history and art: it is the world of agricultural peasantry, of Constable, Benjamin Britten and Akenfield.'[2]

Jennings was also a cosmopolitan intellectual, familiar with the latest art and literature, hugely well read and widely travelled. He was born in 1907 in Walberswick, a village inhabited by fisherman and, from about 1890, artists and architects. Jennings' father Frank was an architect who preferred saving old buildings to constructing new ones; only after the Second World War did he allow indoor plumbing, electricity or the telephone in

1. Jennings, 'Notes on Presentation', for *Family Portrait*, 1949, in *The Humphrey Jennings Film Reader* ed. Kevin Jackson, Carcanet, 1993, p.166. Recently Kevin Jackson has transformed our knowledge of Jennings' life and work and this essay is indebted throughout to his biography *Humphrey Jennings* (2004).
2. David Thomson, 'Humphrey Jennings' in *The New Biographical Dictionary of Film*, 2002.

his home. Both his parents were supporters of Guild Socialism, which had its roots in the writings of William Morris and John Ruskin and sought a social and political ideal that was not based purely on economics. The exotic, spiritual side of Guild Socialism led some of its followers, including Jennings' mother, towards theosophy.

His education was almost entirely in Cambridge, where he was a boarder at the Perse School from the age of eight, and an undergraduate at Pembroke (1926–9), with a double starred first in English. He became a research scholar, though his thesis on the poetry of Thomas Gray was never finished. His friends included Jacob Bronowski, William Empson, Charles Madge, Malcolm Lowry, the poet Kathleen Raine, the painter Julian Trevelyan and future film historian Graham Noxon. We get a sense of this ambitious, confident, vanguard, gifted group from the little magazine *Experiment* (1928–31), 'all written by degreeless students or young graduates'. Film is strongly represented in *Experiment*, with stills and articles on Eisenstein, on Man Ray's recent surrealist film *L'étoile de mer*, Bruguière and others. Jennings was deeply involved in Elizabethan poetry and drama as well as modern theatre, and his first UK production (with Denis Arundell) of Stravinsky's *Soldier's Tale* in 1928, with the ballerina Lydia Lopokva and Michael Redgrave, attracted national attention.

Jennings' problem was an equal enthusiasm for many things. He wrote from Cambridge to a friend: 'As to my progress in art, I am as usual torn among painting, literature and the theatre. I love each infinitely in turn, and I feel that I get on well in each – but where it will all end – in which, I don't know.'[3] He did continue to paint, and many of his last paintings and drawings are of Blythburgh in Suffolk. To say 'last paintings' makes it sound as if he returned to painting East Anglia as an old man, but Jennings was only forty-three when he was killed falling from a cliff on the Greek island of Poros, while prospecting camera angles for a film. It's not easy to get a sense of Jennings as a painter, despite what must have been a prolific output. There are oil paintings, drawings, some surrealist collages. Quite often he painted from photographs. Sometimes the lines are spiky and jagged, sometimes the planes overlap and spaces merge as in cubism. His post-war painting tended to be more pastoral, featuring landscapes and agricultural implements such as ploughs. But it is as a film-maker that he remains best known.

Jennings was as interested in the urban as the rural, though his abiding concern was not so much with a town/country divide as with the larger question of the impact of the machine on human lives. He compiled a vast collection of extracts from writings and images from the last three hundred years concerned with the Industrial Revolution. The idea was not to make a 'picture of the development of machinery itself' but of man's adaptation and response to an altered world. This epic collage-collection of texts remained unpublished during his lifetime; *Pandaemonium 1660–1886* was finally published in 1985. It is probably here, as in the related project, Mass Observation, that Jennings comes closest to his political model, William Cobbett, who in *Rural Rides* recorded his observations on life in towns and villages, and was especially concerned with the plight of the rural poor.

Mass Observation, founded by Jennings, Charles Madge and Tom Harrison, was similarly based on the principle of retrieving evidence, this time of the lives of 'ordinary people' from their own mouths. Mass Observation began modestly but swiftly expanded,

3. Hodgkinson and Sheratsky, 'Humphrey Jennings – More than a Maker of Films', Clark, 1982, p.6.

gathering an army of volunteers who produced quantities of field reports that give an extraordinary picture of everyday life in Britain in the late '30s and early '40s. For Madge and Jennings, though, 'Mass Observation was less sociology than a kind of poetry, akin to Surrealism.' [4]

The film *Spare Time* (1939) drew on Jennings' experience of Mass Observation, although by then he had left the movement. Shot in the North, largely unscripted, taking advantage of what he found, the film celebrates the leisure activities of the steel, cotton and coal workers: brass bands, lurchers, football matches, and a kazoo band parading across a cold, deserted waste ground. Julian Trevelyan described *Spare Time* as Jennings' 'surrealist vision of Industrial England; the cotton workers of Bolton were the descendants of Stephenson and Watt, the dwellers in Blake's dark satanic mills reborn in the world of greyhound racing and Marks & Spencer.' [5]

As his poet friends David Gascoyne and Kathleen Raine recognised, Jennings 'was primarily a poet by nature'.[6] And it is through their particular understanding of surrealism that the conception of poetry shared by Jennings and Gascoyne can best be approached. This has nothing to do with fantasy and not much to do with the Freudian unconscious, more 'a universally valid attitude to experience, a possible mode of living'.[7] Jennings had been familiar with the writings and the films coming from surrealist Paris in the late 1920s, but was temporarily disillusioned after a trip there in 1930. By the mid 1930s, however, he was closely involved with the London surrealist group, and exhibited at the International Surrealist Exhibitions in London in 1936 and in Paris in 1938.

For Jennings, as for David Gascoyne, surrealism was poetry, lived poetry: bringing together two distant realities and striking a spark from their contact. The juxtapositions he makes are seldom as violent as those in French surrealism but involve subtle associations, visual, verbal and aural. The film director Lindsay Anderson wrote in 1954 that he 'had a mind that delighted in simile and the unexpected relationship'.[8] In his practice as a film-maker and as the compiler of *Pandaemonium* he worked with fragments, which are so juxtaposed as to produce unexpected connections and make us marvel at the strangeness of the familiar. In his use of montage he learned from Eisenstein, while he shares with surrealism the attention to the potency of humble signs, coincidences and associations. In the spirit of both surrealism and Mass Observation Jennings rejected hierarchies, and was just as at home filming Myra Hess playing in wartime London at the National Gallery as he was filming the kazoo band.

Jennings was interested in what might constitute modern myth, but there is often a valedictory tone in his work. The frankly nostalgic early colour film *Farewell Topsails* (1937) records one of the last voyages of a tall ship carrying china clay from the Cornish mines. There is an element of the modern primitivist in Jennings, a melancholy sense of the passing of more authentic things; at the same time there is a zest to his films and writings, a delight in texture and detail, and humour – and a profound patriotism which, as a critic said, 'gives his films a universal appeal'.

4. Katheleen Raine, *The Land Unknown*, 1975, quoted in Jackson, 2004, p.188.
5. Julian Trevelyan, *Indigo Days*, in Jackson, op.cit., p.212.
6. David Gascoyne, Introductory Notes, *Journal 1936–7*, Enitharmon, 1980, p.10.
7. David Gascoyne, *A Short Survey of Surrealism 1935*, Enitharmon, 2003, p.24.
8. Lindsay Anderson, 'Only Connect: Some Aspects of the Work of Humphrey Jennings', *Sight and Sound*, April–June 1954, reprinted in *Film Quarterly*, vol. XV no. 2, Winter 1961–2.

Artists in East Anglia

Ian Collins

Art in East Anglia is as old as human settlement here. The fields remain rife with ancient relics. As a child I filled pockets with pieces of decorated Roman pottery, and dreamed of Celtic torcs and the treasures of Angle ships berthed in burial mounds. During the so-called Dark Ages the highest spirit of humanity remained illuminated in the manuscripts and stained glass of local monasteries. And in the Stour Valley church of Wiston a mural of St Francis preaching to the birds was painted by a master from the monastic art school at Colchester within a few decades of the saint's death. However remote, our region was never beyond the reach of creative currents abroad.

For the last 250 years East Anglia has acted as a powerful lure for visual artists. Such success has come despite a lack of those dramatic features traditionally linked in art to the picturesque or sublime. Though far from the uniformly flat terrain caricatured by Noel Coward, the nearest we get to a mountain range is a gentle undulation.

But admiration of the cool and quiet landscapes of northern Europe marked a major advance for art in the seventeenth century. East Anglia came to appeal a century later, chiefly because of its affinity with the Netherlands. Dutch art hung in the homes of certain local collectors – where, doubtless, some of it was seen by a Sudbury-raised lad named Thomas Gainsborough. Looking to the local landscape he found his first and last love.

Gainsborough's belief in the power and glory of the unclassical East Anglian countryside inspired one of the most radical artists Britain has ever produced: John Constable. Summing up his childhood haunts of East Bergholt, Dedham and the Stour Valley – an area little changed to this day save for more trees and the teeming jungle of the A12 – he wrote, 'These scenes made me a painter, and I am grateful.' While Constable celebrated the agrarian and riparian landscape where Suffolk and Essex meet, John Crome and John Sell Cotman were leading the Norwich School of Artists into a discovery of magical Norfolk wilderness – Broadland, Breckland, Mousehold Heath – and of architectural ruins. Again, the Netherlands had set the scene. And a long-overlooked and often watery world was best evoked, it seemed, by a long-underrated but quicksilver medium: watercolour.

Retaining a sense of awe in the face of nature, Constable caught the myriad effects of light and atmosphere which are the true joy of soggy, sunken and sky-dominated East Anglia. He was ridiculed or ignored by local and national audiences for his pains (then again, Turner, who had also wandered the East Anglian coastline, spent his final years of embittered rejection living under an assumed name). But those revolutionary pictures lit a fire in France. A torch carried by Corot was taken up by several pioneering painters who decamped to the village of Barbizon, where their experiences led in turn to the emergence of Impressionism.

An experiment begun in East Anglia was to return in 1884 when Philip Wilson Steer, fresh from France, spent the first of several summers in Walberswick and Southwold. Here he made notes and sketches for some of the most beautiful pictures known to British art, an air of eerie enchantment enhanced by the fact that the paintings were completed in wintry Chelsea. Girls with golden hair, pink sashes and – as someone said – long legs like Sheraton tables, played beside the sea in a kaleidoscope of light and colour. The broken brushstrokes and vivid unmixed colours of Impressionism captured the sun-drenched scene perfectly. How Steer came to develop this daring technique on the Suffolk coast – and why he abandoned it within a decade, as he moved elsewhere – remains unclear. His best pictures were hard to sell and easily mocked: his confidence was knocked. A recent novel and film suggested a passing love affair. Certainly there was an unparalleled passion in his East Anglian pictures of the period.

Walberswick and Southwold have attracted wave after wave of artists who have responded to the glittering eastern light and wild sea and marshscapes without ever constituting a formal school. Along with the climate, the warmth of the local welcome has varied enormously. When a rejected Charles Rennie Mackintosh fled to Walberswick from Glasgow in the summer of 1914, and unwisely stayed on when World War I started, he took long evening walks in the sand dunes and collaborated with his wife Margaret on ravishing watercolour drawings of local flowers. But the 'foreign' artist was rumoured to be a spy who flouted black-out rules to signal to ships at sea – and correspondence with the Viennese Secession (alien revolutionaries!) appeared to provide proof of treachery. Mackintosh was arrested and allowed to continue a southward flight only after high-placed friends in London had intervened on his behalf.

World War I also brought an outpost of Bloomsbury to Wissett, near Halesworth, when the pacifist painters Duncan Grant and Vanessa Bell, and writer David Garnett, left the jingoism of London to struggle with a wayward smallholding. Such a haven proved illusory, despite warm praise from a visiting Virginia Woolf who began drafting her novel *Night and Day* there. The men were threatened with jail terms by the Blything Tribunal before an appeal panel in Ipswich (mindful of a defence from Maynard Keynes) granted exemption from military service but banned self-employment. The artists moved to farm labour, and the creation of the celebrated Charleston household, in Sussex.

War-time land work had taken a young Hilda Carline to Suffolk. When she married Stanley Spencer, in 1925, the service was held at Wangford, near Southwold, where she had been happy. They both painted pictures of local landscapes during their honeymoon, and it may not be fanciful to observe that a shadowy and tangled scene produced by the bride prefigured later mental turmoil. But Stan was in ecstasy – with an imprinted memory of guests leaving the church after the Wangford wedding in clusters and attitudes like the figures in his great *Resurrection* painting, now in Tate Britain.

By the summer of 1937 Stanley Spencer was reluctantly divorced from Hilda, and already estranged from new wife Patricia Preece. He returned to the scene of his greatest romance and painted a brilliant picture of Southwold beach. The 'dirty-washing colour' sea was 'splashed by homely aunties' legs and the air was full of suburban seaside abandonment,' he wrote, having regained his vantage point each morning by measuring the distance between dog messes. Beneath a breezy surface it was a view from a wistful outsider.

In 1950 a passer-by spotted Spencer nudes in a London gallery window and pressed a prosecution for obscenity (causing the pictures to be destroyed). This was Sir Alfred Munnings, president of the Royal Academy. The previous year he had fulminated against Picasso. But the Waveney miller's son had not always been such an arch reactionary. Training as a poster designer in Norwich at fourteen, and losing an eye to a Norfolk briar at twenty, he captured early horse-centred scenes with a bright impressionism. Despite an ongoing cloud over his reputation, he has some claim to being England's Degas.

Peaceful, private, isolated – yet with a network of rural rail links until the 1960s era of Dr Beeching – rural East Anglia has been hugely popular for holidays and hideaways. The sense of being a world away, on one of the edgiest edges of England, could be achieved within striking distance of London. Many have come here for health reasons. Between the wars Mark Gertler had three spells in the tuberculosis sanatorium at Mundesley on the windswept north Norfolk coast. With good reason travel posters of the time proclaimed the slogan: 'Come To East Anglia. It's So Bracing!'

Finance has also been a factor. Local patrons of the arts have long been active [for the particular impact of Benjamin Britten and, especially, Peter Pears, see p.161]. Certain artists have lived in grand style, migrating between London and the countryside according to season and whim. Until recently, others were able to live cheaply in simple cottages and on the fruits of land and sea. Some rural painters, like the prolific Harry Becker (1865–1928), were at times too poor even to buy canvas – being as impoverished as the farm labourers they depicted. Bills may be bigger now, in an age of high utility costs, steep rents and surging property prices. But while the regional cost of living has risen sharply, the quality of life has remained higher still. The inward flow of artists continues. And if the luminaries are more often migrant than native, East Anglia has still nurtured the likes of Michael Andrews (linked to the School of London) and Pop Art's Colin Self.

Remoteness has appealed to reclusive spirits, but the region has also offered more communal activities. The closest we came to a formal twentieth-century arts colony was a motley assembly of artists and craftspeople around Edward Bawden and Eric Ravilious – themselves masters of the lino-cut and watercolour respectively – between the wars at Great Bardfield (with work now showcased in the wonderful Fry Art Gallery at Saffron Walden). Art schools and societies, arts festivals and now open studio schemes have all added to the attraction. Often in Aldeburgh as a set-designer, John Piper criss-crossed the region as part of a self-appointed task to chart Britain's natural and architectural heritage before they were lost. A project begun when the pending Blitz jolted him out of abstraction was to last all his life as the peril from bombers gave way to that from bulldozers. His fluent pen and brush encompassed noble halls and humble cottages, but lingered longest in and around churches – the beacon towers of the Fens looming loveliest among dozens of recorded East Anglian landscapes and landmarks.

In what Sickert so erroneously dubbed 'the sucked orange' of the Stour Valley, landscape painters have continued to find fresh inspiration in familiar scenes. Distinguished help has often been at hand – with the painter-plantsman John Nash once numbered among tutors at the Flatford Mill Field Studies Centre. And for decades from the 1930s Cedric Morris and Lett Haines ran the famous (in some circles, infamous) East Anglian School of Painting and Drawing along French and Bohemian lines. First at Dedham, and latterly at Hadleigh, the school drew students from Lucian Freud to Maggi Hambling [see plate 2] who were encouraged to portray one another, the iris-rife garden

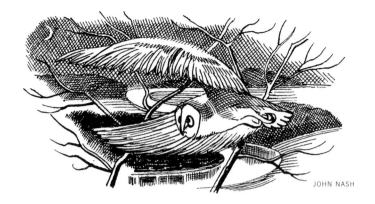

JOHN NASH

and the fields beyond. When depicting the smouldering wreck of the first school (ruin possibly wrought by a Freudian fag-end) the company was assailed by a passing Munnings, who lived nearby in what is now a museum to his memory, crying 'Down with modern art!' The same sentiment gripped a section of Aldeburgh opinion more than 60 years later when Maggi Hambling, lately relocated to a village near Saxmundham, and long memorialising notable people from Beccles-raised scientist Dorothy Hodgkin to the dying Cedric Morris, designed a Scallop tribute to Benjamin Britten for the brow of the beach towards Thorpeness. Approved by a poll in the local paper, the steely monument nevertheless remains a focus of controversy in the locality.

Another Flatford Mill Field Studies Centre tutor was the bird painter Eric Ennion, who in 1946 taught the science-minded Mary Slatford the art of intensely observing nature. As a farmer's wife in the Waveney Valley, the future Mary Newcomb (1922–2008) evolved a painterly vision of deceptive naivety – a personal pictorial poetry firmly rooted in rural reality. A kindred evolution is now working through her daughter, Tessa. Similar (and yet absolutely singular) journeys from representational Suffolk towards a universal abstraction can be clearly traced in the work of Mary Potter, Pears and Britten's great friend, who spent her last three decades dissolving matter into light in Aldeburgh [see plates 8, 9]. It is less obvious in, but also fundamental to, the early art of Prunella Clough, who spent much of her childhood in Southwold, and who then painted the local fishermen and turned the twisted shapes of war-time coastal defences into spiky abstraction. On the other side of Suffolk, at Little Thurlow, a young Elisabeth Frink would convey a landscape dotted not with horses but airbases. She vividly remembered crippled bombers limping home, or occasionally crashing in the fields. The angular forms of some of her bird sculptures from the 1950s would be likened to the jagged fuselage of wrecked planes.

And then there are the complete oddities – such as Arthur Boyd [see p.253], who crossed the world to Constable Country for the inspiration to paint his native Australia. Fiery images of the Outback filled his nest-like thatched studio at Ramsholt, on a bank of the River Deben. Part of a distinguished artistic dynasty, Boyd was brother-in-law to Sidney Nolan [p.249 and plate 12] who came to Aldeburgh in Britten's wake. He might also be a kindred spirit to John Bellany and Anthony Green, memoirists and mythologists of faraway places who find the space for dreams in unlikely corners of rural Essex and Cambridgeshire respectively.

Overall, we can fairly claim that East Anglia has attracted more and better artists down the generations than any other English region, save for Cornwall. But as well as savouring such a fertile record, we may also ponder what might have been.

When the last war threatened, Adrian Stokes and his wife Margaret Mellis searched for a safe house in the country where they were to be joined by a couple of friends and fellow artists. The Norfolk and Suffolk coasts were scoured, and the Martello Tower at Slaughden almost taken. But in the end they found what they wanted in the far south-west, just outside St Ives. Ben Nicholson and Barbara Hepworth arrived as planned, and the rest is art history. Today we could have been visiting a Tate Aldeburgh. Ironically, Margaret Mellis was to live in Suffolk from 1950 with her second husband, the collagist Francis Davison. From a harbourside shack at Walberswick and then a Syleham smallholding, they gravitated to Southwold where Margaret continued in her widowhood to create abstract constructions from driftwood. Friends came in her wake – Roger Hilton very nearly moving to East Anglia (before preferring rugged Cornwall to a region where 'the trees look like parsley'). Guy Taplin, relocating permanently from London to Wivenhoe, a move Francis Bacon managed only briefly, came to share thoughts on the found wood from which he carved talismanic birds. And here a teenage fan of Davison and Mellis, who also tried his hand at driftwood constructions, saw things 'that blew me away'. His name was Damien Hirst.

The lure continues. Alison Wilding has worked at Snape [plate 13], and Louise K. Wilson has lately haunted the nuclear testing ground turned nature reserve of Orford Ness [p.309 and plate 16]. And now Hirst's close friend Sarah Lucas lives in Britten's old house near Eye, having been drawn here by his music.

Brief Lives

Simon Loftus

I love old graveyards, especially those that have not been tidied up. I like the humpy ground, the stoop and totter of disordered headstones, the decayed splendour of family tombs. I relish the vigour of stone-carved lettering, spelling out the evocative names and comforting, customary phrases – or bursting the bounds of decorum with startling frankness, or a brief, heartrending sigh. That vivid immediacy is found surprisingly often in the country churchyards of East Suffolk or inside the churches themselves, etched on memorial slabs sunk into cool floors. It's part of the long local tradition of religious and political non-conformity – plain speaking, but with an ear for the rhythms of language.

These inscriptions can be quietly poignant or fiercely down-to-earth, or surprising in other ways. You might not expect to find evidence of the Industrial Revolution in the graveyard of Leiston church but a couple of cast iron headstones, with bold nineteenth-century lettering, tell their own fascinating story. They were made in Garrett's engineering works, a thriving local business that was soon to become famous for its traction engines, exported to half the world. One of these gravestones commemorates a young man called Robert Fletcher (lovely medieval name, meaning arrow-maker) and the other is a memorial to Henry Newson, who died in 1834 after a long but troubled life: 'No more we hear his spirit moan, His doubts and fear forever gone'. Nearby stands a rectangular stone pedestal, crowned with an elegant iron urn. The pedestal is inscribed with the names of various members of the Garrett family and the urn was cast in their factory – which was founded in 1778 when Richard Garrett married Elizabeth Newson and set up in business as a blacksmith and maker of agricultural tools.

A grandson of that marriage was the great Newson Garrett, who was born in Leiston in 1812 but found the village too crowded with his relatives, so moved to nearby Aldeburgh and made his fortune as a merchant and maltster. He was remembered by all who knew him as a good and generous man and is commemorated in Aldeburgh church with a lovely epitaph – 'God gave him largeness of heart'. Outside, in the graveyard, he lies buried alongside his wife and two of his children, one of whom was the remarkable Elizabeth Garrett Anderson. She became the first English woman to qualify as a doctor, in the face of strong opposition from the medical profession, and founded the first hospital in London to be staffed entirely by women – before retiring to Aldeburgh where she completed her pioneering career as the first woman mayor of any English town [see p.86].

Her father's finest memorial is not in fact in Aldeburgh, for Newson Garrett was the man who built Snape Maltings, one of the grandest of its day, to supply the raw material for brewers in East Anglia and London. Here and there, if you look closely, you will find

JOHN NASH

iron wall-ties embossed with his name, dotting the brick walls of foyers and performance spaces that have been converted from the kiln rooms and drying floors of the old Maltings. Garrett's 'largeness of heart' is everywhere implicit in the beauty of these fine industrial buildings – and wonderfully expressed in the series of portraits that he commissioned of his workers, which now hang in the foyer of Snape Maltings Concert Hall.

That sense of honour for manual work has a strong Suffolk tradition. Few visitors to the Concert Hall bother to stop at Snape Church, but here you can find a beautiful monument of rustic simplicity – a crumbly red headstone which marks the grave of George Alabaster, who died at the age of 37 in 1759. It is carved with the tools of his trade, a pick and shovel.

Such unpretentious expressions of local worth take many forms. One of my favourite examples is the tomb of a seventeenth-century rector who was turned out of his living because of his loyalty to King Charles, during the English Civil War. It is built into the south-facing wall of Theberton church, close to the porch, and made like a bench, where visitors can pause and enjoy the warmth of the sun. 'Here is a stone to sitt upon, Under which lies in hopes to rise, To ye day of Blisse and Happinesse, Honest John Fenn.'

Continue up the road to Blythburgh church and you will find, close to the altar, the memorial stone of one Thomas Neale of Bramfield, 'one of the Best of Magistrates in his time ... who lived much desired and died greatly lamented'. Who could wish for a finer epitaph? But Neale suffered sadness, for close by lies his daughter Mary, 'who with a Straine of piety far beyond her years & a chearfulness to Admiration humbly Resigned her Soule into the hands of her Redeemer', in June 1694 – 'Aged tenn years 4 months & 22 days'. The counting of every day of that short life tells us more than any words how she was loved and mourned.

A few miles away, in Neale's home village of Bramfield, is a hidden treasure – the most startling collection of epitaphs in the whole of Suffolk. To discover them you must make your way past all the other glories of this tiny church (detached round tower, one of the loveliest rood screens in England and magnificent sculptured monuments to Arthur Coke and his beloved wife, who died in childbirth) and concentrate your attention on the floor, immediately in front of the altar. Here, side by side, were buried the members of one of Bramfield's most prominent families – distant cousins of the great Nelson. And here, on the black slate slabs that cover their graves, we can read their lives, summarised with an urgency and eloquence that rings through the centuries. Linking those stories is a scandal, which someone wished remembered.

Whoever that 'someone' was seems to have had extraordinary license to write the frankest epitaphs, mostly with affection but once with barely concealed disdain, and you must read them all to understand the hidden narrative which links them. I like to begin with the memorial to Lambert Nelson who died in his fifties, in 1714. Lambert was a lawyer who married a local heiress, daughter of the delightfully named Reginald Rabett, and together they produced four children. Thus far the inscription is entirely conventional, but then the author launches into a eulogy for a good but unrecognised man. It is worth quoting in full.

> He was a Man of bright Parts, sound judgement, Good Breeding and Pleasant Conversation, Master of the Learned Languages & all ye Liberal Arts, Yet a very Valuable and Right Honest Attorney.

I love that telling 'yet', as if it were astonishing that a man so gifted could also be that rarest of things, an honest lawyer.

> He was Second to None in the strokes of the pen Or Turns of Witt. A true Son of the Church and a Conscientous Subject Of the Crown of England: In either of which Capacities, He was fit for any Emploiment, Had he been less Reserv'd himself, Or better known in time to any Great Minister, Whose Height might expose him To the Necessity of Leaning Sometimes Upon so Steady a Propp, And the Bosom of so Resolute a Confident.

Lambert had a sister, Bridgett, who never married but 'freely underwent the Care of a Wife and a Mother, and often the Fatigue of a True Friend, for any of her Acquaintance in Sickness or Distress'.

> She was a Devout Member of the Established Church, Charitable, Prudent, Chast, Active and remarkably Temperate; yet often Afflicted with great Sicknesses, And for above three Years before her Death, with a Dropsy, of which she Died after having been tapped five times.

This admirable but afflicted woman gave her name to her niece, Lambert's eldest daughter, whose memorial slab lies close to her aunt and is inscribed with this astonishing story.

> Between the Remains of her Brother Edward, And of her Husband Arthur, Here lies the Body of Bridgett Applewhait, Once Bridgett Nelson.
> After the Fatigues of a Married Life, Born by her with Incredible Patience, For four Years and three Quarters, bating three Weeks; And after the Enjoiment of the Glorious Freedom Of an Easy and Unblemisht Widowhood, For four Years and Upwards, She Resolved to run the Risk of a Second Marriage-Bed But Death forbad the Banns – And

having with an Apoplectick Dart (The same Instrument, with which he had formerly Dispatch't her Mother) Touch't the most Vital part of Brain; She must have fallen Directly to the Ground (as one Thunder-strook) If she had not been Catch't and Supported by her Intended Husband. Of which Invisible Bruise, After a struggle for above Sixty Hours, With that Grand Enemy to Life (But the certain and Merciful Friend to Helpless Old Age) In Terrible Convulsions, Plaintive Groans or Stupefying Sleep, Without recovery of her Speech or senses, She Dyed on the 12th day of Sept in ye Year of Our Lord 1737 and of her own Age 44.

That justly celebrated inscription is so full of drama that it's easy to overlook the memorial to Bridgett's husband, Arthur Applewhaite, who lies beside her – but only by reading his inscription can you understand her own. For 'the Fatigues of her Married Life' were provoked by this mean man, who caused her much grief. Arthur's father was 'Favourite and Bailiff' of successive owners of the great estate of Heveningham Hall but Arthur himself, as a second son, had little hope of inheritance. His marriage to Bridgett Nelson was made with a sharp eye to her wealth, as 'sole heiress' to her father's estates. But they had no children, so Arthur's intention that his wife's lands would eventually revert to Applewhaite ownership was frustrated. Such was his rage that Arthur's last act was to collude with his father and brother in a legal action to leave his wife penniless. '(Having by his Father's Instigation made no will) He left no legacy But a Chancery-Suit with his Eldest Brother For her own Paternal Estates in this Town and Blyford.'

That scandalous land-grab seems to have failed, leaving Bridgett to enjoy her 'easy and unblemisht widowhood' – but its memory lingered long and the unknown memorialist who composed these inscriptions seized the chance to record the truth. The story is there to be read, by all who care to do so.

The Composer

W.H. Auden

All the others translate: the painter sketches
A visible world to love or reject;
Rummaging into his living, the poet fetches
The images out that hurt and connect,

From Life to Art by painstaking adaption,
Relying on us to cover the rift;
Only your notes are pure contraption,
Only your song is an absolute gift.

Pour out your presence, O delight, cascading
The falls of the knee and the weirs of the spine,
Our climate of silence and doubt invading;

You alone, alone, O imaginary song,
Are unable to say an existence is wrong,
And pour out your forgiveness like a wine.

(December 1938)

'He who loves beauty
Worships me.
Mine is the spell
That binds his days.'

The voice of Apollo in *Death in Venice*
Act 1, Scene 7

He who
loves beauty

If Wind and Water Could Write Music

Jonathan Reekie

'If wind and water could write music it would sound like Ben's', Yehudi Menuhin

Anyone who has heard *Peter Grimes* and stood on Aldeburgh beach will appreciate Menuhin's words: the screech of seagulls, the clatter of pebbles, the constantly shifting moods of the sea – all are powerfully evoked by Britten's score.

Britten knew these sights and sounds from childhood. He was born in Lowestoft on 22 November 1913 (auspiciously St Cecilia's day, the patron saint of music). His father, Robert, was a dentist who lived and practised just off the seafront. In between drilling, patients could hear the young Ben playing the piano upstairs. Britten knew by the age of eleven that he wanted to compose and was greatly encouraged by his ambitious mother, Edith, a keen amateur pianist and singer. She was said to intend her son to become the 'fourth B' after Bach, Beethoven and Brahms.

After school at South Lodge in Lowestoft and boarding at Gresham's near Holt, Britten went to the Royal College of Music at the age of sixteen. On graduation he began to earn a living in London, writing music for theatre, film and radio, and during this period first worked with and befriended W. H. Auden.

In 1937 Britten, already feeling the pull of Suffolk, purchased the Old Mill which overlooks Snape Maltings, then a bustling malt factory. He had met his partner Peter Pears by this time and two years later, with war looming, they left for America, partly to further their careers but also because of their shared pacifism. In a Los Angeles bookshop, Pears first came across the poems of George Crabbe, and the story of Peter Grimes. Britten also read an E.M. Forster article about Crabbe in *The Listener* (see p.80) and as Britten later wrote: 'I suddenly realised where I belonged and what I lacked.' He returned to his native Suffolk in 1942 and despite the fame and world travel that was to come, he was never really to leave. When Britten was made a Freeman of Lowestoft in 1951 he said:

> Suffolk, the birthplace and inspiration of Constable and Gainsborough, the loveliest of English painters; the home of Crabbe, that most English of poets; Suffolk, with its rolling, intimate countryside; its heavenly Gothic churches, big and small; its marshes, with those wild sea-birds; its grand ports and its little fishing villages. I am firmly rooted in this glorious county. And I proved this to myself when I once tried to live somewhere else. Even when I visit countries as glorious as Italy, as friendly as Denmark or Holland – I am always homesick, and glad to get back to Suffolk. I treasure these roots, my Suffolk roots; roots are especially valuable nowadays,

Benjamin Britten on Aldeburgh beach, July 1959 (Photograph by Hans Wild)

when so much we love is disappearing or being threatened, when there is so little to cling to.

The inspiration of Suffolk is to be found throughout Britten's music. Most explicitly in the two operas *Peter Grimes* and *Albert Herring* that portray Suffolk, but also in many other works – *Let's Make an Opera* (set in Iken) and *Curlew River* (not specifically Suffolk, but so evocative of the watery, mysterious landscape of Orford, where it was first performed). The chorus of Pilgrims in the ferryboat chant:

Between two kingdoms, O River, flow
On this side, the land of the West,
On the other, dyke and marsh and mere,
The Land of the Eastern Fens.

Peter Grimes, which has been performed from Sydney to Santiago, has made audiences around the globe familiar with Aldeburgh, the Moot Hall, the beach, the pub and its community. The regular productions send a steady trickle of the world's great opera directors and designers to poke around the boats and huts on the beach (Brian Upson, the boat builder at Slaughden, even built a replica fishing boat for the great German director Peter Stein's production).

Albert Herring, despite its quintessential Englishness (actually based on a Guy de Maupassant story), has been performed widely overseas, exporting an affectionate portrait of Suffolk village life to the world. Campsey Ash, Saxmundham and Wickham Market, places that Eric Crozier took off the signpost in the village of Tunstall near Snape, are all mentioned, as are Ufford, Orford, Iken and Snape. Crozier also found there the name of his main character, from the then Herring's village store (there are still Herrings living in the parish). The young boy in the opera, Harold Wood, is named after a station on the Liverpool Street-to-Suffolk line and Mrs Herring reminisces about a day out on Felixstowe Pier. The opera's setting is the fictional Loxford, prompting John Piper to base his design for Mrs Herring's shop on one in Yoxford [see plate 11].

In 1947, the year of *Albert Herring*'s premiere, after unsuccessfully trying to buy Iken Rectory, Britten moved to Crag House on Crabbe Street, overlooking the sea in Aldeburgh. The first Festival in 1948, which relied hugely on the help of the local people (the apprentices at Reades, the builders, did the opera scene changes and the shops closed early so that locals could attend), opened with the premiere of *St Nicolas*. Performed by professionals, amateurs and audience, this was Britten saying that he wanted his Festival to be for and about the people of Aldeburgh. In the same year *Albert Herring* was first crammed into the Jubilee Hall. When Sid sings 'Or dance to the band in the Jubilee Hall?' there must have been a great collective titter and a communal sense that this really was an Aldeburgh Festival.

The Festival relied on any performance space it could find, including the Parish Church and Baptist Chapel. As it grew, other venues were commandeered – churches in Blythburgh, Orford and Framlingham, even punts on Thorpeness Meare, where the music during the premiere of Britten's *Six Metamorphoses after Ovid* took flight in the breeze, mid-performance. There was also regular participation by local amateur musicians through the Aldeburgh Music Club and other choirs and ensembles, as well as many children, most notably in *Noye's Fludde* in Orford Church in 1958.

In 1957 Britten needed more privacy and so he swapped houses with his friend, the artist Mary Potter, and moved to the Red House in Golf Lane. It is still preserved much as when he lived in it, now with the adjacent Britten–Pears Library converted in 1963 from an old school for milkmaids. The Red House was to become the social hub of Aldeburgh's musical life, with many a good post-concert party, swimming, games of tennis and Happy Families, and even a Christmas party combining a magician and Britten's Pushkin songs performed by Rostropovich and Vishnevskaya.

In 1970, with Britten's fame reaching new heights and increasing disturbance from the jets based at Bentwaters and Lakenheath, Britten bought a small house in Horham, near Eye, where he would escape to compose. But Aldeburgh was to remain his home until his untimely death in 1976. The churchyard became his final resting place, in a grave lined with reeds from Snape. Britten's memorial is not only his music, which is performed ever more widely, but also the living, vibrant legacy of Aldeburgh Music, which today is responsible for both his Festival and the fulfilment of his initiatives in the nurturing of musical talent at all levels from school age upwards, through emerging professionals, to the musical greats of today. Little could he have imagined in 1948 when he established his nine-day Festival that all this would emerge and, as Lord Harewood predicted (see p.182), that Britten to Aldeburgh would be this country's equivalent of Mozart to Salzburg.

I'm Still Ben

Christopher Matthew

Every time I pass the Wentworth Hotel, I picture the same scene. It is shortly after seven o'clock on a warm June evening. On the beach opposite, the fishing boats are lined up, ready for launching early the following morning. The sky is pale and wispy with clouds. The gulls are wheeling above a dead calm sea. Issuing through the seaside entrance of the hotel is a crowd of smartly dressed people, laughing and chattering as they turn right and head past the Moot Hall. Leading the procession, like a pair of distinguished Pied Pipers, Benjamin Britten and Peter Pears, beaming with their friends.

I have no real evidence that such a scene ever took place – or that Britten or Pears were ever present. I am merely going on the account of a friend who recalled the early days of the Aldeburgh Festival, when some of the composer's greatest operas were performed on the stage of the Jubilee Hall, a couple of hundred yards down the road in Crabbe Street. He definitely remembered the first performance in 1960 of *A Midsummer Night's Dream*, when the only way into the orchestra pit for the composer was via the stage, and the audience spent the interval wandering around the beach next to the lifeboat.

Every year heralded a new Britten work, and every year he and Pears invited old friends like Copland and Poulenc and later Rostropovich to come and make music with them. The splendid and sadly missed Lettie Gifford – one of Britten's oldest friends, whose husband Charles was Festival treasurer for 25 years – once told me: 'In those piping days, there was a considerable feeling of rubbing shoulders with the great.' Landladies, she said, tried to trump each other with names. 'I've got Osian Ellis staying with me this year.' 'Oh yes? Well, I've got Janet Baker.'

It seems hardly credible now, but in the early days, there were many locals who were none too enthusiastic about the Festival and the annual invasion by hordes of – as they saw them – arty types and culture vultures. Golf club stalwarts were to be heard announcing in the butcher's that they were off to North Berwick for the whole of June. Today, the golfers are some of the keenest concert attenders around. The shopkeepers also gave the impression of being unsusceptible to Festival fever and to the big international names seen wandering in and out of the High Street. Legend has it that Marcel – for years the local men's hairdresser – was working his way through the usual patient array of waiting heads when in marched Marion Thorpe announcing that she had Mstislav Rostropovich in the car outside and could Marcel give him a quick trim straight away. 'Rostropovich or no Rostropovich,' Marcel is reputed to have replied, 'he takes his place in the queue like everyone else.'

But, then, one of the great attractions of Aldeburgh has always been its air of informality. And no one epitomised it more than Britten himself. He was, by all accounts, a man of simple tastes and modest friendships. Music critic and erstwhile Aldeburgh resident Gillian Widdicombe cherishes an early memory of seeing him in an Aldeburgh Carnival procession, marching red-nosed behind the local dairy float, smiling broadly and enjoying every moment of it.

'He was a complicated man,' an old friend told me, 'but also one who loved cricket and going on picnics and laughing with his friends.' Not just the likes of John and Myfanwy Piper and William Plomer and the Rostropoviches, but the fishermen (in particular the late Billy Burrell, for years coxswain of the lifeboat), and people like Bob and Doris Ling. Bob started life as a maltster in Snape and spent five years as a gravedigger before becoming concert hall manager at the Maltings [see p.101]. To Bob and Doris, it was always 'Ben' and 'Peter'. 'I'm still Ben, Bob,' Britten told him soon after his ennoblement. 'Don't forget that.'

Often he would drop in on one of them out of the blue, saying he was bored and fancied a chat, and during the the rebuilding of the Maltings after the devastating fire of 1969, in the course of which he lost his beloved piano, he always made a point of chatting with the workmen. At the same time, he was a deeply practical man who knew best how to deploy the Festival's limited financial resources and, despite his appearance of mild academic detachment, something of a showman. Peter Pears once cheerfully confessed, 'His were always the ideas that worked, while mine invariably got nowhere.'

Being a Suffolk man, Britten invariably wrote with an eye to the setting in which each new piece was to be performed – whether it was in Orford Church, where *Curlew River* (1964), *The Burning Fiery Furnace* (1966) and *The Prodigal Son* (1968) were all premiered, or the Jubilee Hall in Aldeburgh. He also drew on local talent whenever and wherever possible. He wrote *Noye's Fludde* (1958), for instance, knowing that there were buglers at the naval school at Hollesley, hand-bell ringers at Leiston Secondary Modern, and plenty of other schools in the district which could provide several arkfuls of masked animals. One of the youthful highlights for a friend of mine, who spent her childhood in Aldeburgh and still has a house nearby, was when a group of them was spotted collecting autographs outside the Jubilee Hall before a performance of *Let's Make an Opera* and invited in to watch the whole thing, cross-legged on the floor at the very front.

Of course, Britten was a lot more in evidence in those early days when he lived in that lovely pink house overlooking Crag Path and could be seen by passers-by every afternoon, standing at a table in a window overlooking the sea, working on his orchestrations. The composer Peter Dickinson – himself a distinguished Aldeburgh resident of many years' standing – remembers coming to the town as a young man in order to be interviewed for a summer job at Sizewell Hall, then a school, and spotting the great man at work. He couldn't believe his luck. Eventually his father had to tell him to stop staring, it was too rude, and the pair of them sat on the beach instead. There they got into a long conversation with one of the fishermen, which ended with the words, 'It was Mr Britten what made this place'.

No one would argue with that – though his fame finally forced him and Peter Pears to withdraw from public view to the more reclusive surroundings of the Red House by the golf course. At Festival time, the house would be as full of old friends as ever, as would many in the area – though in most cases with paying guests. Friends of mine who became once-a-year landlords and -ladies did so with varying degrees of success and pleasure. One, who for several years let his house on Crag Path to some BBC people was understandably

Britten goes
boating with
E.M. Forster (left)
and a couple of
friends, 1949
(Photograph
by Kurt Hutton /
PicturePost /
Getty Images)

irritated when, having vacated his home, as usual, he decided to come to an Aldeburgh concert and not only had to stay with friends opposite, but was not even invited into his own place for a drink. The memory still rankles.

For others, the experience passed off comparatively easily, though young musicians had to be watched, particularly string players. Following concerts they tended to party late into the night, and cellos could make terrible holes in the floor. One friend turned up at her house to find a group of young people about to light a makeshift barbecue which they had built up against one of the outside walls. What the tenants thought of their accommodation was never recorded – though when my cross-legged friend and her husband first let their house, Donald Mitchell's wife came to vet them. As she was leaving, she said, 'Oh dear, Donald should have come. He'd have quite liked you.'

Sadly, most of those whose support and friendship helped to establish the Festival in its early years are no longer with us. One of the greatest and best-loved figures, and one of Britten's oldest friends, was Princess Peg – or, as she was more properly known, HRH the Princess of Hesse and the Rhine. For years the Festival's president, she would stay at the Wentworth with a group of friends who were expected to attend every concert she did. She brooked no dissent. I turned up in the hotel dining room one evening, looking for a friend who was in her party, and – though I protested that I had only just arrived – I found myself bundled off to an organ recital in Framlingham Church. During a pause in the first item – a glorious piece by Bach – Peg turned to me and whispered, 'It's funny to think that my husband's great-great-great-greatgrandfather turned Bach down when he applied for a job.' I spent the rest of the piece thinking up a suitable reply. After the applause had died down, I said, 'I think your husband's great-great-great-great-grandfather made a slight error.' It wasn't the wittiest or most profound thing I have ever said, but I shall always be glad I had the opportunity to say it.

Reprinted from the Festival programme book, 2003.

Double Portrait: Some personal recollections
Donald Mitchell

Edinburgh, 5 May 1971.

I am starting to write this double profile (a daunting task: I wish I were a painter rather than a writer) in a hotel room in Edinburgh where I'm waiting for B.B. and P.P. to arrive, while that peculiarly golden evening sunshine which sometimes engulfs Edinburgh pours in through my window and over the characteristic green and black of the garden and houses beyond. They are driving over this evening, after an afternoon's rehearsal at an old friend's house outside Edinburgh, to spend the night before tomorrow's concert, a lunchtime recital at Edinburgh's National Gallery in memory of Tertia Liebenthal, who died last year. The programme is going to include, besides Purcell and Schubert, an important Britten premiere, the first complete performance of his most recent song-cycle, *Who are these children?*, settings of poems by William Soutar, the little-known Scottish poet who died in 1945. So tomorrow we shall be seeing B.B. in action in those two roles as composer, and as Peter's partner, collaborator and co-creator which for many years now have been the two 'faces' which the public has come to admire in so many outstanding performances.

I sit up on my bed scribbling, and wonder how tomorrow will unfold. Few people have an inkling of the kind of stress and strain to which working artists, however eminent and experienced, are subjected – to which they subject themselves. Of course, that is what is involved in being totally serious and committed, which is the hallmark of a recital by P.P. and B.B. They themselves may be satisfied or dissatisfied with what they achieve, but the premise from which they set out is always uncompromisingly the same, as is their aim: to serve the art of music, above all to release the composer's voice – whether it be Schubert's or Percy Grainger's, Purcell's or Schumann's – and let it speak to their audience as if it were indeed the absent composer himself who was transformed into a tenor voice or seated at the piano. This is why I have always thought that recitals by P.P. and B.B. must be any composer's dream: because the performers in fact are composer-oriented, not performer-oriented. No doubt tomorrow's recital will prove to be just such an event.

Before I rouse myself to go and see if they have arrived I must jot down one memory which always comes to mind when I am thinking of B.B.'s and P.P.'s commitment, their devotion to the notes. We are aloft (in October, 1969), somewhere between New York and Boston, amidst the juddering internal plastic splendour of Eastern Airlines (greenery-yallery with a vengeance, if I remember rightly). The 'shuttle' as it's called takes less than an hour, so there's scarcely time to settle down to a good read, though I make some progress with a remarkable short story by Thomas Hardy which Ben has drawn to my attention ('An Imaginative Woman'). I read, but B.B. and P.P. are already thinking of tomorrow's recital. One of the songs they performed with great success in New York was that inspired folk-song setting of Percy Grainger's, 'Bold William Taylor', but P.P. has found it by no means easy to memorise and is still not sure that he has got it right. The exuberant Grainger makes it difficult for the singer by ingeniously avoiding uniformly regular entries for the voice: there's a beat missing where one expects there to be one, and one added where one doesn't expect an extension.

Up comes B.B.'s briefcase on to his knees, to form an improvised dumb keyboard, and his long, delicately shaped but strong fingers tap out P.G.'s rhythmic patterns on the bulging leather surface. At his side, sotto-sotto voce, Peter sings the song over. Now and again they stop and patiently go over a tricky entry, then continue. A remarkable and entrancing performance, this! Much finger-tapping and head-wagging from B.B., and semi-soundless, under-the-breath singing from P.P. Heaven knows what the commuting gentlemen returning to their businesses in Boston made of it all, but when, next evening, P.P. sings 'Bold William Taylor', everything is exactly in place – or rather, exactly out of place. The mid-air rehearsal had done the trick.

7 May

Yesterday's recital was certainly greatly enjoyed by me and by the audience packed into the rather small gallery, richly hung with splendid paintings. Back-stage, conditions somewhat cramped (doors to be locked and unlocked for a visit to the lavatory, which reminds one of the security arrangements that complicate concert-giving in the midst of a substantial national art collection), and the piano a challenge to B.B.'s pacifying, mitigating, modifying fingers, which somehow manage to summon up the substance of a ravishing tone even when, mechanically speaking, or so one imagines, the instrument has long ago given up the ghost. B.B. achieves a minor resurrection, but certainly the piano can't have helped the wear and tear on his nerves.

One almost writes the 'usual' wear and tear, but that would sound callous and also hardly convey the epic nature of the pre-performance tensions to which B.B. is subjected. I don't think many people are aware of this side of his performing life: on the platform it all seems to come marvellously easy to him. It is true, indeed, that on the platform the nerves largely subside and his musical sensibility fills their place, though without displacing the fine nervousness which is a feature of B.B.'s accompanying and of his interpretations in general – something quite distinct from the nerviness which can assail him before he becomes wholly engaged in the business of making music. After the recital or the concert is over, it's a different story. There's the relief that it's done, enjoyment of the music, and praise for P.P.'s performance. To most compliments on his own performance Ben replies, 'Well, it's a glorious piece, isn't it?', thus cunningly deflecting the tribute. The tribulations and anxieties that constitute the overture to a recital are real enough, but I believe the compensating factors – the music itself and the insights P.P. brings to his performances – eventually come to outweigh the preparatory attacks of nerves. I believe B.B. himself might agree with this last statement, though only after a concert.

This digression has led me away from the concert itself, which opens with a Purcell hymn (an In Memoriam for Tertia Liebenthal), continues with a group of Schubert, and ends with the first complete performance of B.B.'s most recent song-cycle, the Soutar set,

Op. 84 [*Who are these children?*]. I have heard stretches of the Soutar songs at the morning rehearsal – not a complete run-through, but rather a look at those songs and those parts of songs which require a warming-up. How striking it is at the rehearsal that, despite B.B.'s pre-concert nerves, he is absolutely calm in support of Peter, the singer, only anxious to give him the support he needs and to fulfil his precise musical needs. This is 'accompanying' on an exalted level, professionalism carried to the nth degree. Indeed, when one sees these two great artists in rehearsal, neither of them so much conscious of himself as of the composer they are bent on serving, one catches a glimpse of the unique professional understanding which forms the core of their celebrated partnership and which, miraculously, has seen it through decades of ill-tempered claviers, unwanted cocktail parties, inadequate or downright hostile acoustics, exacting audiences, exhausting travel, alarming partners at inescapable formal dinners, and all the other perils associated with a strenuous concert life.

During the actual performance of the Soutar songs I am astonished, not so much by the calibre of the cycle, which I had guessed from the rehearsal and from earlier study of the music, but by P.P.'s projection of this complicated work, which one could never have imagined from the preliminary, partial rehearsal. It was amazing, this sudden opening up of impressive reserves of vocal power and the revealing of a masterly grasp of the total shape of the work. The dramatic span of the cycle was unfolded with complete authority. This taught me anew a lesson which is of profound importance: that the art of the performer lies in just this capacity to produce a performance at the right moment, not the day before or in rehearsal some hours before, but at that arbitrary moment which we designate a 'recital', 'concert', or what you will, and during which we expect something eventful to materialise. Magic has to be heard to be done, whether the time for the artists is propitious or not; and it was precisely the magic touch which those of us present at this Edinburgh recital recognised in P.P.'s launching of the Soutar songs.

Needless to add, neither B.B. nor P.P. was as elated by the performance of the cycle as I was. 'We'll get it better' was about Ben's only comment. I think, though, that he was pleased to sense for himself that the cycle did work as a whole (there's been a good deal of shuffling round of the cards that go to make up this particular pack) and felt too that this performance was a useful step towards the ideal performance at which they are aiming. B.B. was full of praise for the way in which Peter had 'brought it off', less full of praise for his own share in the proceedings. Small wonder, when one sees the kind of problem set for B.B. the pianist by B.B. the composer, e.g. the fiendishly difficult canonic accompaniment of 'Slaughter'. I notice, however, that despite the difficulty (the equivalent of tongue-twisting for the fingers, whatever that may be), B.B. the composer shows no sign of intending to help out B.B. the pianist by moderating the passage in question. (If Ben can't play it, I wonder to myself, who on earth can?)

As for P.P., who needless to add has problems enough on his own account in this cycle (the unmeasured freedom of B.B.'s recent vocal writing introduces its own complications), what struck me afresh at Edinburgh was his unique dramatic gift, his capacity to uncover the inner drama of a work and make it tangible, almost. There's no doubt to my mind that this ability to 'act' with his voice has its roots in the fact that P.P. is a conspicuously gifted actor in the conventional sense of the word. Who could forget his noble performance as the old King in Mozart's *Idomeneo* at the rebuilt Maltings? This was not only beautifully sung but also a commanding dramatic impersonation. It was in fact distinguished by the continuous relationship P.P. achieved between his stage actions (whether a glance, gesture or posture) and his vocal 'acting' (whether the articulation of a crucial phrase, the shading of a dynamic or the finding of the appropriate colour of tone). Stage gestures and musical gestures were precisely dovetailed; and it is surely this synthesis which is a major contribution P.P. has made to the musical theatre in our day. (All this reminds me of a fascinating remark of B.B.'s: that a sympathetic and co-operative producer was an absolute necessity for him because, when writing his music for the theatre, he often imagined, even down to the smallest detail, the kind of physical movement or action that should accompany it; and he found it distressing when a producer ignored or contradicted the movement implied by the music.)

I remember as I write this an amusing instance of P.P.'s gift for impersonation. I don't expect I'm alone in recalling in detail his portrayal of Nebuchadnezzar in *The Burning Fiery Furnace*. A memorable impersonation this, which included the splendid miming of P.P. in the Babylonian feast, which the small boys later satirise. He brought to a very fine art indeed his simulated munching and drinking, above all the plucking of the imagined grapes from the imagined bunches, each grape held fastidiously between finger and thumb, appraised and fastidiously gobbled.

This scene was astonishingly evoked one night in New York (an improbable setting), when B.B., P.P., Sue [Phipps], Kathleen and I were taken off to a Japanese restaurant by our generous New York friend, Laton Holmgren, who was not only a kind host but impressed us all by ordering our dinner in immaculate Japanese. The occasion was further distinguished by the unwelcome fact that P.P. was suffering from a catastrophic throat, had lost his voice and had been obliged to postpone his first New York recital. He had been ordered by his doctor to rest his voice, and I have still a vivid picture of him sitting at the opposite side of the alarmingly hot table on which the food was strewn, thence to be cooked under our noses, wrapped almost up to his ears in a long muffler (a bizarre touch, this) and obediently observing his vow of silence.

We had here of course a special combination of circumstances: an explicit link with Japan (shades of the Noh-play!), a feast of no less than Babylonian proportions, and a compulsory silence which made mime a convenient substitute for speech. At any rate, the next time I looked across at P.P. I was amazed to find that he had vanished and Nebuchadnezzar sat in his place, going through his Babylonian gobbling routine with inimitable verve, plucking food out of the air, and consuming it with evident satisfaction, much to the mystification of the New Yorkers by whom we were surrounded. It was not a long display but I think we were all transported back to Suffolk and Orford Church in a matter of seconds; and I remember it struck me at the time that this brilliant bit of impromptu stage business only went to show how P.P. carries the art of impersonation around with him at his very fingertips.

That entertaining incident was an example of the attention to detail which is certainly one of the keys to P.P.'s vivid stage presence; and one might think that a passionate concern for detail is characteristic of the approach of P.P. and B.B. to their manifold activities, to the multiple lives they seem to lead.

I think of the kind of attention P.P. pays to Festival exhibitions, not only organising them in the most basic sense (i.e. tirelessly driving round the country to collect the paintings from obliging owners), but also supervising and directing the hanging (and a good exhibition has to look as good as a good performance sounds) and preparing the catalogue. It is, in fact, just this pervasive care for detail, bearing the impress of B.B.'s and P.P.'s personalities, which is surely one of the unique qualities of the Aldeburgh Festival and associated events at the Maltings. It seems perfectly logical and consistent to me to discuss all these topics in the context of a performance, because it is just the same care, passion for detail and insistence on 'getting things right' – something wholly different from the merely tidy or pedantically correct – that we experience in P.P.'s and B.B.'s music making.

B.B., like P.P., has this same inexhaustible energy which extends to whole ranges of details that in my more innocent days I should never have imagined that he would have wanted to bother about. But I think that there can be no partial involvement for B.B., at least in those things that matter to him. It is either total immersion or nothing. I well remember once surveying the Maltings with him when the hall was first being built and was still in a pretty skeletal shape. I was amazed by the account he gave me as we stood overlooking the busy site, an account of the building as it was to be in which his interest extended to the very last detail, even (I recall) to the colour of the external guttering. Yes, it was essential to get it – the colour – right. It was a bit like – no, it was precisely like – a composer talking about a composition, not yet fully sketched out, but all the details of which, even the most minute, were already clear and established in his mind. The Maltings, when it was built, matched up to that detailed account which B.B. had given me; and I realised that this was yet another aspect of his fierce mental energy, a capacity to dream detailed dreams and to make them come true, in detail.

Magic! one might exclaim, and rightly, because there is a magical aspect of B.B.'s personality, that whole area from which his music emerges. Sometimes there's so much emphasis given to one prominent feature of B.B.'s outward image – his practical, no-nonsense, energetic and self-effacing approach to the business of making music (in every sense associated with the phrase) – that it is easy to forget the inner nature of his art. Of course, the moment we hear his music we are reminded of the intense 'other' life that this exceptional man lives, a world profoundly different from the everyday world in which we, as colleagues, or friends, customarily meet him. Those who are close to his art know that at the centre of his music there is an intensely solitary and private spirit, a troubled, sometimes even despairing visionary, an artist much haunted by nocturnal imagery, by sleep, by presentiments of mortality, a creator preternaturally aware of the destructive appetite (the ever hungry beast in the jungle) that feeds on innocence, virtue and grace. All this is, as it were, a B.B. contained within the B.B. who is the eminently practical, rational man, the most professional of colleagues and also the kindest and most generous of friends. But that other B.B. is there all the time; and sometimes I think the B.B. one thinks one is talking to or walking beside is actually somewhere else, because for a moment that other world has carried him off. For which reason, however much time I spend with B.B., talking, walking or working, my sense of wonder does not diminish. Though one may know B.B. well on one level, there are other levels where one can in fact only know him through his music. There, of course, one finds B.B.'s own self-portrait, the best likeness one could hope to find; and where Ben's music begins, my words must stop.

Reprinted from *Aldeburgh Anthology*, 1972

Remembering Pears

Roger Vignoles

It is Peter's size that I remember first. Tall for a tenor, at least of the non-*Helden* variety, and the chest of a man who, even in his sixties, kept himself fit doing press-ups in the wings while waiting to go on in the dress rehearsal of *Death in Venice*. Those lungs gave him phenomenal breath-control. On one occasion, when I accompanied him in a demonstration of the first song of *On This Island*, we came to the long dying fall on the word 'break', where instinctively one speeds up to make sure the singer doesn't reach the end out of breath. Gently nudging my arpeggios forward, I realised all of a sudden that Peter was doing the reverse: not just holding to the tempo, but actually slowing down, wringing the last ounce of expression from the melisma's final three notes and suggesting that he was still good for at least another bar. Like all great performers, Peter was not immune to the pleasure of showing off. No one in the masterclass, neither the young singers nor the pianists like myself, nor even the handful of Aldeburgh faithfuls in the audience, was deceived by the apparent diffidence with which he would mutter, as if to himself, 'Well, perhaps I'd better just show you...'. He knew it was worth our while to listen.

I suppose the first time I heard Pears' voice I was in my teens. Still at school, my brothers and I had bought my father for Christmas an LP of the *Serenade* for tenor, horn and strings, and over the soup that evening we sat down to listen to it all together. In the way that first impressions sometimes remain with one forever, I have never forgotten the sunset melancholy of Dennis Brain's horn introduction, the hushed pulsation of the strings, the plangent beauty of the high A flat with which the voice entered:

The day's grown old, the fading sun / Hath but a little way to run

The marriage of words and music was so complete that I felt for the first time that I understood English poetry. I thrilled to the brilliance of the dying echoes in Tennyson's 'The Splendour Falls', to the dark treachery of the horn in Blake's 'The Sick Rose'; to the inexorable march of the Dirge, with its keening Gs and G sharps, so dangerously high for most voices but perfectly pitched for Pears'. Then came the fleet-footed scherzo of Ben Jonson's 'Queen and Huntress', with its scurrying *pizzicati* and the outrageously extended melisma with which each verse came to an end. Just thinking of it still brings instantly to mind the perfectly executed vocal slalom with which Peter negotiated those vertiginous triplets, and the almost Noel Coward-like snap of the final cadence – 'e——-xcellently bright'.

Peter's diction was always remarkable. Paradoxically it was founded on his ability to spin the vowels into a perfect legato, through which the consonants were etched in such a way as to reveal both the surface and the deeper meaning of the text. Nowhere more so than in the final movement of the *Serenade*, Keats's famous ode to sleep, where for bars on end the voice is reduced to a narcotic monotone, against which the strings paint their shifting colours. Again, I have only to think of it to hear once more the heroic climax at 'Turn the key deftly', and the wondrous diminuendo, on a single lingering D, with which the song winds to a close:

And seal the hushèd casket of my soul.

For several years, my only acquaintance with Pears' singing was still on gramophone records – Quint in *The Turn of the Screw* (that melismatic gift again, now turned to infinitely malevolent purpose); *A Midsummer Night's Dream*, the *Spring Symphony*. Then there was an early broadcast of the *War Requiem*, which I played over and over again on my Grundig reel-to-reel tape recorder – 'What passing-bells for these who die as cattle?', 'Out there we marched quite friendly up to death', the lyrical 'One ever hangs where shelled roads part', and, most memorable of all, 'It seemed that out of battle I escaped'.

I came to know the *War Requiem* even better, and Pears' back view with it, singing in performances with CUMS and later the Bach Choir conducted by David Willcocks. Pears, too, was the evangelist sans pareil of the Bach Choir's annual Easter performances of the *St Matthew Passion*. He brought to it an unchallengeable authority, sharing the stage with John Carol Case as the Christus, and the luxury-cast quartet of Heather Harper, Janet Baker, Robert Tear and John Shirley-Quirk singing the arias.

Then as now there were always two performances, one on Passion Sunday, the other on Palm Sunday. For the second performance, Pears often stepped aside for Robert Tear to take his place, with Gerald English taking over the arias. On one occasion a young soprano in the chorus was heard to remark somewhat maliciously: 'Bob Tear sounds as though he's been up all night listening to Peter Pears.' A cruel and probably unjust remark, but reflecting the long shadow that Pears' singing cast across the world of English tenors of the next generation, especially of course in the singing of Britten's music. On the one hand it was hugely susceptible to mimicry – one has only to think of Dudley Moore's famous *Beyond the Fringe* parody. (Only years later, after getting to know Pears' singing much better, did I realise how perfectly Dudley Moore had captured not only the characteristic *glissandi*, but also Pears' uncanny legato – on the words 'and-frightened-Miss-Muffet…'.) On the other hand it was virtually impossible to match, because of Pears' unique combination of a silky smoothness at the top with a dark baritonal weight at the bottom (that great chest again). No tenor can fully negotiate the parts that Britten wrote for Pears without developing that dual nature, so to speak. In it lies the dual personality of Peter Grimes, who in Britten's version morphs from a clumsy fisherman who doesn't know his own strength into a visionary, poetic figure. And in the last role Britten composed for him, it was this quality of believable *gravitas* that gave Pears' Aschenbach such poignancy.

I was lucky enough to work as repetiteur and chorus master for the first production of *Death in Venice* (this is when I happened to observe the press-ups in the wings) and I remember being deeply moved by Peter's depiction of Aschenbach's fall from grace.

Rouged and pomaded like the elderly fop, his singing of the 'Phaedrus' monologue was infinitely touching. Always a master of recitative, he brought a lifetime's experience to the final farewell to Tadzio:

...And when your eyes no longer see me... then you'll go too.

In public I only got to perform with Peter on a handful of occasions. Once it was on television. Anglia TV had proposed a series of short programmes entitled *Musical Triangles*, and here the triangle was, as I remember, Britten, Pears and the Voice, represented visually by a somewhat gynaecological drawing of a pair of vocal cords. Among other songs we performed 'Before Life and After' from the cycle *Winter Words*. At the time, young as I was, I thought it a rather awkward piece of writing, with its thick triads deep in the bass. Only later did I recognise these as a Brittenesque metaphor for the layers of strata laid down during the primeval ages 'when all went well', and the song itself as one of Britten's most intense laments for the loss of innocence.

Among the other occasions that I remember were the programmes of songs and readings that Peter used to devise, together with Norman Scarfe and Colin Graham, for the last Sunday night of the festival. Generally left to the last minute, the three of them would ransack the Red House Library for source material, and for the first time I became aware of the breadth and depth of Peter's literary taste, and his collection of rare books. At about the same time I acquired, via the English Opera Group tombola, a tiny marine watercolour by Henry Bright from Peter's extensive collection of paintings (his was the eye that decorated the walls of the Red House with Mary Potters, John Pipers and Sidney Nolans, among many others; see p.161).

In 1977 we celebrated Roger Quilter's centenary with a handful of songs including the exquisite setting of Edmund Waller's 'Go, Lovely Rose'. It was the summer after Britten died, and Peter and I were rehearsing in the Red House a day or two before the concert. All went well until we got to the final couplet 'How small a part of time they share/That are so wondrous sweet and fair', when all of a sudden Peter broke off, and looking round I found myself left alone with the piano. Not knowing what else to do, I continued practising until Peter returned. Unnecessarily, he apologised to me. 'Frightfully sorry about that – a bit near the bone, you know – but it'll be all right on the night.'

My last memory of Peter is of a class at the Britten–Pears School devoted to Handel. By then he had suffered the stroke that finally ended his singing career, but was still enthusiastically teaching with the aid of a stick, of whose use as a theatrical prop he was well aware. With infinite patience but little success, he had been trying to instil some kind of life into a young tenor's sadly anaemic rendering of Jephtha's great accompanied recitative 'Deeper and deeper still'. Finally, he realised he was not getting anywhere. 'Perhaps I'd better have a go ... Roger, do you mind?' and before our eyes, there in the bare recital room, he became transformed into a figure of prophetic stature, almost as though he had stepped out of the Sistine Chapel ceiling. It was the Pears of old, the Pears of the Evangelist, of Idomeneo, of the Male Chorus in Lucretia, of the Madwoman in Curlew River. It was the Pears of Grimes, and of Aschenbach, and I doubt if any of those present has ever forgotten it.

Britten, His Mentor and Some Colleagues

Peter Dickinson

An already remarkably gifted thirteen-year-old, Head Boy of South Lodge Preparatory School in Lowestoft, attended the first performance of an orchestral piece by a modern British composer with epoch-making results. The work was Frank Bridge's *Enter Spring*, with the Queen's Hall Orchestra conducted by the composer at the Norwich Triennial Festival on 27 October 1927. The boy, of course, was Benjamin Britten and, although he had heard Bridge's *The Sea* three years earlier and had been 'knocked sideways', it was after *Enter Spring* that he met Bridge himself, who agreed to teach him.

Born in 1879, Bridge was an exact contemporary of John Ireland and Cyril Scott. Of that generation, Vaughan Williams was a little older: Bax slightly younger. Before World War I Bridge had a career as a relatively conventional composer, whose output included perfectly crafted piano miniatures with floral titles and music for small orchestras; he also played chamber music professionally. But in reaction to World War I his whole orientation changed and a mood of profound anger seems to have driven him towards more advanced musical techniques. His Piano Sonata (1924), written in memory of a colleague who was killed in the war, is at times viciously dissonant. Consequently, in the period of his full maturity between the wars, Bridge was misunderstood by the conservative British critics who would soon under-estimate his pupil. Bridge admired Alban Berg, although Britten was discouraged by the Royal College of Music from studying with him, and Bridge's String Quartet No. 3, with its well-absorbed continental influences, was first performed in Vienna before it was heard in London. Bridge owed much to his friendship with the generous American patron Elizabeth Sprague Coolidge, who would soon provide opportunities for Britten. It was her financial support and promotion of Bridge's music at festivals in America and Europe that enabled him to maintain his independence in spite of a dwindling public in England, where he was active as a conductor but undervalued in that capacity, too.

In several significant ways Bridge was a role model for the young Britten. He was a non-conformist because he was not part of the parochial English folksong school of composers; he was a pacifist; and he was also a practical musician – a viola player and conductor. Britten responded to this background and his own music shows Bridge's fingerprints right into maturity. Bridge's visits to America may also have given Britten the idea of transatlantic success when things at home were discouraging. In 1930 Britten noted in his diary that Bridge was getting a good reception there and added: 'It is pretty disgraceful that England's premier composer should have to leave his country to get some recognition.'

Bridge's earlier career involved string teaching rather than composition, but by the time he met Britten he had given this up. However, he was so impressed by Britten that he took him on right away. Ethel and Frank Bridge had no children and virtually adopted the boy, taking charge of his artistic development. Bridge realised the exceptional nature of the talent he was nurturing which gave rise to a kind of partnership that must have meant a lot to the older man too.

Ten years after he first met Bridge, Britten publicly acknowledged what he owed him. His *Variations on a Theme of Frank Bridge* for string orchestra was based on the second of Bridge's *Idylls* for string quartet (1906) and the manuscript, but not the published score, shows that each variation represented a characteristic of Bridge himself – 'His integrity, his energy, his charm, his wit, his tradition', and so on. It is almost as if Britten had created his own *Enigma Variations* in which all the characters are aspects of Bridge himself rather than different people. And there is no enigma here, except that Bridge's music was not sufficiently well known for listeners to recognise the quotes from it in the fugal section.

Britten did not enjoy his subsequent studies with John Ireland at the Royal College of Music and was consistently loyal to his first teacher. He took part in performances of Bridge's chamber music; he copied parts for him and read proofs; Bridge gave him copies of his scores; and later Britten and Pears recorded some of Bridge's songs. In 1967 Britten conducted *Enter Spring*, which had not been heard for thirty-five years, and recorded the cello sonata with Rostropovich.

Accustomed to Bridge's high standards, Britten found most contemporary British music defective but there was one composer he approved of five years before he actually met him. That was Lennox Berkeley, whose connections with Britten are particularly fascinating. Berkeley came from an aristocratic family and was ten years older; he, too, had attended Gresham's School in Norfolk but then studied with Nadia Boulanger in Paris, the centre of activity in new music. In March 1931 Britten went to a chamber concert at the Grotrian Hall in London that included, according to his diary, a 'very interesting suite of L. Berkeley for Vlc & Oboe'. This was Berkeley's *Petite Suite* (1927), a distinctly neo-classical set of five movements strongly influenced by Bach. After a Prelude and an Allegro the movement titles reflect their Baroque inspiration – Bourrée (cello solo), Aria (oboe solo) and Gigue.

What did the seventeen-year-old Britten find 'very interesting' about Berkeley's student work? Probably his exploitation of the two instruments in independent two-part counterpoint that was not always consonant. Britten might have remembered the Aria for oboe solo when he wrote his *Six Metamorphoses* for solo oboe twenty years later.

Britten finally met Berkeley when they were both at the International Society for Contemporary Music Festival held at Barcelona in 1936, only three months before the start of the Spanish Civil War. He flew from Croydon airport, with various changes of plane, and got there on 17 April, meeting Berkeley shortly after his arrival. The programme included Berkeley's *Overture*, which the composer conducted, and Britten's *Suite* for Violin and Piano, performed by Britten and Antonio Brosa.

This was before Britten had met Pears and the two composers got on splendidly. They sat at café tables in the park, transcribed tunes played by folk musicians and then turned them into the four-movement orchestral suite *Mont Juic* as a collaboration. They enjoyed working together. Britten acknowledged Berkeley's help with *Our Hunting Fathers*, premiered at the 1936 Norwich Festival, but for years they preferred not to reveal who wrote which parts of *Mont Juic*. Because their approach was so similar at that time, it has always been hard to tell that Berkeley wrote the first two movements and Britten the last two. The third movement is a lament that became particularly poignant, since the Spanish conflict was well under way by the time *Mont Juic* was first performed in a BBC broadcast in January 1938 and a much larger war was looming – to Britten's increasing despair.

The previous autumn Britten had been with friends to the Leeds Festival where he heard Berkeley's oratorio *Jonah* and reported in his diary: 'he conducts very well and has a good show. It has some good things in it & is even more promising for the future.' *Jonah* is based on set numbers like the Bach passions but with touches of Stravinsky's neo-classicism. Britten would have approved of its independence from the English choral tradition, which was one reason why it was not well received.

When he saw the score of Berkeley's *Domini est terra* he reported in a letter to his friend the singing teacher Ursula Nettleship: 'Lennox Berkeley has just written a fearfully good PSALM for chorus & orchestra. It's the goods all right. You must see it.'

The premiere was at the Queen's Hall in June 1938 and the previous month Britten had been to Sadler's Wells and admired Berkeley's ballet score *The Judgement of Paris*, choreographed by Frederick Ashton. By this time Berkeley and Britten had become close friends and decided to share the Old Mill at Snape where Britten was writing his Piano Concerto, which he dedicated to Berkeley. He seemed pleased to be able to tell his publisher that the work had the approval of both Bridge and Berkeley, but later – after Britten had played it at a Prom – Bridge and his friends were disappointed by what they probably regarded as the concerto's showy superficiality. Britten was painfully aware of his idol's disapproval, which coincided with carping reviews. Meanwhile he and Berkeley could admire each other professionally, although on a domestic level Berkeley would soon be eclipsed by the arrival of Peter Pears. Britten had been collaborating with W. H. Auden on films and was setting his poetry. Both he and Berkeley set 'Night covers up the rigid land' and Berkeley set 'Lay your sleeping head, my love', dedicating his songs to Britten as well as his *Introduction and Allegro* for Two Pianos and Orchestra, which he played with William Glock at a Prom in September 1940. By then Britten and Pears were in America – they left England in April 1939 and returned just under three years later.

Britten first met Aaron Copland at the Festival of the International Society for Contemporary Music held in London in 1938, at which both of them and Lennox Berkeley had works performed. Britten saw more of Copland in America and he would have found him complementary to Berkeley – they were both Boulanger pupils and venerated her as intensely as Britten did Bridge. But times were changing and Britten's international career enabled him to grow out of the Bridge circle. He and his colleagues now supported each other with conspicuous success. It was Britten who introduced Copland to his publisher, Boosey and Hawkes, and Copland drew Britten to the attention of Koussevitsky, whose Foundation commissioned *Peter Grimes*. Copland had visited Britten at Snape, where they shared scores [see p.246]; after the war he met Britten and Pears whenever he came to London; and he was featured at the Aldeburgh Festival in 1960. Later Copland said that Britten's training was 'impeccable'.

However, Britten's support of Berkeley was greater – his *Four Poems of St Teresa of Avila* were written for the English Opera Group and three of his four operas were premiered at Aldeburgh. Right from their first meeting Berkeley hero-worshipped Britten, promoted him at the BBC when he was on the staff there, and eagerly awaited every new score. Their friendship continued after Berkeley's happy marriage to Freda Bernstein in

Benjamin Britten and Lennox
Berkeley picnic on a beach,
September 1961.

1946 and two years later Britten became godfather to their eldest son Michael, now an established composer. In Britten's lifetime there were twenty-four performances of works by Berkeley at Aldeburgh Festivals. This can be set alongside twenty-seven by Bridge, which included several short songs; ten by Copland; and twenty-two by Tippett – these figures include repeated works.

Britten's connection with Tippett, who was Director of Music at Morley College, London, started much later. In May 1943 he wrote to Elizabeth Mayer, who had looked after him and Pears in Long Island: 'One great new friend Peter and I have made, an *excellent* composer, & most delightful & intelligent man, Michael Tippett...'. Britten had seen the score of *A Child of our Time*; admired it and its message; and subsequently attended the first performance in March 1944. Berkeley also liked the work and saluted another British composer, apart from Britten, who could write 'real, living music', although he feared Tippett had a tendency towards complication which would certainly become more pronounced later.

Tippett wrote two song cycles for Pears and Britten – *Boyhood's End* (1943) and *The Heart's Assurance* (1951). In 1943 Tippett was jailed for three months as a conscientious objector who refused to undertake non-combatant military duties. Ironically, he was an inmate at Wormwood Scrubs prison when Pears and Britten gave a recital there and, by special arrangement, was allowed to turn pages. In 1963 Tippett dedicated his Concerto for Orchestra to Britten for his fiftieth birthday and in return Britten gave Tippett the dedication of *Curlew River* for his sixtieth birthday two years later.

The admiration between Tippett and Britten was mutual, but unlike Britten's connections with Bridge, Berkeley and Copland, there is little common ground in their music. By the time they met, both composers had achieved maturity and Tippett's apparently disorderly idiom was far removed from Britten's fastidious approach inherited from Bridge or the polished techniques emanating from the Boulanger *atelier* reflected in different ways in the music of both Berkeley and Copland. Berkeley's melodic and colourful music is now receiving greater attention – Britten's admiration was justified – and Copland's position as a major figure on the international scene from the mid-twentieth century onwards can be seen as an American counterpart to that of Britten.

A Wolf in Tweed Clothing

Paul Kildea

Before Purcell there was no composer in England to speak of, so we learnt as kids, although in retrospect this is a little rough on Tallis and Byrd, two of Christianity's more beguiling pimps. And after Purcell there was really no one until Parry and Stanford almost two hundred years later, so long as one is content to draw a veil discreetly over the latter's Irish origins. Arthur Sullivan was a court jester who longed to be thought of as a serious artist; Frank Bridge, a John-the-Baptist figure, preaching in the wilderness, a prefigurement of great but as yet unrealised things; while Delius was far too French for his own good. Elgar, Vaughan Williams and Walton were three wise men who wrote music that spoke to the English soul, although their gifts were subsequently considered somewhat wanting when placed beside the child they came to honour, Benjamin Britten, whereupon VW recast himself as more shepherd than wise man, wandering bucolically through the pastures of English folk tradition, greeting his herds and hay. Britten, born providentially on the feast day of the patron saint of music, St Cecilia, would himself come to be recognised as the One True Saviour – at least of English music, although broader claims have not been ruled out, in this life or the next. His opera *Peter Grimes* was thrown down on the table like a winning hand in a late-night poker game; in this one gesture it became evident that it was really *his* music that defined the English soul, the first to do so since Purcell's, etc, with all necessary apologies to his supporting cast. That's about it, actually. And it is just as I thought: there is nothing to it, this whole music-history lark.

Except … A happy ending should never be allowed to get in the way of a good story. And the story of English music is vastly more entertaining and scandalous than any reduction would have us believe. At its core is this 200-year dry spell, which goes some way towards explaining why England became so intent on discovering musical prophets and saviours from among her own people. Finding them was no easy feat, for England in the nineteenth century had in place none of the continent's cultural infrastructure through which to cultivate her own music and musicians. This made England in the first half of the twentieth century particularly sensitive to charges of musical imitation and unoriginality – all the while she was plundering continental models in her attempt to build her own Valhalla-on-Thames. Partly because of the cultural cold war that grew out of the traumatic events of 1914–18 and 1939–45, England's music-history shorthand contains few acknowledgements of the significant debts to Austria and Germany – for the music, naturally, but significantly also for the post-1945 institutions that are now such an important and ingrained part of English culture. Yet even before hostilities commenced between the countries, Elgar's close affinity with Richard Strauss, say, or Stanford's with

Brahms was not allowed to contradict emerging notions of nationhood. In much this way was Edmund Hillary's inconvenient New Zealand nationality skimmed over by those in England looking for imperial assertion when, as part of John Hunt's 1953 English expedition to Everest, he was actually the first to reach the peak.

There is nothing surprising in any of this, and it is only worth stating here because English musical insecurity coincided absolutely with the period in which Benjamin Britten was learning and then practising his craft. The shattering success of *Peter Grimes* only one month after the armistice was merited for the work alone, yet without doubt the timing of the premiere invested the opera with a symbolic weight that affected its reception and, consequently, performance history. *Grimes* was viewed as a symbol of regeneration, a symbol of a country gaining artistic maturity and triumphing in a field dominated by the recently vanquished enemy, Germany. It is not that *Grimes* is an 'un-English' work; the prosody, the weather-whipped rural community and its depiction of the two great institutions of English life – church and pub – position it firmly in the English social vernacular. On the other hand, continental models have been acknowledged – by composer and commentators alike – Berg's *Wozzeck* and Strauss's *Der Rosenkavalier* being just two of them. Yet the determination to claim Britten as an 'English composer' at a time when his country most needed him – helped to no small degree by Britten's own proclamations and behaviour, incidentally, which played up this idea, no matter how genuine a motivating factor in his decision to return to England from America in 1942 – and the sheer originality of his music have worked together to disguise his strong, ongoing continental debts.

Britten was not electing to join a club by returning to England. Although for some decades there had been a distasteful mixture of soul-searching and back-slapping with regards the *idea* of English music, in a way that would be inconceivable today, London in the 1940s no more constituted an English sound or aesthetic than did Vienna an Austrian aesthetic in the 1820s. Each city facilitated the music of those composers and performers who assembled there. Vienna had the tradition and infrastructure that London lacked, and was also what Britten termed 'the spiritual home of the most extraordinary number of great composers'.

Yet for all of Britten's talk about his spiritual ties to Suffolk ('I am native, rooted here' he has Peter Grimes sing near the beginning of the opera), from Vienna he learned that composers were a form of currency. In 1946 he wrested control over his current and future dramatic works from an existing opera company, Sadler's Wells (and would soon reject overtures from another, the new company at Covent Garden, to become its music director) and formed his own, which really did affect his compositional aesthetic through its limited resources and touring schedule. Two years later he rejected the very idea that an urban existence was necessary for the creation and propagation of musical works when, along with his partner Peter Pears and the opera director Eric Crozier, he founded the Aldeburgh Festival, for which he wrote the majority of his music.

In his tweed suits and woollen ties and plummy RP (Received Pronunciation) accent Britten was the perfect English gentleman. He was no Beecham, that railroading, rambunctious upper-class playboy, who begat music companies much as a street cat does kittens; he was simply a man who astutely recognised that he had accumulated huge political capital through the fantastic events of June 1945 and set about spending it. Why couldn't a composer be a form of currency in England, too, no matter that one had never been before? He pushed his case to the Arts Council over funding for the English Opera Group or the Aldeburgh Festival. He gave evidence to panels or informally to the BBC about the 'future of English music'. He was waspish about Covent Garden, a stern critic who urged the opera company to put its house in order. He spoke out about the parochialism of nationalist music and of its clumsy, folksy manifestations in England. He charmed friends and colleagues – yes, the word needs to be reclaimed in connection to Britten owing to its almost total excision from Humphrey Carpenter's pervasive biography of the composer – and ran a sort of black market at Aldeburgh where audiences encountered rare and seemingly illicit treasures.

It is possible to identify in *Der Rosenkavalier* an influence on Britten far greater than the Act 3 trio, which made its presence felt in the Act 2 trio of women's voices in *Grimes*. For with *Der Rosenkavalier*, so the historical shorthand goes, Strauss stepped back from the expressionist brink he had stood before so precariously with *Salome and Elektra*. Is this not what Britten did after *Grimes*, a score full of modernist gestures, a story every bit as dispiriting as Berg's expressionist masterpiece *Wozzeck*? Yet to think this way is to be blind to the implicit content and purpose of his later dramatic works, and also to misread what Britten set out to achieve through the Aldeburgh Festival and the English Opera Group.

Those commentators who spoke of Britten's 'retreat' to Aldeburgh, who somehow equated his predominantly rural life as affirmation of his Englishness, who identified in his rejection of America a confirmation of the tottering British Empire have missed the point about what a radical composer he was. Every new award, from being appointed Freeman of Lowestoft in 1951 to his peerage in 1976 only months before his death, kept this image alive, as did the tea parties with the Queen or her mother and his increasing distance from the experimentation in English music in the 1960s and 1970s. And it took an American to see through the disguise. 'When you hear Britten's music, if you really *hear* it, not just listen to it superficially', said Leonard Bernstein in 1980, 'you become aware of something very dark. There are gears that are grinding and not quite meshing, and they make a great pain.' It is a remarkably succinct definition of modernism, from the industrial metaphors to the evocation of searing pain – the twentieth-century condition, after all. The fact that Britten achieved this from within a simple English exterior marks him as a paradox, certainly. Yet it is these contradictions that fuelled his life and art.

See Rupert Christiansen, *Britten's Britishness: the operas viewed from abroad*, p.341, for further discussion of Britten's international standing.

Fire and Iron: Britten and Pacifism

Andrew Plant

Isaac the first-born spake and said, My Father,
Behold the preparations, fire and iron,
But where the lamb, for this burnt offering?

Wilfred Owen (1893–1918) from *The Parable of the Old Man and the Young* (1918), set by Britten in *War Requiem*

On the night of 14 November 1940 the burnt offering was Coventry Cathedral, victim of Luftwaffe bombs. The circumstances of its destruction dictated that the festival in 1962 to mark the consecration of its successor would have a distinct soberness, quite unlike the celebratory atmosphere surrounding the completion of the new cathedral at Guildford in 1961. When Britten was asked to write a work for Coventry's new cathedral, he took the opportunity to make his most profound statement: *War Requiem*.

It was surely inevitable that as a committed pacifist from an early age, Britten would seek to emphasise the building's turbulent history, but this commission was by no means the first occasion on which the composer seized a concept in order to promote his own viewpoint or ideology. In 1971 Britten speculated that 'it' (his pacifism) may have grown from his horrified reaction on hearing a boy being beaten at his prep school, a statement that Pears corroborated. His final year at this school, South Lodge, was marked by a vehement essay denouncing blood-sports and war, an attitude which plunged him into considerable disgrace. During his period of study with Frank Bridge he continued to discuss pacifism; in his first year at the Royal College of Music he produced a brief polemic, *Sport*, a setting of W. H. Davies disparaging organised violence.

Britten's diary for 1936 contains frequent bitter reflections on the Spanish Civil War: he records his deep empathy with the youth of that conflict and rails against his own Government being 'willing to spend £300,000,000 on men-slaughtering machines'. In March 1936, against this horrific background, he wrote the music for the brief but hard-hitting pacifist film *Peace of Britain* (made by Paul Rotha's Strand Films), comprising three minutes of military statistics and a vehement appeal, 'Write to your MP … Demand peace by reason'. Also from this year comes his still-neglected masterpiece *Our Hunting Fathers*, a ferocious diatribe against man's inhumanity to animals and men, first performed at the Norfolk and Norwich Triennial Festival to a fairly impenetrable libretto by Auden (not himself a pacifist) and seemingly contrived with at least one eye on scandalising the audience who were probably anticipating a cosy celebration of their domestic companions. In 1937 came a slighter *Pacifist March* written for the Peace Pledge Union. The next year saw a radio cantata *The World of the Spirit*, whose format evidently influenced the composer when compiling later works, as it comprises an intriguing assembly of texts by various authors. Among them is the story of a Jewish rabbi, killed in battle after bringing a crucifix to a dying soldier. In April 1940 in an interview with the *New York Sun*, Britten spoke of his new *Sinfonia da Requiem*: 'I'm making it just as anti-war as possible ... by coupling new music with well known musical phrases, I think it's possible to get over certain ideas ... I'm quoting from the *Dies Irae* of the Requiem Mass'. This was a curious choice for a commission to celebrate the 2,600th anniversary of the founding of the Japanese Empire and an evident misunderstanding or misinterpretation of the work's inherently Christian subtext caused the *Sinfonia* to be rejected by its recipients.

Britten and Pears had left for Canada and the USA in April 1939, before war was thought inevitable, and were already there when it was declared. Their return at the height of hostilities three years later through seas infested with U-boats shows clearly their dedication to return to do the work for which they were best fitted. They were, of course, obliged to face a local tribunal. The opening phrase of Britten's defence, 'Since I believe that there is in every man the spirit of God, I cannot destroy...' recalls words of Ivan Turgenev included in *The World of the Spirit*: '...the face of Christ, a face like all men's faces'. Britten was registered as liable to be called up for service involving non-combatant duties but appealed against this, citing the work he had already undertaken in the cause of pacifism and writing that he could not conscientiously abide by the ruling, since he would be no less actively participating in the war than if he were a combatant. 'I appeal to be left free to follow that line of service to the community, which my conscience approves & my training makes possible.' Fortunately perhaps, the chairman on this occasion had known Britten for some years and decided that the composer should be completely free to carry on with his work.

These undertakings included a concert tour with Yehudi Menuhin in 1945 to German concentration camps, including Belsen. From their disturbing experiences emerged Britten's feverish and virtuosic song-cycle, *The Holy Sonnets of John Donne*. Mention should also be made of *The Ballad of Little Musgrave and Lady Barnard*, a miniature cantata for male voices and piano, written for the inmates of Oflag VIIb at Eichstätt, where it was first performed in 1944. Based on a folksong, it tells of true but illicit love betrayed by a spy, outnumbered and destroyed by opposing forces and lamented by a threnody no less affecting for its modest scale. Having already experienced the seizure by the authorities of some of his other manuscripts for fear they contained code, Britten must have relished the success of this little work, whose subtle appositeness has rarely been fully acknowledged.

Two of Britten's five Canticles deal with violence or war and although both end in benediction, parts of *Canticle II*, 'Abraham and Isaac', were reworked in *War Requiem* for the setting of Wilfred Owen's horrific version of the story, with its devastating dismissal of the interceding angel and the completion of Isaac's sacrifice: 'But the old man would not so, but slew his son / And half the seed of Europe one by one'. His verse is given a still darker patina by the prayer of the boys' choir which Britten placed immediately afterwards as a commentary: 'Hostias et preces tibi Domine laudis offerimus'. *Canticle III*, 'Still falls the Rain', is a setting of Edith Sitwell's extraordinary description of the Blitz as the

The opening of the *War Requiem* in Britten's composition draft 'nineteen hundred and forty nails / Upon the Cross'; yet there is redemption on its final page, when mankind is blessed by 'the voice of One'. In the *War Requiem* the only completely consoling movement is its still centre, the timeless appeal for peace that is the *Agnus Dei*, juxtaposed with Owen's *At a Calvary near the Ancre*. However, neither poet nor composer shrank from condemning the ecclesiastical hierarchy who fell into the sin of pride, thus denying their God and condoning the sentencing of young men to their deaths: 'The scribes on all the people shove / And bawl allegiance to the State'. One thinks too of another Owen poem, 'The Kind Ghosts', set by Britten in his *Nocturne* (1958) with such mellifluousness and calm simplicity that its overwhelming cynicism sometimes passes unnoticed in performance. Britannia's wilful refusal to acknowledge the cost of maintaining her status quo was censured with even greater directness in Auden's 'A Summer Night', the dark troubled heart of Britten's *Spring Symphony* (1949):

And, gentle, do not care to know,
Where Poland draws her Eastern bow,
What violence is done;
Nor ask what doubtful act allows
Our freedom in this English house,
Our picnics in the sun.

Britten once commented to Sidney Nolan, 'It's a kind of reparation. That's what the *War Requiem* is about; it is reparation.' However, *The Times* commented of the work: 'It is not a *Requiem* to console the living; sometimes it does not even help the dead to sleep soundly. It can only disturb every living soul, for it denounces the barbarism more or less awake in mankind with all the authority that a great composer can muster.'

Another form of recompense was fashioned in 1969 to mark the fiftieth anniversary of the Save the Children Fund. Britten again chose not to shy away from stark realities, writing an immensely powerful setting of Bertolt Brecht's *Children's Crusade* for children's voices, two pianos, organ and a large battery of percussion. Its cataclysmic opening pages, a vivid depiction of aerial bombardment, bring the horrors of war unnervingly close and Nolan later made a series of paintings recording key moments in the drama, part of a considerable legacy based on Britten's music. Less bombastic, yet much more chilling, is the late song-cycle *Who are these children?* (1969) to words by William Soutar, some of which detail the consequences of war in starkly economic verse. For one of the songs, the wailing of an air-raid siren is recreated in the piano part.

Immediately following this work, in 1970, came *Owen Wingrave*, an opera originally written for television, with a libretto by Myfanwy Piper based on the story by Henry James, in which a young military student rejects his ancestors' oppressive history of soldiering for a life of peace. Britten seized in particular on the word 'scruples' as a catalyst for the infuriated family, producing a terrifying ensemble of malice and contempt. James writes: 'They talked of his scruples as you wouldn't talk of a cannibal's god'. Britten was reading the novel during the composition of the *War Requiem* and some of the *Dies Irae* fanfares from that work were recast in *Wingrave* – they also recalled *Ballad of Heroes*, Britten's cantata from 1939. In *Wingrave*, particularly in the protagonist's aria, 'Now you may save your scornful looks', the composer's personal creed may be found:

Oh you with your bugbears, your arrogance, your greed,
your intolerance, your selfish morals and petty victories,
peace is not won by your wars.
Peace is not confused, not sentimental, not afraid.
Peace is positive, is passionate, committing –
more than war itself.

'I'm strong, and I know it, and I'll stay strong' he might have added, as does Billy Budd at the similar emotional climax of that great opera: Budd, who has also struck one blow and regretted it, who abjures further violence, who goes to his death with utter self-confidence in his belief. Britten also agreed that, in some ways, *Wingrave* is a 'companion piece' to his earlier opera, *The Turn of the Screw* (1954). The two stories have close similarities but whatever may comprise Wingrave's nemesis, 'the power that makes men fight', it is a force less corporeal than Quint and more deadly than Claggart's twisted emotional discharge in *Budd*.

Myfanwy Piper again had little help from James, who has Wingrave remark of the house, Paramore: 'There are strange voices in it that seem to mutter at me – to say dreadful things as I pass ... It's what my aunt calls the family circle. It's all constituted here, it's a kind of indestructible presence, it stretches away into the past.' Britten marked two passages in his copy of the novel: the story of the father who killed his son in a fit of passion later became the ballad holding the work together. A shorter remark, not in fact used entire, provided the view against which the boy must struggle: the opinion that voicing pacifist views is 'corrupting the youth of Athens' and 'sowing sedition'. Once more the Apollonian vision of beauty recurs as a metaphor for Britten's concerns, as it did five years earlier in the final section of *Voices for Today* (1965), written for the twentieth anniversary of the United Nations. The potent libretto of this work is entirely concerned with Peace, being a series of quotes on the subject drawn from prophets throughout the ages. It concludes with an extract from Virgil, foretelling 'the birth of the boy who shall at last bring the race of iron to an end, and bid the golden race spring up all the world over ... thine own Apollo is at length on his throne'.

Perhaps Wingrave's personal requiem may be discerned in the closing movement of the composer's *Suite on English Folk Tunes* ('A Time There Was...') from 1974. In this valedictory work, Grainger's transcription of the haunting war song 'Lord Melbourne' is stripped of its military livery and transformed into a lament of heartbreaking poignancy. However, in its addressing of universal suffering, the *War Requiem* is an elegy for more than one conflict and for more than one Owen.

At the end of *The Rape of Lucretia* (1946) the Female Chorus poses a despairing question, 'Is this it all?', answered by the Male Chorus uncertainly but with some degree of optimism: 'It is not all ... In His Passion is our hope'. Tippett preferred a humanistic viewpoint for his war-torn oratorio *A Child of Our Time* (1941), which closes with an affirmation that the cycle of life will bring eternal renewal: 'Here is no final grieving, but an abiding hope'. There is little such reassurance in the *War Requiem*. Peter Evans wrote: 'If [Britten] refuses to portray a God of wrath, his man-made *dies irae* must appear the more terrible a denial of the God of pity so sublimely invoked elsewhere.' Evans's remarks apply particularly to the immensely cathartic closing pages of the work, as the soldiers' refrain 'Let us sleep now' is gradually overwhelmed by the *In Paradisum* of the choirs and chorus. However, this mood is not allowed to remain: the vision appears to recede and the tolling bells which punctuate the final 'Requiescat in pace' return the listener to the mourning world before a final unsettling harmonic sidestep (heard twice before in the work) underlines a curious and strangely cold Amen to the concluding prayer. Unlike *Lucretia*, Britten forbears to end with the equivalent of 'It is not all' and we are left with Owen's lines placed at the head of the score: 'All a poet can do is to warn'.

However, if Owen was able only to warn, others have attempted to understand. Among them was fellow pacifist Ronald Duncan, the librettist of *Lucretia*, who in 1945 produced a post-Hiroshima cantata entitled *Mea Culpa*, that he hoped Britten would set. The composer did not do so but the libretto survives at the Britten–Pears Library: in its general tenor and use of Biblical phrases, it is not unlike *A Child of Our Time* but is also notably influenced by classical Chinese poetry. Another such visionary was Edwin Muir, who drew extraordinary comfort from the flawed nature of man, so exemplified in human conflict, seeing the Fall as the truly 'felix culpa', the 'blessed fault' of the Easter Exsultet ('O truly necessary sin of Adam ... O happy fault which was counted worthy to have such and so great a Redeemer!'). This amplifies Owen's telling phrase incorporated into Britten's setting of the *Agnus Dei*: 'But they who love the greater love / Lay down their life; they do not hate'. Although Britten did not set any of Muir's poetry, he possessed a volume containing the following lines:

But famished field and blackened tree
Bear flowers in Eden never known.
Blossoms of grief and charity
Bloom in these darkened fields alone.
What had Eden ever to say
Of hope and faith and pity and love
Until was buried all its day
And memory found its treasure trove?
Strange blessings never in Paradise
Fall from these beclouded skies.

Edwin Muir (1887–1959) from *One Foot in Eden* (1965)

Writing an Opera
Eric Crozier

To collaborate with a composer in writing an opera is one of the most stimulating and enjoyable experiences that an author can have – yet few people seem to know how such a collaboration works in practice. I have been lucky. I have not only written librettos myself; I have also, on several occasions, acted as a dramatic adviser for other librettists, and have thus been able to watch and share in the whole process of collaboration from start to finish.

In 1949 Benjamin Britten was commissioned by the Arts Council to compose a full-scale opera for performance at Covent Garden during the Festival of Britain. He had no subject in mind; but he had been eager for some time past to persuade the distinguished novelist, E.M. Forster, who was a friend of his, to write a libretto for him. Forster was attracted by the idea. He was, however, diffident about his own ability to write for the theatre. So it was agreed between him and Britten that I should be asked to join them.

We had one or two abortive meetings to discuss possible stories. Then, one winter's evening, my telephone rang, and Britten asked me to travel to Aldeburgh as soon as possible. I left home very early next morning, and arrived to find Britten and Forster still at breakfast. They gave me some hot coffee. Then they shut me up in a room to read Melville's *Billy Budd*.

This short novel was Melville's last work. The manuscript, an almost incoherent mass of scribblings and crossings-out and over-writings, was found among his papers after his death and was not published until twenty years or so afterwards. The action takes place aboard a British man-of-war during the Napoleonic wars: there are no female characters; the atmosphere is stark and tragic; and the central problem concerns the eternal conflict between good and evil, and the inadequacy of human justice in exceptional circumstances.

Britten and Forster were very much impressed with the book. While I was reading it, they fidgeted about the house wondering if I would be equally impressed, and what I would think about the possibilities of using it for an opera. We spent the rest of that day discussing the merits of the story, which were considerable, and its demerits for our purpose, which were many. The central conflict, the strength of the characterisation, the poetic and almost parable-like nature of the subject – all these were admirable. The practical difficulty, however, of an opera without women's voices seemed insuperable. Britten believed that he might be able to score the work in such a way that this defect would be transformed into a virtue. This, however, did not dispose of the fundamental objection that a work with an all-male cast could only have a very limited currency in the opera repertory. (The subsequent history of the opera has shown that this objection is a more serious one than we allowed it to be at the time.)

A point comes in the planning of every opera when an act of faith has to be made. After thorough discussion of all the advantages and disadvantages, we decided that Melville's novel was so excellent that we would go ahead.

The three of us now began to study the book in the closest detail. We drew up lists of characters: we set down a table of the crucial scenes in the dramatic action: we drew a rough sketch of a sailing-ship so that we could understand more clearly the physical pattern of events and follow Melville's characters about from the commander's cabin to the orlop-deck. At this stage, I must admit, we often seemed to be groping about in a fog. Our list of crucial scenes had no recognisable dramatic shape, nor could we tell if the action would fall into two, three or four acts. We were like people trying to complete a jig-saw puzzle with half the bits missing.

In these circumstances the best thing to do was to separate for a time and to digest the ideas that had emerged so far. It was also necessary for Forster and myself to set about filling in the gaps in our knowledge of the period with which we were dealing, and to learn all that we could about how men lived, worked and fought aboard an eighteenth-century man-of-war.

We read a great many books; we spent a valuable afternoon on the *Victory* at Portsmouth; we pored over scale-models at the National Maritime Museum; we visited a training-ship for young seamen and sought advice from its commander. And, time and time again, we turned back to Melville's story, trying to understand it and interpret it in the light of our newly found scraps of knowledge.

One day in March (some two or three months after our original meeting), Forster and I travelled down to Aldeburgh. We had done all the preparation that we could: now we had to settle down to work in earnest. For a whole month we lived in Britten's house. Each morning after breakfast, the two of us went to our study. Britten – who was busy with another composition – went to his study at the other end of the house. Our first task, which took almost a week, was to plan a detailed synopsis of the action of the opera. This obliged us to invent new scenes to serve as links between those scenes that we proposed to take directly from Melville. We also had to invent new characters, or to fuse in a single character those functions which Melville had distributed among two or three minor figures. Midway through each morning, Britten would come in to see how we were getting on. At lunch, during afternoon walks, and at dinner, the three of us discussed the problems arising from our day's work. Sometimes the problems were of a purely practical nature. At other times, they took us deeply into considerations of psychology, and into long arguments about metaphysical questions arising from Melville's concepts of good and evil.

As soon as our ground-plan had been firmly established and approved by Britten, Forster and I began to write the actual text. We would both read the relevant passages from Melville's novel – or perhaps one of us would read aloud, while the other listened. Then we would decide how that particular incident could best be presented dramatically. The discussion of one small scene might take us ten minutes, or it might take the whole morning. When we had reached agreement about the style and contents of the scene, each of us would write a draft. (Sometimes Forster alone made the draft: sometimes – and especially with the more technical scenes, such as the preparations for battle in Act Two – I would make it.) We then read the draft aloud, criticised it frankly, amended it, and showed it to Britten. He would have alterations to suggest, affecting either the structure of the scene, the contents or its verbal expression, and we would do our best to satisfy him.

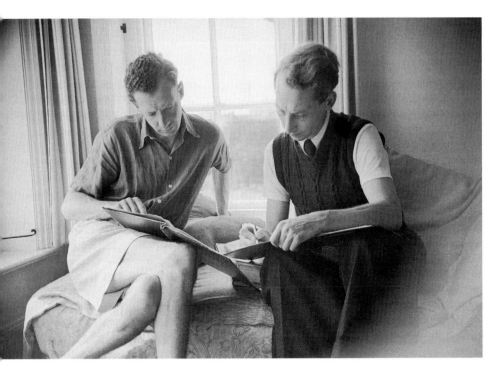

Benjamin Britten and Eric Crozier at work on *Billy Budd,* 1949 (Photograph by
Kurt Hutton/Picture Post/Getty Images)

Gradually, in this way, we built up our first version of the text. At the end of March,
I typed out three copies of the complete script, so that each of us could take a copy away
when we separated.

In August we met again. At this stage, Britten joined us. He, in fact, now became leader
of our discussions. Between March and August he had been studying our first draft in
detail. His musical ideas were taking definite shape, and in consequence he had radical
criticisms of our text and many suggestions for improvement. What Forster and I had
given him was a dramatisation of the novel. This had served its purpose by providing the
composer with material to stimulate his musical invention. Now we had to adapt our text
accordingly, and to translate what was still more or less a play into a libretto.

The distinction between these forms is not easy to make in a short space and without
giving actual examples from the scripts. A play is usually written in rational and logical
language. It speaks from the author's mind to the minds of his audience: it aims to make
everything explicit. Poetic drama, on the other hand, uses more highly charged and
evocative language; it discards many of the realistic details of the naturalistic play; it
speaks to the heart, and may leave much unsaid. Poetic drama is more concerned with
expressing fundamental human passions and emotions than with illustrating the
superficial aspects of human behaviour: it is, for that reason, more universal in its scope,
and less likely to be popular with mass audiences. A good opera libretto has the same force
and directness as poetic drama. It ignores trivialities of behaviour and concentrates upon
deeper motives. Unlike poetic drama, however, it needs a spare, simple and singable

language, without the elaboration of images upon which the poet relies for his complete expression. By definition, a libretto is incomplete. It exists only as a springboard for music. If it reads uncommonly well, and seems almost a play or a poem in its own right; it is probably trying to usurp the composer's function and will seem over-elaborate and ornate when sung.

During our second month together, Forster and I had to revise almost every line of our March version. We shortened many scenes, and rewrote them in more direct terms. We removed one character altogether. We tautened the dramatic conflict. We also discovered that at certain moments Britten needed opportunities for the emotion of particular situations to 'flower': it was our task then to provide suitable words for these moments of lyrical expansion.

It is this stage of collaboration that provides the most gruelling test of the relationship between composer and author. Many authors cannot revise. Some resent the necessity for revision, and get restless and irritable when they are forced to discard their original ideas. In the case of *Billy Budd*, it was remarkable to see with what humility Forster, a much older man than Britten or myself, accepted this necessity, and how eagerly he shared in the task of picking our first libretto to pieces and remaking it under the composer's direction. Great credit must also be given to Britten for the tact and sympathy with which he put his ideas and helped us to understand the reasons for so many alterations.

Our work together was marked by gaiety, enthusiasm and good humour. All three of us, in fact, felt some regret when August came to an end. By then, we had succeeded in transforming the first draft of the libretto into a second version that is almost identical with the published text. Not quite identical, however. Invariably, during the composition of an opera, the composer requires further alterations to be made. As his own ideas crystallise, the text must be adjusted to suit them. The librettist's job then is to provide such adjustments as swiftly and as willingly as possible. His telephone may ring at any time with an urgent appeal for a couple of extra verses, or for six new lines for a particular character to sing in an ensemble. By then he will probably be busy on other work – but it is essential for him to remember that collaboration continues until the final stages of rehearsal, since even at that late date singers may find certain phrases awkward to sing, or parts of his libretto may prove ineffective in performance.

Reprinted from *Aldeburgh Anthology*, 1972

Working with Britten

Janet Baker

Ben was a king. When he walked into a room the air began to crackle; everyone came alive, became more than themselves. When he left, he made us feel as though we had been better than our best, pleased with ourselves.

Approaching his kingdom, which begins for me where one leaves the AI2 and makes that right turn 'to Aldeburgh', feels exactly like going home. It must have rained a lot over the years during Festival time but in my memory the town is everlastingly bathed in sunlight, the cornfield behind the old rehearsal hall is for ever gently moving in a soft breeze, and colleagues are sitting in shirt sleeves enjoying a coffee break in the open air.

They have been marvellous years. People would look at us, the young ones, as though we'd been given the *Good Housekeeping* 'seal of approval' if we were appearing at Aldeburgh; working with Ben did indeed 'seal' us – with quality. Once exposed to him a musician could never be quite the same again. It wasn't that Aldeburgh concerts were given endless rehearsal; on the contrary, I can remember a number of occasions when we felt decidedly pushed for time, but that's part of professional life in general; it was rather a widespread longing to do great things because Ben would be listening; after that it wasn't enough just to be at one's best for Aldeburgh, one tried to give the same dedication to every situation.

One of the most touching aspects of his personality was his deep understanding of performers and their problems. He was a performer of the very highest calibre himself and he knew from the inside exactly how we felt. This was the only level on which I could attempt to communicate with him. We talked once about the difficulty of the *Lucretia* rape scene; this is awkward for me since the tessitura lies just on the break in my voice around middle C. The entire scene is full of drama, which is hard for me to achieve so low in the voice. Ben's comment when we spoke of this was, 'Oh! dear, it's my fault, I've written it all wrong.' Of course he had not written it 'all wrong'; he had scored the piece for Ferrier whose voice was rich and full in that area but who had difficulty later in the opera where I felt more comfortable.

He once gave the cast of *Albert Herring* a piece of advice which I have never forgotten. He had watched a run-through which had not pleased him but which we all thought had gone well. He explained that in playing comedy one must not think the situation amusing oneself; that the characters were not in the least amusing or eccentric to themselves, which is precisely why an audience thinks them to be so. We must therefore take ourselves seriously and not try to make the characters funny; this fact is well known to actors but I had not come across the theory before and found it illuminating and true.

Ben was always ready to talk over problems. He discussed the character of Kate in *Owen Wingrave* at length as we were sitting among the tombstones in Blythburgh churchyard. He warned me that she was not an easy person to play but that he wanted me to tackle her because of my ability as an actress [...].

People would often say to me during the weeks of rehearsal for *Owen Wingrave*, 'Does Ben see you as this sort of character, because he has type-cast you all so carefully?' In that case, he must also have seen me as a teenager when I was already a woman of over thirty; that sort of logic is nonsense. What he did see was a singer who had to be capable of acting a difficult role and who looked right enough in shape and size to pass for a younger woman. The real key to Kate's character lies in the score at the moment when Owen's body is discovered and she realises that she will spend her entire life suffering the most dreadful remorse for what she has done. Ben portrays Kate's anguish most vividly. A bad person feels no remorse; Kate is not a bitch and she is not bad; she is young, and she is without security of any kind, dependent upon the charity of the household, constantly and desperately mortified by her own mother.

To work under Ben's baton was a joy of a special kind. The clarity of his beat and the sureness of his tempi gave a rare security. One was upheld by his marvellous shaping of the phrase but at the same time given room, a sort of freedom, to yield to the inspiration of the moment. Only the very greatest conductors have this ability. I imagine his accompanying at the piano was the same but I never had the opportunity to sing Lieder with him on my own. There was an occasion during the English Opera Group's tour of Russia in 1967 when he played for Peter and me in a performance of *Abraham and Isaac*, which I shall always remember.

Whether he directed his own or the music of another composer, there was a feeling that the tempo he chose was the right one. The sheer kindness of his personality and the infinite patience with which he would iron out problems never made one feel restricted or dominated. People with his sort of charm allied to immense talent must find relationships easier than lesser mortals do. Of course there must have been a 'dark' side to him; after all, he was a genius, not a saint; all I can say with perfect honesty is that I never saw it.

Ben's personal magnetism drew everybody towards him. My own decision not to allow myself to approach too close too often is one which I do not regret. I must have appeared at most of the Aldeburgh Festivals since the early sixties except for the odd year when Glyndebourne performances made it impossible to make the journey to Suffolk. Ben would get a bit huffy about Glyndebourne interfering with his projects but I would grin to myself and think, 'It's a jolly good thing not to be always available at the Master's call!' He knew perfectly well that I considered Aldeburgh home and he knew also of the huge musical debt owed both to him and to Peter. So did many musicians. One couldn't really do anything for him, though, except try to perform at one's very best, of course. But there was no way of returning a fraction of what he poured out to us and to his profession.

Now that he is gone, I feel very differently. The one thing he would ask is continued loyalty in every sense, to the place and to the School that is his superbly fitting memorial. That, at least, I can give; it is especially important that the musicians who fell under his spell and were polished by his methods of working should pass on as much as possible to the young people involved in the Snape project. It is very greatly Ben's doing that English musicians have become a truly important international force in the years since 1945. If it is possible to sum up the reasons for this tremendous flowering of talent it might be in the word 'Excellence'.

It is quality which divides the professional from the amateur, a dedicated, single-minded search for the best – in oneself – allied to the best in others. In work with Ben everyone was concerned with this search because it was his search too.

I have always believed that the creative person inhabits a world unknown to others. The gulf which exists between his world and that of the re-creative artist is wide indeed. Even at their most sublime, performers are still only able to go as far as the entrance and look from afar towards the land where the composer is perfectly at home. The suffering such a homeland exacts from an individual as the price he must pay for the original ideas he brings back to us is unimaginable. And yet, while there is no doubt that the composer wants no other country, it must be frightening and lonely there. Contact is far more easily made on the performing level and many people consider it to be as important as the creative one because performers bring a work to life. I cannot agree; even if a composition is never heard, the process of seizing an inspired idea, and shaping it into concrete form, makes the composer what he is. A woman is not less a mother because her child dies at birth; she has undergone the psychological and physical processes which make her so; the same with the creative genius, whether his music is heard or not, he has gone through the agony, and there it lies, the material for others to use.

I often used to wish I could communicate with Ben on his own level, the level of his creative work; an utterly futile wish. Yet when he was conducting and one gave him, heart and soul, of one's best in performance, the look in his eyes, the expression of gratitude on his face, made such moments memorable and the best sort of communication one could possibly wish for.

The last rehearsal I did with Ben was on *Phaedra* during the summer of 1976; this is the piece he wrote for me, a dramatic cantata. Dramatic indeed, full of passion and nobility. Phaedra – the words of the Robert Lowell translation which Ben used make her a woman who has loved, betrayed, suffered remorse – attempts to put right the terrible wrong she has done, and nobly dies; a character to glory in. Her music is towering, full of contrast, and the bars in which she announces the progress of the poison surging through her veins are among the most sublime of all Ben's music. I now have copies of the printed score but the much-thumbed, tatty, yellow-paper-bound, awkward-sized manuscript I had at first is more precious to me. I always revise from it. I began to memorise the score during my annual tour of the USA in January 1976, in a train going from New York to Washington. The first rehearsal was in the spring of that year and when Steuart Bedford and I met Ben in the library at the Red House the music was tucked safely away in my head; Ben was pleased I knew it so well at that early stage.

We worked for two hours that day. Steuart and I had run through the piece on our own the day before and he had started to play the first recitative section rather fast for me. It is marked 'agitated crotchets' and I could not manage the words 'My lost and dazzled eyes' clearly enough. I said to Steuart, 'I'm sure Ben will want me to sing the phrase at a speed which makes the words possible' and sure enough, the following day, Ben did comment on this very point. He would always see at once how to solve a difficulty according to the individual need. He also mentioned that the word 'Aphrodite' a little further on should be sung *marcato*, a marking which is not in the printed vocal score. I asked him if I could start the final phrase 'My eyes at last give up their light', on C, instead of E as he had

Janet Baker and Benjamin Britten in
the Working Men's Club, Thorpeness,
during a rehearsal of Britten's
Phaedra, Op. 93, for the first
performance on 16 June, 1976
(Photograph by Nigel Luckhurst)

written it, because it gives the voice a moment to relax before that extremely taxing end; this he immediately agreed to.

On the day of the first performance, Ben, who had been at the previous day's rehearsal, appeared at the final run-through. He saw I was without the score and said, 'You're a brave girl to do the first performance from memory.' I was suddenly terror-stricken and thought, 'My God! Perhaps I'm not as brave as I think I am!' and then that night I thought of the five months of study and decided to trust my memory. Responsibility for the work of any composer is a heavy burden, but the premiere of a piece with the creator sitting in his box twenty feet away is a terrifying one. I opened my mouth and out rolled the words 'In May, in brilliant Athens', beautified by the perfect acoustic at the Maltings. The performance went very well and everyone was stunned by the power and passion of Ben's writing at a time when he was so frail physically.

The following year, we repeated the performance and this time Ben was not in his box. Somehow the first summer without him was not a sad one. The air, the fields, the buildings were all filled with his joyous spirit, free of the frail body at last.

A composer belongs to the whole world; but a composer has to live at a specific time in a certain place and is a human being like the rest of us; so Ben is also the special property of his country, and of the people who knew him. As a man, a musician, and a friend he belongs particularly to those of us who were lucky enough to know him, to work with him, and to love him.

Reprinted from *The Operas of Benjamin Britten*, edited by David Herbert, 1979

Versatility and Restraint: Benjamin Britten and John Piper

Frances Spalding

The creative exchange between Benjamin Britten and John Piper was among the most lasting and productive relationships in the composer's career. It thrived on, and deepened, a friendship based on mutual admiration and respect. Piper had a vast, sprawling, ungainly career that took him into many fields and left him divided between his own work, designs for book illustrations, murals, tapestries, stained glass and the stage, photography for the *Shell Guides* and the writing of reviews, essays, books and gazetteers. He had started to make his name as a stage designer before his working partnership with Britten began. But his reputation, in the third quarter of the twentieth century, as one of the England's leading theatre designers is closely linked with the work he produced for all Britten's operas after *Peter Grimes*, excepting the childrens' operas and *Owen Wingrave*. As this last, written specifically for television, followed the successful filming of *Peter Grimes*, Britten appears to have accepted John Culshaw's television team which included the designer David Myerscough-Jones. Piper acted as adviser, taking full responsibility for design only when *Owen Wingrave* moved to the stage. In total, Britten's working association with John Piper lasted twenty-seven years. This essay traces the onset of a partnership that was to raise English opera, as an art form, to a new level.

Britten and Piper first met in 1932 at a concert in the Queen's Hall. No real friendship developed at this stage but they met again, in the late 1930s, when both allied themselves with the Group Theatre. They must have met at advisory meetings; perhaps on other occasions too, for in addition to its productions the Group Theatre mounted an impressive programme of lectures, exhibitions and debates. But its creator, Rupert Doone, was neither entrepreneur nor good organiser, and the company suffered friction and dispute. The meeting of the Group Theatre during the 1937 August Bank Holiday at the home of John and Myfanwy Piper – Fawley Bottom Farmhouse, near Henley – has become legendary. Somewhat against his wishes, Benjamin Britten was among the party. 'Pretty grim outlook,' he noted in his diary. '– house filled with people – I have to sleep on the floor – no accommodatory luxuries...'[1] However, he and John Piper enjoyed a conversation about music and musicians which revealed a shared enthusiasm for Poulenc.[2] Things went awry when the Group Theatre playwrights Auden and Isherwood arrived to announce that they were aiming their next play at a West End production. As the identity of the Group

---

1. Benjamin Britten, quoted in *Letters from a Life: The Selected Letters and Diaries of Benjamin Britten 1913-1976: Volume One 1923–1939*, Faber & Faber, 1991, p.452.
2. Recorded in *Alan Blyth, Remembering Britten*, Hutchinson, 1981, p.28.

Theatre was by then bound up with these two authors, this was bitter news. 'Rows – & more rows,' Britten recorded in his diary, disappearing into the garden to have his first cigarette. Nor was the gloom dispelled by Auden vamping hymns and picking out with one finger 'Stormy Weather' with Britten providing the accompaniment. For one entire day Doone shut himself away in a room with Isherwood and Auden before emerging to announce that *On the Frontier* would, after all, be produced by the Group Theatre.

Through this group Britten and Piper became familiar with the ideal of a close collaboration between playwright or composer, producer, designer and cast. Over time, Piper noticed that Britten's 'passionate insistence ... on the unity of the parts' increased.[3] He also discerned in Britten a 'restrainedly violent character', which, he said, was 'a type I've always liked',[4] perhaps recognising in it an aspect of himself. Both men were also extraordinarily versatile: Piper adapted his style or ideas to the opera or ballet in question, yet always worked in a vein that was absolutely his own, while Britten, in an interview, admitted that he saw no reason why he should lock himself inside a personal idiom: 'I write in the manner best suited to the words, theme, or dramatic situation which I happen to be handling.'[5]

There is no indication that Britten and Piper remained in contact during the war; and during the summer of 1945, when Piper was intent on a return to North Wales, both he and Myfanwy missed the first performance of *Peter Grimes*. It was Rudolf Bing, Glyndebourne's General Manager, who brought the two men together again early in 1946, sending Piper the synopsis for a new opera, *The Rape of Lucretia*.

Bing and Piper first met in September 1945, in connection with a proposed production of *Carmen* for the 1946 Glyndebourne Festival. The project collapsed, but Bing retained the hope that Piper would work for him. Then, in December 1945, Eric Crozier brought to Bing an idea that Britten and his circle had evolved in the wake of *Peter Grimes*, for an independent opera company which would commission new work and perform for a season in London, the provinces and on the Continent. Encouraged by the promise of financial support,[6] Bing persuaded John Christie to take overall responsibility for the venture, at this stage called the 'Glyndebourne English Opera Company'.

The synopsis of *Lucretia* left Piper keen to be involved. As scenery and costumes were needed by early June, his designs would have to be completed by mid-March, giving him just two months to work on his ideas after consultation with the producer (Eric Crozier) and with Britten. In February 1946 Britten and Peter Pears stayed with the Pipers at Fawley Bottom while giving a concert in Henley-on-Thames and the following month Piper accepted a fee of £150 for his designs for the opera.

In this instance, Britten had begun work on *Lucretia* before Piper was brought in as designer, but his preference, which became more insistent over time, was to have some idea of what was happening on stage before he began to compose. (In turn, Piper would protest that he could not design a set until he knew what the music was going to sound like.)[7] Overall, Piper's conceptions for *Lucretia* show careful attention to the musical ideas: in the

3. John Piper, in *The Operas of Benjamin Britten*, edited by David Herbert, The Herbert Press, 1979, p.6.
4. JP, in 'Folio: John Piper at Aldeburgh', Anglia TV, 27 October 1983.
5. *Observer*, 27 October 1946.
6. By Leonard and Dorothy Elmhirst, the owners of Dartington, and from the Arts Council.
7. John Piper recollects this altercation in 'Folio: John Piper at Aldeburgh', Anglia TV, 27 October 1983.

first scene, for instance, the brooding sense of stifling heat conveyed by the music was intensified by his storm-laden background and brilliantly illuminated scarlet tents. Overall, his designs avoided anything too realistic or naturalistic. He read D.H. Lawrence's *Etruscan Places* (1932), noted his admiration for the ease, naturalness and abundance of life in Etruscan tomb decoration, and had the sculptor Willi Soukop commissioned to make freely modelled dancing statues to ornament the hall of Lucretia's house. The second time this set appears, in Act 2, Scene 2, after the rape has taken place, the arcading is fully open and flooded with early morning sun. Here Piper used a vivid primrose yellow sky to convey the freshness and relief that follows a storm. But when *Lucretia* moved to Covent Garden, the producer took advantage of his absence and had the primrose sky replaced with the kind of familiar blue used in musical comedies.

Lucretia would have demonstrated to Britten that Piper, no prima donna, was by nature well suited to collaborative work. When at a late stage in the initial production an Epilogue and an Interlude were introduced and Crozier suggested the latter needed a drop curtain, Piper immediately set to work. The new passages introduced Christian themes and a redemptive interpretation that, as Claire Seymour points out, unequivocally equates Lucretia's suffering and death with Christ's Crucifixion.[8] Piper immediately recognised that the Christian moral needed a scenic equivalent. He brooded on this at length, and solved the problem by incorporating into his design allusions to medieval images of Christ in Majesty, such as that found in a tympanum at Vézelay, and by echoing the colours used in previous scenes. He wanted the simplicity and intensity that are found in stained glass, which he hoped would reflect the tenor of Britten's music.

Throughout the opera he tried to align colour with meaning, in order to further its visual and emotional unity. He wanted Collatinus to wear red, as he said, 'like the generals' tent in which he is first disclosed – a good, positive, constant red that would proclaim itself in a dim or strong light'. He continues: 'Junius, the trouble-provoker, should have a pictorially trouble-provoking pink; Tarquinius a scurrilous, blue-bottle greenish blue. Lucretia, before the rape, must be in white; and the bedroom, we said, should be – partly, at any rate – in a disturbing purple, and after the rape Lucretia should be coloured by this purple of the bedroom until her death....'[9]

Critical reactions to the opera were mixed, but Cecil Gray, in the *Observer*, was unambiguously in favour of 'the superb sets designed by John Piper, who here shows himself to be in the first rank of contemporary stage designers.'[10] In the drab post-war period Piper's colours had a startling eloquence. *The Times* pronounced his sets as 'simple in design and rich in effect',[11] while the *Manchester Guardian* thought them 'sombre and handsome'.[12] Desmond Shawe-Taylor in the *New Statesman and Nation* admired their contribution to the dramatic tension. Strange, he remarked, 'that we should have had to wait all this time to see a stage decorated by so evidently a dramatic painter!'[13]

Such critical acclaim must have confirmed Britten in his choice of designer. Piper, however, was now aware of how time-consuming work for the stage could be, and in

8. See Claire Seymour, *The Operas of Benjamin Britten*, Boydell Press, 2004, p.86.
9. John Piper in *The Rape of Lucretia: a symposium*, Bodley Head, 1948, p.72.
10. *Observer*, 14 July 1946.
11. *The Times*, 13 July 1946.
12. *Manchester Guardian*, 15 July 1946.
13. *New Statesman and Nation*, 20 July 1946.

September 1946 he turned down an opportunity to work on *Otello* with a producer he admired, John Moody. But the following year he again agreed to work with Britten (and the newly formed English Opera Company) on *Albert Herring*. And this time he was involved right from the start, for Eric Crozier sent him for comment the initial draft of his libretto.

Because Britten had greatly admired Piper's model for Lucretia's house, further models were made for *Albert Herring*, for Mrs Herring's shop, Lady Billows' house and the marquee at the Vicarage.[14] All were conceived in a very different style to *Lucretia*, being gaily but not fussily realistic, for, whether designing for a comedy or tragedy, Piper disliked any too lavish display of scenery or too much clutter on stage. Instead he preferred a succinct use of prop or detail. (His role model in this was Picasso, whose stage designs, Piper thought, embodied Jean Cocteau's remark: 'I want to write a play for dogs, and I have got my scenery. The curtain goes up on a bone.')[15] Again his sets were praised, Desmond Shawe-Taylor greatly enjoying their 'stylised late-Victorian profusion'.[16]

At the premiere of *Herring* at Glyndebourne, Britten was presented on stage with a Piper oil painting, based on his drop curtain for the opera [see plate 11].[17] This had been Crozier's idea, and he had collected sufficient donations to commission the picture. The gift confirmed the association between Britten and Piper, and soon after, Britten gifted Piper the score of *Albert Herring*, the three acts separately bound and inscribed: 'For dear John P. with affectionate admiration – lots of it – and everlasting thanks for his great work on Albert Herring. June 20, 1947, Benjamin B.' Britten, it seems, had recognised in Piper's work a sensitivity to texture and nuance that matched his own. Over the years to come, the two men took much pleasure in each other's company and enjoyed an easy and affectionate working relationship. Piper once said of Britten: 'I've never known anyone who left me so much alone on the job or was a better supporter when it was finished.'[18]

He went on to design sets for *Billy Budd*, using untreated timber for the boat and a completely black surround to suggest the sea; to enliven *Gloriana* with costumes that mingled in their hundreds on stage and fused together in subtle changes of colour harmony; to echo in his sketchy gauzes the lack of fixity in *The Turn of the Screw*; to catch, in silvery tones of grey, the disembodied, detached mood of *A Midsummer's Night Dream*; to suggest, by means of a transparent set, the idea that in *Owen Wingrave* Paramore, the ancestral house, in spite of being so solid and so military was really insubstantial; and to capture visually the seductive mystery and sheer improbability of the city for Britten's *Death in Venice*. Is it any wonder that this man is referred to several times in Britten's letters as 'a dear'?

14. Reproduced in David Herbert, ed., *The Operas of Benjamin Britten*, p.149.
15. Quoted by JP in 'The Design of Lucretia', in The Rape of Lucretia (Bodley Head, 1948), p.68.
16. *New Statesman and Nation*, 28 June 1947.
17. The picture still hangs at the Red House, the house at Aldeburgh which he shared with Peter Pears and which is now in the care of the Britten–Pears Foundation.
18. JP in 'Piper at Sixty', in *The Sunday Times*, 22 March 1964.

**7 Owlbarrow from the Top of the
Town Steps**
Kathleen Hale
From 'Orlando's Seaside Holiday'

8 **Aldeburgh Beach** (above)
Mary Potter, 1953
*Julian Potter writes: 'Aldeburgh
Beach was submitted for a Tate
competition with the theme of
'Figures in their Setting'. With the
exception of her portraits, figures
in my mother's work were only
Lowry sized, but for this one there
was, originally, a large figure in the
foreground – myself – sprawled
across the shingle. The picture
hung in the tate like that, but did
not win the competition. When she
got it back, she erased me and put
in more pebbles.'*

9 **Benjamin Britten dressed for the
Opera Ball** (left)
Mary Potter, 1952

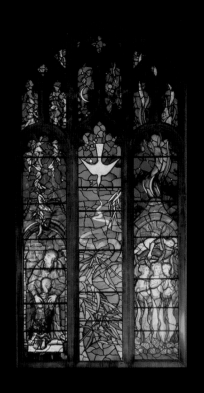

10 **Britten memorial window in Aldeburgh Parish Church** *(left)*
John Piper, 1979
These depict Britten's church operas: The Prodigal Son, Curlew River *and* The Burning Fiery Furnace

11 **Albert Herring drop curtain** *(below)*
John Piper, 1947
'Loxford'

12 **The Initiation** *(overleaf)*
Sidney Nolan, 1971
One of several working designs for The Initiation, *a ballet on which Nolan was to have collaborated with Britten. The project was discussed during the composer's visit to the Adelaide Festival in 1970 but remained unfulfilled.*

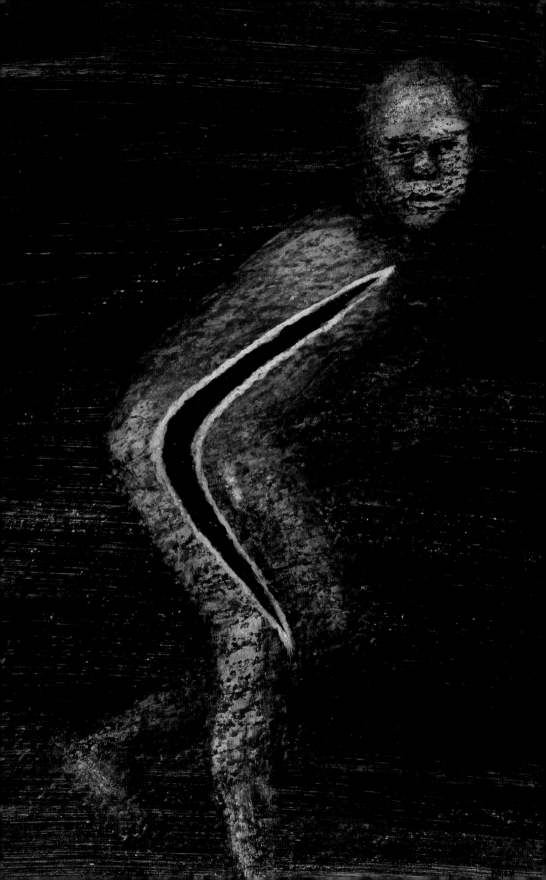

The Britten–Pears Art Collection
Frances Spalding

Visitors to the Red House, the home of Benjamin Britten and Peter Pears at Aldeburgh from 1957 until their respective deaths, quickly become aware that its domestic interior is warmed and enlivened by works of art. There had been no hint of this interest while Britten lived at the Old Mill at Snape, but soon after he moved to Aldeburgh, initially to Crag House, pictures began to appear on the walls. This was the start of his and Pears' collection and the seriousness of this project, for Pears at least, is suggested by the large notebook he obtained at this time, inside which is the heading 'A list of pictures belonging to Benjamin Britten and Peter Pears'. Beneath are their addresses, in Suffolk and London. Each time they moved, Pears would cross out the old and write in the new, the collection continuing to grow while houses and flats came and went.

There is no doubt that most of the paintings and sculptures were bought by Pears. Whereas Britten claimed he had no real visual sense, Pears told his biographer: 'Ever since I can remember I have been mad on pictures.'[1] He acquired the habit of visiting museums and galleries in the cities where he performed, conveying enthusiasm for what he saw in his letters. Humphrey Carpenter points out that as Crag House belonged to Britten and was not jointly owned, Pears had very little call on his high earnings, and was, therefore, able to tour West End galleries and to get to know certain artists, bringing back trophies to share with Britten. Myfanwy Piper tells how there was always something new to be shown with pride and excitement, and that Pears had 'a sensitive, very personal eye'.[2] The pleasure he obtained in showing his collection led to the installation in the library (built in 1963) of an expensive system of spotlights. Though the effect was suitably dramatic, the system was not easy to adjust when paintings were rehung and a simpler method of lighting was eventually introduced.

The motivation behind the making of this collection was neither a desire for prestige nor financial gain. Pears once said: 'I need to feel a love and immediate contact with a picture. I do not like to be lectured by it or instructed to work out a puzzle. Why shouldn't art please immediately?'[3] He did, however, regret not buying a Picasso for £300 which, many years later, could have brought in enough money to solve the problems caused in 1969 by the fire at the Maltings. Though, in time, some works of art were sold, to give help and support to music students or to the Aldeburgh Foundation, this was merely a

1. Christopher Headington, *Peter Pears: A Biography*, Faber & Faber, 1992, p.327.
2. Ibid., p.328.
3. Ibid., pp.327–8.

Henri Gaudier-
Breszka, *Horace
Brodsky*, 1913

side-benefit. Primarily, buying pictures was for Pears, as Myfanwy Piper acutely remarks, 'a relaxation and a life-saver'.[4] The collection is sufficiently eclectic to suggest that Pears was led not by any conscious decision to collect this or that, but by an alert eye and a mind ready to act on serendipitous finds.

His most active period as a buyer appears to have been during the late 1940s and 1950s. It is astonishing to discover that in 1947, as the ledger book records, he acquired five oils and one drawing by Constable. Though the attribution of one of these oils, a landscape, has been questioned, this cache included the charming tiny portrait of his eldest son John Charles Constable absorbed in work at his desk, as well as a portrait of his

4. Headington, p.327.

Cecil Collins, *Resurrection,*
1952, © Tate, London 2008

younger brother, Charles Golding Constable. Two years later Pears bought another gem,
William Blake's *St Paul and the Viper,* one of the illustrations to the Bible which the artist
painted for his patron Thomas Butts. It was an apt addition to the collection, given that
Britten had first set one of Blake's poems ('O rose though art sick') to music in 1943, in
his *Serenade* for tenor, horn and strings, and later, in 1965, based an entire song cycle on
writings by Blake.

But Pears was primarily a collector of his own time and the core of the Britten–Pears
Collection is a confident selection of modern British art. If Pears liked to encourage young
artists, such as Keith Grant, he was also keen to own pictures by recognised figures. He
frequented, as did many other collectors at this time, the Leicester Galleries in London,
which annually mounted exhibitions titled 'Artists of Fame and Promise'. Here, in 1950,
Pears found two paintings by Walter Sickert, *Santa Maria della Salute* and one of his most
haunting music hall scenes, *Minnie Cunningham,* her red dress marvellously offset by the
dingy green background as she stands, stilled in mid-action on the stage.[5] If this is a
masterpiece of twentieth-century British art, so too is Henri Gaudier-Breszka's pastel of

5. This was one of the pictures sold towards the end of Pears' life.
6. Headington, p.327.

Horace Brodsky which Myfanwy Piper reckoned 'brilliant, aggressive, demanding'.[6] Pears added to this collection other names: Henry Lamb, Duncan Grant, Josef Herman, William McTaggart and Gilbert Spencer, the gifted but lesser known brother of Stanley, to name a few. He found a rare Gwen John oil of a tiger, an equally unique portrait of Percy Grainger by Maxwell Armfield, and two of Cecil Collins' finest visionary drawings, the *Resurrection* and *Agony in the Garden*. Though four years apart in date, they are both in the same precise yet lyrical vein.

Pears was alert too to developments in sculpture and in 1950 purchased from Gimpel's in London a piece by Kenneth Armitage, *People in the Wind*. Armitage produced an entire series of works on this theme, merging the figures into an organic unit and only indicating as many heads or limbs as he felt necessary. Like other works in this vein, they are composed on the slant to convey movement and urgency. In the aftermath of the Second World War, of Belsen, Buchenwald and Auschwitz, these small sculptures chimed with a view of man that was vulnerable and anguished, no longer confidently at the centre of things.

Britten's contribution would surely have been his belief in the importance of places, roots and associations, for many of the pictures in the Red House reflect awareness of the East Anglian landscape, its churches and the sea. Hence the Thomas Gainsborough *Suffolk Landscape,* Harry Becker's drawing of a marsh 'dyker' and the superb embroidered paintings made in his retirement by the Norfolk fisherman John Craske, to whom Pears was introduced by the author Sylvia Townsend Warner, whose own bequest of Craske's pictures was given to the Aldeburgh Foundation [see plate 6].

There is also evidence in the collection of the collaborative relationships Britten sought to establish with certain artists, such as Sidney Nolan [see plate 12]. More fruitful and long-lasting was his working association with John Piper, and dotted around the house can be found various mementoes of the operas on which they collaborated. Piper's fine watercolour of Aldeburgh Church as well as his oil of Corton Church remind that he and Britten sometimes went church crawling together. Their correspondence reveals that Britten played a key role in the acquisition of John Piper's *Clymping Beach*, a major 1953 oil, showing a land- and seascape which Piper loved because of its combination of the man-made and the natural, a row of stones, ready for future building blocks, leading the eye into the distance. 'All change is ripeness, not destruction,' Piper wrote of *Clymping*, when he based a large mural for the Mayo Clinic in Connecticut on the same scene.[7]

But the artist best represented in this collection and closest to both Pears and Britten was Mary Potter. As is well known, she exchanged houses with them, gaining Crag House in return for the Red House, when they felt a need to move away from the sea front in order to gain greater privacy. Here, in the late 1950s and early '60s, in the wake of her divorce from the writer and BBC producer Stephen Potter, she painted the beach at Aldeburgh and views of the sea, and began to experiment with a more elliptical, abstract style, suggestive of moments suspended in time. She did so with the encouragement of Bryan Robertson, who offered her a retrospective exhibition in 1964 at the Whitechapel Art Gallery, London, and also encouraged her to produce some paintings on a larger than usual scale.

In 1963 she had moved back to Golf Lane, to the Red Studio which Britten had had

7. From information supplied to the Mayo Clinic on the scene of this mural.

John Piper, *Clymping Beach*, 1953

built by Peter Collymore in the grounds of the Red House. There she remained for the rest of her life. Britten and Pears asked for no rent but instead accepted a picture each year. (Another was added after her death, when her will instructed Pears to select a painting from her studio.) The Red House therefore became the recipient of a fine collection of her pictures. Her late style is wonderfully oblique, the starting point often something glimpsed in passing – a gap in a hedge, the sight of bonfire, the sheen of light on a puddle or in a sink, the fall of leaves or the movement of a bird. Her habit of mixing bees wax with her paint had given her a taste for close tones among which small touches of stronger notes sing out. Though her shapes are allusive, often half-stated, the marks used can have an almost abrasive vigour, poetry and toughness going hand in hand. She was more restrained in her handling of portraits, as can be seen in the Red House in her likenesses of Pears and Imogen Holst, but her small watercolour of Britten's housekeeper Nan Hudson is intensely characterful. Overall the Mary Potter oils and watercolours in the collection struck Myfanwy Piper as introducing 'pools of perceptive calm' into the lives of Britten and Pears [see plates 8, 9].

Words, Music, Theatre, Song

James Fenton

An extract from James Fenton's Prince of Hesse Memorial Lecture, 2005

Britten's many virtues as a dramatist include what may seem an eccentricity: that he thought of the first performance of any of his works as the definitive one, because he was writing for particular voices, and for those particular venues, many of which dot this landscape, and for particular instrumental ensembles. So it is that when we hear a Britten opera for the first time, one of the first things we think is: ah! this is going to be the sound, and that sound varies from piece to piece (in the way that, for instance, the sound of Rossini's orchestra does not). The ensemble varies according to the budget, and the piece is designed to fit the venue in its present state of repair or disrepair. There are times also when Britten comes close to realising the ideals for drama which Auden sketched out in a brief manifesto of 1935. 'Drama', Auden wrote, 'began as the act of the whole community. Ideally there would be no spectators. In practice every member of the audience should feel like an understudy. Drama is essentially an art of the body. The basis of acting is acrobatics, dancing, and all forms of physical skill. The music hall, the Christmas pantomime, and the country house charade are the most living drama of today.'[1]

That choice of genres is eccentric, but in practice what Auden meant included folk forms such as the Mummer's Play, and would have certainly included the Miracle or Mystery plays, as is evident from a further passage in the same document: 'The subject of drama ... is the commonly known. the universally familiar stories of the society or generation in which it is written. The audience, like the child listening to the fairy tale, ought to know what is going to happen next.'

Auden himself never achieved this sort of drama in the 1930s, when he and Britten worked together. But Britten did, rather later, with works such as *Noye's Fludde* and *Curlew River*. And it seems appropriate to mention today, in connection with the second of these, that it was in the company of his friend Prince Ludwig of Hesse and the Rhine, the founder of this lecture, that Britten first witnessed the Japanese Noh-play:

It was in Tokyo in January 1956 that I saw a Nō-drama for the first time; and I was lucky enough during my brief stay there to see two different performances of the same play – *Sumida-gawa*. The whole occasion made a tremendous impression upon

1. *The English Auden*, Faber & Faber, 1977, p.273.

me, the simple touching story, the economy of the style, the intense slowness of the action, the marvellous skill and control of the performers, the beautiful costumes, the mixture of chanting, speech, singing, which with the three instruments made up the strange music – it all offered a totally new 'operatic' experience.

There was no conductor – the instrumentalists sat on the stage, so did the chorus, and the chief characters made their entrance down a long ramp. The lighting was strictly non-theatrical. The cast was all male, the one female character wearing an exquisite mask which made no attempt to hide the male jowl beneath it.[2]

This strikes me ... as a good example of a composer coming to a clear idea of what he wanted – what he wanted as the dramatist-of-last-resort. He goes on to suggest that surely the medieval religious drama of England would have had a comparable setting, 'an all-male cast of ecclesiastics – a simple austere setting in a church – a very limited instrumental accompaniment.' And so he began what might have seemed an ill-advised attempt to marry the Japanese drama he had seen with the English medieval church tradition. He avoids the mistake he made in *The Rape of Lucretia*, where he tacked a Christian ending on to a story that did not seem to warrant it. In this case the drama of *Curlew River* begins with a hymn, from which as Britten said the music of the whole piece is derived. Anyway in performance it would not escape notice that the whole piece, including the instrumental parts, is performed by monks.

Debussy said that he would have liked to see *Pelléas* put on in Japan, by which he meant he would have liked it staged away from the European theatre from whose traditions he was in revolt. And Debussy came near to the ideals of Britten and Auden when, talking of People's Opera on a quite different scale, he has Monsieur Croche beg us:

Let us rediscover Tragedy, strengthening its primitive musical setting by means of the infinite resources of the modern orchestra and a chorus of innumerable voices; let us remember at the same time how effective is the combination of pantomime and dance accompanied by the fullest possible development of lighting required for a vast audience. We could glean valuable hints for this from the entertainments arranged by the Javanese princes, where the fascination of speech without words, that is to say of pantomime, almost attains perfection, since it is rendered by action and not by formulas.[3]

Britten and Pears and the Prince and Princess of Hesse and the Rhine, a remarkable sight in their Balinese costumes, went 'gleaning valuable hints' in this way, Britten bringing back a knowledge of the gamelan orchestra along with his Japanese musical booty. But with *Curlew River* his intention is to tell a Christian parable not by implicit reference to ancient ritual, but by means of ritual itself.

In the same way in *Noye's Fludde*, Britten takes the medieval drama, which was enjoying a revival at the time in places like the Edinburgh Festival. But here we can certainly see Britten the dramatist at work. He cuts the text a little, and perhaps surprisingly. Then he, as far as I can tell, adds some crucial musical inventions of his own,

---

2. *Britten on Music*, ed. Paul Kildea, Oxford University Press, 2003, p.381.
3. *Three Classes in the Aesthetic of Music*, Dover, 1962, p.83.

Boys reading a score during pre-production of Benjamin Britten's *Noye's Fludde*, June 1958.

which enrich the ritual sense of the piece – that is the very simple devices whereby the children, the animals going into the Ark, sing *Kyrie Eleison*, and coming out sing *Alleluia*.

And then Britten makes a big decision which tells us that authenticity, in the historical sense, couldn't be further from his mind. He places a hymn at the start, the middle and the end of the drama, and these hymns are not medieval, they are – at least two of them are – exceedingly familiar from the Anglican services of the day. By this means he can call on the audience to behave as a congregation, and join in the singing. This is how he achieves Auden's ideal of making the drama 'an act of the whole community' so that there are no spectators. The central hymn, 'Eternal Father Strong to Save', has a profound resonance for any maritime community, since it is the hymn for sailors, fishermen and lifeboatmen's services.

The last hymn, on the other hand, 'The Spacious Firmament on High', used to be notorious among Anglicans as being not really a Christian text at all but a piece of eighteenth-century deism or theism (I can never remember which is which). But by that point in the Mystery Play, all bets are off, and Britten seems only to be led by Blake's great dictum: 'Exuberance is beauty'.

What is curious about these two very happy examples of Britten's dramatic skill as a composer, and what I had not quite anticipated when I set out to write the lecture, is that they take us back to the principle with which we began: No music without song, no song without words, no words without the praise of God. Within that ancient aesthetic, Britten is very happy indeed. He is like a cat with a clear conscience. Word, music, theatre, song, bugles, hand bells – whatever he wants he uses with freedom, working on his chosen ground and with his chosen instruments, borrowing, inventing . . . because the fit is on him and there can be no delay.

From Britten with Love

Ian Bostridge

The great thing about Benjamin Britten's song cycles with orchestra is that they exist at all. The orchestral repertoire for tenor is all too small. The influence of Berlioz is there in Britten's teenage assurance of the *Quatre Chansons Françaises* for Orchestra and Soprano, and later, too, Mahler is the other colossus in this repertoire, something Britten obliquely reflected when he dedicated the *Nocturne* to the composer's wife, Alma. It was left to Britten, a precocious admirer of Mahler's music, to create for a tenor a similarly extraordinary body of work in this genre. Just as in opera, he created peerless dramatic and poetic opportunities for what was, in conventional terms, an unheroic voice, that of his life's companion, the tenor Peter Pears.

If the protagonist of *Peter Grimes* was originally intended to be a baritone (like the role he was modelled on, Berg's *Wozzeck*), Britten's early works in orchestral songs were written for the Swiss soprano Sophie Wyss. *Our Hunting Fathers*, his opus 8, written under the influence of W.H. Auden, has all the devastating energy and aggressive edge of the *enfant terrible*. That urge to shock is more successfully tamed and engaged in the other piece he wrote for Wyss, *Les Illuminations*. The choice of text is a surprising one. Rimbaud is not a poet whose work has been part of the French song tradition, but Britten's use of French functions as a sort of theatrical mask. The role-playing it permits opens up a realm of freedom and fantasy that expands into and beyond Rimbaud's linguistic virtuosity. Ferocity of invective is yoked with the humour of the flâneur and a melting sensuality, making *Les Illuminations* the great masterpiece of Britten's first period.

Britten's choice of Rimbaud is striking in so many ways: the overt homoeroticism; the identification with the predicament of the exile, Britten in (or close by) New York, Rimbaud in London, both cities evoked in 'Villes' in all their excitement and horror; and the not-at-all coincidental juxtaposition of an English musician setting French and a French poet using the unfamiliar structures of English.

Les Illuminations is a work of transition. Containing, in 'Being Beauteous', an erotic vision dedicated to PNLP (Peter Pears), it was also professionally the work that represented Britten's allegiance to his companion. Musically, *Les Illuminations* is both the climax to the work of early mature Britten and the bridge between the overt radicalism of *Our Hunting Fathers* and the elegiac tone of the *Serenade* for tenor, horn and strings. *Les Illuminations* is full of a young man's anger, with a fizzing satirical edge that is missing from the later works.

If he had been born 100 years earlier, Britten claimed, he would have been writing Romantic music. The *Serenade*, despite Britten's diffidence ('not important stuff, but quite pleasant, I think'), is a thoroughly Romantic piece, phantasmagorical and death-laden, a quality underlined by the use of the horn, that iconic instrument for Romantic composers, conjuring up forest depths and an inexpressible longing.

Les Illuminations is for strings only; the *Serenade* for strings and horn. The *Nocturne* is for strings and seven obligato (Britten's spelling) instruments that, soloists in each of the central seven movements, join forces only at the last. There is no prologue or epilogue, no fanfare or envoi; the piece melts into and out of existence. It is one of those works, like Britten's *A Midsummer Night's Dream*, that emerges from nothingness, crystallizing a music that has somehow hung in the air before the piece has even begun. In emotional contours, the *Nocturne* is similar to the *Serenade*, with its central nightmare (Wordsworth's vision of Paris following the September massacres, a masterful piece of suffocating claustrophobia in Britten's setting), a movement of virtuosic release (the Keats ditty for flute and clarinet that is preceded by the aching lament of the Wilfred Owen setting) and an elegiac last movement, a Shakespeare sonnet.

This last song of the *Nocturne* is often given a vague Mahlerian provenance, and interpreted as a straightforward love song for Pears. Love songs in Britten are never uncomplicated. The *Michelangelo Sonnets* had originated as an idea before Pears' appearance in the composer's life, during Britten's unconsummated obsession with Wulff Scherchen, which awkwardly overlapped with his relationship with the tenor.

If 'Being Beauteous' is dedicated to one, the almost equally erotic 'Antique' from *Les Illuminations* was for the other. Britten's parting gift to Pears, his last opera, *Death in Venice*, written more than thirty years later, dealt with the subject of a world-famous artist marooned in Venice and obsessed with a beautiful young man. The choice of subject is notable, given that one of the most painful periods of Britten's time with Pears had been during rehearsals for *The Turn of the Screw* in 1954, when Britten's infatuation with the Miles of that production, David Hemmings, had teetered on the edge of scandal.

Throughout Britten's partnership with Pears, his attraction to young men or boys had both inspired and unsettled him, and *Death in Venice* tried to address the inspirational forces at work, as well as the dangers, for the man and his art. The same complex emotions are at work at the end of the *Nocturne*. Tchaikovsky suffered similar feelings, and the homosexual scandals surrounding him have sometimes been associated with his possible suicide and with the supposed death embrace of the *Pathétique*. What is certain is that he dedicated the symphony to his nephew, with whom he had been infatuated since the boy was eleven or twelve. The thematic basis of the last movement of the *Nocturne* is obviously related to Tchaikovsky's notion of his own last movement 'dying away'. The rhetorical grandeur of Britten's score at this point, compared to the rest of the cycle, has clear practical roots in the scoring – chamber orchestra, rather than the strings, plus soloist of the earlier movements – but it is used to convey something rather clotted; the overwhelming sense is of struggle, and at one point the vocal line almost breaks down ('when in dead night'). The quotation from Tchaikovsky points at an assimilation between his sexual struggles and Britten's.

Only at the very end of the song, as we return to the clearer texture of the opening of the whole piece, do we find the resolution that we might expect, and it is, indeed, one founded in a vision of sustaining love: 'All days are nights to see till I see thee, / And nights bright days when dreams do show thee me.'

Britten Remembered

Hans Werner Henze

One of the first pieces of modern music that I heard as a student was *Peter Grimes*, in Mannheim in 1946. What struck me above all were the orchestral interludes, which had an organ-like beckoning and resonant quality, informed by a sense of remoteness; they seemed to me like echoes thrown back by the horizon of the sea. Hearing the work again on subsequent occasions confirmed this impression. This dement of landscape, of making a landscape visible in its colours and contours, seems to crop up in many of his works, and the landscape is always that of England. Three works immediately come to mind: the *Serenade* for tenor, horn and strings; *Les Illuminations*; and the *Nocturne* for tenor and chamber orchestra. In all three you can sense the vicinity of the sea; you can hear the facets of grey, silver grey, ash grey, white and mother-of-pearl of which the low-lying sky is composed, and amid which all the things of the world that appear in this music – men, animals, plants and flowers – have taken on a matt, withdrawn and quiet quality. When I describe it in this way, however, all I am providing is a description of the terrain, and I have so far been speaking only of colours, atmospheres, of the scent of the Suffolk meadows and of the wind whispering or howling across them. Not of the syntax.

I never had a conversation with Ben about music. Only on one occasion did I hear him talk about it, in the late 1950s in the little hall in Aldeburgh. He was standing next to me during the rehearsal of a piece by a contemporary whom he did not admire, and was confiding his displeasure to the dachshund under his arm; after a while he left. We shared a kind of wordless friendship; there were always others around whenever we saw one another, and so neither he nor I spoke about music or related subjects. But I did dedicate my *Kammermusik* (1958) to him, as a true act of homage and an expression of gratitude for the inspiration that his works had given me. Ten years later he dedicated his setting of Brecht's *Children's Crusade* to me. During the period after the 1968 Hamburg Medusa scandal, when my political views had suddenly been thrust into the limelight in a hostile and almost intolerable fashion, thanks to a massive media campaign, and performances of my works in the Federal Republic were rapidly decreasing and the theatres were rejecting my pieces, I saw him one night in London at the house of mutual friends. He put forward Aldeburgh as a place where my new works could be performed, and I took up this offer soon enough – which is how it came about that *El Cimmarrón*, which had been written in Cuba, received its first performance on 22 June 1970 chèz Britten at the Snape Maltings.

Several years previously he had been present at the German premiere of my *Novae de Infinitio Laudes* in Cologne (1962). On the morning after the concert he came to my hotel and left for me a long letter about my piece; it was a letter full of sympathy and warm-hearted comradeship. This gesture had something of the politeness and good manners that were once perhaps taken for granted between artists, but have now completely been lost in the wake of that ludicrous so-called competitiveness – a better word would be marketing – which makes the producers of works of art into individuals who have to corner sectors of the market for themselves.

I should have written Ben a letter at least as long, after hearing his *War Requiem* for the first time - but I didn't get round to it. This work had a shattering impact on me; it found me exhausted and perplexed after the 1966 premiere of *The Bassarids* in Salzburg. The *War Requiem* seemed to me to be a work whose urgency had banished all stylisation, and had drawn its expression from an intense capacity for suffering. Moreover the connection with the great Requiems of the past seemed natural and unproblematic; it seemed to result from a necessary affinity with Bach, Berlioz and Verdi, to whom Ben had built a bridge that, even after the completion of the *War Requiem*, could still be used by him and us, his younger colleagues. It was as if the demands of the subject had mobilised new forces in him, which is why it is like a battle fought with armour and heavy artillery: it is not just a work with a mass appeal unrivalled in our time, composed in profound seriousness and with an enormous investment of effort, but at the same time a compendium of significant answers to the questions of construction, syntax and semantics. This work represents the other side of Ben's music: a world in which the lyrical is denied, and whose contours have been elaborated in a hard and indeed temperate and unornamented manner. This is no doubt the product of maturity. It has been fully realised for the first time in the *War Requiem*, as great drama, but it can also be found in the earlier works, if not as a predominant factor. And if in the early works he still employed parody and stylisation, such characteristics increasingly gave way to a more chiselled manner, which no longer admitted anything but austerity, dismissing every superfluous effect, every trace ornament.

I have no difficulty in outlining Britten's historical background. I see as his first ancestor William Blake. I come to this of course by way of Ben's setting of 'O rose, thou art sick' in the *Serenade*. (The first time I heard this piece it scared me to death. I have tried again and again to set this poem myself, without success.) There is Elizabethan music; there is magical poetry that has been married to it. In its delicate fragility it is this music that reaches back to the early works I've mentioned, and it reappears in the late works, transformed, rethought, in a new shape. Because there is a strong national sense of history in his thought and action, there is Britten the pacifist with socialist tendencies, and Britten the young composer who worked with the literary avant-garde, primarily with W.H. Auden, and came to elaborate his own aesthetic, not without their influence. More background is provided by a number of English composers of the late nineteenth century. You can detect an emphatically non-Continental musical thinking; no trace of the Vienna School, not even of its traditionalistic side; on the other hand there is perhaps an English variant of the *Neue Sachlichkeit* of 1930–35, and French elements (already conveyed in English models) in so far as these are worth mentioning outside of the world of Debussy. For there is not a trace of Debussy to be seen, and Ravel too is by-passed: the one, I suppose, on account of his overstraining of the concept of style, the other because of his artificiality and his lack of passion; both must have struck Britten as unusable.

For the rest, he in fact was born with his own style, and had merely to develop it in a consistent manner, with eyes open to what was going on in the world, with a sense of

Benjamin Britten rehearsing the *War Requiem* in Norwich Cathedral with Peter Pears (left), Thomas Hemsley and members of the Melos Ensemble, 1-2 December, 1967

reality that subsequently also determined his practice. He is one of the best examples of pragmatic musical thinking, which is why you can find pieces for children and beginners that are easy to sing and to play – indeed his oeuvre contains a remarkable amount of music for young people. But there is also technically and intellectually demanding chamber music; the development of the *Lied*; and the operas – virtuoso and dramatically sophisticated works full of popular appeal – almost all written for the touring English Opera Group and its practical and financial constraints.

There was also Britten the conductor, and the unusually gifted pianist. (Whenever did he find the time to practise?) Ben was a practical man, a modern musician, an inspirer and initiator. To return once more to his oeuvre, I feel that the relationship between his native lyricism and his dramatic manner, something that he worked and struggled for, is a source of conflict inherent in almost all of his works. The one allays the other; the one corrects the other; the result is a tense, shaping interaction that also ensures constant development, and prevents stagnation and repetition.

It was painful to see how illness overcame him and made his work more difficult, and *Death in Venice* seems to me already to bear traces of the weakness that would soon overpower him. The 'in memoriam Benjamin Britten' at the head of my Fifth String Quartet is meant to convey my empathy with this remarkable man; my grief at his death, which came thirty years too soon; my respect for his work, for his struggle; my joy at his victories, and my admiration for his mastery.

Reprinted from *Music and Politics: Collected Writings* 1953–81, translated by Peter Labanyi, Faber & Faber, 1982

On Receiving the First Aspen Award

Benjamin Britten

Britten was the first recipient, in 1964, of the Robert O. Aspen Award in the Humanities, established to honour 'the individual anywhere in the world judged to have made the greatest contribution to the advancement of the humanities'.

Ladies and Gentlemen, when last May your Chairman and your President told me they wished to travel the 5000 miles from Aspen to Aldeburgh to have a talk with me, they hinted that it had something to do with an Aspen Award for Services to the Humanities – an award of very considerable importance and size. I imagined that they felt I might advise them on a suitable recipient, and I began to consider what I should say. Who would be suitable for such an honour? What kind of person? Doctor? Priest? A social worker? A politician? Well, ...! An artist? Yes, possibly (that, I imagined, could be the reason that Mr Anderson and Professor Eurich thought I might be the person to help them). So I ran through the names of the great figures working in the Arts among us today. It was a fascinating problem; rather like one's school-time game of ideal cricket elevens, or slightly more recently, ideal casts for operas – but I certainly won't tell which of our great poets, painters, or composers came to the top of my list.

Mr Anderson and Professor Eurich paid their visit to my home in Aldeburgh. It was a charming and courteous visit, but it was also a knock-out. It had not occurred to me, frankly, that it was I who was to be the recipient of this magnificent award, and I was stunned. I am afraid my friends must have felt I was a tongue-tied host. But I simply could not imagine why I had been chosen for this very great honour. I read again the simple and moving citation. The key-word seemed to be 'humanities'. I went to the dictionary to look up its meaning, I found *Humanity*: 'the quality of being human'(well, that applied to me all right). But I found that the plural had a special meaning: 'Learning or literature concerned with human culture, as grammar, rhetoric, poetry and especially the ancient Latin and Greek Classics'. (Here I really had no claims since I cannot properly spell even in my own language, and when I set Latin I have terrible trouble over the quantities – besides you can all hear how far removed I am from rhetoric.) *Humanitarian* was an entry close beside these, and I supposed I might have some claim here, but I was daunted by the definition: 'One who goes to excess in his human principles (in 1855 often contemptuous or hostile)'. I read on, quickly. *Humanist*: 'One versed in Humanities', and I was back where I started. But perhaps after all the clue was in the word 'human', and I began to feel that I might have a small claim.

II

I certainly write music for human beings – directly and deliberately. I consider their voices, the range, the power, the subtlety, and the colour potentialities of them. I consider the instruments they play – their most expressive and suitable individual sonorities, and where I may be said to have invented an instrument (such as the Slung Mugs of *Noye's Fludde*) I have borne in mind the pleasure the young performers will have in playing it. I also take note of the human circumstances of music, of its environment and conventions; for instance, I try to write dramatically effective music for the theatre – I certainly don't think opera is better for not being effective on the stage (some people think that effectiveness *must* be superficial). And then the best music to listen to in a great Gothic church is the polyphony which was written for it, and was calculated for its resonance: this was my approach in the *War Requiem* – I calculated it for a big, reverberant acoustic and that is where it sounds best. I believe, you see, in *occasional music*, although I admit there are some occasions which can intimidate one – I do not envy Purcell writing his *Ode to Celebrate King James's Return to London from Newmarket*. On the other hand almost every piece I have ever written has been composed with a certain occasion in mind, and usually for definite performers, and certainly always *human* ones.

III

You may ask perhaps: how far can a composer go in thus considering the demands of people, of humanity? At many times in history the artist has made a conscious effort to speak with the voice of the people. Beethoven certainly tried, in works as different as the *Battle of Vittoria* and the Ninth Symphony, to utter the sentiments of a whole community. From the beginning of Christianity there have been musicians who have wanted and tried to be the servants of the church, and to express the devotion and convictions of Christians, as such. Recently, we have had the example of Shostakovich, who set out in his 'Leningrad' Symphony to present a monument to his fellow citizens, an explicit expression for them of their own endurance and heroism. At a very different level, one finds composers such as Johann Strauss and George Gershwin aiming at providing people – the people – with the best dance music and songs which they were capable of making. And I can find nothing wrong with the objectives – declared or implicit – of these men; nothing wrong with offering to my fellow-men music which may inspire them or comfort them, which may touch them or entertain them, even educate them – directly and with intention. On the contrary, it is the composer's duty, as a member of society, to speak to or for his fellow human beings.

When I am asked to compose a work for an occasion, great or small, I want to know in some detail the conditions of the place where it will be performed, the size and acoustics, what instruments or singers will be available and suitable, the kind of people who will hear it, and what language they will understand – and even sometimes the age of the listeners and performers. For it is futile to offer children music by which they are bored, or which makes them feel inadequate or frustrated, which may set them against music forever; and it is insulting to address anyone in a language which they do not understand. The text of my *War Requiem* was perfectly in place in Coventry Cathedral – the Owen poems in the vernacular, and the words of the Requiem Mass familiar to everyone – but it would have been pointless in Cairo or Peking.

During the act of composition one is continually referring back to the conditions of performance – as I have said, the acoustics and the forces available, the techniques of the instruments and the voices – such questions occupy one's attention continuously, and certainly affect the stuff of the music, and in my experience are not only a restriction, but a challenge, an inspiration. Music does not exist in a vacuum, it does not exist until it is performed, and performance imposes conditions. It is the easiest thing in the world to write a piece virtually or totally impossible to perform – but oddly enough that is not what I prefer to do; I prefer to study the conditions of performance and shape my music to them.

IV

Where does one stop, then, in answering people's demands? It seems that there is no clearly defined Halt sign on this road. The only brake which one can apply is that of one's own private and personal conscience; when that speaks clearly, one must halt; and it can speak for musical or non-musical reasons. In the last six months I have been several times asked to write a work as a memorial to the late President Kennedy. On each occasion I have refused – not because in any way I was out of sympathy with such an idea; on the contrary, I was horrified and deeply moved by the tragic death of a very remarkable man. But for me I do not feel the time is ripe; I cannot yet stand back and see it clear. I should have to wait very much longer to do anything like justice to this great theme. But had I in fact agreed to undertake a limited commission, my artistic conscience would certainly have told me in what direction I could go, and when I should have to stop.

There are many dangers which hedge round the unfortunate composer: pressure groups which demand true proletarian music, snobs who demand the latest *avant-garde* tricks; critics who are already trying to document today for tomorrow, to be the first to find the correct pigeon-hole definition. These people are dangerous – not because they are necessarily of any importance in themselves, but because they may make the composer, above all the young composer, self-conscious, and instead of writing his own music, music which springs naturally from his gift and personality, he may be frightened into writing pretentious nonsense or deliberate obscurity. He may find himself writing more and more for machines, in conditions dictated by machines, and not by humanity: or of course he may end by creating grandiose clap-trap when his real talent is for dance tunes or children's piano pieces. Finding one's place in society as a composer is not a straightforward job. It is not helped by the attitude towards the composer in some societies. My own, for instance, semi-Socialist Britain, and Conservative Britain before it, has for years treated the musician as a curiosity to be barely tolerated. At a tennis party in my youth I was asked what I was going to do when I grew up – what job I was aiming at. 'I am going to be a composer', I said. 'Yes, but what else?' was the answer. The average Briton thought, and still thinks, of the Arts as suspect and expensive luxuries. The Manchester councillor who boasted he had never been to a concert and didn't intend to go, is no very rare bird in England. By Act of Parliament, each local authority in England is empowered to spend a sixpenny rate on the Arts. In fact it seems that few of them spend more than one twentieth of this – a sign of no very great enthusiasm! Until such a condition is changed, musicians will continue to feel 'out of step' in our semi-Welfare State.

But if we in England have to face a considerable indifference, in other countries conditions can have other, equally awkward effects. In totalitarian regimes, we know that great official pressure is used to bring the artist into line and make him conform to the State's ideology. In the richer capitalist countries, money and snobbishness combine to demand the latest, newest manifestations, which I am told go by the name in this country of 'Foundation Music'.

V

The *ideal* conditions for an artist or musician will never be found outside the *ideal* society, and when shall we see that? But I think I can tell you some of the things which any artist demands from any society. He demands that his art shall be accepted as an essential part of human activity, and human expression; and that he shall be accepted as a genuine practitioner of that art and consequently of value to the community; reasonably, he demands from society a secure living and a pension when he has worked long enough; this is a basis for society to offer a musician, a modest basis. In actual fact there are very few musicians in my country who will get a pension after forty years' work in an orchestra or in an opera house. This must be changed; we must at least be treated as civil servants. Once we have a material status, we can accept the responsibility of answering society's demands on us. And society should and will demand from us the utmost of our skill and gift in the full range of music-making. (Here we come back to 'occasional' music.) There should be special music made and played for all sorts of occasions: football matches, receptions, elections (why not?) and even presentations of awards! I would have been delighted to have been greeted with a special piece composed for today! It might have turned out to be another piece as good as the cantata Bach wrote for the Municipal Election at Mühlhausen, or the Galliard that Dowland wrote as a compliment to the Earl of Essex! Some of the greatest pieces of music in our possession were written for special occasions, grave or gay. But we shouldn't worry too much about the so-called 'permanent' value of our occasional music. A lot of it cannot make much sense after its first performance, and it is quite a good thing to please people, even if only for today. That is what we should aim at – pleasing people today as seriously as we can, and letting the future look after itself. Bach wrote his *St Matthew Passion* for performance on one day of the year only – the day which in the Christian church was the culmination of the year, to which the year's worship was leading. It is one of the unhappiest results of the march of science and commerce that this unique work, at the turn of a switch, is at the mercy of any loud roomful of cocktail drinkers – to be listened to or switched off at will, without ceremony or occasion.

VI

The wording of your Institute's Constitution implies an effort to present the Arts as a counter-balance to Science in today's life. And though I am sure you do not imagine that there is not a lot of science, knowledge and skill in the art of making music (in the calculation of sound qualities and colours, the knowledge of the technique of instruments and voices, the balance of forms, the creation of moods, and in the development of ideas), I would like to think you are suggesting that what is important in the Arts is not the scientific part, the analysable part of music, but the something which emerges from it but transcends it, which cannot be analysed because it is not in it, but of it. It is the quality which cannot be acquired by simply the exercise of a technique or a system: it is something to do with personality, with gift, with spirit. I quite simply call it – magic: a quality which would appear to be by no means unacknowledged by scientists, and which I value more than any other part of music.

It is arguable that the richest and most productive eighteen months in our music history is the time when Beethoven had just died, when the other nineteenth-century giants, Wagner, Verdi and Brahms had not begun; I mean the period in which Franz Schubert wrote his *Winterreise*, the C major Symphony, his last three piano sonatas, the C major String Quintet, as well as a dozen other glorious pieces. The very creation of these works in that space of time seems hardly credible; but the standard of inspiration, of magic, is miraculous and past all explanation. Though I have worked very hard at the *Winterreise* the last five years, every time I come back to it I am amazed not only by the extraordinary mastery of it – for Schubert knew exactly what he was doing (make no mistake about that), and he had thought profoundly about it – but by the renewal of the magic: each time, the mystery remains.

This magic comes only with the sounding of the music, with the turning of the written note into sound – and it only comes (or comes most intensely) when the listener is one with the composer, either as a performer himself, or as a listener in active sympathy. Simply to read a score in one's armchair is not enough for evoking this quality. Indeed, this magic can be said to consist of just the music which is *not* in the score.

Sometimes one can be quite daunted when one opens the *Winterreise* – there seems to be nothing on the page. One must not exaggerate – the shape of the music in Schubert is clearly visible. What cannot be indicated on the printed page are the innumerable small variants of rhythm and phrasing which make up the performer's contribution. In the *Winterreise*, it was not possible for Schubert to indicate exactly the length of rests and pauses, or the colour of the singer's voice or the clarity or smoothness of consonants. This is the responsibility of each individual performer, and at each performance he will make modifications. The composer expects him to; he would be foolish if he did not. For a musical experience needs three human beings at least. It requires a composer, a performer, and a listener; and unless these three take part together there is no musical experience. The experience will be that much more intense and rewarding if the circumstances correspond to what the composer intended: if the *St Matthew Passion* is performed on Good Friday in a church, to a congregation of Christians; if the *Winterreise* is performed in a room, or in a small hall of truly intimate character to a circle of friends; if *Don Giovanni* is played to an audience which understands the text and appreciates the musical allusions. The further one departs from these circumstances, the less true and more diluted is the experience likely to be.

One must face the fact today that the vast majority of musical performances take place as far away from the original as it is possible to imagine: I do not mean simply *Falstaff* being given in Tokyo, or the Mozart *Requiem* in Madras. I mean of course that such works can be audible in any corner of the globe, at any moment of the day or night, through a loudspeaker, without question of suitability or comprehensibility. Anyone, anywhere, at any time, can listen to the B minor Mass upon one condition only – that they possess a machine. No qualification is required of any sort – faith, virtue, education, experience, age. Music is now free for all. If I say the loudspeaker is the principal enemy of music, I don't mean that I am not grateful to it as a means of education or study, or as an evoker of memories. But it is not part of true musical experience. Regarded as such it is simply a substitute, and dangerous because deluding. Music demands more from a listener than simply the possession of a tape-machine or a transistor radio. It demands some preparation, some effort, a journey to a special place, saving up for a ticket, some homework on the programme perhaps, some clarification of the ears and sharpening of the instincts. It demands as much effort on the listener's part as the other two corners of the triangle, this holy triangle of composer, performer and listener.

VII

Ladies and Gentlemen, this award is the latest of the kindnesses for which I am indebted to your country. I first came to the United States twenty-five years ago, at the time when I was a discouraged young composer – muddled, fed-up and looking for work, longing to be used. I was most generously treated here, by old and new friends, and to all of these I can never be sufficiently grateful. Their kindness was past description; I shall never forget it. But the thing I am *most* grateful to your country for is this: it was in California, in the unhappy summer of 1941, that, coming across a copy of the Poetical Works of George Crabbe in a Los Angeles bookshop, I first read his poem *Peter Grimes*; and, at this same time, reading a most perceptive and revealing article about it by E.M. Forster [see p.80], I suddenly realised where I belonged and what I lacked. I had become without roots, and when I got back to England six months later I was ready to put them down. I have lived since then in the same small corner of East Anglia, near where I was born. And I find as I get older that working becomes more and more difficult away from that home. Of course, I plot and plan my music when I am away on tour, and I get great stimulus and excitement from visiting other countries; with a congenial partner I like giving concerts, and in the last years we have travelled as far as Vancouver and Tokyo, Moscow and Java; I like making new friends, meeting new audiences, hearing new music. But I belong at home – there – in Aldeburgh. I have tried to bring music *to* it in the shape of our local Festival; and all the music I write comes *from* it. I believe in roots, in associations, in backgrounds, in personal relationships. I want my music to be of use to people, to please them, to 'enhance their lives' (to use Berenson's phrase). I do not write for posterity – in any case, the outlook for that is somewhat uncertain. I write music, now, in Aldeburgh, for people living there, and further afield, indeed for anyone who cares to play it or listen to it. But my music now has its roots, in where I live and work. And I only came to realise that in California in 1941.

VIII

People have already asked me what I am going to do with your money; I have even been told in the post and in the press exactly how I ought to dispose of it. I shall of course pay no attention to these suggestions, however well- or ill-intentioned. The last prize I was given went straight away to the Aldeburgh Festival, the musical project I have most at heart. It would not surprise me if a considerable part of the Aspen Award went in that direction; I have not really decided. But one thing I know I want to do; I should like to give an annual Aspen Prize for a British composition. The conditions would change each year; one year it might be for a work for young voices and a school orchestra, another year for the celebration of a national event or centenary, another time a work for an instrument whose repertory is small; but in any case for specific or general usefulness. And the Jury would be instructed to choose only that work which was a pleasure to perform and inspiriting to listen to. In this way I would try to express my interpretation of the intention behind the Aspen Institute, and to express my warmest thanks, my most humble thanks, for the honour which you have awarded me today.

Poster for the first Aldeburgh Festival, 1948

'Golly! What a party!
Talk of eating hearty . . . !'

Albert in *Albert Herring*
Act 2, Scene 2

Introduction to the First Festival Programme in 1948
The Earl of Harewood

Since the war ended, the Festival in this country has become something of a national habit. Music has been the basis of many of them, and they have been as various as they have been frequent. There have been Festivals of contemporary music, of ancient music, of English music, of choral music; new Festivals, old Festivals; Festivals in usual and Festivals in unusual halls; in industrial towns and in watering places; Festivals to honour the old and Festivals designed for the young. Some of them have been original in their intention, some frankly imitative. Some of the programmes have had shape and purpose, others have been too exclusive or the opposite. To yet a few more – a minority, fortunately – one's reaction has been the same as Albert Herring's: 'Golly! What a party! Talk of eating hearty!' The Aldeburgh programme has been planned with a view to avoiding the mental indigestion which is the result of an overloaded programme as well as the emptiness of the imitative. It has, in fact, been planned round Aldeburgh itself.

In any community, local patriotism is a strong factor, and it need not be aggressive to be effective. The art of a town or county is as logical a local product as, for instance, the county cricket team, and as much a source of pride. If the friendly rivalries of neighbours and the shades of opinion, which to the visitor may seem infinitesimal, are not integral parts of the Festival programme, the intimacy, which results from them, is. The various items on the programme 'belong' to Aldeburgh and Suffolk in the sense that Mozart did to Salzburg. They are at the same time, many of them, of world-wide fame. Through them, local patriotism, with its enhanced sense of physical relationship with its surroundings and its intimate local associations, finds its point of contact with the national and the international. The contrast – and the unity – of local and national is not emphasised in this Festival, but its presence provides a nucleus for the programmes. One hopes that visitors to Aldeburgh may feel that the hosts have at least not hired the entertainment for their guests, but have provided it themselves.

The Origin of the Aldeburgh Festival
Eric Crozier

In August 1947, several of us were driving across Europe from Holland, where our English Opera Group had just given the first Continental performances of *Albert Herring*, through Belgium, Luxembourg and France, to Switzerland. The rest of the artists were travelling by train: our scenery was on its way in three enormous lorries. We were to stage *Albert Herring* and *The Rape of Lucretia* at Lucerne, in a Festival programme that would include Menuhin, Fürtwangler, Ansermet and other international artists. We were proud to be presenting – for the first time – a group of forty British artists in such distinguished company; proud of the warm and appreciative response our new operas could draw from European audiences; proud that England was at last making some contribution to the traditions of international opera.

And yet – there was something absurd about travelling so far to win success with British operas that Manchester, Edinburgh and London would not support. The cost of transporting forty people and their scenery was enormously high: despite packed houses in Holland, despite financial support from the British Council in Switzerland, it looked as if we should lose at least three thousand pounds on twelve Continental performances. It was exciting to represent British music at international festivals, but we could not hope to repeat the experiment another year. 'Why not', said Peter Pears, 'make our own Festival? A modest Festival with a few concerts given by friends? Why not have an Aldeburgh Festival?'

During our stay at Lucerne we discussed this idea – analysed, criticised, objected, amplified – till it was agreed that if the stage of the Jubilee Hall proved large enough to accommodate a simple form of opera, we would try to plan a Festival for 1948. On our return to England, Benjamin Britten and I hurried to Suffolk, saw the Jubilee Hall and called on Colonel Colbeck, the Mayor, and Mr Godfrey, the Vicar, for their advice. Some days later we gave a tea-party for local friends and acquaintances and discussed the plan with them. There were many problems. Would permission be given to have concerts in the Church with paying audiences? No Festival could hope to succeed without this, for no other building in the town was large enough. Would the ration of basic petrol be restored by the following summer? Was there sufficient accommodation for visitors to Aldeburgh? Should the Festival be given during the normal holiday season, when the town was full anyway – or earlier in the summer? Could it be early enough to precede the school examination period, so that children might take part in the performances of *Saint Nicolas* – then unwritten? How could expenses be met if no one bought a single ticket for any of the performances?

A Committee was appointed under the chairmanship of the Countess of Cranbrook, and it was agreed that the artistic direction of the Festival should be entrusted to the English Opera Group, whose performances of opera would form the nucleus of the Festival week. Opera with, or without, orchestra? This would make a vast difference in expenditure, and it seemed that a building as small as the Jubilee Hall could only support opera with piano accompaniment, until Benjamin Britten and Peter Pears offered to contribute to the cost of the orchestra by giving a recital in the Parish Church without fee.

In arranging the performances, we tried to plan a balanced programme that would include only outstanding works and artists, giving fair representation to local interests, and remembering – without chauvinism – that this was a British festival and should chiefly centre on British music and painting. We hoped, by pleasing ourselves, to please many people: if we had tried to please everybody, the result could only have been a timid and half-hearted mixture of oddments.

The Committee was magnificent in its open-minded acceptance of our proposals, and in the determination with which it set about the organisation of practical affairs through its sub-committees for accommodation, catering and transport.

In January 1948 there was a public meeting at the Jubilee Hall, when a great many people came through the piercing rain of a winter's night to hear about Festival plans. At the end of the evening, nearly two hundred pounds were subscribed in the form of guarantees against loss – an encouraging beginning, though little enough in comparison with the estimated expense of £2,500. During the following weeks, the total rose steadily till it reached £1,400. Enquiries began coming in for tickets and programmes, but there was considerable delay before these could be ready, and the booking office did not open till the beginning of March. Then there was a great rush for seats, and within a week one quarter of all tickets had been sold. Confidence was increased to certainty by a generous offer of support from the Arts Council.

Since our very first talks in Switzerland about the idea of a Festival, it had always been our intention that this should be an annual and growing event, making Aldeburgh a temporary home for leading contemporary artists in opera, drama, ballet, chamber music and painting. Expansion would depend on the creation of a demand from Suffolk audiences, for although many visitors may attend a Festival, it was on support from local people that planning for the future had to be based. Plans for the next year and several years to come were determined by the buildings available for performances – the Jubilee Hall, the Parish Church, the Baptist Chapel and the Cinema – but was it over-fanciful to look forward, through a series of annual Festivals, to Aldeburgh as the centre of arts in East Suffolk, with its own theatre for the annual visit of its Festival artists? To judge by the enthusiasm of local support in the first nine months, and all that has happened since, I do not think it was.

Reprinted from the Festival programme book, 1948

Looking Back on the First Aldeburgh Festival

E.M. Forster

Festivals are not always attractive. Sometimes they are just an excuse for overcharging. Put on *Bohème* and *Butterfly*, call it a Puccini festival and try to get half-a-guinea for the five-shilling seats. At other times, though genuinely local, they have not enough local material to build with, and remain at the flower-show level, the amateur-theatrical level, and my old enemy, the Morris Dance, once more comes forth and foots it defeatedly on the tussocks of the village green. A festival should be festive. And it must possess something which is distinctive and which could not be so well presented elsewhere. Aldeburgh on the Suffolk coast fulfilled these conditions. Its festival could be built round the considerable figure of the poet the Rev. George Crabbe.

Crabbe was born there, about two hundred years ago, in a gloomy building which the sea has now demolished. He did not like the place, he grew up in poverty and discomfort, but his early impressions of it helped him to become a poet. He has described it in *The Borough* and other writings, and even when he left it and was not directly concerned with it, it continued to work in his imagination. When he was a young man, he came across a scamp of a fisherman, whose story interested him, and he worked him up into Peter Grimes, the sinister hero of his best-known poem. The fisherman died, Crabbe died, but Peter Grimes has lived on, and in our day another Suffolk man, Benjamin Britten, has made him the subject of an opera. So there exists in Aldeburgh the natural basis for a festival. It can offer a particular tradition, a special atmosphere which does not exist elsewhere in these islands: nothing overwhelming, but something that is its own, something of which it can be proud. And George Crabbe lies at the centre of its spiritual heritage.

What does the place look like? It is described in a gazetteer of the year 1844 as a 'seaport, fishing town, and delightful bathing place, pleasantly situated on the side of a picturesque acclivity, rising boldly from the German Ocean'. Which as far as it goes is all right. The church stands on the summit of the acclivity, at its base runs a long High Street, parallel to the sea. Still nearer the sea runs a sort of parade, and by 'sort of' I mean the sort of parade I enjoy. There is a sense of space, of unfussiness, and in the midst of the gentle area, in the midst of the shingle and the windswept grasses, rises a tiny Elizabethan Moot Hall. North and south of the town stretch marshlands, which prevent it from expanding, and the southern lands are intersected by the River Alde. The conduct of the Alde is peculiar. It flows straight towards the sea, and when only a bank of shingle intervenes, it bends, and follows a course of many miles before it debouches. On this bank of shingle was built Slaughden Quay, where Crabbe used to roll barrels of butter when he was a boy.

I have only to add that Aldeburgh is connected with our majestic British Railways by a local locomotive, locally known as the Aldeburgh Flier [the Aldeburgh Flier was Beechinged in 1963], and I have told you as much as an outsider can tell outsiders. The outsiders who know it best are the golfers and the yachtsmen, who have frequented their paradise for years, and who may well have found this irruption of the arts vexatious. To all who hit little balls about or who float upon bits of wood in the water, apologies are perhaps due and also apologies to the inhabitants. They, and they alone, can really know what Aldeburgh is like.

The Festival opened with a choral and orchestral concert in the Parish Church. This is a spacious sixteenth-century building. The nave is broad, the two side aisles are broad, so that it wavers in appearance between a gothic edifice and a public hall. Some of the windows are filled with pretty painted glass of the present century. Others have plain glass, and through these could be seen pink chestnut trees. There is a Jacobean pulpit from which Crabbe has preached. Behind it is a monument to him, wherein he is justly described as the poet of nature and of truth. His parents lie in the churchyard.

The Mayor opened the proceedings in a short dignified speech. Standing between the town clerk and the vicar, he welcomed the visitors, and indicated the troubles through which the town is passing. For the sea is advancing all along the East Anglian coast, and at Aldeburgh it is trying to break through the narrow neck of shingle which separates it from the Alde. The chaos there is already most alarming. Slaughden Quay, which I remember as clearly defined fifteen years ago, is now in confusion. Buildings are cracking. A notice board inscribed 'Do not park here' is buried up to its throat in pebbles. If the sea does break into the Alde, the town itself will be threatened, and extensive defence works are in progress.

The chief item in the first concert was Benjamin Britten's *Saint Nicolas*, conducted by Leslie Woodgate. This had been written for Lancing College, and was only performed at Aldeburgh by its courtesy, so a full account of it would be out of place. But I may refer to the birth of the saint, when, after choral rejoicings, a single little boy piped out. Also the miracle of the three little boys who had been pickled, and whom the saint raised to life out of their respective jars. Here again the sudden contrast between elaborate singing and the rough breathy voices of three kids from a local 'Co-op' made one swallow in the throat and water in the eyes. It was one of those triumphs outside the rules of art which only the great artist can achieve. Wonderful too was Britten's throwing about of a tune from the main choir in the church to the girls' choir up in the gallery under the tower. The church seemed alive and at the end the whole congregation was drawn into a hymn.

Saint Nicolas was not the only novelty. A cantata by another East Anglian composer, Martin Shaw, was also presented: *God's Grandeur*, setting a poem by Gerard Manley Hopkins. Here I remember vividly the entry of the soprano solo to the words 'Nature is never spent', after which the music lightened, lifted, and spread into tranquillity. It was an impressive afternoon. About 60 per cent of the audience, I was told, came from the town or the immediate neighbourhood. I listened to their comments as they streamed down the hill. Most of them were enthusiastic, though I did overhear one hard-bitten man say to his womenfolk, 'Not my cup of tea'.

That was the Saturday. On the Sunday there was a piano recital in the cinema by Mewton-Wood. His chief items were Schumann's *Davidsbündler*, and a sonata with jazz tendencies by Constant Lambert. As he was going happily ahead, the cinema was shaken by two loud bangs. Most of the audience knew what they meant, but the visitors did not learn until the end of the concert. They were maroons. They signified that the Aldeburgh lifeboat was going out, and they summoned the 'floaters', the men who pull the boat down the slips into the sea. The boat went to the aid of a disabled yacht. It had to go to Lowestoft and was away all night. And by a strange coincidence, while it was in action there was a broadcast in London about an Aldeburgh lifeboatman of the past, and about an autobiography which he had written [see James Cable, p.64]. Next morning we heard the maroons again. The boat was back safely. The episode, coming in the midst of our pleasure-going, had allowed us to reflect on the life of the town. On the sea-front of the Jubilee Hall are a number of white boards, on which are recorded the many achievements of the lifeboats in the past. There have been disasters also, and indeed I was told that the launching that Sunday afternoon had been difficult and dangerous.

Next day, a series of lectures opened in the Baptist Chapel. I gave one on the subject of George Crabbe and *Peter Grimes*. The hall, which dates from 1822, is a convenient and dignified little building, very pleasant to speak in. It had been painted up in cream and chocolate – indeed Aldeburgh generally seemed to have got a good allocation of paint. Oh for a little brightness in life! How one appreciates it, even when it takes the form of paint upon someone else's house! And how happy I was, in the course of a drive from Aldeburgh to Orford, to pass through a district which had lately been released from the grip of the military authorities! There had, of course, been wanton destruction, and the fields were covered with weeds. But the district had got a high rehabilitation priority, or whatever the phrase is, cottages and barns were being rebuilt, a pub was bright with flowers in front, roofs were being thatched. I had got the idea that thatch was dying out. That cannot be true of Suffolk, for the thatch was being put on everywhere – gleaming angles and surfaces of whitish gold. I contrasted the happy scene with a village I once knew and loved in Wiltshire – Imber: little Imber in the downs, nine miles from any town. The British Army has sat down upon Imber for ever and for ever, and has wiped it off our country's map. I envied these East Anglian villages their happier fate.

But to return to the Festival. In the evening came the main event: the performance of Britten's comic opera, *Albert Herring*, with Peter Pears in the title role. The full company of the English Opera Group, and its orchestra, had come down from London, and much fitting into the Jubilee Hall had to be contrived. There was not room for the harp and percussion down amongst the other instruments. The harp had to be up in the auditorium with a screen in front, and the percussion on the opposite side was blanketed by gaily coloured eiderdowns to deaden the sound. The stage too was congested. The naughty children had to bounce with discretion, and Albert's sack of turnips to be dumped where no one would trip. I had seen the opera before in the immensities of Covent Garden, where the problem was not so much to avoid collisions as to get into touch. I preferred the Aldeburgh performance. It was lively and intimate. The audience, after a little hesitation, started laughing, and Joan Cross, in the part of a dictatorial lady, seemed inspired to every sort of drollery. The music kept going, balance between voices and instruments was attained and maintained, but the feeling in the Hall was not so much 'Here we are at last having an opera in Aldeburgh' as 'Here we are happy'. That the Jubilee Hall got excessively hot cannot be denied. It was delightful to burst out in the intervals on to the beach, or to watch the crowd who were partly in evening dress and partly dressed anyhow, and exempt from the drilled smartness of Glyndebourne. During the first interval a man in a pub said: 'I took a ticket for this show because it is local and I felt I had to. I'd have sold it to anyone for sixpence earlier on. I wouldn't part with it now for ten pounds.'

During the day there were several exhibitions to be visited – two Constable shows (pictures and drawings), model sets of *Peter Grimes* in the Moot Hall, contemporary East Suffolk painters, and a book exhibition. This included first editions of Crabbe and Edward FitzGerald, and that rare selection from Crabbe by FitzGerald, of which only forty copies were printed. FitzGerald was the subject of a brilliant and provocative lecture by William Plomer in the Baptist Chapel which I have already mentioned. Dealing with FitzGerald's character rather than with his work, Mr Plomer examined the oddness in it, the independence, the refusal to be rattled by contemporary judgements, whether literary or social, the agnosticism, the belief in tolerance, in leisure, and in pleasure [see p.91]. FitzGerald, he told his audience, was a drone, and only a drone could have written the *Omar Kháyyâm* they so much admired. The civilisation that produces no drones, and reckons everything in terms of man-hours, is doomed. We came away convinced that FitzGerald was at all events not an old dear. There were other lectures, to which I was not able to go, and more recitals and concerts, and poetry readings in the Parish Church.

Such was the Aldeburgh Festival, and two questions suggest themselves: can it happen again, and could it happen elsewhere? Aldeburgh means it to happen again, and is supported by the English Opera Group, which was founded by Benjamin Britten, and his friends Peter Pears the singer, John Piper the painter, and Eric Crozier the librettist, and which has a special line on East Anglia. The situation here is hopeful. Other towns may be equally well placed and governed by equally enlightened local authorities, and perhaps festivals will spring up everywhere, and people stop trailing up to London for their art.

But there are difficulties. The chief is financial. And there is the difficulty of offering something distinctive, which I have already mentioned. An eminent and sympathetic civil servant who was visiting Aldeburgh thought that the Festival problem might be solved by having a permanent orchestral and operatic company in London, which could be sent out where required. My objection to this is that as soon as you start being central you centralise. You obliterate distinction. You amuse the provinces from the metropolis. Whereas the provinces ought to amuse themselves – and those who have the good fortune to visit them. Possibly the present physical decay of London may help. No one who looks at its dishevelled and disheartened streets today could well mistake it as a Mecca for anything, least of all as a Mecca for art.

Reprinted from the Festival programme book, 1949

Early Days in Aldeburgh: Memoirs of a Railway Enthusiast

George Behrend

What has Aldeburgh to do with Lucerne? For most people, nothing. Yet whenever I visit Lucerne, I never pass the Post Office without a thought for the telegram I dispatched there in 1947 to Crag House, Aldeburgh. 'Thinking of you', it ran, 'on this great moving day', and it did not bear my signature. But it was a great and moving day, for while I was in Lucerne listening to *Albert Herring* for perhaps the eighteenth time – the premiere had been conducted in my (borrowed) socks – the Maestro's chattels were being shifted from Snape Mill to Aldeburgh. Not that we called him 'Maestro' in those days; we were considerably shattered that Ansermet did, for he was by far the oldest and most respected English Opera Group member at Lucerne. We felt suitably small.

There were five of us at Brunnen when the Aldeburgh Festival was born there. Nancy Evans, Eric Crozier and I had returned, depressed, from a reconnaissance of the Lucerne Theatre, where the E.O.G. [English Opera Group] would perform in the forthcoming week. Its only advertisements were for a local schoolchildren's road safety exhibition. The E.O.G. might just as well not have existed. The others had spent the day in a field, where they decided to have their own festival, at Aldeburgh. Henceforth the conversation seldom deviated from this topic, and I was somehow amazed, when eventually we got back to Harwich, that they all wished to return direct to London.

So on my first visit to Aldeburgh in 1948 I was full of curiosity. Would the sea really enter the new orchestra pit of the Jubilee Hall, a matter on which there had been so much discussion the summer before? Petrol was still rationed, so I had travelled by train, crawling up Brentwood bank behind an old 'Sandringham' class steam engine, so slowly that it was quite easy to see how the boy character in Herring got his name. Nowadays the expresses rush far too fast for anyone to read the nameboard on Harold Wood Station.

At Saxmundham, where everyone except the privileged changed into the 'Aldeburgh Flyer', I encountered the first of Aldeburgh's characters whose fame had spread to Lucerne, but who, alas, has gone on: a small but extraordinarily striking lady in flat sandals and what would nowadays be called Carnaby Street or 'with it' strange attire, who had obviously driven over to meet her guests. Most unceremoniously she bundled one of them, followed by a mountain of luggage of the others, into my compartment of the 'Flyer' (which by now was panting furiously on its Westinghouse pump, to recover from the outmoded manoeuvres needed to back into our platform). From the caricature descriptions I guessed Margery Spring Rice's identity correctly, but who my fellow traveller was I never knew. In any case the appearance of 'Sirapite' alongside us at the Leiston stop completely absorbed me. 'Sirapite' was a traction-engine locomotive, the like of which I never knew existed, which used to take wagons down the steep private siding to Garrett's Leiston works.

The opening performance of *St Nicolas* 'sprang upon the church' with a burst of excellence from which the Festival has never looked back. Not many people knew that the composer himself had cut off the legs of one of his wardrobes, to make it fit into the church as one of the rostra. Strolling along Crag Path afterwards, I was interrupted by a voice from the gate into one of the gardens asking, 'When did you arrive?'

My forty-eight hours' passivity ended abruptly. I was one of the few people in Aldeburgh who knew all the E.O.G. members by sight, and from that moment the rest of the Festival became a kaleidoscope of moving artists about – also timpani, harps and pieces of furniture. The motto for this surprising activity was emblazoned on a van for all to read: 'Always get WIGGS' estimate first', and Wiggs performed wizardry with grand pianos, coming all the way over from Lowestoft to move them from one part of Aldeburgh to another.

There was a curious cameraderie. As Joan Cross (I think it was) put it, there was no room in the ridiculous back-stage facilities of the Jubilee Hall for opera stars to bring their temperaments with them; so they left them behind. Unions did not seem to come into it much either, as in company with the engineer in charge of the sea-wall defences (as well as the regular stage staff) we successfully changed the scenery of *Herring* without causing the music to stop. Not for nothing is the Cross Keys next door to the Hall: as German railwaymen would say, it was a case of 'Gut geschmiert, gut gelaufen'.

Despite the many foreign visitors, the Festival was as wholeheartedly Suffolk as Adnam's magnificent beer, and Aldeburgh at that time was well safeguarded by Sergeant Bird of the East Suffolk Police. Not all the Aldeburgh inhabitants wholly approved the invasion of London highbrows, and someone, having read a criticism which favourably compared Aldeburgh's newly-arrived composer to Mozart, stuck up a notice on the Jubilee Hall as a joke. The notice objected to such a comparison, and gave a date and time at which the signatory would appear on the steps of the Hall to meet the upstart and answer the challenge.

Sergeant Bird could see nothing japish in this. 'Putting up unauthorised notices is not allowed', he declared. 'Who is this Mozart, anyhow? Sounds like an alien.' He demanded the immediate presence of the Maestro at Aldeburgh Police Station, to affirm that the offending poster had the Town Council's permission, precisely at the moment when the Maestro was due on the air. Caring nothing for the BBC, Sergeant Bird considered his non-appearance as an effrontery. It fell to Eric Crozier to explain matters – and, somehow, he managed to do so.

The early Festivals were far removed from the present-day royal grandeur of The Maltings. Yet some of the best music I have ever heard emanated from the Young People's Club near the station, which was used for orchestral rehearsals. The thought of a pipe-smoking lady harpist seeking the seclusion of the Jubilee Hall ladies' lavatory in which to rehearse may seem far-fetched today, but it really happened. Almost anything could be expected.

The only man actually to ask me how the first Aldeburgh Festival was going did so on Saxmundham Station. I was meeting the London Express for one of the Maestro's as yet unpublished manuscripts, needed by the founders for a recital even then in progress at Aldeburgh. It wasn't there, and I shall not easily forget nearly being carried off to

Benjamin Britten and Peter Pears with George Behrend on tour, about 1949

Halesworth in the guard's van, where I unearthed it. After the interval would have been too late.

The standard of the Festival has always been high, but my passion for transport unwittingly assisted at the downfall of a certain terrified quartet, whose concert in Aldeburgh Church was not up to it. The day before I had discovered that, while Eastern Counties had assigned their most modern buses available to their Aldeburgh routes in honour of Festival Week, Saxmundham's remote garage still contained some of the very same Tilling Stevenses that Southdown used when Glyndebourne opened in 1934. I remarked to some bus official about the splendid tone of their sonorous gearboxes, and the next afternoon the unfortunate quartet, already nervous, was totally drowned as one of them – put on specially, no doubt – came grinding up the hill outside. By 1949 they had been scrapped, but to me their presence was an augury for the lasting success of the Festival – chariots of destiny! Everybody else cursed the Eastern Counties Omnibus Company for using such antique buses.

Let us hope the founders will enjoy this twenty-fifth Festival, and the succeeding ones, at least as much as the audience always seems to. For the raison d'être of the Festival is, and indeed always was, to perform the kind of music that the founders wished to share.

Reprinted from the Festival programme book, 1972

Imogen Holst and the Early Music Revival at Aldeburgh
Christopher Grogan

The story of the early music revival in Britain in the twentieth century is peopled by a gallery of colourful, sometimes idiosyncratic, yet often visionary, performers and scholars. From Arnold Dolmetsch through to David Munrow and beyond, the movement was fuelled by the energy of personalities who, while often at odds with each other and the wider musical world, shared a common zeal to disseminate the treasure trove of early repertories and forgotten performance practices that they were rediscovering. From the early 1950s Aldeburgh was fortunate to embrace one of the most knowledgeable, wide-ranging and enthusiastic of these early music advocates, Imogen Holst ('Imo' to all her knew her), who used the theatre of the annual Festival to develop new audiences for this music both locally and, through broadcasting, internationally, and whose legacy continues to dominate the Festival's early music programming to this day [see also p.105].

Imo's openness to the qualities of pre-Classical music was instilled in her by her father Gustav, who once remarked that 'there are two kinds of musical Philistine: he who considers musical history to have begun at a definite date, and he who believes it to have ended at an equally definite date'. When Imo went to the Royal College of Music in 1926, this entrenched attitude was still prevalent in the teaching of music history. Moreover, standard performing editions of Baroque music were highly Romanticised, and as Imo recalled, 'my fellow pianists and I used to work hard at the accompaniments of [Bach's] violin sonatas, endeavouring to obey all the instructions ... and seldom questioning anything that the editors had asked us to do.' Then a chance comment that she should consult the *Bach Gesellschaft* led her to a new discovery:

> What we found there was exciting but unsettling. Some of our accompaniments had no right-hand part for the keyboard player, which meant that the expressive bits we had practised so carefully must have been composed at the end of the nineteenth century ... there were no indications of loud or soft, although in the copies we were using the editors had given us definite instructions ... the words *ritt* and *rall* never appeared ... Thrilled by this discovery, we began to make pencil corrections in the copies we were using, crossing out all unwanted slurs and dynamics. The result was a mess, and it was difficult to read the notes. So we tried scratching out the editor's contributions with a penknife, but the result was a worse mess (and it wore holes in the pages). We then decided to make our own manuscript copies for our own use ... in that instant, we became embryonic editors.

So it was as an editor, armed with the scholar's eager anticipation of new discoveries, that Imo started out on her career as a pioneer of early music. During her extensive European travels she would bury herself in library collections of manuscript and early printed music, transcribing materials that she might at a later date be able to bring to performance and publication.

By 1951, Imo was already a regular visitor to Aldeburgh and had become a trusted friend and musical collaborator of Benjamin Britten, having worked with him on an edition of Purcell's *Dido and Aeneas* for the English Opera Group. For the Festival that year she was invited to write an article on 'Elizabethan Music' and took the opportunity to expound ideas of performance practice that had matured within her over the previous two decades. Key themes were the need for scholarly humility, and the responsibility of audiences to overcome their grounding in post-1750 music and listen to early music with 'pre-tonal' ears:

> One cannot help wishing that it were possible to get some idea of what their music-making sounded like during those flourishing years – whether their oboes were as raucous as some modern writers would insist, and whether their singers invariably put on the brakes and slowed down as they approached their final cadence in the way that some present-day conductors, nurtured on the music of the nineteenth century, would have us believe.

Imo already felt that Aldeburgh's cultural soil would provide a fertile bed for the sowing of the seeds of her early music enthusiasms, and when in 1952 she became part of the administration and planning of the Festival she seized her opportunity. For 1953 she persuaded Britten to include an unknown duet by Arne in the opening concert, and herself conducted Handel's *L'Allegro, Il Penseroso, ed il Moderato*, for which she cajoled Britten into playing the harpsichord continuo.

The following year, she conducted a famous performance of Bach's *St John Passion*, introduced her enthusiasm for the music of Heinrich Schütz in the form of his own *St John Passion* and directed a programme of choral music that took the audience to both ends of the historical spectrum by including both Pérotin's 'Beata viscera' from *c*.1190 and the first performance of Priaulx Rainier's *Cycle for Declamation*. The thinking behind these concerts provides an early insight into Imo's instinct for 'joined-up' programming. Famous 'masterworks' were set into their historical context to demonstrate that the 'great' composers had not (as much music teaching and literature supposed) fallen fully formed from the sky but were both subject and indebted to a host of precedents and influences. And the sound world of medieval repertories was given contemporary resonance by means of programming pieces alongside modern music conceived for the same forces.

In 1956 Imo became an Artistic Director of the Festival and immediately intensified its engagement with early music. That year she edited and realised John Blow's *Venus and Adonis*, a task that helped her define an individual and pragmatic attitude towards the competing demands of scholarship and performability. The subject had been contentious ever since Arnold Dolmetsch had dismissed musicological insights and trusted to his instincts to produce performances that were characterised, as Thurston Dart remarked, by the sort of 'wild guesses' without which 'no musician and no musical scholar will ever get anywhere'. Opposing this approach was a purist musicological school for whom 'authenticity' – developing a true understanding of how a piece would have been originally performed and how it would have sounded – was essential before any performance could be undertaken. As both a performer and a scholar (although never a musicologist) Imo steered a course between the two: while neglectful neither of scholarship nor the need for authenticity, she would never let a piece that excited her on the page lie unperformed through scholarly timidity. She was not afraid of shaping music into performing editions that she thought would be more attractive to modern audiences, nor of taking editorial liberties with music that she felt would benefit from her creative input. Of *Venus and Adonis*, she commented in the programme book that 'The prologue has been left out; a short passage in the huntsmen's scene has been transposed to suit the compass of the voices and throughout the work the recitatives and arias have been freely "graced".' More mischievously she enthused to Britten:

> It's such fun being reckless – he [John Blow]'s easier to deal with than Purcell, because there's not so much there to begin with … I'm having it all my own way … and am putting in parodies of Thurston Dart at 'Hast thou been reading those lessons in refined arts?' complete with *very* slow trills.

On the other hand, if she regarded the work as a masterpiece – as with *Dido and Aeneas*, again edited with Britten – her editing eschewed such liberties and left the text largely untouched.

Together with the promotion of Baroque opera, Imo's main focus in her early years at Aldeburgh was on choral music, primarily through the vehicle of the group she had formed, at the suggestion of Peter Pears, in 1953 and which became the Purcell Singers. The importance to Imo's achievement of the Purcell Singers' ability to perform music from such a wide range of centuries and styles cannot be underestimated, and was recognised more or less from the group's inception, as this review of a London performance given on 21 April 1956, from the *New Statesman and Nation*, demonstrates:

> Miss Holst has an imaginative response to the music of the remote past, which she has imparted to her group of youthful singers: they sing, not cautiously, but with infectious enthusiasm. A well-chosen medieval group made a quite startling effect of immediacy, and the choir further demonstrated their versatility in the Choral Dances from Britten's *Gloriana* and in a selection of madrigals from all over Europe, among which a brilliantly gay and flirtatious piece by Monteverdi was outstanding.

The Purcell Singers were to prove equally vital to the next stage of Imo's cultivation of early music at Aldeburgh, through the involvement of the BBC. The Corporation had been significant in the revival of early music since 1946 when it had established the Third Programme, aimed at 'the alert and receptive listener'. For the 1957 Festival, Imo decided to establish a series of late-night concerts, lasting for about half an hour, in which she could explore some of the byways of early music that her scholarship had opened up. Working within an extremely tight budget, she had to demonstrate to the other Artistic Directors that her new initiative would not be a drain on the Festival's resources, and so approached the BBC Transcription Service for support. Their acceptance marked the beginning of a collaboration that broadcast the Aldeburgh late-night concerts to appreciative audiences in more than forty countries, the only minor drawback being that Imo and her singers often had 'to re-record the programme after midnight, in order to get rid of the extraneous noises' of coughing in the audience.

Buxtehude's *The Last Judgment*, under the direction of Charles Mackerras, was chosen to inaugurate the series, which was scheduled at 10.45pm in the Parish Church across five nights. For the following year, 1958, Imo devised a series of Magnificats, comprising settings 'chosen from different periods of music and different countries of Europe'. The performances were revelatory and illuminating, prompting Andrew Porter, in the *Financial Times* of 20 June 1958, to write:

> Each night, in Aldeburgh Parish Church, the day closes with a Magnificat and other motets, sung in sweet sure tones, beautifully chorded and phrased, by Miss Imogen Holst's Purcell Singers. Dunstable, Obrecht, Josquin, and most wonderful of all, Monteverdi's first Magnificat. These unforgettable performances should be preserved on gramophone records.

That the Purcell Singers never did commit their interpretations of early music to disc was, and indeed remains, disappointing. such was the paucity of available recordings; the previous year Gilbert Reaney had complained: 'It is a shock to anyone who does not believe music was invented around the year 1500 to find how little medieval music is available on gramophone records'.

For the next fourteen years, Imo brought her unique knowledge and insight to the programming of her late-night concerts. No two series were the same in conception. Some celebrated anniversaries (Purcell in 1959, Dowland in 1963), while some looked at antecedents and influences. And frequently she would juxtapose the ancient and the modern: in 'English Church Music of the Fifteenth and Twentieth Centuries', Leonel Power, Dunstable, and the anonymous 'Passion of St Luke' rubbed shoulders with BBC commissions from the likes of Birtwistle, Mathias, Gordon Crosse and Jonathan Harvey. Her mission was always to entertain, but also to challenge her increasingly discerning audiences, while continuing to tread her own path between the demands of authenticity and her passion to bring to life what she saw on the page.

And it was not only the Purcell Singers who thrived at Aldeburgh. Imo brought to the Festival many leading exponents of early music, and also younger performers and ensembles who were later to make their mark internationally. The controversial Raymond Leppard was invited to open the 1958 Festival with a groundbreaking performance of Monteverdi's *Il ballo delle ingrate*. Imo would have been attracted to Leppard's unconventional approach to the performance of early opera, which closely echoed her own philosophy; in 1966 he remarked: 'It is foolish – and finally impossible – to adopt a prissily "pure" attitude to these works ... It is equally foolish to resent or reject the element of compromise which must play a part in their modern-day performance.' Over the following years the Deller Consort, the Julian Bream Consort and the Philip Jones Brass Ensemble were all regular visitors, while in 1967 Roger Norrington, a former member of the Purcell Singers, brought his highly accomplished Heinrich Schütz Choir. 1968 saw the first appearance of the inspirational David Munrow, who returned the following year with his Early Music Consort, comprising James Bowman, Oliver Brookes, Mary Remnant and Christopher Hogwood. The encouragement of this next generation of performers, and her own willingness to step aside as they came to the fore, remain among Imo's enduring achievements in the early music revival.

In the final analysis, Imo's genius lay less in her abilities as a scholar, or even as a conductor, of early music, but as a communicator, who could bring her enthusiasms alive through the intoxicating combination of her speech, writing and performances. The enormous breadth of her knowledge far exceeded that of most early music repertory specialists, embracing as it did choral and instrumental repertories from Gregorian chant, medieval and Renaissance forms, through to the high Baroque in Europe and the domestic eighteenth-century music of the Vauxhall Garden concerts. But this knowledge would of itself have been of little use had she not been able to transmit her joy in this music to her audiences. In 1966 she gave a lecture at the Festival entitled 'What *is* Musical history?', prompted by her 'coming across an astonishing sentence in Grove's *Dictionary* (1954) stating that "Lully's harmony is not always correct"'. Illustrated by the Purcell Singers, the lecture urged its audience to rid themselves of Romantic notions of harmony and form as a means to rediscovering and connecting with early music. Immediately afterwards, on 16 June, Joyce Grenfell, by now one of Imo's staunchest admirers, wrote to her:

> The whole thing gave enormous delight to me – from timing, humour & wit & above all from perfect communication with us, the audience. You are a born communicator … I found I could very nearly make myself believe that I'd never heard 2 parts before & felt I was in a spare, light monastery somewhere a long time ago suddenly making a discovery [see also p.256].

In an obituary of Imo published in the journal *Early Music* in November 1984, J.M. Thomson remembered that 'she was startlingly individual … and she stamped everything with an unmistakeable presence and personality. Any scholarly assessment of her role in the early music revival would need to draw together her manifold activities.' This essay has dealt with only one aspect of these activities – her contribution to Aldeburgh – but even in this single context her enduring influence can be still be felt. The 2008 Festival featured a concert of William Byrd, juxtaposed with music by Wolfgang Rihm and Iannis Xenakis; evenings devoted to Imo's favourite Purcell and Bach; and the challenging *Messe de Notre Dame* by Machaut, programmes that had she been alive she might well have devised herself, and the sounds of which she would have certainly have relished. In 1951 she had written: 'We owe a debt of gratitude to the Aldeburgh Festival … for proving to us … that there is no longer any such thing as a "revival" of Elizabethan music: it exists in its own right, as a necessary part of everyday life in 1951.' That the same is yet more true in 2008, and not only of Elizabethan music but of a wealth of early repertories, is very much a tribute to the lasting achievements of Aldeburgh's own pioneering 'twentieth-century explorer' of early music.

Folk-Songs
Imogen Holst

Cecil Sharp knew Aldeburgh well. His last visit to the town was in 1923, when he played some of his own folk-song accompaniments, with a buoyancy that was unforgettable, on a well-worn piano in a wooden hut in the garden of 49 Park Road. It was his work as a preparatory school teacher that had first started him off on his search for genuine English songs that would bear any amount of repetition.

There had been other English collectors before him: the Rev. John Broadwood had published the first collection of English folk-songs in 1843. And there were other great collectors during Sharp's lifetime, including Vaughan Williams, whose large manuscript collection of folk-songs (which have been copied out by an Aldeburgh Festival soprano) contains many unfamiliar tunes from East Anglia.

It was Sharp himself, however, who did more than anyone else for the revival of folk-music in England. My father used to say that when the time came for the history of twentieth-century English music to be written, Cecil Sharp's name would stand out above all others. That was many years ago, when English composers were still overwhelmed with gratitude for the 'miracle' of folk-song, which had saved them from a surfeit of nineteenth-century translations and had taught them to listen to the musical possibilities of their own language.

Today we take our folk-songs for granted. Cecil Sharp would have been one of the first to agree that this is as it should be, for he knew that work such as his could never be completed until it had become unnecessary.

He was only just in time with his collecting, for most of the singers who gave him the best songs were already in their sixties and seventies. They sang with tremendous conviction, telling the stories of their ballads with a fervour that was dramatic and yet impersonal. Every word mattered to them, even if they were not always sure about the exact meaning of all the verses. (When Sharp had noted 'The Death of Queen Jane' from a singer in the Kentucky mountains he began telling her some of the historical background of the song. 'There now,' she exclaimed, 'I always said it must be true because it's so beautiful.')

Traditional singers have a freedom in their rhythm which is almost impossible to convey in written notes that keep to a given number of beats in the bar. One of the earliest collectors of Scottish folk-songs, the Rev. Patrick MacDonald, was complaining in 1760 that he found it difficult to write down the tunes because they were sung by the natives in a 'wild, artless and irregular manner'.

The most successful attempts to convey this freedom were made by Percy Grainger when he recorded Lincolnshire folk-songs by phonograph, more than fifty years ago. He felt very strongly that any noting down of a traditional singer's songs should give all possible details of all the different verses. With the skilful use of written-out ornaments, phonetic spelling and generous supply of dynamics, he managed to bring the printed page to life in the most startling fashion. Looking through the early volumes of the *Journal of the Folk-Song Society* we can almost hear the 'twiddles and bleating ornaments' of Mr Joseph Taylor, carpenter; and the broad, even notes of Mr George Gouldthorpe, lime-burner, who 'gave his tunes in all possible gauntness and barrenness'; and the 'pattering, bubbling, jerky, restless and briskly energetic effects' of Mr George Wray, brickyard-worker and ship's cook, who had a grand memory at the age of eighty and sang his innumerable verses with a jaunty contentment.

Percy Grainger used what he called 'the nearest writable form' of what he actually heard. There were no accurate symbols for the elaborately varied embellishments that were introduced at will, like seventeenth-century 'graces'; or for the changing levels of pitch that can only be approximately conveyed as 'B flat (*slide*)(?) B natural'. Nowadays, with the help of tape-recorders, it is possible to experiment in new systems of noting traditional songs, and soon we may hope to read the levels of pitch in an African herd-boy's call with something of the assurance of an Indian musician, who, knowing the name of the raga he is to sing in, is able to move from the lowest of his three A flats to the highest of his four F sharps with an exact precision in the timing and expression of the slide that connects the two notes.

Inexperienced collectors of folk-songs in the British Isles have often complained that traditional singers are 'out of tune'. Brought up exclusively on the equal-tempered scale of the keyboard, they have been unable to listen to the strange intervals with open and unprejudiced ears. It is true that collectors, as well as arrangers, are inclined to fit a folk-song into their own way of thinking. But, with arrangers, this crime can often turn out to be a blessing in the long run, for if the songs were to be rigidly protected from the approaches of adventurous outsiders they would soon shrivel to the insignificance of ethnological exhibits in a museum.

Tom Moore was accused of altering a traditional Irish folk-song when he turned it into 'The Last Rose of Summer', but Aldeburgh Festival audiences would probably agree that the alteration was an improvement. Burns was accused of 'patching' the words of Scottish folksongs. He replied: 'Better mediocre words to a tune than none at all.'

Perhaps the most astonishing changes that folk-songs have ever lived through are the alterations that Luther made to a number of sixteenth-century traditional German love-songs, when he borrowed them and transformed them into the hymn tunes that were afterwards used by Bach as the foundation of his cantatas and Passions.

It may be that there is an excitingly unpredictable future for some of the English folk-songs noted by Sharp and Grainger and Vaughan Williams and the other collectors. One thing seems certain: the tunes themselves have a good chance of surviving, for they were made to last.

Reprinted from the Festival programme book, 1959

John Dowland
Peter Pears

He called himself Doleful Dowland, and nobody will contradict him. One does not expect merry songs from texts which start 'In darkness let me dwell' or 'Mourn, mourn, day is with darkness fled' or 'Die not before thy day, poor man condemned'; these were his favourites. He did not live exclusively, however, in inspissated gloom. Some of his loveliest songs are coloured with a gentle silvery sadness, like 'Weep you no more', or 'Flow not so fast', and there is a noble and radiant resignation quite without bitterness or self-pity in 'Time's eldest son' and 'Far from the triumphing court'. But the tavern song, unbuttoned and rumbustuous, is not to be found in Dowland's four volumes, and one is led to imagine that had he chosen such a text he would have flavoured it bitter, not mild. It is no great loss in any case, for his colleagues could supply such things in quantity. His gifts lay elsewhere.

It is arguable that his songs were the first great art songs of modern times, and that we have to wait for Schubert for their equal. For though we have between them the whole range of Monody, one has for a century and a half to depend on a variable element in songs, the realisation of the figured bass, an improvised accompaniment which cannot by definition have the living authority of Dowland's own lute accompaniment or Schubert's piano. And these two masters are alike in the richness of their invention for the voice's partner, the so-called accompaniment. That Dowland, as a lute virtuoso, should write superbly for the lute is no more surprising than that Liszt or Chopin should write superbly for the piano, but a great player is not always a great composer, which Dowland certainly was.

How, we would like to know, did Dowland sing? For one must presume that he mostly sang and played his own songs. His writing for the voice does not, apart from one or two out of his eighty songs, demand a great range, nor is a huge volume required to compete with the lute. There is very little ornament, virtually no florid passages, and yet the singer who called Dowland's songs simple would be a fool. The most straightforward of them – melodies like 'Awake, sweet love', or 'If my complaints' – can sound charming when sung sweetly and truly, and many of the songs were played as lute solos almost as they stand. In the bigger songs there are more serious problems of interpretation and performance. His way with words would seem arbitrary to those accustomed to the practice of song-writers since, from Purcell to Britten. The word-accentuation in 'In darkness let me dwell' is a case in point. The longest notes in that first sentence belong to the least important words, 'in' and 'me', and the important work word 'dwell' is thrown away. The clue to this strange emphasis lies in the great weight which Dowland gives to the line of the voice.

In all these big songs of his the voice is one of the strands of counterpoint – the most

Benjamin Britten and Peter Pears at Snape Maltings Concert Hall, May/June 1969

important – of which the song is made, and it is the job of the singer to find and reveal the shape of his line in relation to the other lines which Dowland so richly and inventively supplies to the lute, that instrument which being plucked has naturally a dying sound and is therefore not apt for sustained counterpoint. Dowland certainly knew how to play his own lute music, but we had to wait 300 years for his successor, and it is one of the achievements of Julian Bream that he can reveal to us the rich and subtle counterpoint and sustain it, by means of a 'modern' colour-and-dynamic technique wholly right for this expressive music. Thus the 400-year-old composer – and his dear instrument – still lives.

Reprinted from *Aldeburgh Anthology*, 1972

How the Festival Developed
Nicholas Clark

Determination, hard work and above all a strong desire to bring music to the local community have been the fundamental building blocks of the Aldeburgh Festival. Stephen Reiss, Festival manager from 1956 to 1971, acknowledged this in the earlier edition of the *Aldeburgh Anthology* in 1972, when he presented a concise resumé of the Festival's financial history to date and briefly took account of the time and energy involved in the creation of a new concert hall. This essay takes the story forward, but underlines what I believe is implicit in his writing: that the Festival's development will continue to hark back to the vision of its founders and early supporters to create, in the words of Lord Harewood in 1948, 'a Festival around Aldeburgh itself'.

The sea and coastal surroundings have played an essential part in the Festival's development, both from a practical and artistic point of view. A great deal of the success of the Festival has relied on the goodwill and tireless efforts of the people of Aldeburgh, who have accommodated a veritable invasion of visitors to their town every June. From the very beginning Britten was a familiar figure to many, often taking an afternoon walk along the seafront when time permitted to work out the musical ideas already in his mind. Aldeburgh was not only the place he found most conducive to work, but also the setting from which much of his musical inspiration came. What could therefore be more natural than to bring music to Aldeburgh in the shape of 'our local Festival'?

Its origins lay in Peter Pears's famous suggestion ('Why not have an Aldeburgh Festival?') while touring in 1947, as recounted by Eric Crozier in his article on p.183. Imagination, ingenuity and determination ensured that the first Festival took place some ten months later in June 1948. From the beginning, organisers, administrative staff and volunteers alike were united in bringing a very high standard of musicianship to the intimate setting of this small fishing town. Various locations in Aldeburgh served as venues for concerts, lectures and exhibitions, the Jubilee Hall primary among them, but supplemented by the local Parish Church among others. Elizabeth Sweeting, first Festival Manager, reminds us however that in 1948 it was not yet accepted practice to use churches for performance, and dispensation had to be sought from the authorities for such innovations as allowing applause at the conclusion of concerts.

Artistic and administrative concerns aside, in order to survive the event also had to prove its financial viability. The 1948 Festival garnered £2,800 in receipts with subsidies from the Arts Council of £600 – an impressive tally given the financial difficulties under which post-war Britain was still struggling at that stage (perhaps this is seen in proportion when noting that the equivalent value of that total sum of £2,800 in 2008 is slightly in excess of £73,240). The support offered in kind by the townspeople was critical and it has always made the difference between success and failure. Not only were Britten and Pears at the helm, in charge of artistic management and performing in numerous concerts throughout its duration, but, in addition, Britten took an active interest in financial matters. Elizabeth Sweeting recalls that Basil Douglas, later manager of the English Opera Group, once showed amazement at the composer's ability to present him with an exemplary budget for an opera.

Reiss referred to a period of serious financial sagging in the early 1950s which no doubt caused some concern amongst the Festival's organisers. A noticeable decline in receipts occurred in 1952, 1953 and 1954. Yet the dedication of staff and supporters and the fact that Britten and Pears were able to draw some of the most important and influential names in the artistic world, in turn attracting audiences both local and from further afield, brought a return to economic stability from 1955 onward. Receipts showed a steady increase and by 1967, twenty years on, were recorded at £44,000.

Patterns of growth and weakness were in evidence in ensuing years, the 1980s in particular showing a comparatively fallow period financially. This was of course a time when funding for the Arts, not just in Aldeburgh but nationally, was an increasingly competitive business. That notwithstanding, the Festival's artistic directors remained faithful to the expectations of their audience and throughout the decade they managed continually to schedule artists of the highest calibre. Subsidies provided by the Arts Council were supplemented by a series of generous donations and programmes of sponsorship from individuals and corporate organisations alike, which have become vital to the existence of the Festival and to the maintenance of its standards. The Festival's gradual growth in scope and structure has meant increases in expenditure that are greater than ever foreseen: the first Festival was nine days long and comprised three opera performances, ten concerts (including two verse and music recitals), ten lectures and five exhibitions. Sixty years later fifty-three major events took place throughout a two-week period, and the costings for the sixty-first Aldeburgh Festival in 2008 were in the region of £500,000.

Turning again to 1967, the Festival's twentieth anniversary also marked a major turning point in the history of its development with the opening of a much needed concert hall. Although there was a great deal to be said in favour of Aldeburgh's unique ability to facilitate concerts in local venues, the lack of a theatre which could accommodate full orchestral and choral forces and seat a large audience was now a serious drawback.

In 1954 the Earl of Harewood, then Festival president, presented plans in his Foreword to the programme book to create a new hall in the town which would 'fit in with the character of Aldeburgh and its Festival as we have always known them'. A diorama of the proposed new building which, when finished, would be on a site to the south of the Parish Church, was displayed. After further deliberation the architect H.T. Cadbury-Brown explained some of the most crucial challenges in his *Notes on an Opera House for Aldeburgh* in the 1957 Festival programme book. He maintained that much could be learnt from some of the world's most celebrated performance spaces, not only such theatres as those in Milan or Bayreuth but also the 'great unroofed auditoria of antiquity or buildings designed for a different but just as clear theatrical and musical tradition, such as the Japanese Noh and Kabuki'. The description of a versatile space such as this must have found favour with Britten who, less than a decade later, was to compose the Noh-inspired *Curlew River*.

This ideal performing space was achieved, but the prohibitive costs of constructing such a hall from scratch and the lack of enough available land prevented it from being built in Aldeburgh itself. After much discussion and planning it was finally confirmed in late 1965 that the disused Maltings at Snape would be converted for the purpose.

The River Alde provides a long historical as well as geographical link between the Malt House at Snape and Aldeburgh, but with the closing of operations at the Maltings in the early 1960s new links were forged again, primarily through the Festival. It was the ideal choice for the new auditorium for both historical and artistic reasons. Britten commented during an interview with John Warrack for the BBC television programme *Music International* in 1967, whilst standing amid the construction of the interior of the new concert hall, that a primary objective was preservation. From a personal point of view it was essential that nothing interrupt the character of the environment that had obviously inspired him as a composer and had provided a site for the 'local', but at the same time ever-growing, Festival. The composer observed that the Maltings had remained a landmark in this part of Suffolk for over a hundred years and that he had looked out on the building while resident at the Old Mill at Snape as he wrote *Peter Grimes*. He surely spoke on behalf of everyone who cherished history when he stated that no one wished to see any fundamental changes in what he termed 'a wonderful building'.

Britten recognised that this major new development was an encouraging extension of his and Pears' ambition to bring music to Aldeburgh, but that their celebration of the arts now extended well beyond its boundaries. Acknowledging that this was still a Festival whose focus was Aldeburgh, however, was important to him. He went on to explain that the Jubilee Hall would remain the Festival Opera House, but he was clearly inspired by the possibilities afforded by the new performance space and added that from time to time operatic works would be featured at Snape. Indeed, the selection of venues for the four operas that were staged during the 1967 Festival bore witness to this. Britten's own *A Midsummer Night's Dream* was performed in the newly opened concert hall, the first performances of Lennox Berkeley's *Castaway* and William Walton's *The Bear* (both one-act operas) took place at the Jubilee Hall, and performances of *The Burning Fiery Furnace* were held in Orford Church.

Britten also composed a new work for performance that year, the appropriately named *The Building of the House*, Op. 79, which he described as 'a true example of Occasional Music'. This is an overture with or without chorus (on this occasion the chorus was of course in attendance) with text taken from *The Scottish Psalter* that proclaims humility in recognition of the wonder of God. It concludes with the couplet:

But they shall thrive whom God doth bless,
Their house shall stand through storm and stress.

What was undoubtedly unforeseen when those celebratory lines were first sung was the damage that fire would bring to the newly converted concert hall. The devastating set-back caused by the blaze that destroyed the Maltings on the opening night of the 1969 Festival inspired the same generosity of spirit that in the attitude of workers and volunteers that had ensured the success of previous Festivals. There was an immediate re-organisation of concerts in alternative locations, perhaps the most famous of which involved the offer by the diocesan bishop and vicar of Blythburgh of the use of that Parish Church to stage a now legendary production of Mozart's *Idomeneo*, conducted by Britten, directed by Colin Graham and performed by the English Opera Group.

Britten and Pears remained remarkably undaunted by the setback and almost immediately embarked on the mammoth task of ensuring that the Maltings would be rebuilt and open for business in time for the following year's Festival. The Queen, who had officially opened the concert hall in 1967, returned to Snape to re-open the new Maltings in 1970 and quipped, with a candour appreciated by everyone, that great as the occasion was, she hoped that the building would remain intact so that she did not have to perform this particular official duty for a third time.

Nowadays festival locations such as Aldeburgh beach and Bentwaters Airbase revive the idea of open air Festival events like those held formerly on Thorpeness Meare, and the presence in Aldeburgh has been strengthened by the addition of the Pumphouse, the town's redundant Victorian pumping station, for the Festival's fringe. The addition of new facilities to the Maltings site from 2009 will inevitably have an important impact on the future development of the Festival. We might ask how will this affect the original desire to plan a festival around Aldeburgh itself? The answer to this question can be found in Britten and Pears' wish not only to bring music and the arts to the local community but to foster its growth through knowledge and learning. A significant part of the new development will be devoted to enhancing the facilities for music education.

This aspect of Aldeburgh Music's remit extends to school and community programmes but at its heart is the School for Advanced Musical Studies, now the Britten–Pears Young Artist Programme. Britten and Pears first made plans for such a school as early as 1953 and it was finally realised, albeit in modest origins, in the form of a masterclass in September 1972. This was loosely modelled on the summer school for young musicians at Tanglewood in the United States (where *Peter Grimes* had its American premiere) and at the Banff Centre in Canada. Today the founders' ideas have been expanded to include Aldeburgh Residencies, giving talented musicians at all levels access to the inspiring surroundings of the Suffolk coast, and the Aldeburgh Young Musicians scheme for 8–18-year-olds of exceptional potential.

The new buildings at the Maltings site focus directly upon expansion: increased room for rehearsal, performance and learning spaces for musicians, actors and dancers. There is a new studio for writers and artists – fulfilling the desire of the Festival's founders that the place should be a celebration of creativity. Significantly, and perhaps not surprisingly, this expansion closely resembles a masterplan that Britten and Pears commissioned in the early 1970s. Realising the creative potential of the Snape Maltings site, they drew up plans for what they called an 'Arts Centre' there, plans that thirty-five years later are finally and imaginatively coming to fruition.

For a musical overview, see in addition Paul Griffiths, *Music that Belongs Here*, p.346.

The Maltings

Derek Sugden

The Maltings at Snape, built by Newson Garrett, are perfect examples of what J.M. Richards called 'The Functional Tradition' and are well illustrated in the book of that name that he wrote with Eric De Maré.

They are traditional nineteenth-century industrial buildings of red brick from the local Snape brickworks, with timber floors and deep timber roofs. The Malt House roofs were once finished with Welsh and Italian slates and the turning bays and stores with red clay pantiles. When these roofs were replaced they were covered with asbestos tiles or asbestos sheets which rapidly grew moss and fitted well with the industrial scale of these buildings. This tradition was maintained throughout the last hundred years, including the latest extension in 1955, which is in reinforced concrete with an asbestos roof. Because it has been carried out in a direct and unselfconscious way it still follows the tradition at Snape.

The brief was for a concert hall to seat about 750 people, with a restaurant and bar if possible. We were to consider the provision of some opera-house lighting and a removable proscenium. We were also asked to make the auditorium suitable for stereophonic recording by Decca and to provide in the plan for a recording room with wiring for Decca and the BBC. We thought it very important that this building should be designed either as a concert hall or as an opera house. Many post-war auditoria have failed because they have tried to fulfil too many functions and have not succeeded in fulfilling any one properly. It was agreed that the Maltings should be a concert hall, and, although opera lighting was to be provided, it was felt that the single auditorium space would create its own type of opera production. As the design developed this became clearer, and the introduction of any temporary proscenium within the auditorium would have been quite wrong.

Our main aim in the design was to create a single auditorium which would take a large symphony orchestra and chorus and yet keep the building, both inside and outside, in sympathy with the traditions at Snape. In producing the plan for the conversion we tried to use the existing walls of the Malt House wherever possible. The internal walls, the brick hoppers and the suspended drying floors were removed down to the lowest floor-level. This left a large space of 155ft x 60ft for the auditorium and a space 19ft wide running the full length for the foyer, lavatories and cloakrooms.

At first we thought it would be necessary to design a large, removable stepped floor in order to provide a level surface for stereophonic recording. This idea was quickly abandoned when Decca said they were quite happy with the space on the stage and the flat area in front of it. We could now provide a permanently stepped floor, creating at the rear of the auditorium a space underneath for the lavatories, plantroom and sub-station. Thus the foyer could be left completely free for circulation.

The roof design became the key to the whole building, and we looked for a design that would keep the shape of the old roof. Studies were also made of various heating and ventilating schemes at this early stage to ensure that we could use roof ventilators similar to the old Malt House smoke hoods. The old roof trusses had been mainly of heavy timbers reinforced with the later addition of steel tie-rods. We felt that the design of this roof, wholly exposed within the auditorium, should be in the same materials and of very direct and simple construction. The final solution was for a timber and steel roof with a flat top, similar to the old roof, to accommodate the ventilators. The roof trusses are constructed of douglas fir and all the ties are of high-tensile steel.

The plan still did not work until we took the decision to raise the main brick walls by 2ft. This now made it possible to walk up the stairs and into the restaurant without banging one's head. These walls were also stiffened with piers, arches and beams. Then the main walls in the auditorium were finished with a ring-beam which tied the old walls together and carried the new roof. The stage was planned 4ft above the floor, which was fixed at such a height that lorries could load and unload at stage-level. In addition to the orchestra pit there were requests for holes through the stage and access from underneath it to the dressing-rooms and the loading-bay.

All these ideas led to a decision to excavate the whole of the stage area below the auditorium level, to suspend the stage on steelwork, and to provide a system of jacks so that the rake could be altered to suit different opera productions or concerts.

There are no finishing materials, as such, at Snape; the fabric of the building forms the finish both inside and out. The roof and the pine joists in the foyer are exposed and left natural. The brick walls in the auditorium have been patched and raised with old red facing bricks saved from the demolition, and the new piers and arches in the foyer have been built in new red facing bricks. All the old walls have been grit-blasted and finished with a sealer to restore the original soft red colour of the bricks. The stage and auditorium floor are finished with a hardwood, but for quietness the sections under the fixed seating have been covered with cork. The foyer floor and staircase are finished with red pammets which are continued outside in deep steps to form the main entrance.

Seating in the concert hall presented a formidable problem because it had to look right in a building which still retained a marked mid-nineteenth-century atmosphere. Then it was suggested that perhaps the right material was cane, as used at Bayreuth. Wolfgang Wagner, the director at Bayreuth, sent us photographs of the seating there and assured us of its robustness – most of the chairs still in use are those originally made in 1876. We prepared some designs with cane seats and ash frames and these have been made by a firm in Ipswich. To maintain the same character throughout the building we have chosen Thonet bentwood cane chairs for the orchestra and restaurant. Space does not allow me to mention all the detailed work on the acoustics, the mechanical and electrical services and the opera-lighting and controls.

Demolition began in May 1966, and real construction began about two months later. By this time we had made the final decision to excavate the whole of the area under the stage. Trial holes had been dug and we knew the ground water-levels, but the flow of water into the excavation was much greater than was expected because of the large areas of peat on the riverside. The hole rapidly filled with water, much to the alarm of the regular Snape visitors. Any attempt to use a mechanical digger in these conditions turned any clay present into a soup-like slurry which was nearly impossible to remove. The contractor had quickly to change to a much larger pump, and confidence was restored as the water-level dropped.

Old, heavy foundations were discovered and took a long time to break up and remove. All this time the sides of the excavation were exposed, making the peat shrink, and it had to be removed in sections and replaced with concrete. This excavation also exposed very poor and and sometimes non-existent footings to the main north and south walls of the auditorium and these had to be extensively underpinned.

The other problem met during construction was the building of the septic tank. In the position chosen we found the water-level about 2ft higher than that shown in the trial holes, and in addition it did not vary with the tide. To overcome this, we have had to insert an additional chamber and to provide a lift-pump, otherwise the entire drainage system for the concert hall would not have worked.

Erection of the roof was due to start in November, but was delayed for three weeks. However, the roof ventilators, complete with their dampers and motors, were finally erected one fine Monday in February, and from then on work continued independently of the weather.

Designing and building a concert hall-cum-opera house in just over a year meant getting together an impressive number of people. Their enthusiasm made it all possible.

Reprinted from the Festival programme book, 1967

Auditorium interior (Photograph by Jeremy Young)

A Novelist Visits the Britten–Pears School

Susan Hill

It all began with the sea. I was born by it – the same North Sea as Aldeburgh sits by, but higher up this bleak east coast, in Yorkshire. The sea haunted my childhood – I walked by it, played in it, feared it – its smell, its spray, the boom and hiss of it and all its colours of grey. I watched trawlers put out of the harbour, and fishermen throwing nets on to the foreshore wall to dry, pungent of oil and herring in the sun. I saw the lifeboat disappear into a howling tunnel of snow and spume. I loved everything about the life around, upon and beside that sea, and took it entirely for granted. Until I was parted from it. We moved to the industrial Midlands when I was sixteen, and to a city I found ugly and bewildering, yet stimulating, too; I knew I needed my horizons to open up towards adulthood, I was busy and happy. But I missed something, something ... who knew what thing?

One June afternoon, I found out. I heard it. I was sitting on an uncomfortable chair in the music block of my new school, with the sweet smell of phlox, the sound of tennis ball on racquet coming through an open window behind me. How extraordinary, the way one remembers things so vividly! This was a general music appreciation lesson for A-level students of other subjects, and our teacher was enthusiastic, with richly varied tastes – just the right person to awaken a response in a well-disposed but musically ignorant person like me. So far, I had enjoyed her classes, but in a relaxed sort of way. I was quite unprepared for what was to happen to me that afternoon – to be thunderstruck, turned inside-out by what we heard on the gramophone – the *Sea Interludes* from Benjamin Britten's opera *Peter Grimes*. I don't think I had ever really been affected by music before. Now, it catapulted me back into my childhood and to that magic sea, and a full realisation of how I missed it, how much a part of my inner life it was still. More. As I listened, to the *Interludes* and then to extracts from the opera itself, I felt a sort of answering vibration within my own imagination, a curious, altogether certain awareness that this music, the story of the opera, and the place in which it was set, and the man who composed it, too, had aroused an excitement which would be vitally important for the rest of my life, in ways I could not yet grasp.

I shall never forget the impact of Britten's sea music on me, that summer day. My ears rang with it, all the way home. I went to the record library and borrowed the opera. I read books about the Suffolk coast, then Crabbe himself. But more than anything else, as I sat, listening, listening, I remembered the sea, felt the tug of my own roots, drawing me back to it and yet back not for escape or nostalgia; it was altogether more positive than that. I was going back, into the imaginative future.

I was not a musician, of course, and although my enjoyment and awareness of a whole sound world began to open out from then on, I was not going to become a musician. I would be a writer, for that is what I had always been, I had invented imaginary worlds, used words to describe what I saw, sensed and dreamed, ever since I could hold a pen. Nothing had happened to change that. Music beckoned me, I did not yet know where, but it would be in words that I would express my own creative excitement, my vision of the past and the sense of place that was becoming so important.

Britten was one of the most literary composers – not because the word ever dominates the music, but in that he read so widely and was so deeply sensitive to literature and the worlds of poet, novelist, playwright. But I was not merely responding to the stories of his operas, the poems he turned into songs. It was the music itself that I heard and loved – the voices, the melodies, the individual instruments which so affected me.

Ten years passed before I came to Aldeburgh, though I was on the road, as it were, all that time. I was serving my apprenticeship as a writer, mainly by reading, though I wrote some early fiction, and it was altogether bad, because I was at odds with the subject matter. I hadn't found my own voice. Or rather, I had, but I didn't realise it. Not until I drove through thin February sunlight down a long ribbon of road, beside scrubby heath-grass and bright gorse, came to the top of a short, steep hill – church to my left – dropped between huddled houses through a narrow lane and abruptly out into the light. Saw sky everywhere. I got out, to stand in wonder, facing the beach, the boats and the sea, the sea. The Moot Hall was just behind me. I touched its wall. Peter Grimes! The waves hissed up, sucked back, over the shingle. I tasted salt on the wind. A gull cried. And that music again filled my heart and my head.

There has never been another moment quite like that in my life. It was compounded of absolute joy, the 'shock of recognition' and a sense of disbelief in the reality of it all that made me faint. I felt at home in this town I had never visited, more than in my own birthplace. Then everything – the words I would spin out of this place; the imaginary people and events, down to tiny details, of their lives; all my books which would have their origins and deepest roots here – all of it fell into place, I really did grasp it in one flash before it was gone, whirling away on the sea wind, to be followed, strained after, coaxed back to me, over years to come.

A writer has a hundred ideas which he examines then rejects, because they are not 'right', do not trigger off the fertile stream of creative emotion and invention. Then comes the right one, instantly recognisable, the spark that lights the bonfire. All my sparks in those days flew up from Britten's music and from the coast and countryside around Aldeburgh, so that I owed everything to him, even though the ideas took a form which was entirely and independently mine. The process is not one of imitation but of cross-fertilisation – though I dare say it was a good thing I was not a composer!

So every winter, I came to live and write books, and walk and walk, and there never was a place like it for inspiration. And all the time, in the dark evenings, I returned to the music, my touchstone.

On a different level, I was also beginning to learn in all sorts of ways how wide Benjamin Britten's influence was on the musical life of his time, most particularly among the young, whom he understood and loved and for whom he was always writing. I knew cathedral choirboys who sang and played his music as naturally as they breathed, responding with freshness and delight, and older students, working single-mindedly at instruments and composition, who hitch-hiked to the Festival. I realised how the man, the music, everything that Aldeburgh and the Snape Maltings represented, enriched and inspired those who grew up to a love of it – some of them talented enough to be making music their career, others just throwing themselves into school performances of *Saint Nicolas* or *Noye's Fludde*. If I, who was no musician, had benefited so much, think how it must be for them! And if Britten's imaginative world could make such an impact all round the world, imagine the effect on aspiring musicians if they could not merely visit, but stay, study, practise, perform their music in the place itself!

In a sense, the Britten–Pears School began when the Festival itself began, over thirty years ago. It is one more stepping-stone in a path we can now trace backwards. It has not sprung up, new and raw in 1979, and it is not alone and unsupported in the world; it has loving parents and friends, to whom it owes its existence, and on whom it may depend for inspiration, help and example as it grows up. It is the youngest member of a close and gifted family. How I wanted to write about it, yet how distant it seemed. Five years since I wrote a book in Aldeburgh, with only fleeting visits since, and marriage, the birth of my daughter, new work, have preoccupied me and pushed the past away. So much forgotten and the new building unimaginable.

March. A certain smell in the air. Sea fever. I would come!

It was perfect weather, twenty-four hours of it, like a gift encapsulated between the snows and cold of this appalling winter. Warm enough to walk on the beach without a coat, the sea smooth as silk, blue, blue with a silver rim and the sky a quite different blue; houses, streets and pebbles looking freshly washed and rinsed in the sun. We drove to Snape. Quiet. Shelduck on the mud, and the reeds just stirring drily.

We went inside the School building. Smells of new wood, varnish, piano felt and putty, and the sunshine making lozenges on a honey-coloured floor. Everything is pale, cream, stone, white, grey, except for the ceiling of curving, rose-red brick and some nutty-coloured carpet. Footsteps rang, voices echoed. We plonked a piano. Resonant note, a bit hollow, but the lovely Recital Room has acoustics as fine as those of the Concert Hall next door. On the top floor, the Holst Library, so silent you could hear the dust seethe. What a place to work in! It is a most satisfying building, calm and sure and beautiful, a perfect conversion, with a new quiver to it, like a set of young strings within a mellow frame. Seen from outside, it blends with the rest of the Maltings complex in a delightfully homely mixture of roofs, windows and old walls.

I was impressed, interested, admiring, but I still felt detached, cool. Until we went into a practice room at the far end, and I saw it. Two windows, set exactly at eye level, and beyond them, the view. Marshes, reed beds, the silver curve of the river, and sky all above and around. Some redshanks, long legs like pencils, piercing the mud. Everything bleached as bone left out long in the sun – except that there is also a suffusion of pink in the light itself – hardly there, but there. I went outside quickly. Stood quite still. Far away, a bird cry. The wind keening faintly. *Curlew River*. High notes.

Then it all came rushing back, that feeling of years ago, and I wanted to stay because I had sensed something just ahead, work I might yet do. I turned to look at the School and imagine how it would be for those to come here, full of talent and energy and passionate determination, to play music in the beautiful rooms. It is the most hopeful memorial to Britten's genius.

When I was at Snape, that extraordinary day, I made a wish. That everyone should, together with all the musical benefits and delights they receive, be touched by that magical other thing, when the spirit of man, the music and the place fills you like a great breath. It happens suddenly and its effect is overwhelming and everlasting. Standing, first on the shingle by the Aldeburgh sea, then looking out over the marshes, beside this exciting, utterly down-to-earth and practical new Maltings building, I knew that for certain.

Written in 1979 for the Aldeburgh Festival programme book. Megan Peel brings the story up to date:

Since Susan Hill's piece, the Britten–Pears Young Artist Programme (as it is now called) has grown into the largest UK programme for developing the talents of emerging professional musicians, both singers and instrumentalists. The aim is to bridge formal musical education and professional life. The auditions, held in Amsterdam, Boston, Frankfurt, Helsinki, New York, Lucerne, Stockholm, St Petersburg and Toronto, are very competitive: in 2008, over 800 students auditioned for the Masterclass and Orchestral courses, which last between 6 and 10 days. Since the first course in 1972, more than 10,000 young artists have experienced this unique programme, many of whom have gone on to make a real mark in music.

The faculty has included Dame Joan Sutherland, Elly Ameling, Elisabeth Söderström, Sir Thomas Allen, Harrison Birtwistle, Murray Perahia, Oliver Knussen, Malcolm Martineau, Sergei Leiferkus, Philip Langridge, Ileana Cotrubas, Imogen Cooper, Roger Vignoles and Galina Vishnevskaya. The string quartets have had the opportunity to work with the Amadeus, the Borodin and the Alban Berg Quartets, among many others. The Beaux Arts Trio and the Florestan Trio have led masterclasses, and yearly opera productions are musically directed by the likes of Michael Chance, Richard Egarr, Yvonne Kenny, Ann Murray, Emmanuelle Haim and Hans Peter Blochwitz. Alumni include Thomas Adès, Gerald Finley, Simon Keenlyside, Adrienne Pieczonka, Diana Montague, Dame Felicity Lott, Ian Bostridge, Ian Storey, Eva-Marie Westbroek, the Endellion String Quartet and many leaders and principals of the world's orchestras.

As the programme develops and expands, particularly with the new facilities at Snape opening in 2009, even more young musicians will be able to take advantage of the opportunities it offers, which remain true to the wishes of its founders, Benjamin Britten and Peter Pears.

GRAHAM MURRELL

Rediscovering Music
Mark Padmore

We shall not cease from exploration
And the end of all our exploring
Will be to arrive where we started
And know the place for the first time

These oft-quoted words from T.S. Eliot's 'Little Gidding' served as an inspiration for the John Passion project, one of the first Aldeburgh Residencies that took place in September 2005. Our familiarity with the great works of the classical music canon makes it very difficult for performer and listener alike to find a way to approach them with a sense of exploration. Usually we rely on the conductor to interpret a work and to give instructions to the players and singers in order to realise their vision of it. The musicians become a sort of sophisticated instrument upon which the conductor plays. This situation is made worse by the economic realities of modern music-making where time is money and rehearsals cannot be spent in discussion. A week's residency at Aldeburgh gave the Orchestra of the Age of Enlightenment and I Fagiolini, along with Peter Harvey as Christus and myself as Evangelist, the chance to throw out the rulebook and see what happened.

We started not with a read-through of the piece but with a seminar led by John Butt, Professor of Music at Glasgow University and author of a wonderfully thought-provoking book, *Playing with History*. He talked about what is known about the genesis of the John Passion and the four different versions that Bach performed, and reminded us that it achieved no definitive form in Bach's lifetime. When Bach started a fair copy of the full score in 1739 he only got as far as the first ten numbers, but these show very clearly that he was constantly revising – the opening chorus alone contains nearly 200 changes. This led to questions about which version we should use and whether one edition was better than another, and on to a discussion of what we mean by 'historically informed performance'. Can we ever realise the composer's intentions; indeed, can we ever be sure of what they were? And if we could realise them, would we like the result?

Our first musical rehearsal concentrated on the chorales. Words are rarely printed in orchestral material and often players are wholly in the dark as to what they are. By asking everyone to sing the chorales we began to understand the shape and meaning of the text. We sought to find a naturalness in our inflexion of the German and a real acquaintance not just with the melodies but with the inner parts and bass lines as well.

Two rules were agreed: first, that everyone should be present for all rehearsals. Bach's Passions are often rehearsed in disjointed ways to save money: continuo players for the recitatives, *obbligato* instruments for the arias and tutti only for the choruses. We wanted everyone to feel responsible at all times for how the piece unfolded. The second rule was 'no pencils'. The pencil was only just invented during Bach's lifetime and was not used by musicians. Often the pencil markings that litter modern-day scores actually cut off the question of intention and become an end in themselves. Without being able to mark up the parts we had to become more engaged and attentive to what was going on around us.

It is this quality of attention that was at the heart of what we were after. Declan Donnellan in *The Actor and the Target* devotes a chapter to the difference between attention and concentration. Concentration in performance can be likened to going on a walk in the mountains with a guide who tells you what to look at, where to go and at what pace; the guide may be knowledgeable and experienced but whilst you travel safely and arrive in good time for supper, you might miss much along the way. We were trying to create a situation through attentiveness where we knew the way well enough not to get hopelessly lost but where any member of the group could surprise us with an insight. All eyes and ears would be open but not necessarily all looking at the guide.

The differences between classical music and theatre are worth pondering. Nowadays, it is almost impossible to imagine a Shakespeare play being put on with less than four weeks' rehearsal, but Beethoven's Symphonies and Bach's Passions are frequently performed with no more than a warm-up. The problem is that we think we know how these pieces 'go'. We recognise them; we've played them before; we've got the recording. But why not ask what we don't know about a piece? Have we ever truly listened to the viola line in the opening chorus of the John Passion? Have we noticed that Peter's denial of Jesus has a verbal rhyme and the same melodic shape as the end of the previous aria? Do we know what that aria is about without having to look up a translation? Or which chorale melodies are repeated and in what context? So much can inform our understanding of this masterpiece, yet we so rarely open ourselves up to it.

To help with this process we invited two speakers to come and give us insights into related fields. John Drury, former Dean of Christchurch, Oxford talked about the theology of the John Gospel and about the irony of redemption coming through suffering (the theme of the opening chorus, and central to the whole work). Nigel Spivey gave a lecture on the iconography of the Passion and the depiction of suffering in art. These lectures and most of the rehearsals were open to the public. It seems vital to me that the process of music-making should be accessible to audiences. For most people the possibility of reading a score in the way one might read a play script doesn't exist; we go to recordings. But recordings are, of course, interpretations. It is very hard to encounter music before it is interpreted except in rehearsal.

The other great stimulus to seeing a piece afresh is to have an educational project running alongside. Cherry Forbes, education officer of the OAE, organised one in two local primary schools. Various players went in to the schools to talk about the John Passion and the children learnt to sing the first crowd scene. They also wrote a translation for the chorale that Bach weaves into the aria *'Mein teurer Heiland'*. At our dress rehearsal we had 60 children on stage with us to perform these two sections and then to listen to the rehearsal. Our aim was not to produce a highly polished performance of the John Passion; it was rather to admit that we don't know the piece as well as we think do, and to give ourselves back the excitement of discovering it for the first time. Aldeburgh gave us that opportunity and a transforming encounter with the John Passion ensued.

The Value of Music in Prisons

David Ramsbotham

In April 1996, shortly after I had been appointed Her Majesty's Chief Inspector of Prisons, I was invited to meet the organisers of the International String Quartet competition, and Yehudi Menuhin in particular, who apparently wanted to talk to me. I am not a musician, so there was no musical reason why I should have been invited. But I had had the great pleasure and privilege of meeting Yehudi once before, ten years earlier, staying at the house of the then Commandant of the British Sector in West Berlin. He was there because he had been awarded the Mendelssohn Prize for services to Jewry since the end of the Second World War. I remembered asking him about the subject of his acceptance speech to which he replied 'toleranz', because, he said, it was the only remaining word with that meaning that had not been hijacked.

Naturally, at the thought of meeting him again, I accepted, being told by the chairman that Yehudi really wanted to talk about prisons, in which he had an abiding interest. On the day he was kind enough to say that he had been interested in the things that I had been saying about the conduct of imprisonment and explained that he would dearly like to help in any way he could. In particular he wondered whether music played any part in the lives of prisoners, particularly young prisoners, because it had so much to contribute. I had to admit that, having only been in post for a bare six months, I did not yet know what was or was not going on around the whole prison system, but that having been alerted I would look into it.

On doing so, not surprisingly I found that while immense amounts of red tape had been laid down from on high, everything that was actually done with and for prisoners depended on individual prison governors. If they saw value or interest in anything, they could invest money in it, at the expense of something else. This meant, and means, that no introduction is permanent because it is likely to be overturned by the next governor, whose interests or priorities may be different. For the future, this built-in inconsistency must be changed in the interests of common sense if nothing else, but that is not the subject of this article.

Quite by chance the International competition that year was won by the excellent Schidler Quartet from Leicestershire. At the same time Glen Parva, the only Young Offender Institution (YOI) in Leicestershire, had a very humane and forward-looking governor. So when, during one of our subsequent conversations, Yehudi said that he wished that he could get a string quartet into a YOI, because of what the young offenders could learn from the exposure, the outcome seemed obvious. The young men of the Schidler were enthusiastic; the Governor of Glen Parva was keen and receptive; Yehudi

gave his name to the venture. But the authorities remained totally opposed and refused to give permission.

There then began a most frustrating eighteen months, during which 'toleranz' was tested to the limit. Firstly the Governor was diagnosed with cancer and, having tried bravely to continue in post, was forced to hand over, temporarily at first, to his deputy. Secondly, activity funding in prisons fell under even greater pressure, particularly for education. Yehudi had let it be known that the main reason why he felt that a string quartet was so relevant was because it had so much to teach young people about life – individual skill, self-discipline, team work, determination in particular. He felt that seeing and hearing a quartet in action could not fail to impress itself on people, admitting all the while that he was biased.

Eventually the great day came and the Quartet was allowed in, to play to and engage with as many young offenders as wished to attend. Because Yehudi could not himself be there, the Governor arranged for a video to be made of the event, which he later sent to him. True to his forecast, those who came were amazed and fascinated. Having played, the Quartet explained how they put a piece together, and then sent the boys to get paper and combs, with which they were encouraged to put together a piece of music that they all knew. It was, clearly, one of those magic moments, from which good things should have come.

But it was not to be. That was the only time to my knowledge that a Quartet has been invited to teach its lessons in a YOI. The Governor had to retire and his replacement had no time for such activities. Sadly, Yehudi died soon afterwards. No one thinks as far as eighteen months ahead in a prison, because governors change with such rapidity that short termism reigns. But the lesson remains.

In 1996 I was also introduced to the annual competition and exhibition organised by the Koestler Trust, founded almost fifty years ago by the writer Arthur Koestler, himself a former political prisoner. Each year individuals in prisons, young offender establishments and special hospitals have the opportunity of entering any one or more of more than fifty classes covering every aspect of the arts from painting, through music to needlework and matchstick modelling. Each entry is professionally judged and commented upon and a number of them are included in an annual exhibition. The artists receive both prize and sale money.

The ethos of the whole exercise is that every work of art is an individual achievement. Achievement develops self-esteem. Self-esteem is a vital ingredient of rehabilitation and the ability to lead a useful and law-abiding life. Therefore, because they are a means to that vital end, which amounts to protecting the public, the arts are, or should be, a compulsory ingredient in the programmes available in every prison. Armed with new skills and burgeoning self-esteem, offenders may go on to engage with the work, education or training that are essential for successful rehabilitation.

I was therefore delighted when, in 2002, I learned that Aldeburgh had embarked on a most imaginative venture, involving the boys of Carlford Unit at the nearby HMP and YOI Warren Hill and the children of Debenham High School, under the guidance of Phillipa Reive. Those who came to the Festival that year may remember the remarkable video made by the two groups in which they declared their hopes, fears and aspirations to a background of music that they had written themselves. It marked the beginning of an ongoing relationship between Aldeburgh Music and the Unit, to the credit of both and the benefit of many. Carlford Unit contains young people serving long sentences for very serious offences, many of whom have lived Dickensian lives in conditions that the press loves to sensationalise. Winston Churchill once said that those involved in the criminal justice system must be aware that 'there is a treasure in the heart of every man, if only you can find it'. The media's current vogue for demonising feral young people suggests otherwise, but the programmes that Aldeburgh has initiated and run are living proof of its validity. The enthusiasm of the staff of the Unit for the benefit to those taking part in the Aldeburgh ventures is a testament to their value.

This imaginative outreach of the spirit of Aldeburgh demonstrates as clearly as the experience of the Schidler Quartet in Glen Parva the positive and multifarious contribution that music can make to everyone's lives. Not every kind of music appeals to every ear or indeed taste, but there can be few people whose daily lives it does not touch. Ask any group of young people about what brings them together and most of them will say 'music'. That characteristic ability to unite can be turned to advantage as, for example, is currently being practised in Manchester as a way of integrating young immigrants from many different countries. On a number of evenings each week they are encouraged to play, sing or dance from their own national repertoire. Afterwards, as they mingle with one another they refer to each other not as 'that Pakistani' or 'that Chinese' but 'the person who sang that song'.

I am one of those who believe that the only raw material that every nation has in common is its people. Woe betide it if it does not do everything possible to identify, nurture and develop the talents of its people – all of its people – because, if it does not do so, it has only itself to blame if it fails on the world stage. Music is a wonderful medium for identifying talent, which, once encouraged, can be channelled and deployed to best advantage. It can help in the rehabilitation of those who appear to have nothing to contribute by teaching them about life, as Yehudi Menuhin believed, or developing their skills and self-esteem, as Arthur Koestler demonstrated. I warmly congratulate all those at Aldeburgh who, on behalf of the nation, are practising what they preached.

Two poems from HMP Young Offenders Unit Warren Hill at Carlford Unit, Hollesley Bay, where Aldeburgh Music conducts regular education work

The Only One

The deepest bars, inspired
    by scars
Product of the deepest, far reaches of
    a heathen's past.
They say the deepest pain is a gift
    from the start
A gift to word the experiences of a curse
    in a way to touch a heart.
Behind bars I'm kept from my heart.
Just after my heart, my love, broke
    through the bars on my heart
And I'm left trapped, a chain on a bicycle
Moving so quickly toward a
    recidivist cycle.
I wonder if they can find a way.
A way to play a dangerous game
Where all of the participants but one
See me and my crimes.
As exactly the same.

This Person

I've been fighting this person,
For far too many years.
His eyes are the same to me
Even though they've changed.
The look upon his face
Has been with me for years.
My death won't release me
From his strong hold.
He follows me everywhere
Though you can't see him.
He stares back at me
Through my lone mirror.
Its funny how this person
Is me.

Composing a Concert

John Woolrich

Frank Zappa claimed he could compose with anything, any 'data', he called it, that you gave him. Even, he said mysteriously, with a large group of people. Devising a concert is composing, but with pieces of music rather than notes. The process is the same: material has to be chosen and organised. Not surprisingly, then, composers often make the most interesting programmers, and can give you more than just an original choice of pieces. 'If you ask a composer to plan a series of concerts', says Harrison Birtwistle, 'you expect the results to carry forward some of his own creative occupations, and also to have a more eccentric view of music than is usually demonstrated in programme planning.'

How can this work in practice? Birtwistle is interested in symmetry – he describes the structure of his piece *Tragoedia*, for instance, as a 'bilateral symmetry'. A note in the programme for a concert he planned in 1970 (called 'Spring Song') said that the aim of the evening was 'to conceive a concert as an overall structure … without the punctuation of applause, and that its formal bilateral design, arranged symmetrically around the interval, be underlined through lighting and spatial organisation. Rather than merely separating the halves of a programme, the interval becomes part of the total musical experience.' So Birtwistle built a concert in exactly the same way that he built a piece of music. Oliver Knussen's programmes are as intricate and deeply considered as his own compositions.

That isn't to say that the choice of repertoire isn't significant in itself: Stravinsky-the-conductor's choice of non-Stravinsky repertoire is fascinating, both the ancient (Cherubini, Mozart, Schumann, Glinka, Tchaikovsky and Mozart) and the modern (Debussy, Dukas and Manuel de Falla). It is just as intriguing to discover that Mahler conducted Debussy, Tippett conducted Ives, Webern conducted Milhaud, and Brahms conducted William Byrd.

Benjamin Britten's selection of repertoire for Aldeburgh is also revealing. Some names crop up frequently: Purcell (the first composer in the first festival), Dowland, Mozart, Schubert, Berg and Frank Bridge (his teacher). This isn't just the music that Britten loved, it's also music that illuminated and gave a context to his own work. Even if Britten had left his own music out of the concerts, a self-portrait would have emerged from his choice of works by other composers.

So how to start planning? Britten programmed the music he loved: 'We are planning some pretty scrumptious programmes', he told Lennox Berkeley in 1950, 'with lots of Bach & Mozart.' 'Programmes', Thomas Adès says, 'are designed purely for my own pleasure.' So, start with something you love, and don't assume or try to guess what the audience wants. It is just as important to create new expectations in listeners as to satisfy the old. William Glock said he wanted to offer Third Programme listeners 'what they will like tomorrow'. (Glock was the most radical, creative and influential of programme planners, at Dartington Summer School – which he founded – the Proms, the BBC Symphony Orchestra, the Third Programme, and the Bath Festival.)

Given that these days we have access to so much music on CD or on the radio, and that the core repertoire, at least, is well represented in the concert hall, it makes sense for a small festival like Aldeburgh to specialise in the less visited byways of music. Nearly sixty years ago Britten described the Aldeburgh Festival as concentrating on 'works which do not fit into the usual repertoire'.

But why not simply leave the choice of music to the performers? There can be a substantial gap between music that's good to perform and music that's good to listen to. William Glock had a strong sense of how to exploit his relationship with performers: 'I have always been convinced that the most stimulating programmes arise from making definite proposals to the artists concerned, and never from asking "What would you like to perform?" Of course compromise may often be necessary. But the difference between one approach and the other is between maintaining a clearly defined policy and ending with a mere pot-pourri, however good the individual works.' 'I hate those programmes that look like baskets in a supermarket,' says Pierre Boulez, 'with everything thrown in together.'

How do you fit pieces together to avoid what Boulez calls 'completely incoherent progammes'? One way is simply to trust instinct: William Glock said that he programmed intuitively. 'The nose scents and it chooses,' said Stravinsky. 'An artist is simply a kind of pig snouting truffles.' In his autobiography Glock describes the difference between this approach and Pierre Boulez's more theoretical one. He once proposed a programme of Boulez's own *Eclat* and Berlioz's *Symphonie Fantastique*:

> There was a dark and unsettling silence. During the next two or three minutes I decided that my suggestion must have seemed quite preposterous. But then he said that he found the programme not so bad, after all. It could be presented as a programme of virtuosity and invention. That was characteristic of him, of his impulse to draw things together and find an underlying basis. I, on the other hand, tried out one idea after another. But our different approaches, one belonging to a theorist and thinker, the other governed by trial and error, worked well together.

Programmes, Boulez says, 'should have some meaning'. A good concert can show the deep connections between things that appear different on the surface. As William Glock said, 'ideally, the pattern and the content should grow together'.

In 1985 Claudio Abbado and Hans Landesmann devised a series of concerts, 'Mahler and the Twentieth Century', to show that 'today's music is not an isolated occurrence, but the logical continuation of the great composers we all love'. So Abbado performed Mahler alongside Berio, Rihm, Maderna and Boulez, showing how Mahler had anticipated and influenced later composers. It made Mahler sound like the first great twentieth-century composer. Setting his music alongside that of, say, Weber and Schubert would have told another story.

One of William Glock's first decisions at the BBC was to break down 'the old segregation of past and present'. His first invitation concert consisted of Boulez's 'Le Marteau sans Maître' sandwiched between two Mozart string quintets. Another had a symmetrical structure: a Byrd motet, followed by a Boulez piece, Machaut's *Messe de Notre Dame*, a repeat of the Boulez and then finally another Byrd motet. A recent Aldeburgh concert mixed modern Italians (Nono, Sciarrino, Castiglioni and Scelsi) with sixteenth–seventeenth-century ones (Monteverdi and Gesualdo). Members of the audience without a programme were duly foxed ('Was that Nono or Gesualdo?'), proving that the eccentricity and extremity of recent Italian music belongs firmly in a 400-year-old tradition and that news from the seventeenth century stays news.

Composer programme-planners seem oblivious to the 'old segregation'. A typical Boulez programme in the 1960s might present the Mass of Barcelona (by anon.) alongside Messiaen's *Chronochromie* or thirteenth- and fourteenth-century Coronation music next to Stravinsky's *The Flood*. Harrison Birtwistle once interwove John Cage's Clarinet Sonata with Machaut's *Messe de Notre Dame*.

Benjamin Britten deployed this technique back in the 1950s. Even today his placing of pieces by Berg in Aldeburgh concerts (the *Four Pieces* for clarinet and piano between songs by Purcell and Schubert in 1953) looks startling, and would have made both the Berg and the Schubert sound more intensely themselves. Berg's *Three Pieces* from the *Lyric Suite* coming after Britten's own *Nocturne* (dedicated to Alma Mahler) at a concert at Orford in 1959 looks less unusual, but following the Berg with Handel's 'Praise of Harmony' for tenor and strings must have been bracing. Britten locked the concert together in a symmetrical structure: Handel–Britten–Berg–Handel.

The strangest context Britten found for Berg must have been in a concert he proposed to Norman Del Mar: 'The programme of your orchestral concert at Aldeburgh looks a little like this at the moment: Siegfried Idyll, Berg double concerto (with Noel, & Parikian perhaps) & the Carnival des Animaux. The latter I'd like to play with Noel, with you conducting ... Can you think of a nice English piece to start off with?' In the end Britten modified his plans and dropped the Berg but kept the strangeness: the programme was Boyce's Symphony No.3, Schoenberg's Chamber Symphony No.1, Chausson's Concerto for piano, violin and string quartet, Wagner's *Siegfried* Idyll and Saint-Saens's *Le carnival des animaux*.

This is such a typical Aldeburgh programme: independent, quirky, adventurous, eccentric, and both serious and fun. It is a spirit that has survived and prospered for sixty years in the hands of creative programme builders of the stature of Benjamin Britten, Oliver Knussen and Thomas Adès. If you want original insights about music, ask a composer.

The Problem of Ultra-Modern Music

David Toop

I have been asked to write about problems of contemporary music. To be a little more precise, I have been asked to reflect on Hans Keller's essay, *The Problem of Modern Music*, first published in 1961, then reproduced in the 1972 *Aldeburgh Anthology*. That was his opening salvo, and so shall it be mine. After all, a perception lingers that contemporary music continues to be weighed down with problems, multiple rather than singular, so we should ask if these problems are in any way similar. Have they changed, diminished, or multiplied, and was Keller's text an accurate prediction of the future, which is our present?

What he wrote, elegantly and succinctly, was an ambivalent overview of one part of classical music. Schoenberg is examined and found culpable, if only because he arrived before his time; Britten and Stravinsky are mentioned and exonerated. He ends with a slightly forlorn plea: 'The contemporary crisis can only be resolved in practice, by practice – practice in listening, in playing, in composing. There is a lot of talk about education nowadays, but the most essential part of education has always been self-education.'

Forlorn or not, I'm in broad agreement, though what Keller and his colleagues lacked was practice in listening to all the musics of that contemporary crisis. Wondering if I had kept any references in my personal archive to Aldeburgh or Keller, I came across an intriguing cutting from *The Sunday Times* of June 1971. Both Felix Aprahamian and Desmond Shawe-Taylor seized upon a convergence of festivals as an opportunity to use Aldeburgh as a rod with which to beat the International Society for Contemporary Music (ISCM). Nicolaus A. Huber's now obscure electronic work, *Versuch über Sprache*, was thrashed to within an inch of its life, the *coup de grace* administered with a note that 'the cognoscenti of the ISCM endured the cipher for a very long time until finally Hans Keller dared to lead the general exodus.' Returning to the Queen Elizabeth Hall a few days later for the same column, Aprahamian throws a roundhouse right hook at AMM, the pioneering improvisation ensemble then containing Cornelius Cardew, Eddie Prevost and Keith Rowe, among others. 'Most of it', he deadpans, 'consisted of endless microtonal inflections and percussive accretions to a held organ chord – B flat major, second inversion – a chord with which, as Sir Jack Westrup recently declared in similar circumstances, I am not unfamiliar.'

Very droll, though as it happened, I attended that concert and remember it with fondness and in some detail, despite the intervening passage of years. I was in the company of a friend from Hornsey art college, the late Stuart Marshall, and at a point when proceedings were becoming inert, the two of us decided to leave. Like Hans Keller, we led a general exodus, though our reasons were less to do with protest or boredom and more a realisation that events lacking a conventional narrative arc leave many openings for an audience to leave or stay. One wouldn't expect Aprahamian to show any enthusiasm for such notions but for those of us who felt constrained by the entrenched rituals of the concert hall, they were liberating. More revealing, perhaps, is Shawe-Taylor's review of *Islands* by Elisabeth Lutyens. 'Wearisomely devoid of movement,' he observed, concluding with a backhander that concedes a modest achievement of 'wan charm'. Poor Lutyens suffered greatly at the hands of many British critics, partly because she had the temerity to be a woman who composed, partly because she was an unashamed modernist working within an aggressively conservative milieu.

Too late for her to enjoy it, but the Lutyens star has risen somewhat of late, illuminating for a new generation the particularity of her vision. Just in case anybody thinks that this recent flicker of interest in Lutyens is the dawning of modernity revisited, there is a parallel excavation of music by composers perceived as quintessentially English. The emergence of yet another folk revival has pulled Vaughan Williams, Warlock, Ireland and Moeran into its vortical and sometimes esoteric enthusiasms. We live in confusing times.

Our cultural climate may be blighted in certain respects, not least in the marginalisation of serious debate about serious musics, but on the positive side, women are not derided with such flagrant sexism, music from beyond the so-called developed world is no longer described as primitive, and microtonal inflections, percussive accretions and stasis, wearisome or not, are recognised as techniques of our time. They can also be heard in other musics, historically, geographically and culturally remote. This expands a point made by Keller. Most music works with identifiable elements and retains a link with the past, though such links may require unpicking before they can be recognised. 'For on the whole,' he wrote, 'music is still music, even though most electronic music may not be.'

Here is one significant difference between the topic of his essay and mine. Electronic music has become a democratised language, an affordable tool available to composers via downloads or from a variety of off-the-shelf boxes, and so its spread and diversity is now far wider than Keller could have envisaged at the time of writing. The period when electronic music was solely an experimental branch of the classical tradition has long gone; though we might feel suffocated under the volume of electronic music emerging from all points of the globe, there is a satisfying proportion that negotiates a line between broad accessibility and experiment. Keller made the point that nobody had grown up with atonal music. 'The culture whose end we are approaching is old,' he wrote, 'and old age is inevitably retrospective.' Keller accepted some of the changes of this culture, but there has been a tendency in recent years to condemn the majority of twentieth-century music as a gross mistake. Whereas other art forms are reconciled to the avant-garde upheavals of the past century, or so the argument goes, music will return to its basis in harmony, melody and rhythm.

To some extent, this has been the case. The radical deconstructions of the 1950s through to the 1970s can seem rather nostalgic now. Subjects for rediscovery, reconstruction and academic analysis, they have become embedded in the way music (or soundwork, to acknowledge sound art, phonography and other contemporary forms) is experienced, performed and presented. This means that their true legacy, beyond controversy, is taken for granted. One obituary of Karlheinz Stockhausen claimed that after the breakthroughs of *Kontakte, Momente, Telemusik, Hymnen* and so on, his later music was increasingly irrelevant. This may be true, though the jury is out and a retrial seems imminent, but the more important point is that Stockhausen's electronic works have influenced entire genres of popular music. What we now call electronica is a hybrid, fused on the one hand from the influence of Stockhausen and his contemporaries, and on the other hand the vitality and innovation of African-American musics such as soul, funk and disco. Some still find this traversing of boundaries – race, class, high art and low art – uncomfortable, but the history of twentieth-century music abounds with fusions. There is an audience whose formative years have been informed by a vast range of musics – popular, experimental, global, historical, good, bad, silly and serious – and these versatile, knowledgeable, adventurous listeners no longer have to struggle in the face of dissonance, electronic noise, arrhythmic outbursts, impossibly eclectic references, or the outstayed welcome of a B flat major chord, second inversion.

One week before writing this essay in May 2008 I was performing in the Royal Festival Hall Ballroom space with the ensemble I direct: Unknown Devices: the Laptop Orchestra. This is a large group of students from London College of Communication, most of them playing laptop computers, and on this occasion augmented by six students from the Royal College of Music and two musicians from the London Sinfonietta, all of them playing conventional acoustic instruments. The performance was completely improvised; the audience was large, mostly young, and very enthusiastic.

Earlier that evening I had joined a capacity audience in the Royal Festival Hall to hear *In Seven Days*, a new piano concerto by Thomas Adès. The previous day I was in Leiden, listening to a performance of new pieces, including one written by the American composer David Behrman, for an extraordinary ensemble of recreated sirens, based on the inventions of an early twentieth-century Dutch physicist named H. A. Naber. Again, the concert was sold out. The week before that, I was in Cambridge, hearing immersive playbacks of pieces by sound artists John Levack Drever and John Wynne. Anybody who arrived late was obliged to stand, as the venue was full. The week before that I had been to the Young Vic to hear Olga Neuwirth's opera, *Lost Highway*, loosely based, seemingly by way of *West Side Story*, on David Lynch's film of the same title. Some seats were empty, though not many. Yes, contemporary music of this kind is not sufficiently popular as a platform on which to build a successful radio station, nor does it trouble television schedules, but its outreach goes far beyond the bad old days when performers might outnumber their audience.

Keller spoke of a culture of change. Those changes generating the crisis of which he wrote have persisted, multiplied, and in some ways intensified. We live in a world of increasing media saturation, globalisation, social anxiety and rapid technological development, though wars and economic instability remain a constant. In 1971, dismissal by a mainstream newspaper like *The Sunday Times* underlined the marginality of experimental music; now newspapers are losing their claim to be mainstream; for better or worse, every fragment of taste and belief is represented online. Societies are far more diverse and so the overarching ideal of a unified culture stands revealed as a lost utopia, just one transitional moment in the struggle to understand and reconcile ourselves to the bewildering complexity of the twenty-first century.

In the past few years, digital technology has transformed many aspects of music, from distribution, production, promotion and accounting at one end of the spectrum to composing, performing and listening at the other. The looming question of how to make sense of diversity, how to evaluate it all and bring together audiences, is exemplified by iPods and other MP3 players. All this esoterica, now collected together in one tiny personal device: Alfred Schnittke and Autechre, Bo Diddley, Frescobaldi and Takemitsu, Mary J. Blige and An Sook Sun, Weddel seals under Antarctic ice and the sound of a dry leaf blown about in a quiet street. Some identify this as the problem of all problems: sonic solipsism; music detached from human interaction; music as a global sweetshop.

This ignores the curiosity of humans. There are those who wish to cut themselves off from everything other than their own clan, their own identity, and those who wish to know what lies over the fence, behind the wall, beyond the ocean. 'Only madmen invent entirely new languages,' Keller wrote. Yet music is too vague and subjective to be a language in this sense. We can learn new ways of hearing – with redefinitions of what music might become, alien sounds, or methods and systems of organisation that initially seem incomprehensible – because humans possess a remarkable capacity to adapt.

Musical eclecticism did not begin with MP3 players. Debussy and Ravel, along with most of the composers I have mentioned above, have all played their part in opening the ears of the world to the extravagant, contradictory beauty of its own sound. As a young teenager at school in the 1960s I was lucky enough to be taught by an inspirational art master, Michael Evans, who not only eased me over the hurdle of Picasso's Cubism but loaned me his 10-inch records of Bartók String Quartets and Louis Armstrong's Hot Five. Again, this was an existing tendency, brought about by the growing ease of accessing the world's cultures. As recordings and broadcasts of music became more diverse and plentiful, musicians, composers and sound artists such as myself, Christian Marclay and John Zorn developed a practice built upon unexpected juxtapositions and extreme inclusiveness. This inclusiveness is one of the dominant themes in Alex Ross's recent book, *The Rest is Noise*. Ross can write without doubt or embarrassment of the Velvet Underground, Public Enemy or Tibetan Buddhist liturgy and consider these musics alongside Britten, Sibelius and John Adams. Unlike Hans Keller, I feel it is pointless to conclude with a prescription for our ills. If these are our problems, we are lucky to have them.

GRAHAM MURRELL

13 Migrant

Alison Wilding, 2003

Wilding writes: 'Snape is shaped by water, and Snape Maltings is now a concert hall which bears the traces of serious flood defences. In high summer you can lie on your back in the grass and watch the brown sails of boats gliding past, just visible through purplish reed beds. 'Migrant' is about travelling, not destination. Its nature is changeable, secretive – a glimpse of bird and boat.'

14 **Creek Men**
Laurence Edwards
Snape marshes, Summer 2008

15 **Lost on the Beach** (left)
Lines of Defence (bottom)
Bettina Furnée and Simon Frazer
From the project 'If Ever You're in the Area'.

'Lost on the Beach', East Lane, Bawdsey. On selected days during the summer of 2005 a helium balloon reading HOLD SWAY was flown from the crumbling searchlight emplacement.

'Lines of Defence', when installed on 15 January 2005 at East Lane, Bawdsey, consisted of 38 flags in five lines, each one metre apart, positioned on the eroding cliffs 60m south of Martello Tower W. Letters on the flags spelled out SUBMISSION IS ADVANCING AT A FRIGHTFUL SPEED, a text sourced by Simon Frazer for its reference to climate change and the essentially fearful reaction which prompts people to go to war.

16 **Orfordness** *(top)*
Louise K. Wilson

17 **'Faster than Sound',
Aldeburgh Festival** *(bottom)*
Bentwaters Airbase, 2008

Thomas Adès and the Festival, 1999–2008
Tom Service

It seemed like a radical appointment in 1999: the 28-year-old composer, pianist and conductor Thomas Adès became the sole Artistic Director of the Aldeburgh Festival. After more than a decade of collaborative artistic direction from Oliver Knussen and Steuart Bedford in the wake of Peter Pears' death in 1986, Adès joined Chief Executive Jonathan Reekie, who had started his job in 1997, and was charged with continuing and renewing the traditions of Aldeburgh. Ten Festivals later, the partnership of Adès and Reekie – and John Woolrich, who has held the position of Associate Artistic Director since 2004 – leaves Aldeburgh a changed institution: new performing venues, new partnerships with performers, and new relationships with composers. Which is to suggest, paradoxically, that Adès bequeaths the Festival to pianist Pierre-Laurent Aimard, who takes over in 2009, in largely the same state he found it back in 1999. That's to say, the Festival continues to make a unique mark on Britain's musical landscape, after ten seasons that have mixed new music with older repertoires in often revelatory concerts, making the familiar sound new-fangled and the strange, familiar. The ethos of Aldeburgh remains unchanged: a place in which inspirational artistic directorship sheds light on music history, and in which performers have the freedom and the challenge to explore their limits. Precisely in his innovation and individualism, Adès has been a consolidatory custodian of the essential Aldeburgh spirit.

Adès' programmes, when you look back at the programme-books of the last ten years – or, if you're lucky enough to have been there, when you sift through your musical memory – have achieved a similar magic to that which his music performs. There's a symbiotic relationship between Adès' programming priorities and the achievements of his works over the last decade, nearly all of which (the only large-scale exception is his 2004 opera, *The Tempest*) have been performed or premiered at the Aldeburgh Festival, beginning with a staging of his opera *Powder Her Face* at the opening of the 1999 Festival. Just as music like his Piano Quintet reimagines the archetype of sonata form, making this most tradition-bound of all musical structures seem surreal and uncanny, so too have his programmes managed the same paradoxical trick with the way we think of different repertoires. The Arditti Quartet concert in 2002, when Adès gave the British premiere of his Piano Quintet, is a case in point: surrounded by music by György Kurtág, Conlon Nancarrow (two composers whose music runs like golden threads through Adès' Aldeburgh decade), Bartók and Xenakis, Adès' work was at the centre of a web of musical connections that made the concert more than the sum of its parts.

One thing that Adès' time as Artistic Director certainly has changed about Aldeburgh is the repertoire on which he has focused, his special enthusiasms as performer and composer that have inspired the imaginations of any listener who has visited the Festival since 1999. There's an individualism to all this, inevitably, as he said to me in 2000, early on in his tenure. 'The programmes are designed purely for my own pleasure. I don't believe in the idea of a collective "audience" and a generalised response, or in giving "the people" what they want. An audience is a collection of individuals. I'm trying to create a vision of the world as I would like it to be and appeal to listeners as if from one individual to another.' That vision encompasses composers like Janáček, Busoni, Fauré, and Ives, all of whom Adès' programmes have celebrated with typical insight (with special revelations in Fauré's chamber music and Busoni's orchestral and solo piano works), but you can see the priorities of Adès' musical world most clearly in the living composers whose music he has performed and programmed. Kurtág is one such, whose music was again a feature of the 2008 Festival, but younger generations of composers have benefited most of all. One is Richard Ayres, the Cornwall-born composer who has made his life in Holland, whose NONcerto, No.30, was one of the important premieres of 2001, performed by the City of Birmingham Symphony Orchestra and Sakari Oramo; his fable-like anthropomorphic opera, *The Cricket Recovers*, was commissioned by Aldeburgh and given its beguiling world premiere at the opening of the 2005 Festival.

But it's Adès' admiration and love for the work of Irish composer Gerald Barry that he has shared most often and most passionately with Aldeburgh audiences, an association that began in 2000 when he conducted the world premiere of Barry's *Wiener Blut* (with the Birmingham Contemporary Music Group, one of the ensembles who have given signature concerts at nearly every one of Adès' Aldeburgh Festivals). The staging of Barry's opera, *The Triumph of Beauty and Deceit*, which opened the 2002 Festival and which Adès also conducted, was only the first of that year's celebrations of Barry's uniquely iconoclastic musical voice. Barry was also the centrepiece that year of one of those Aldeburgh concerts that burns itself on the memory, one of the most illuminating concatenations of music that I've ever heard. His *Cheveux-de-Frise* was the climax of the first half of Adès' programme with the City of Birmingham Symphony Orchestra at Snape, with a phalanx of local children's choirs, as well as the Britten–Pears and Tallis Chamber Choirs. They had started with another Barry work, his brilliantly subversive setting of 'God Save the Queen', and Adès' own 'Brahms', a setting of Alfred Brendel's 'Brms' [see p.229]. This music takes Brahmsian melodic and harmonic tics and pushes them to their limits, making what Adès sees as an 'anti-homage' to the composer, with whom he has a complex, ambivalent relationship (echoing Britten's own infamous loathing of Brahms). Next was the pulverizing energy of *Cheveux-de-Frise* (whose title comes from the up-turned stakes or rocks used to impale oncoming cavalry), music that was shockingly intense in Snape's intimate acoustic.

There could be no greater contrast with the music of the second half, you would have thought: Morton Feldman's quiescent, shimmering *Coptic Light*, and the rapt radiance of Brahms' *Schicksalslied* – an act of genuine homage from Adès to Brahms. But that's when something mysterious happened. Barry's music found an echo in Feldman's: both pieces are pitched at extremes of orchestral possibility, and both works turn the material of music into a tangible physical experience, albeit at opposite ends of the dynamic spectrum. The Elysian vision of Brahms' Hölderlin setting received a performance whose epic contrasts between radiant stasis and expressive violence were a consummation of the programme's poetic extremes. It was a concert that liquefied distinctions between old and new, in which Brahms' *Song of Destiny* became as contemporary an experience as the Feldman or Barry.

That's a sleight of hand that Adès has long cultivated in his Festival programmes, as he described eight years ago. 'I try not to programme a famous piece from the core classical and romantic repertoires unless it is going to be kicking and screaming in the concert. Last year [1999], we put Haydn's hurdy-gurdy concertos alongside Nancarrow and Beethoven's Symphony No.4. The Haydn was shocking because you can't make the hurdy-gurdy conform to modern sensibilities – it sounds exactly as unrefined as it did in the 1790s. It makes you start to think that maybe Haydn isn't supposed to sound polished and nice, and wakes you up to the realisation that we could never survive in the eighteenth century with our notions of taste and beauty. The juxtaposition between Nancarrow and Beethoven made the conductor take the Beethoven very fast... But the point of the whole concert was to say that even if we've heard the Beethoven 160 times, it is still a live animal, not some conventional piece to end a programme.'

Jonathan Reekie has also explained this sort of programming serendipity. 'I think composers, when they programme, are very good at making the kinds of mysterious connections that you wouldn't have thought about between composers and between pieces. It's easy to put together programmes that have historical, social, or cultural connections. It's much harder to put together pieces of music that, on the face of it, don't have anything in common, but which, deep down, have a creative resonance with one another. Tom and John are really good at feeling those sorts of connections, the most exciting kind.' Any number of individual programmes since 1999 could be used as evidence of how this has worked in practice: the CBSO's concert with Sakari Oramo that put lesser-known British works alongside Nielsen's Fifth Symphony; one of Oliver Knussen's programmes that juxtaposed *The Rite of Spring* with Debussy, Knussen's own music and more Stravinsky; a Composer Portrait of Italian composer Salvatore Sciarrino in which pianist Nicolas Hodges played the world premiere of two pieces next to music by Alessandro Scarlatti; a Tchaikovsky Cabaret; one of Adès' concerts with Ian Bostridge which mixed Kurtág and Liszt, Schumann and Britten; or the choral group Exaudi's unforgettable pairing of Ockeghem with Brian Ferneyhough's *Missa Brevis* in Orford Church in 2006, among the most visceral musical performances I have experienced, and continuing a relationship with Ferneyhough's music that Adès began in 2001 when the Arditti Quartet played his Fourth Quartet.

Diverse repertoire, dizzying connections across music history, and different performing contexts, too: Adès opened the Pumphouse in 2000, a venue whose importance has grown steadily every year, a 'miniature Maltings', as *The Sunday Times* put it, in which cabarets, electronica, improvisation, and straight-ahead chamber concerts provide an Aldeburgh Fringe that has become essential to the life of the whole Festival. In 2006, *Faster Than Sound* was inaugurated at the brilliantly bizarre military setting of Bentwaters Airbase, a disused Cold-War relic in which you encountered geodesic domes, sound installations and electronic performances; an event developed in subsequent years.

So what will be the lasting effects of the Adès years at Aldeburgh, the legacy of his partnerships with Jonathan Reekie and John Woolrich? One of the most important is the intimacy with a handful of performers and ensembles that has been fostered over the last ten festivals: especially close partnerships with Ian Bostridge, the Belcea Quartet, the City of Birmingham Symphony Orchestra and Birmingham Contemporary Music Group, with

Alfred Brendel, who gave his last Aldeburgh Festival recital in 2007, with the Arditti Quartet, and, more recently, with the Northern Sinfonia, and with Pierre-Laurent Aimard, who has been part of the Festival every year since 2004. Even more importantly, in the context of British music festivals as a whole, the last ten years have reinforced the sense that Aldeburgh offers the greatest chance to have your ears opened, to hear music you thought you knew resound with fresh meanings, and experience genuinely new music in the company of its composers and the performers closest to them. Adès' programmes have animated Aldeburgh's alchemy of place and music as much as those of any previous director, as well as taking the Festival in unexpected directions.

To take one of the many experiences that embody all of this: in the final concert of the 2006 Festival, Adès conducted the CBSO in a programme that was stark in its simplicity and boldness, yet astonishingly subtle and powerful in its realisation. The first half was Stravinsky's *Rite of Spring*, and the second, Tchaikovsky's *Pathétique Symphony*. The shattering parallelisms between these two pieces were magnified in these performances, revealing new dimensions to both of them. The resonances of that single concert reverberate in the memory, profoundly altering my thinking about these two masterpieces. I'm not alone. Over ten Festivals, it's not just individual programmes that resound with the spirit of discovery and adventure for anyone who is part of the Aldeburgh audience, but whole repertoires, whole visions of musical possibility. Such is the sustaining magic of the Aldeburgh experience.

GRAHAM MURRELL

Brms

Alfred Brendel

One could stand there
left foot slightly forward
concentrated yet relaxed
a mature man
neither arrogant nor subservient
and wait for the audience to be silent
silent and attentive
before one started to laugh
explosively
to the point where somebody joined in
or
in a serious country like Italy
shook his head

One could then
aim a fire-hose at the first row
unless one preferred to bow politely
sit down
and play something by Brom Brehm Brums
sorry Brahms
while releasing simultaneously a handful of mice
in order to make the ladies climb onto their chairs
squeak in terror
and pull their skirts over their heads
a manoeuvre
that unfailingly makes the mice
take flight

One could leave the hall via the fire escape
equipped with beard and cigar
to sign autographs at the nearby coffee-house
Sincerely Brahms
on napkins and handkerchiefs
blouses and bosoms
on ear-lobes just Brms

Thomas Hardy on journeying to Aldeburgh

My dear Clodd

… the bustle at Liverpool Street, the lively conversation in the carriage, the gradual sense of the nearing sea & its cool salt air as you get on to the branch line, the real taste of it on arrival, & the jolly dinner after. But, as the poet says, 'O the difference to me!'.

Letter to Edward Clodd, Max Gate
Friday night, 28 May 1909

Where

6   VISITORS

have you come from

'Where have you come from? Where have you been?
Wrecking the whole of our daily routine!
Tearing the town from its regular labours
To run up and down and around with the neighbours'

Chorus in *Albert Herring*
Act 3

Hardy and Suffolk
Ronald Blythe

Thomas Hardy was a frequent visitor to Aldeburgh. He was a member of the intellectual group lured by Edward Clodd each Whitsun to Strafford House, Crag Path. Clodd was a tireless Rationalist whose popularisation of the work of Darwin and Huxley had brought him fame and fortune. Although a determined Mr Leo Hunter, the celebrities Clodd entertained at Aldeburgh found his company, the pretty house which he had got Charles Voysey to decorate and his brig the *Lotus*, sufficient attraction to tempt them to the Suffolk coast again and again. They included Sir J.M. Barrie, George Meredith (whose chief defect, Clodd discovered, was that he had 'no pity'), George Gissing (who, when asked for his address, said sadly, 'I haven't one'), Holman Hunt (whose palette hung on the dining-room wall), Grant Allen, Edward Whymper (who, when asked if he would take porridge, said, 'I would rather leave the house') and Clement Shorter.

Edward Clodd and Thomas Hardy on Aldeburgh beach.

H.G. Wells was also a visitor. In *Boon* he describes Clodd as a 'dear compact man, one of those Middle Victorians who go about with a preoccupied carking air, as though, after having been at great cost and pains to banish God from the universe, they were resolved not to permit Him back on any terms whatever. He has constituted himself a sort of alert customs officer of a materialistic age ...'.

Thomas Hardy managed to slip past the 'customs officer'. Clodd was shocked when he discovered that the poet who had once described his Maker as 'that Vast Imbecility' was in the habit of praying in church. His letter to Hardy demanding an explanation received no answer. Hardy enjoyed Aldeburgh and 'the sensation of having nothing but sea between you and the North Pole'. Clodd, however, never forgave him his Christian lapse and after his death he described him as 'A great writer, but certainly not a great character'.

Benjamin Britten's settings of eight of Hardy's poems, *Winter Words*, were composed in 1953 and first sung by Peter Pears at the 1954 Festival.

Boudicca's Chariot Horse and the Mink

Gathorne Cranbrook

A vehicular bridge crosses the upper Alde at the east end of the Straits, White House Farm, Great Glemham. Underneath the bridge there is a concrete ledge on each side of the river, raised somewhat above normal water level but submerged in flood. From time to time, on no particular routine, I check these ledges for evidence of mink or otter. Both have left their signs in past years. In early August 2007 it appeared that the exceptional high waters of July, which overflowed the river banks, had cast up onto the broader (eastern) ledge an old brick and a large bone (fig.1). On these prominent objects, including both ends and the shaft of the bone, mink had deposited their characteristic smelly scats. This is normal behaviour, but it is interesting that these sites were well used so soon (within two weeks) after being exposed by the return to normal water levels.

The bone is a complete left femur (thigh bone) of an equid, stained dark brown as from long immersion in water or mud (fig. 2). It is too large to be the femur of a donkey, but is shorter than the femora of two Arab horses in the Natural History Museum, London. In length and mid-shaft diameter the Alde femur does, however, fall within the dimensions of horses excavated at the Danebury Iron Age fort.

Fig 1.
The horse femur and brick, on the ledge under the Alde bridge; Dr P.J. Piper

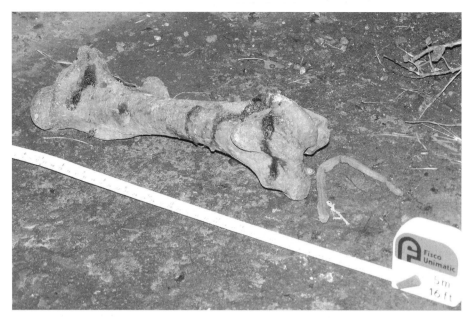

Fig. 2. The femur in situ. Mink scats are visible at both ends and at points along the shaft

Finds from a late Iron Age and Roman site in Essex indicate that the mean height of the Iron Age horses was 12.2 hands and the Roman horses 13.2 hands. Dr A. Grant, an expert in equine anatomy, sums up: 'The picture for horses in England is of general increase in size over time from the early Iron Age onwards in respect of the largest animals, but of much variation at the same time. The conclusion might be drawn ... that [the Alde] femur is of a size compatible with animals of the late Iron Age or Roman period.'

Taking a jump from the reasonable certainties of comparative anatomy, let us envisage a Romano-British scenario. Famously, a bronze head of the Roman Emperor Claudius, unceremoniously ripped from a statuette, was found in the river Alde at Rendham, a mere 2 km north of the Straits bridge. It is generally accepted that this relic was loot taken at the sack of Colchester (Camulodunum) in AD 61 by Boudicca's Iceni army. After being carried so far, would such an object be thrown unceremoniously into the river? Is it possible that an accident occurred at the Rendham crossing? Did a tired horse finally founder at the muddy ford, overturning a chariot and spilling its contents? Hot-tempered and impatient to be home, did the Iceni warrior cut free his broken beast, maybe killing it or leaving it to die in the mire? In either case, its bones would slowly work their way downstream with each winter's flood, until finally being cast up 1946 years later, for the delectation of the river's mink and the interest of the riparian landowner!

Science, by Carbon14 dating or some other technique, may support or dispose of this hypothesis. For the time being, the femur is stored at Glemham House and available to any interested researcher.

Adapted from a note appearing in *White Admiral*, Spring, 2008

Ancestral Airs: Snape and Sutton Hoo

Martin Carver

Under the turf of the Sandlings lie many hundreds of Anglo-Saxons, the local people of the Alde and the Deben, who lived and died here in the fifth, sixth and seventh centuries AD. Sometimes East Angles of our own era encounter their remains by accident, like the decorated bronze bucket ploughed up at Bromeswell in 1988, or the gold ring found at Aldeburgh in the nineteenth century. But other dead Angles have been sought out deliberately, for their beauty and mystery, and then lovingly drawn, cross-examined, interrogated and admired by archaeologists of our day. Over 1,400 years the bodies of the once vigorous pioneers have turned into dark sand, the 'sandmen' of the Sandlings. Their clothes have mostly gone too: colourful weaves of trousers, tunics and cloaks, leather belts and shoes, all reduced to scraps or smears. They now lie in their graves, like brown people in a sandy bath, their limbs full and naked and their round brown heads glistening with traces of white tooth enamel [fig.1].

And yet these were persons of great talent and variety, farmers, fighters, land-owners, poets, artists, criminals. These were the makers of East Anglia who lived through the most

crucial period in our history: the transition from pagan folk to Christian nation. We know this because along with the sandy elegy of their bodies they left us a mass of objects made out of gold, silver, bronze, iron, wood and pottery which have largely survived the gnawing acids of the centuries. From about AD 450, black-stamped pottery urns were placed in holes. They contained the remains of men, women and children cremated on a pyre, wearing their clothes and ornaments and often accompanied by sheep, cattle, horses and dogs. Some of these will have been immigrants from Germany and Denmark, Angles from Angeln on the Jutland peninsula. Grave 84 at Snape contained the remains of a woman with a comb, beads and spindle whorl for spinning, all much

Fig. 1. A sand-body under excavation at Sutton Hoo distorted into fragments by the heat,

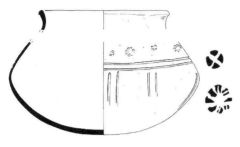

Fig. 2. Cremation urn 84 from the cemetery at Snape

gathered up and placed in a pot decorated with stripes and rosettes [fig.2].

Through the irresistible powers of love, sex and marriage, these incomers were soon mixed into the British population that had farmed the land through the era of imperial Rome, and before that when their ancestors had been members of the Iron Age kingdom of the Trinovantes, and before that, and before that. The new mixture began to create their own regions – the north folk and the south folk, together East Angles – to distinguish themselves from their brothers in the Midlands. Building an identity means building more than a closed community with loyalties to village and valley. In the Europe of the sixth century it meant putting down roots deep into the soil, burying ancestors who were well-labelled and would be recognised easily in the next world. The men were carriers of weapons – the spear and shield – and the women were bearers of brooches and beads, both dressed for parade. The women's brooches secured the *peplos* – a back-and-front pinafore fastened at the shoulder, with strings of coloured glass and amber beads festooned between the brooches. Brooches – and some weapons – are decorated with strange patterns of animal heads, feet, jaws and claws, all locked in some fossilised struggle. Much bronze, often gilded, was put into the ground in the sixth century. This was a wealthy, conservative, kin-based society, whose artists incidentally deserve to be much better known [fig.3].

But this stable world was not destined to last. From Europe in the late sixth century came the champions of the new political agenda, led by Christian thinkers. The new deal had both its demands and its promises: one family to rule all the others, a college of priests to regulate their morals, loyalty to a European ideology; and, in exchange, access to the commercial honey-pots of France, Italy and the Mediterranean. Of course the pagan Anglo-Saxons already had an aristocracy and had their own holy men and more significantly holy women – their 'cunning women'. But now there were hard decisions to make: should we go into Christian Europe, or keep faith with our north sea ancestors; embrace the new order or shore up the old?

At this point the story is taken up by the most famous burial site of them all: that at Sutton Hoo. Opposite Woodbridge a small promontory (*hoo*) overlooks the River Deben at its tidal limit. In the sixth century

Fig. 3. Square-headed brooch from an unlocated grave in Suffolk

a group of furnished graves and cremations of the usual type was placed there, showing that one or more families were in residence. Towards the end of the century, some of the funerals were putting on airs: a cremation not in a pot but in a bronze bowl, and small earth mounds heaped to aid the powers of remembrance. At this moment, roughly coincident with the arrival of St Augustine at Canterbury, one family decided to bury one of their number in a new place and in a specially grand manner. They choose a patch of ground 300 yards to the south, where the earthworks of an old field system still showed. And there they celebrated someone who had died in battle, from sword-cuts on the head. They cremated

Fig. 4. Strap-ends from the horse harness in Mound 17 at Sutton Hoo

him with a horse and sheep and placed the burnt bone in a bronze bowl, with a silver-mounted cup, a comb, iron shears, a knife, something made of glass, something made of ivory. Over the pit containing the bowl, a mound was raised by groups of people digging pits and throwing the soil onto a rising heap, 10m across (Mound 5). Then cattle were killed and eaten and the heads tossed back into the quarry pits. So the Sutton Hoo cemetery began.

This mound was soon joined by others: young men cremated with horses, sheep and cattle and placed in bronze bowls with fragments of weapons and board games (Mounds 4, 6 and 7). The newly prominent aristocracy of the area was signalling its independence with emphatic burial rites, Germanic, pagan and princely. The next young man to be celebrated, a warrior less than 25 years old, rang the changes of pagan practice. He was not cremated but placed in a wooden coffin, with sword, shield, spears, a cauldron for cooking and a bronze bowl for drinking. Stacked outside the coffin at one end was a pile of leather, with gilded links and strap ends and silver pendants: a horse's bridle with a snaffle bit and head piece, all resplendent in gilded bronze and vivid with animal ornament and human faces [fig.4]. Buried under the same mound but in a separate pit was the young man's horse.

In the first twenty years of the seventh century the pagan changes were rung again, this time to favour burial in boats. This practice is widely known in Scandinavia, from the second century to the tenth. But in all England the only boat burials known are from the Alde and the Deben. It started modestly with boats that were dug out of a log, or made of bark or lashed planks. In Grave 47 at Snape the dead man had a sword, a spear, a shield, a knife and an iron-bound bucket. All were placed in or beside the boat – now a shadow in the ground pointed at both ends and about 3m long [fig.5]. It had the ghost of a thwart too, and it is easy to imagine the Alde estuary full of such things, scudding about like canoes, ferrying people and animals on regular journeys.

Then came the great ships: one at least at Snape and two at Sutton Hoo. In the first Sutton Hoo ritual (Mound 2), a clinker-built ship 20m long was dragged over the top of a subterranean chamber grave containing a nobleman flanked with weapons and feasting equipment. The ship was pointed at both ends, and its planks were fastened to each other with iron rivets. The earth mound was then thrown over the top of it. The same kind of ship, but bigger, was used for a burial at Snape (Grave 1) and most famously at Sutton Hoo Mound 1, where by good fortune the ship and its contents escaped the attention of tomb robbers and early archaeologists, and thereby left us one of the richest burials to have survived in Europe.

The Mound 1 ship, 30m long, was dragged down below ground level into a giant trench. Then a burial chamber was erected amidships [fig.6]. It had a wooden floor and was roofed by solid beams; within its dark interior was a great timber coffin dug out from a tree trunk about 1.6m (5ft) in diameter. Inside the coffin lay the dead man and a heap of his clothes: tunics, shoes, a cap of otter fur. Thrown

Fig. 5. One of the boats under excavation at Snape, with Angela Evans and Tim Pestell

Fig. 6. The Mound 1 ship under excavation in 1939, with Basil Brown in the background and Charles Philips

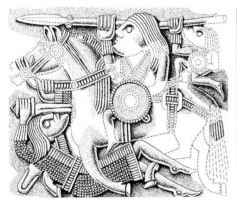

Fig. 7. (above) Horseman and fallen warrior, a detail
from the Sutton Hoo helmet

Fig. 8. (right) Animal art from the Sutton Hoo purse-lid

over the lid of the coffin was an exotic yellow cloak, and on this was laid the glittering parade uniform of a commander: a 'Sam Browne' with strap distributors and epaulettes of solid gold inlaid with garnets, an ornamented sword, an iron helmet inlaid with gold and decorated with scenes celebrating the doings of warriors and gods [fig.7]. Outside the coffin, an iron standard, a sceptre, cauldrons for feasting and a Maplewood lyre. The art of the Sutton Hoo ship burial is the best of its day; with its writhing animals and geometric grids, its dancing figures and swirling spirals it alludes to Britain, Scandinavia, France and Rome, both the ancient Rome and new Rome of Christ [fig.8]. But everything taken from abroad is suborned to the special message of the Sandlings. Here we can peer a little into life in the great hall, where the leader and his companions were drinking, munching, gossiping, arguing and then doing a bit of pompous speechifying. And then they fall into a tearful silence for the bard, who chants long lines of melody in memory of great deeds, no doubt embroidered in words as well as music. And then more drink and more argument about the rise and rise of political pressures, from north, east, south and west, and the perpetual question: what are our people to do?

The occupant of Mound 1 had achieved some kind of kingship, and his burial, around AD 625, is a theatrical vignette of his struggle to reconcile the forces competing for the future: an attempt to combine the best of the new world, with its nation building and its 'first family', with the best of the old, with its ancestral loyalties to Scandinavia and the sea. Membership of Christian Europe had its advantages but it was a closed system, shutting out the Danes and Norwegians. East Angles planned for an autonomous future as a pagan kingdom with equal access to the markets of north and south. However, in the event the force of the European project was too great. In the mid-eighth century the last pagan burial took place: a wealthy dowager, refusing to bend to the times, was interred in a plank-lined chamber on a couch, bedecked with silver.

That marked the end of the burial ground of the East Anglian princes, but not the last of its use. Under the management of Christian kings, Sutton Hoo became a place for the disposal of dissidents. From the eighth to the tenth centuries some thirty-nine people were executed and buried around two gallows sites – one on the fringe of the burial mounds, and the other on Mound 5, Sutton Hoo's founder grave. The sandy limbs of their bodies

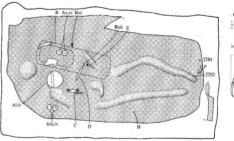

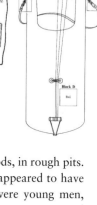

Fig. 10. The Musician's grave (Grave 32) excavated at Snape, with (right) the reconstruction of his lyre

Fig. 9. Decapitated victim from the Sutton Hoo 8th-century execution cemetery

lay, bent and mutilated without grave goods, in rough pits. Some had certainly been hanged, others appeared to have decomposed on a gibbet [fig.9]. Most were young men, that cadre of dissent; but in other graves a man and woman lay together, and in one a middle-aged man lay decapitated and face down with two young women, face down, on top of him. Of which misdemeanours, what offensive customs or what cruel misfortune had brought these anonymous victims to their fate, we know nothing.

We see only that the burial ground which had hosted kings now only hosted outcasts. The old pagan families reinvented themselves swiftly as Christian princes, and their kingdom, refashioned in the European mode, became one of the key building blocks of the new England.

Nevertheless, country people do not forget. Beneath the ground a multitude of edged weapons and the gilded costumes belonging to the many fine women of the day continued to lie undisturbed and respected. There might be a new order, but the roots of the old, as intended, lay deep. Politicians love to organise and manage, but the land has its own long logic. Among the ancestors that lay near to Aldeburgh was the *Snape musician*, whose sand body lay on its back, with a shield and buckle, knife and bowl, and, cradled in his arms, the fragments of a six-stringed lyre [fig.10]. A soldier poet then, a bard, a scop, who did the honours at the feasts, and was remembered with such affection that those who missed him, and his music, buried him with his lyre. Of eight lyres known from Anglo-Saxon England, five lie in East Anglian graves within 20 miles of Aldeburgh. Our current expert on Anglo-Saxon music, Graeme Lawson, calls it a sixth-century centre of artistic activity and patronage. So music too lies among the deep roots beneath the Maltings and the world of Peter Grimes and Benjamin Britten.

Sources

Martin Carver, *Sutton Hoo. Burial Ground of Kings?*, British Museum, 1998, 2001, 2005.

Martin Carver, *Sutton Hoo. A Seventh-century princely burial ground and its context*, British Museum, 2005.

William Filmer-Sankey and Tim Pestell, *Snape Anglo-Saxon Cemetery Excavations and Surveys 1924–1992* (East Anglian Archaeology 95, 2001).

Stanley West, *A Corpus of Anglo-Saxon Material from Suffolk* (East Anglian Archaeology 84, 1998).

Aldborough

Wilkie Collins

Wilkie Collins set the crucial confrontation of his novel No Name *(1862) in Aldeburgh on the coast of Suffolk, using the contemporary spelling of Aldborough. Local people complained that there were at least six ways of spelling the name of the town. In the 1860s train timetables and local newspapers used Aldborough, though at some point since, Aldeburgh has become standard. Collins seems to have visited the town at the end of August 1861.*

No documentary evidence of his stay in Aldeburgh has been found, though local folklore says that he arrived 'in the summer, on the train'. Direct trips from London had been possible since 12 April 1860 when the last section of the branch line from Ipswich, off the main London-to-Norwich route, which was opened in June 1859, was extended the final 5 miles from Leiston to the coast. At the time in which the novel was set, July 1846, the line ran only as far as Ipswich and that line had only been extended from Colchester on 1 June 1846. From Ipswich to Aldeburgh was a 30-mile coach journey, taking several hours – a fact not mentioned in No Name.

But when Collins made the journey, if he did, it was all by rail, starting at Bishopsgate Station in east London and taking four hours in total, nearly half of that being the relatively short trip from Ipswich. At Aldeburgh the station was nearly a mile from the town and travellers were met by coaches from the East Suffolk Hotel in the High Street to be conveyed to their lodgings. The following descriptions of the town are from Scene 4, part 1 of No Name.

The most striking spectacle presented to a stranger by the shores of Suffolk, is the extraordinary defencelessness of the land against the encroachments of the sea.

At Aldborough, as elsewhere on this coast, local traditions are, for the most part, traditions which have been literally drowned. The site of the old town, once a populous and thriving port, has almost entirely disappeared in the sea. The German Ocean has swallowed up streets, market-places, jetties, and public walks; and the merciless waters, consummating their work of devastation, closed no longer than eighty years since, over the salt-master's cottage at Aldborough, now famous in memory only, as the birthplace of the poet CRABBE.

Thrust back year after year by the advancing waves, the inhabitants have receded, in the present century, to the last morsel of land which is firm enough to be built on – a strip of ground hemmed in between a marsh on one side and the sea on the other. Here, trusting for their future security to certain sandhills which the capricious waves have thrown up to encourage them, the people of Aldborough have boldly established their quaint little watering-place. The first fragment of their earthly possessions, is a low natural dyke of shingle, surmounted by a public path which runs parallel with the sea. Bordering this path in a broken, uneven line are the villa residences of modern Aldborough – fanciful little houses, standing mostly in their own gardens, and possessing here and there, as horticultural ornaments, staring figure-heads of ships, doing duty for statues among the flowers. Viewed from the low level on which these villas stand, the sea, in certain conditions of the atmosphere, appears to be higher than the land: coasting vessels gliding by, assume gigantic proportions, and look alarmingly near the windows. Intermixed with the houses of the better sort, are buildings of other forms and periods. In one direction, the tiny Gothic town hall of old Aldborough – once the centre of the vanished port and borough – now stands fronting the modern villas close on the margin of the sea. At another point, a wooden tower of observation, crowned by the figure-head of a wrecked Russian vessel, rises high above the neighbouring houses; and discloses through its scuttle-window, grave men in dark clothing, seated on the topmost story, perpetually on the watch – the pilots of Aldborough looking out from their tower, for ships in want of help. Behind the row of buildings thus curiously intermingled, runs the one straggling street of the town, with its sturdy pilots' cottages, its mouldering marine storehouses, and its composite shops. Towards the northern end, this street is bounded by the one eminence visible over all the marshy flat – a low wooded hill on which the church is built. At its opposite extremity, the street leads to a deserted Martello tower, and to the forlorn outlying suburb of Slaughden, between the River Alde and the sea. Such are the main characteristics of this curious little outpost on the shores of England as it appears at the present time.

* * *

Slowly and in silence the two walked on, until they reached the southern limit of the houses, and entered on a little wilderness of shingle and withered grass – the desolate end of Aldeburgh, the lonely beginning of Slaughden.

It was a dull airless evening. Eastward was the gray majesty of the sea, hushed in breathless clam; the horizon line invisibly melting into the monotonous misty sky; the idle ships shadowy and still on the idle water. Southward, the high ridge of the sea dyke, and the grim massive circle of a Martello tower, reared high on its mound of grass, closed the view darkly on all that lay beyond. Westward, a lurid streak of sunset glowed red in the dreary heaven – blackened the fringing trees on the far borders of the great inland marsh – and turned its gleaming water-pools to pools of blood. Nearer to the eye, the sullen flow of the tidal River Alde ebbed noiselessly from the muddy banks; and nearer still, lonely and unprosperous by the bleak waterside, lay the lost little port of Slaughden; with its forlorn wharfs and warehouses of decaying wood, and its few scattered coasting vessels deserted on the oozy river shore. No fall of waves was heard on the beach; no trickling of water bubbled audibly from the idle stream. Now and then, the cry of a sea-bird rose from the region of the marsh, and, at intervals, from farm-houses far in the inland waste, the faint winding of horns to call the cattle home, travelled mournfully through the evening calm.

John Craske and Sylvia Townsend Warner

Ian Collins

In 1927 the poet Valentine Ackland called at a fisherman's cottage at Hemsby on the Norfolk coast to buy a model boat and found pictures of ships sailing, waves surging and lighthouse signalling on every surface – doors, lids, trays, ornaments and pastry board. Valentine (well-named because she looked the spit of matinée idol Rudolph Valentino) had just discovered John Craske, one of Britain's greatest naive artists. Craske was frail but the visitor was amazed by the vitality of his paintings. She begged to buy a portrait of a ship called *The James Edward* for 30 shillings (£1.50) [see plate 6]. Although the image was Mrs Craske's pride and joy, so vast a sum was gladly accepted in a stricken household often reduced to barter.

Two years later the work was spotted in Valentine's London flat by a West End art dealer and the poet was sent back to Hemsby to trawl for an exhibition. First fearing a demand for a refund, the painter's wife sorted the transfer of paintings and tapestries while her spouse was in one of many comas. Successful shows followed in London and the United States, along with a commission for the Courtauld family yacht. But the disabled fisherman, who died in 1943, never himself saw his work exhibited. After Valentine's death, in 1969, the images she had collected formed an Aldeburgh Festival show arranged by her partner, the writer Sylvia Townsend Warner, who bequeathed them to Snape Maltings to celebrate her friendship with Peter Pears. By that point other Craske pictures had been given to the Red House.

Born in Sheringham in 1881, one of nine children, Craske had followed generations of forebears to sea. He worked out of Grimsby for a time, before the family moved in 1905 to East Dereham, to open a fishmonger's shop. The staunch Salvation Army member married Laura Eke in 1908 – the bride recalling their first meeting in the town thus: 'There was a soap box in the centre of the ring upon which a tall young man in a fisherman's blue jersey stands, his black curly hair is ruffled by the breeze. He is nervous. But he starts to sing: "Since Christ my soul from sin set free…".' For the next nine years the couple worked in happy hardship, smoking and curing fish which the tireless young man then hawked around mid-Norfolk from baskets on two ponies – toiling seventeen-hour days bar Sundays.

Saved from the trenches on health grounds, Craske appealed and was called up in May 1917. Within weeks he was felled by influenza and, after a 'brain abscess' left him prone to nervous collapse, moved to the mental wing of Norwich War Hospital. He then became one of those veterans for whom an internal war never ceased. In October 1918 the invalid was discharged with 'harmless mental stupors' into the care of his stalwart wife. In fact, his nervous afflictions were compounded by undiagnosed diabetes. The couple opened a fish shop in Dereham but in 1920, on the death of his father, John Craske collapsed and was confined to a wheelchair. During a bid for recovery at Wiveton he carved, painted and sailed to Blakeney Point in a little boat. This period is recalled in an epic feat of needlework – a 4.5-metre map of the North Norfolk coast, now in Glandford Shell Museum, near Holt.

The materials of his art were found oddments – old wood, lining paper, distemper, housepaint, whitewash, children's watercolours. Home-made frames were decorated with shells and pebbles. To save the price of nails, models were held together by old gramophone needles. However poor the media, the artist's imagination was rich. His talent was wholly free.

As Craske told his tale: 'I was ill in bed for three years, which I remember very little about, after which I just felt something that I cannot explain urging me on to make pictures of the sea and ships. Continually fresh ideas are flashing through my mind and when I hear the thrilling stories of sea rescues on the wireless, I make a note of them and hope some day to put them in pictures. I thank God for this gift as I realise it comes from Him!' Sylvia Townsend Warner wrote: 'He painted like a man giving witness under oath to a wild story.... Most artists know the sea from its edge. Craske knew it from the middle, from experience of being a small upright movement in a vast swaying horizontality...'.

When those coastal vigils failed to secure convalescence, John and Laura returned to Dereham. Here they were visited in 1931 by Valentine and Sylvia – the latter recording in her diary: 'He was lying in bed by the window, a crumpled-faced man with darting eyes, and large pale hands. Mrs C was short, upstanding, pale, sallow. Her knobbed hair and folded hands gave her the air of something by Craske – a model of a woman.' Guided by his wife, the bed-ridden artist now took to weaving nautical pictures from scraps of wool and cheap silk thread. The first was sewn on a piece of calico intended for a Christmas pudding, with a blue bag and distempered clouds completing the sky when the wools ran out.

There is a striking parallel with Alfred Wallis – the Cornish fisherman-turned-shopkeeper and abiding Salvationist whose naïve paintings, produced amid mounting infirmity, now fetch many thousands of pounds. Both men depicted a marine world of storms and shipwrecks, of boats afloat or berthed on slipways and of cottage terraces seemingly set to slide into the sea. Each scene may be read as a metaphor for rocky life encrusted with firm faith and wild beauty. Craske often recalled prayer meetings on rolling ships as the moon's reflection on the sea was scanned for shoals of whiting. And a final piece of needlework, held by Norfolk Museums and Archaeology Service, is a 3.5-metre Dunkirk panorama with soldiers wading towards waiting vessels beneath flaming, falling planes. Unfinished on the artist's death, the last campaign in a life of struggle contains a hole in the sky – where a doggedly devout artist was sure God would be.

Without the devoted Laura Craske there would have been no art, and the unbegun artist would almost certainly have died in 1918. In the Aldeburgh Festival exhibition catalogue of 1971 Sylvia Townsend Warner wrote: 'After Laura Craske had shown him the way to fill in the boat he had drawn on the pudding-cloth, he developed his stitch technique unguided. He liked approval, and was pleased with earnings, but neither affected him. The one exception was his dreams about the sea. A particular dream of a tempest with much lightning was so compelling that when he woke and asked what day it was, and heard it was Sunday, he broke through the Sabbatarianism of a lifetime and worked all day, making sure of the lightning. That picture he gave to his wife. But in a truer sense, all his pictures were hers. But for her devotion they would not have come into being. Against all reason, all regulations, she set herself to get him, lying senseless as a log, out of the Norwich Asylum.'

And as for Valentine and Sylvia – well, the latter produced two fine historical novels set in Norfolk, *The Flint Anchor* and *The Corner that Held Them*. The two writers were sustained by Sylvia's earnings, chiefly from short stories published in the *New Yorker*. The couple often visited Valentine's family in Winterton and lived for a time at Sloley, near North Walsham. They braved the winter of 1950 at Great Eye Folly – a gaunt turret on the exposed shore at Salthouse, built by Victorian speculative builder and womaniser Onesiphorous Randall and later used as a coastguard station. They subsequently tried to buy this forbidding fortress, where Sylvia noted in her diary that 'The east wind sobs and whimpers like a Brontë in the kitchen', but wisely moved on, for the building was to vanish beneath the Great Flood of 1953.

What remain are words and pictures. Sylvia's poem 'John Craske's Country' throws lines about stoic and even heroic life into a refrain about icy winds and salt water – as in:

Love on this coast is something you must dispute
With a wind blowing from the North Pole and only salt water between.

John Craske

A Visit to Snape

Aaron Copland

One thing that growing old denies one is the kind of camaraderie that creative youngsters share at the beginning of their careers. This is particularly true in music, where the line between young and old is often sharply drawn. Young composers need one another, for they learn more from the attentive eye and sensitive ear of a fellow-craftsman than from almost any other source. Long before you are afforded the luxury of hearing your own orchestration in actual sound there is the possibility that a young colleague will 'hear' it for you. Peering at the same four measures of orchestral score for fifteen minutes, carefully weighing the pros and cons of instrumental balance while you wait with bated breath, your composer friend is likely to come up with some completely unexpected judgment such as you never would have thought of yourself.

It is this kind of composer rapport that I connect with a visit to Snape a quarter of a century ago. Despite my usually stumbling memory, I can still recall the weekend I spent there and the excitement of exchanging ideas with a new-found composer friend, Benjamin Britten, then aged twenty-four.

We had only recently come to know one another at a concert of the International Society of Contemporary Music. The 1938 International Festival was being held in London that year and I had come from America to hear Sir Adrian Boult give the European premiere of my *El Salon Mexico*. A few days before that performance, I had heard my first Britten piece, the *Variations on a Theme of Frank Bridge*. My delight at the technical adroitness and instrumental wizardry of that early composition is still vivid in my memory. Perhaps the fact that we were both represented by the lighter side of our wares drew us together. In any event, our chance meeting had the happy result for me of an invitation to Snape, where the young composer was living at that time.

The address I was given had an air of quaint charm – at least, for an American it had: The Old Mill, Snape, Saxmundham, Suffolk. And the places themselves, both the old mill and the village, were no less charming and quaint. I hadn't realised before my arrival that we were in East Anglia, nor had I any idea of Britten's strong attachment to his home territory. His studio in a converted windmill was in strong contrast to the studio in the loft I had in my own home territory of New York. Our backgrounds and circumstances were clearly different, but the affinity of our musical interests was soon apparent.

Taking advantage of a sunny spell, we spent a day with family and friends on the nearby shingle. (Why have we no shingle in America?) Before long it became clear that the assembled group was in danger of 'roasting'. When I politely pointed out the obvious result to be expected from lying unprotected on the beach, I was told: 'But we see the sun so rarely'(!)

246

What I remember best, of course, was the exchange of musical impressions of all sorts. I had with me the proofs of my school opera, *The Second Hurricane*, composed for young people of fourteen to seventeen. It had been performed the previous year for the first time by a group of talented students at a Lower East Side settlement school in New York. It didn't take much persuasion to get me to play it from start to finish, singing all the parts of principals and chorus in the usual composer fashion. Britten seemed pleased. Sometimes I flatter myself that his subsequent preoccupation with young voices may have been in part an offshoot of his pleasure in *The Second Hurricane*. Occasionally I've even had the illusion of hearing an echo of one of the choruses of the opera ('What's happened, Where are they?') in a fleeting moment of a Britten work. Illusion or not, I like to think of it as a souvenir of Snape.

In return for my playing of the opera, Britten played me his recently completed Piano Concerto No. 1. I was immediately struck by the obvious flair for idiomatic piano writing in the concerto, but had some reservations as to the substance of the musical materials. Here was a delicate moment: I felt my enthusiasm was half-hearted by comparison with his own. As it turned out, I had no need for concern: if anything, my frankly expressed opinion helped to cement our growing friendship. (For the record, it should be added that what I heard was a first version of the Piano Concerto; it was revised by the composer seven years later.)

Less than a year after this visit, Britten was on his way to North America. Perhaps our meeting in Snape had some part in his decision to try his luck abroad. In any case, it is certain that the few years he spent in America were deeply formative ones. They will have to be studied in depth by anyone who wishes to follow the steady growth in stature of this greatly gifted composer and warm friend.

These memories of his earliest meetings with Benjamin Britten form Copland's contribution to a collection of essays, letters, poems and pictures gathered together by Anthony Gishford and published as A Tribute to Benjamin Britten on his Fiftieth Birthday. *The book – a complete surprise – was given to Britten at a celebratory dinner on 22 November 1963. A few days later he wrote thus to Copland:*

'I was so touched by your wire ... and also by the warm & gay bit you wrote for my handsome birthday tribute! How well I remember, & how I enjoyed your visit to Snape – not least your gentle but firm rubbing down of my scarlet & blistered back! (What fools we English are about the sun.) It was noble of you to spend time on writing this for the book, knowing how busy you are – but it was much appreciated.'

Clerihews on Visitors to Aldeburgh

Craig Brown

Algernon Swinburne
let his skin burn.
He forgot the Skin Factor Five
On a trip to Covehithe.

Thomas Carlyle
Might permit himself a smile
If it would cause his wife Jane
Visible pain.

Thomas Hardy
Said, 'Hey gang – let's pardee!'
But he omitted his wife
From his Aldeburgh life.

W.H. Auden
Took a day-trip to Slaughden
In the footsteps of Gissing
But, alas, found it missing.

Paul Theroux
Is not keen on *Who's Who*
He says, 'It's no good at all
It includes V.S. Naipaul'.

Algernon Swinburne wrote *By the North Sea*, inspired by the coast between Dunwich and Covehithe. *Thomas Carlyle* called Aldeburgh 'a beautiful little sea town' but this rare bout of happiness did little to improve his stormy relations with Mrs Carlyle. *Thomas Hardy* paid regular clandestine visits to Crag Path, Aldeburgh, with his mistress Florence Dugdale, while the first Mrs Hardy remained home in Dorset. *W.H. Auden* was a friend of Benjamin Britten, for whom he wrote the libretto of *Paul Bunyan*. George Gissing, author of *New Grub Street*, was an occasional guest of Edward Clodd. *Paul Theroux* visited Aldeburgh on his literary journey around England in 1977. More recently he published a sullen memoir of his former friend V.S. Naipaul.

Sidney Nolan on Britten

During the 1990 Aldeburgh Festival, on 11 June in the Jubilee Hall, Sidney Nolan, interviewed and encouraged by Donald Mitchell, remembered his long professional and personal association with Benjamin Britten. Nolan responded creatively to Britten's music, often with extended series of paintings, and he also unlocked for Britten other worlds – the exposed landscape of his native Australia, an ancient indigenous civilisation, an atavistic inner world – that chimed with and informed the composer's vision. Sadly, although collaboration was discussed between them (a ballet, a sea symphony, Coleridge's Ancient Mariner) – *and their informal mutual influence is perhaps unquantifiable – proposed projects remained unfulfilled. The final connection between the two artists was for the 1991 Aldeburgh Festival Japanese production of* Sumidagawa *(the Noh play on which* Curlew River *is based), for which Sidney Nolan agreed to design the obligatory pine tree. He died on 27 November 1992.*

What follows here are edited extracts from his conversation with Donald Mitchell.

I started coming to the Festival in 1950, but I didn't know anybody for some years. When Britten was writing *Billy Budd* I was here with Kenneth Clark and he kindly offered to take me to meet Ben. He was writing at that particular time the piece of music where the captain, Vere, tells Billy that he's going to die, he's going to be hanged - the most terrible sort of human thing to have in your brain, but the most wonderful artistic thing. He told me what an intense experience it was to envisage the scene and to write it. I was enthralled by this description of the creative process, when it steals into you in some way and then reaches a peak and you can do things under the influence of that situation that you can't otherwise do. You can only do it at that moment when there's been a build-up of some mysterious nature, and he was right in the middle of that. So that's what started our understanding of each other. We either had a shared innocence or a shared opposite.

It made a big difference to my life. I had the choice between going back to Australia and coming every year to the Aldeburgh Festival, or staying in England for the Aldeburgh Festival and going out to Australia every year to see my family. I opted for the latter.

* * *

I had an exhibition here of, I think, twenty-four *Shakespeare Sonnets* [in 1964]. That was triggered off by the Shakespeare Sonnet of Ben ['When most I wink' in *Nocturne*]. I read the Sonnets and I took the last two lines, which are often very sombre, where Shakespeare has a kind of whiplash, and I produced these twenty-four or twenty-five paintings and had an exhibition here. Ben came along and said, 'Mmm. That looks a bit like Peter. That looks a bit like you and that looks a bit like me. Nobody seems to look like Shakespeare.'

It was a very sombre exhibition. It was all about a personal experience of mine, a hidden relationship in my life that I never discuss – rather like the Vere thing – but I was able to put it into the *Sonnets*. Shakespeare was exactly it and Ben's treatment of the Sonnet had kind of opened them up for me. Everybody has these things in their lives, a hidden relationship or a hidden desire or loss or whatever it might be. You don't talk about it, you don't ever express ... I mean, some things in one's life one will never paint, but it only needs something on the same wavelength, as Ben's music was, to unlock it. That's a fortuitous thing, kind of like fate; you might miss the performance, you might never hear the work.

Everybody knows what a piece of wheat is like. Everybody understands the nature of wheat and how it grows. Everybody understands what a bird is like, how it's built – but nobody understands the moment that the bird's going to swoop. That's where the fate comes in. That moment is unknown. It's unpredictable when the bird is going to just dive down. It's a bit like that. It's that unpredictable, fateful moment when the key is in the lock and – [Mitchell: And a mysterious hand turns it.] And it's just turned.

✳ ✳ ✳

[Our friendship] was always steady, polite. On one occasion he said, 'Shall we go for a walk? Schubert liked to go for a walk with somebody as long as they didn't speak.' Sure enough, we walked for about a quarter of an hour around the landscape and we said nothing, and when we got back he said, 'I enjoyed that.' It was like that. We had an instinctive understanding of silence.

✳ ✳ ✳

One of the reasons for the trip [to Australia, with the English Opera Group in 1970] was that we should all go together and that Peg [HRH Princess Margaret of Hesse and the Rhine} should see Australia and experience it. It was not only the [Adelaide] Festival; it was also personal. We were all going to make a big journey together and travel all round Australia.

We went up to Ayers Rock. It's an extraordinary place and very beautiful. As we got out of the aeroplane at Alice Springs, Ben saw these Aboriginal boys at the airport. They're terribly graceful – not elegant, but beautifully graceful. The light was crystal clear and the landscape was pink and it was just at that moment, [with] these boys just walking across, and Ben said, 'Isn't that marvellous?'

Next to Ayers Rock there's another extraordinary clump of mountains, called Mount Olga, rather like Kubla Khan. From a distance they're amethyst and purple and lavender and all kinds of things. From five miles away it's one colour and from ten miles away it's another and from fifteen – it's a marvellous transition of colour. I went with Ben up to a rather inaccessible place that I knew about in the middle of these mountains, where there was an Aboriginal water hole. It was a sacred water hole. It was completely silent and a marvellous sort of atmosphere, this peculiar silence that we'd agreed upon should exist between us like Schubert, and he suddenly said, 'Australia hasn't made a sound yet.'

And my heart leapt because I realised that something had clicked in him and he was going to be the one who was going to make the sound that Australia hadn't yet made. One has to point out very quickly that the Aboriginals had been making the most marvellous sounds for forty thousand years. Ben investigated all that with computers and musicologists and all that, but what he was really thinking of was that he would do something to sum up his feelings toward these Aboriginal boys and the beauty of the landscape, this extraordinary colour, and this uncanny silence that exists in Australia for Europeans. I feel it when I'm there and I was born there. Just uncanny silence – not discomforting – it's quite comforting ...

We were going to go up the Barrier Reef. We flew to Brisbane and we came to a place called Townsville. Well, this was the place where my young brother, who drowned in the war, was buried. So I got out of the aeroplane and I went over to a corner of the compound and I stood there in very hot sun. Ben came over and said, 'Why're you standing here like that?'

And I said, 'Well, my young brother's buried here.'

And he said, 'Do you mind if I stand with you?' Once again we did the same thing; we stood for about ten minutes in silence, And then comes something which is rather complicated to explain.

He told me about a kind of ballet that he would plan to do for Covent Garden. He'd decided not to do an opera but he would do a ballet and it would be on Australia, and he wanted me to work out something to do with Aboriginals. He had a story of a friend of his who tragically hanged himself on the morning of his wedding, I think it was at Oxford. He didn't tell me who it was, but it was quite a deep thing in him. [Nolan is slightly misremembering an account of the suicide of Piers Dunkerley, a dedicatee of the *War Requiem*. An important childhood friend of Britten, Dunkerley was wounded at Dunkirk and spent a time in a German prison camp. He died of an overdose (seconal and alcohol) in June 1959, depressed by redundancy and tensions with his fiancée.]

* * *

[Britten] had the feeling that Western civilisation wasn't bringing up its children properly and he felt that the Aboriginals in the past had. They reared their children to deal with life and be at one with it, and we hadn't done that. We'd got it more kind of complicated and more difficult. He was going to try and show on the stage the two things simultaneously: the life of the boy growing up in the Australian Aboriginal tribe and the life of a boy growing up and going to Oxford and everything ... and have the tragic ending on the one hand, of the English boy, and the kind of ordeal of fire and water the Aboriginals have, a kind of *Magic Flute* ending for the Aboriginal.

In the telling of it he became very – and this is difficult for me to explain – boyish and very happy and very approachable. Just completely easy. It was a side of him that I had actually never seen. It lasted for about an hour and a half and I was overwhelmed by this revelation of his identity. And then we were due to land at Cairns and he suddenly said, 'Well, that's the end of that. When we get back to England I won't be like that any more. My destiny is to be in harness and to die in harness. There won't be any more of that.'

What I'm trying to explain, I think, is that the task of a creative artist in Ben's position is so immense, so overwhelming, that it [took] over all of his life and perhaps hid this other boyish, open, very touching thing. I knew all about being a painter and what that means – that you have to sacrifice part of your life to go through this complicated ordeal of producing something out of yourself. Ben obviously had this uncanny knowledge of what he was and what he had to be.

I prepared a kind of synopsis and between us we worked it all out. It led to my doing an enormous series of flower paintings called *Snake*, a panel of 1,500 paintings, 120 feet long and 20 feet high. It more or less consists of all the wild flowers that can come up in the desert in central Australia. There's a kind of paradise. When it rains there these flowers come up; some of them have been dormant for fifty years. The idea was that almost invisibly every four seconds [one of these flowers] would 'pulse' on stage - the kind of subliminal thing they do in advertising on television. I did thirty or forty of them and [Ben] came to dinner and we went upstairs and he looked at them and he said, 'They're very silent.'

Well, I took that as the greatest compliment. The man with the most wonderful ear in the world was able to hear the silence of the paintings.

So that was a project which of course I'm very sorry didn't come off. [But] he asked me to do something; he wanted me to do a boy as a memory of the ones he'd seen at Alice Springs, and to do something else to indicate the nature of it and so I did the boy with the boomerang painted on him [*The Initiation* – the same title as the proposed ballet; see plate 12].

* * *

I'd gone to Auschwitz in 1960, I think, for the *Observer*, to do some drawings there of the camp. I was so overwhelmed by the experience that I told Ben about it. Ben played the piano with [Yehudi] Menuhin in a concentration camp immediately after the war. I think we both felt that we knew something about what would be the situation with the invasion of Poland and the treatment of the children ... We had that link – a very tragic and terrifying link. But I think it was Auschwitz, really, which was behind our thinking [on *Children's Crusade*, the Brecht setting that inspired a series of paintings from Nolan].

I did a series of drawings for Britten, the sonnets of Donne, *The Holy Sonnets*. They were extremely tough and tragic. I showed them to Peter [Pears] and he said, 'Well, I wouldn't show them to Ben because they're very disturbing.'

And I said, 'Well, I'm sorry they're rather like that, but I had a temperature.' (I got flu one year and it lasted.)

And Peter said, 'Well, the extraordinary thing is that when Ben wrote the music for the Sonnets [after returning from Belsen] he also had a temperature.'

* * *

I just have a feeling that there's something to do with Britten that's rather like Mozart. It's as if fate didn't actually alter their original position as from children to grown men to death. They went straight through, always giving out this gift they were born with, that they had at the age of five, six, or seven; it just keeps on sort of flowing out of them . . .

Reprinted from the Festival programme book, 1993

A Memoir of Arthur Boyd

Brian Whelan

Arthur Boyd, who died in 1999, is commonly acknowledged as one of Australia's most significant artists. He was born in Murrumbeena, Victoria, in 1920 into a prodigiously creative family and was painting impressively from the age of fourteen. His subjects ranged from landscape to portraiture to social realism. An original member of 'The Angry Penguins Group', his work has given voice to a wide range of social, mythical and religious subjects, from his 'Half-Caste and Bride' series which echoed the plight of the Aboriginal condition to several series of paintings on St Francis, Narcissus, Australian landscapes and associated mythologies. The first time I had seen Arthur was in around 1978, in a film my mother had recommended I watch; she being interested in anything on artists, thinking I was 'quite artistic'. I still remember in the film how enthusiastic he was and the very physical way he engaged in landscape painting using long-bristled brushes that I had never seen before.

One damp November evening in 1983 I was visiting the National Gallery in Trafalgar Square, London, and was browsing in the bookshop when I spotted Arthur Boyd, heading for one of the many galleries. He was about sixty-three years old at the time. Under his long white fringe, I recognised his face immediately. With some cheek and with little to lose, I followed Arthur who stopped in one of the rooms to look at a painting. I took my opportunity to introduce myself but he surprised me by shaking me by the hand like an old friend and apologised for not remembering my name. It took a little time to disillusion him. The confusion of the next minute or so concluded with us sitting in front of the picture he was excited about and discussing it. Then instead of me engaging him in conversation about his career, he quickly engaged me in what I was doing. Where was I studying? How was I getting on? He declared how wonderful it must be to be able to see these great works all the time and how he didn't get into London as often as he would have liked to. After looking in his pockets for his phone number in Suffolk he said, 'Why don't you pop down to Fischer and ask them for it? I can't remember my number.' He then shuffled along to see the Rembrandts before the gallery closed.

I knew of Fischer Fine Art. Founded by Austrian Jews in Vienna, it transferred to London before the War. It had a reputation for showing some of the very best artists and hosting some of the city's most prestigious exhibitions and I was sure would not let me have Arthur Boyd's phone number. I was no more likely to get Madonna's phone number from a concert hall ticket office. They wouldn't do it. That night I left the National Gallery and stepped out into the gloomy London weather and went back to the studios where I worked until they kindly asked me to leave. My conclusion was that Boyd was just being polite and I put the whole incident to the back of my mind. But when the weather picked up, so did my optimism.

The story I told to other art students and friends and family of having met Arthur Boyd always seemed unsatisfactory because the next thing asked was, 'And did you go to Fischer?' 'No!' I said. 'You might as well try,' they said. And so I did. I popped into Fischer and told the young lady on the desk that Arthur Boyd had asked me to get his phone number from them as he couldn't remember it. 'Yes I know it sounds silly – you know what artists are like.' The girl was a temp and said she knew nothing about anything and there was no one around to ask. She tried to look helpful and rummaged in a desk, pulling out a book with telephone numbers in it. 'What was his name? Boyd? Arthur? Oh, here it is.' The next afternoon I gave Arthur a ring. He answered the phone, and remembered me. Could I come down on Sunday?

I had never been to Suffolk. In fact my knowledge of England, apart from London, was quite sketchy. I knew Ireland like the back of my hand as my Irish parents took us there every year to see family and friends, but Suffolk, a short train ride north-east from Liverpool St Station? No. I got to a place called Woodbridge early afternoon by changing at Ipswich. Arthur's wife Yvonne very kindly picked me up from the station and drove for half an hour to their house. It was a thatched cottage on the edge of an estuary. Arthur welcomed me and invited me to sit down with a group of people all having lunch. The other guests were trading paintings over the meal. After lunch, with all the deals struck, the guests left with Arthur, who offered to accompany them back to the station. Before he left, he took me into his studio, apologised for the mess and encouraged me to knock out a picture or two while he was gone, at which I laughed.

The studio was a large out-house. It wasn't a typical barn but may have been once used as one. It had a very high ceiling with skylights. It was a scene of utter chaos. Tubes of paint, tins and drawings, were left scattered and paintings were propped up precariously. Enormous newly primed canvases were stacked against the wall; some so big he used brooms, not brushes, to paint them with. Racks of music cassettes and piles of rags and overalls filled the corners. What surprised me was that all around me were paintings, not of Suffolk, but of Australia: what I took to be the outback and the wildness of bush and desert. As I looked at these paintings I felt the heat coming off the pictures. Boyd carried Australia in his heart and soul. They say 'You can take the Australian out of Australia but ...'

I knew Arthur had chosen to live in England for part of the year because he considered the English landscape tradition the core of the Australian landscape tradition. Of all the places in England to choose to live, Arthur chose an estuary near the home of one of England's greatest landscape painters, Constable. East Bergholt, where Constable painted *The Hay Wain* and *Dedham Vale*, was just a short drive away. He only had to step out of his studio door to see the famous big sky of East Anglia and to feel the wind and the rain. A very short walk would give him a full view of the estuary. The soft liquid colours and light of the Suffolk coastline were in stark contrast to the hot, parched, dusty ruggedness of the Australia that Arthur liked to paint.

Boyd's presence in this landscape could be seen simply as 'touching base'. A visit to the garden that had sowed a seed in Constable, which in turn had planted a seed in him that blossomed into an exotic, hybrid flower. In Australia Boyd had built order, design, structure, and found a new palette of colours for his work, but he remained anchored to this place. Boyd was aware of English gardens in Australia: rose gardens, topiary hedges and ponds, cultivated by homesick ex-patriots from England. He had returned the compliment. In his Suffolk studio the Australian outback burned off the canvas.

On Arthur's return we had more time to talk and despite a lot of cajoling I could not be persuaded to paint so he showed me what he was working on. A series of landscapes. He showed me how he used the surface of the canvas or board as an integral part of the making of the picture and then I caught sight of them. The brushes. A stack of long-bristled brushes on sheets of cardboard. I asked him where he got them from. He said he had them made specially.

Later we walked over to the house where again there were paintings everywhere. Behind wardrobes, in cupboards, under and on the beds. Some were even, more conventionally, on the walls. A million ideas for pictures. An energy that was breathtaking. And all the time asking my advice. 'What do you think, Brian? What would you do with that part of the picture? Is that too bright, too blue?' His kindness and enthusiastic engagement with a young student of art were very generous. I asked Arthur the question all art students wrestle with. How do you make a living out of art? He said he had no idea – but it was getting easier. Once there were only about six people who could make a living out of art and not resort to teaching. Now there are lots more. Arthur said the only way he could teach was by example and then told me how he had been invited to speak about his work at an English public school and the slide projector broke down so he had to describe the pictures and then talk about them. He said he never wanted to do that again.

He wanted to know about my background and the subject of Ireland came up. Irish culture was rich, he said. Did I know the work of Sidney Nolan? The Ned Kelly series? His own ancestors were Irish and he and Yvonne had visited Ireland a while back but he said he had been informed his ancestors were Ulster-Scots. 'The wrong kind of Irish!' he laughed. 'They have offered me a show there – but I don't think I can make it. Why don't you do it?' he asked with all seriousness. 'You can fill in for me.' If only real life was like that.

He was determined that I should look at my heritage more closely as a source of inspiration. As an artist he said I had to dig deep into all those stories and take what I needed. 'An artist has many facets. As an artist you must give people a facet they can enjoy and/or relate to. But don't worry about what to do. Do everything. Don't waste time.' He expressed shock and dismay at my confession of painting over old pictures and told me I was being indulgent. So far I had only felt indulgence if I bought a new canvas. 'Hey, you will have to come out to our home in Shoalhaven in Australia, you will love it there.' And I promised I would.

On that day we finished off at the local pub with a couple of pints and then Yvonne and Arthur drove me back to the station and I caught the last train just in time. I jumped on board, closed the door behind me and opened the window to say goodbye and thank-you to them both. Arthur thrust a handful of long-bristled brushes into my hand and stuffed a £5 note into my top pocket. 'Come and see us again!' he shouted as the train took off.

I never got to Shoalhaven but I did visit Arthur several times in Suffolk. The last time I saw him he said he was leaving England for Italy, basing himself there because he had decided the English couldn't see colour. He felt frustrated and needed a change. In typical Arthur Boyd fashion he said 'Give me a ring' and this time managed to find his phone number in Italy and encouraged me to come out. I said I would and shook his hand. I never saw him again.

One of my Pleasant Places

Joyce Grenfell

Joyce Grenfell and her husband Reggie visited the Aldeburgh Festival every year from 1962 until her death in 1979. For fifty years, between 1929 and 1979, Joyce Grenfell and her friend Virginia Graham exchanged letters, amounting to some six thousand documents. This correspondence, edited by Janie Hampton, was published in 1997 as Joyce and Ginnie: The Letters of Joyce Grenfell and Virginia Graham. *A selection of extracts is reproduced below.*

1962

I do love this Festival and this hotel [the Wentworth]. Everyone is concerned in the goings on and there is the sea and yesterday the sun shone. 'Amadeus' last night in a packed church. R. says he liked it. Liked the slow movement of the Mozart best. Then back to the church for the Deller Consort doing very early Flemish music. Ooh such sounds. Marvellous squeezed harmonies and cool soaring sounds rising out of richness. I thought it marvellous. The church floodlit, a moon and a warm night to walk in.

We saw nothing but sky above pale bending reeds. We saw marsh harriers (only two pairs in all England and Scotland and Wales), and bearded tits and beautiful giddy coloured redstarts. Etc.

Today is Blythburgh and some Tchaikovsky! Tonight harpsichords in the Parish Church.

Coming on Hans Keller, the musicologist, and his artist wife in a state of panic – they had no transport and he had to be at Blythburgh to supervise the concert, being broadcast by the BBC. So we took them over, taking a picnic with us. Heavenly church. Full of light it was and radiant. Lovely concert. Tchaikovsky and Mozart – interestingly unexpected mixture. Nobly I think I must give up the morning Debussy I crave and go early with R. to Minsmere for birds.

1966

I went to hear Imogen Holst give a lecture on 'What *is* Musical History?'

Dull you might think? It was utterly fascinating and absolutely first class. She came on trippingly, head down. Not a trace of powder or lipstick on that fifteenth-century head painted on wood. A pale beige dress blending in with face and hair. Almost invisible really. And then she began. It was a miracle of erudition, simplicity, interest, passion and wit. Haven't enjoyed anything more during the whole Festival, and it's been a very good Festival.

When Ben was nine years old and at prep school he went to a music shop in Lowestoft, and he found an early two-part song for women's voices by Gustav Holst. It was his very first contact with modern music.

Imogen Holst was caustic about critics who write of 'tendencies' and say that a composer is 'paving a way', etc. 'What they are doing', she said, 'is making music .. .' (or words to that effect) 'not creating tendencies.' She made us all sing a ten-part round, and that was a triumph for we did – first time.

The Festival Party in the Jubilee Hall was really great fun. Julian Bream prayed some jazzed-up Bach – superb. Surprise item Peter Pears singing 'The Owl and the Pussy Cat' in an amusing setting. Then a jam session with Emanuel Hurwitz (first fiddle of orchestra), Julian B. and a double-bass, and, unrehearsed, Peter, doing 'Night and Day'. His rhythm was appalling! No feel for the beat at all. Wasn't it interesting. A gay evening.

Aldeburgh has been *such* fun. Best year so far for weather and birds and music.

1967

We came in via Snape and went to see the new Hall. It's so attractive. The walls inside are red brick and the wood appears to be blond and unstained. The chairs are the same, with cane seats and backs. All so light and rural looking, without being in the least 'folksy'. Very spacious and gay looking.

We found John Piper putting the finishing touches to some large posterist coloured panels in the foyer. All a bit garish. The place was stiff with people doing last-minute jobs. Drink was being delivered to the fascinating restaurant with big windows looking straight out over the marsh. The BBC were everywhere. So were the film boys who are making the documentary I'm to be in on Thursday.[1] We had a good look round while it was comparatively empty, for tomorrow's crowds won't allow much exploring and HM [The Queen] will be in all the best places. I'd say it's a great success as a building – lots of parking space, a big lawn with a huge Henry Moore on it looks well, and the theatre skilfully built within the walls of the original Maltings.

I bought a little red sailing cap with a bobble on top to wear for 'Ethel' - the girl who goes mad at football games. I've revived it and it's really far more apt in 1967 than it was in 1954. Thank heaven.

My show is tonight and this a.m. Bill [Blezard] and I rehearse our Ben song[2] at 10.30, and then at 12 go up to the Red House and sing it to the Master himself. Bill spent all yesterday afternoon writing out his jazz accompaniment so he gets it right! I have never toiled, polished, worked on anything as I have on this ditty. Let us pray he likes it. I do! Bill does!

1. *Benjamin Britten's Festival*, broadcast 23 June 1967.
2. A 'recitative aria' full of puns on 'Ben': 'benevolent', 'benign', 'benefiting', etc.

At noon Bill and I went to the Red House and did the Festival song in praise of Ben to him and Peter [...] I sang it well and the reaction was so extraordinary that I was quite flummoxed. Ben ran to me and embraced me, weeping! He was very touched and moved. It was very dear and entirely unexpected. Clearly it had moved him. Peter too. So we were rewarded.

Permission granted [...] we had a tremendous discussion about treating creative artists. I said we all have a need for kid gloves – certainly in the early stages of work. Encouragement is vital at that stage and must come before criticism. Joan [Blezard] agrees with Viola [Tunnard] that the objective is the point – the music in their instance – and this must always come first and, roughly, to hell with feelings of artists. But I know that unless the artistic creature is reassured (or this artistic creature, anyhow!) in the very early stages the objective isn't reached.

Then Bill and I met at the theatre and worked. Under difficulties. The piano had no pedals! It had been moved in but not totally reassembled and the man responsible was not to be found. However, dear Bert Pearce, Steinway's genius and charmer, came to tune it and got it together for us. There was a lot of dust about because tabs [stage curtains] were used that hadn't been used before and whoosh there were motes and beams everywhere.

The programme went well and our song was rapturously received. I was dying to sing it again but didn't feel there had been quite enough specific call for that! Later everyone said, 'Why didn't you sing it again?' Damn. Lost me only chance. For it's a one-occasion song.

1968

We were bowled over by *The Prodigal Son* and Orford and the dusk and the setting. It was a heavenly occasion. A pretty dove-coloured evening-into-twilight. Soft and subtle. The air tense with the excitement that Ben's new works always brings with them.

All the regulars were there in force and we had wonderful seats. When it was over there was a long sustained and powerful silence. It's a lovely piece. Peter Pears was the Tempter-narrator and looked rather awful in a high black (net and wire?) hat as if made of petals in flame shapes. He had an eye mask and a blond wig and beard and was not exactly tempting! but very evil. Alas, I detected rather a sign or two of wear in that remarkable voice, and after hearing the young ones in such form it showed rather. Sad. But he was, as always, such a real craftsman that one was full of admiration. It is full of invention and movement. We loved it. Many are saying it's the best. I still love *Fiery Furnace*, but this is a very close second.

1969

A feast of Purcell, Mozart and Schubert with the Amadeus. What a dream of a hall the Maltings is. The Trout Quintet as a finale with Ben at the piano. It was magical. The whole thing rose and flew – or maybe swam is a better verb. Anyway a lovely treat.

We heard the news of the fire at 8 a.m. on our radio and can hardly believe it. There it was yesterday, so beautiful, so airy, so absolutely the dream of what a concert hall in a country place should be. Now ... The mind boggles at the mammoth task of coping with all of us and our tickets for concerts at the Maltings. R. has gone down to offer our help in any clerical or practical way as needed.

To Blythburgh, where a real job has been done in two days to turn it into a concert hall. Amazing. Carpenters and elecs. have worked all night; wardrobe, too, I believe, and we were given an impeccable performance of *Idomeneo*. It is full of such beautiful music and of course Ben got every nuance out of it. I found the whole occasion a triumph of spirit. Very moving to know how hard people will work when they feel it is needed. A great tribute to Ben and all who have made the Festival such an actual thing.

1977

I am longing to write about Aldeburgh for my next book. The Festivals have been such a very enjoyable part of our lives, and Ben's invitations for me to do my programmes were the highest accolade I've ever been awarded. This is certainly one of my Pleasant Places.

Reprinted from the Festival programme book, 1997

Mstislav Rostropovich playing
at Aldeburgh

The Russian Years
Marion Thorpe

In the 1960s, well before the time of *glasnost* and *perestroika* in the Soviet Union, Aldeburgh experienced the golden years of the Russian connection. Personal and musical friendships with some the greatest Russian musicians of the time brought to Aldeburgh a standard of unsurpassed performances. Mstislav Rostropovich, Galina Vishnevskaya, and Sviatoslav Richter were frequent visitors. Their repertoire consisted of solo recitals, chamber music, orchestral concerti and mixed programmes with the artistic directors – Pears and Britten. To savour but a few of these events in retrospect, let us recall Rostropovich in the recently discovered Haydn Concerto in D, or his Schumann concerto in Orford church, Richter on two pianos with Britten, or his Mozart concerto in Blythburgh church with the English Chamber Orchestra. There were memorable performances by Vishnevskaya of Russian works as well as the Pushkin song cycle, which Britten had specially written for her, and solo cello works written for Rostropovich over the years.

It all began in 1960 when Britten, at Shostakovich's invitation, attended a concert at the Royal Festival Hall and heard for the first time Rostropovich in Shostakovich's First Cello Concerto. It was a stunning performance and when Britten congratulated the cellist after the concert, Rostropovich at once requested that Britten write something for him. The first such work, 'by request', was the Sonata for Cello and Piano.

This was the beginning of a rich cross-fertilisation between musicians in both countries. Britten was always keen to write for performers who had special qualities that inspired him. This was certainly true of Slava Rostropovich and Galya Vishnevskaya. Their first visit to Aldeburgh in 1961 was followed by many more and resulted in some of Britten's most important compositions. Over the years he wrote three solo cello suites, and an orchestral cello symphony in the form of a concerto. For Vishnevskaya he set a song cycle to poems by Pushkin and had her voice in mind for the soprano part in his *War Requiem*. Richter too became a frequent visitor, but despite his frequent requests, Britten did not compose anything for the solo keyboard.

Shostakovich's music was often performed and the mutual admiration of the two composers was made manifest in the dedication of works to each other – Britten to Shostakovich of the church opera *Prodigal Son* and Shostakovich to Britten of his Fourteenth Symphony. Shostakovich never attended the festival itself, but on one occasion (I believe) he and his wife visited Britten in Aldeburgh on a return journey from Ireland, and there was much personal and musical understanding between them. I remember one occasion at which I was present when Britten visited Shostakovich in his Moscow flat. Shostakovich sat down and played an excerpt of a piece he was working on. Britten was

On holiday
in Moscow,
1963: Pears,
Vishnevskaya,
Britten,
Rostropovich
and Marion
Thorpe

persuaded to play something of his. At the end, Shostakovich in his practically non-existent English said to Ben, 'You big composer, I little composer.'

The three performing Russians, however, entered into the spirit of the festival and felt at ease in its relaxed and friendly atmosphere. Playing together, and sometimes with Britten and Pears and other artists in mixed programmes, was a source of joy and unexpected pleasure to them and festival audiences alike.

Aldeburgh must have been a great and welcome change from the restrictive atmosphere of the Ministry of Culture and Gosconcert in Moscow headed at the time by the powerful Madam Furtseva. She controlled all travel abroad and all concert arrangements and the portion of salaries allowed to the Russian artists. On the occasion of a visit to the USSR by a group of British Council artists (I was included in the visit) she received us most hospitably and gave a big luncheon for us, including outstanding personalities in the Moscow musical world. She and Britten enjoyed a certain rapport and there was considerable correspondence between them about permission for the visits of Russian artists to this country. Even so, permission was not always granted. Britten had written his *War Requiem* with Vishnevskaya's voice particularly in mind – the other solo roles to be performed by an English tenor (Peter Pears) and a German (Fischer-Dieskau). The work was to be performed for the re-dedication of Coventry Cathedral, which had been destroyed in the war. In spite of urgent pleading Vishnevskaya was not allowed to participate – although she knew the part and was at the time in London, singing Aïda at Covent Garden. Heroically, Heather Harper took on the role and sang it splendidly at short notice. The reason for Vishnevskaya's ban was believed to be the participation of the West Berlin Philharmonic Orchestra (West Berlin not being recognised by the USSR) in the Coventry Festival. A few months later, however, she was allowed to sing in the recording of *War Requiem* under the direction of the composer.

On a visit to the USSR in 1963 the Rostropovichs took us to visit the church of Zagorsk, a little way out of Moscow. It was before the Russian Orthodox Easter and there was snow on the ground. The church was brightly lit by a multitude of candles, which lit up the walls covered with golden icons. Priests dressed in splendid robes were chanting during the service. The church was crowded and outside old women were kneeling in the snow, bowing their heads to the ground. It was an amazing scene, straight out of ancient Russia. Slava in the meantime had gone to find the Archimandrite in charge of the religious community. Father Poemen was an impressive figure in his black cassock and long flowing beard. He received us with hospitality and a warm contact was established. He and Ben corresponded with each other and Ben sent him several recordings of his work; he even sought his advice on an ancient Russian tune, which he incorporated in his Third Cello Suite.

Britten and Pears had spent a memorable holiday in Armenia in 1965, arranged by the Rostropoviches and the local composers' union. Slava and Galya decided at the end of the holiday to drive to the Pushkin house near Pskov in Northern Russia to mark Ben's setting of the poems he had written for Galya during their stay in Armenia. Peter recounted what happened there in his diary, 'Armenian Holiday':

> The last song of the set is the marvellous poem of insomnia, the ticking clock,
> persistent night-noises, and the poet's cry for a meaning in them. Ben has started
> this with repeated staccato notes high-low high-low on the piano. Hardly had the
> little old piano begun its dry tick tock tick tock, than clear and silvery outside the
> window, a yard from our heads, came ding, ding, ding, not loud but clear, Pushkin's
> clock joining in his song. It seemed to strike far more than midnight, to go on all
> through the song, and afterwards we sat spellbound. It was the most natural thing
> to have happened, and yet unique, astonishing, wonderful...

These musical and other experiences in Russia were reciprocated by the visits of Russian friends to Aldeburgh and its festival. Communication between the artists was profound and clear in spite of having no language in common. Music has no barriers, but the language barrier was overcome by the improvisation of a new 'pidgin' form of language spoken between Slava and Ben, which became known as 'Aldeburgh Deutsch'! Some of it was based on musical terms; it was very expressive and perfectly understood between them.

After the Rostropoviches' exile from Russia in 1974 they continued to visit Aldeburgh. They bought a house there in which Galya and her family spent a considerable amount of time. Galya taught at the Britten–Pears School in the summer song masterclasses. During those difficult years of exile, Aldeburgh was a safe base for them where they felt close to Ben and Peter and continued to uphold their legacy long after their deaths.

Aldeburgh: A Magical Festival

Steven Isserlis

I believe that Snape is the only place I know which has been responsible for changing my attitude to a particular style of music. Of course, there are many locations in which I have absorbed great musical influences, and have been hugely inspired by the surroundings; but my experience in the wilds of Snape was a little different. I am ashamed to admit it, but I grew up with a resistance to the music of Britten. I could hear that it was very special – but it just didn't appeal to me. In particular, the Cello Symphony I hated on sound (as it were); this wouldn't have mattered much, except that in the late 1980s EMI asked me to record it for them. This was to be my first recording with orchestra, and was a wonderful opportunity. But – I knew I couldn't do it if I didn't like the work. So I started to look at it closely, in the hopes that the veil would be drawn away from my heart. Of course, I would eventually have fallen in love with it, because it is a masterpiece. But my epiphany came much sooner than it would have under normal circumstances: I happened to be playing at around that time in the Snape Maltings, and decided to take a walk across the marshes before the concert. At one point I stood still and listened to the haunting silence; suddenly the thought came to me: 'This is it. This is where Britten's music comes from!' And from then, everything changed – and I remain a passionate fan of the Cello Symphony, and of much (though I must admit, not all – for the present, anyway) of Britten's music.

My first performance at Aldeburgh was as part of a short masterclass seminar given by the distinguished Danish cellist Erling Blondal Bengtsson. I remember playing the Prelude of Bach's fifth suite at the end-of-course student concert; about ten minutes after I'd finished, Britten arrived. So alas, I just missed my only chance to play to him. I did, however, get to play Bach to Imogen Holst, who was a friend of my teacher, Jane Cowan. As a result of that, I became friends with 'Imo' (well, if a rather bumptious teenager and a distinguished eccentric in her late sixties can be called friends), and she invited me to play her lovely piece for solo cello, *The Fall of the Leaf*, at a concert that marked her seventieth birthday in 1977. (I received my first-ever national review for that, the *Telegraph* graciously describing me as 'the talented Roger Isserlis'.) Later, she invited me back to the festival to give the first performance for many years of her father's only work for cello, *Invocation*. So my early memories of Aldeburgh are very much bound up with her. I really don't think that a character like Imo's could exist now. I remember her speeches to audiences: bending from the waist down, she would inform them, in the sort of voice now heard only in nursery schools, that they were about to have a 'lovely, lovely time'. They would sit there meekly, putty in her hands.

At the concert in which I played *The Fall of the Leaf*, Peter Pears sang songs by Quilter and his contemporaries, with Roger Vignoles at the piano. I listened backstage and was bowled over by the performance; when they came offstage, I was ready for them. 'That's the best performance I've ever heard of British music!' I gushed. Peter Pears looked at me a little strangely, as well he might; to him, having introduced so many of the greatest works ever written by a British composer, it must have sounded very foolish. Well, it was a silly thing to say; but I was young...

Another striking memory is from 1974, when Rostropovich was finally allowed out of the Soviet Union and was able to give the premiere of Britten's Third Suite for solo cello, which had been written for him some years earlier. Again, Britten was sitting in the box; I remember thinking how frail he looked – but he was still a strong presence. We knew that we were listening to history in the making. Since then, I have performed that same Suite (the only one of the three that I play) several times at the Maltings; on each occasion, I have glanced towards the darkened box and imagined that Britten's ghost was sitting there. It is quite an eerie feeling!

As I think of Aldeburgh and Snape, other memories come tumbling into my brain: the sight of Joyce Grenfell striding into a concert, seemingly oblivious to the excitement she was stirring up among her fellow audience members; Peter Pears and Murray Perahia getting to the very heart of Schumann's *Dichterliebe*; Olly Knussen's torso heaving with enjoyment of a somewhat risqué joke, with his co-director Steuart Bedford sitting with cocked head and knitted eyebrows, doing his good-natured best to understand it; my friend the pianist Paul Coker watching with amused concern a temper tantrum of mine backstage including (I'm ashamed to admit) some kicking of a dressing-room wall, when I felt my cello hadn't been speaking properly during the first half of a recital; my mother attending a Bach recital I gave in the beautiful Blythburgh church, shortly before she died; Stephen Hough being thrilled by the sound of Britten's piano, kept at the Red House; and so on. Variety has always been a hallmark of the festival and its associated activities, every visit offering a new and different experience.

From a musical standpoint, it is remarkable how the Aldeburgh Festival has kept its place, through many changes of direction, as a central pillar of the contemporary British scene. Audiences go to the concerts to be challenged as much as to enjoy themselves. (The two should not be mutually exclusive!) The residencies in which Aldeburgh specialises allow audiences, composers and performers to get to know each other far better than they could during normal concert life. As Thomas Adès reaches the end of his exciting tenure – full of surprises and unexpected treats – and Pierre-Laurent Aimard gears up for the beginning of his, the festival is off on another new track. It will be a different sort of event entirely, I'm sure; but it will remain unique, invaluable – and vital in every sense.

On the A12

Michael Laskey

Towards the end of a long drive home,
your nervous system subdued by pistons,
your children, gone through the quarrelsome

miles, mild now in the back of your mind,
and the road once more your own, the known
camber of a bend, horizons, signs

you read for the sake of their refreshed
welcoming names, not to tick them off,
Ufford, Hacheston, Campsey Ash.

And it's almost over, you're all but back
unpacking, when for a sudden split
second the road, that must know the make

and colour of your car and your number plate,
turns towards your returning smile
a quite blank unfamiliar face

so out of place you can't remember
where in the wheeling world you are
or what time it is of what day, month, year.

Darsham

Blake Morrison

From here it's only miles to the House in the Clouds,
a madcap water-tower pretending to be home,

and for you a chapter in the same tall story
of the Blythburgh angels and Cromwell's guns.

So these skies press on and turn out to be childhood,
a red tractor on a curved brown field.

We go down to the water and are sand-flies.
We rejoin the lugworm and the celandine.

We listen for cathedral bells at Dunwich
tolling from the graveyards of the sea.

When jets come trailing glory from Lakenheath
you bury your great head between my knees.

Water
married
to stone

'What lies in wait for me here,
Ambiguous Venice
Where water is married to stone
And passion confuses the senses?'

Gustav Aschenbach in *Death in Venice*
Act 1, Scene 3

Figuring the Landscape

Paul Heiney

Just after the turn of the year, we gathered in our small parish church to bury a grand old countryman of eighty-two. To an outsider, passing by, it would have appeared to be no more than yet another pensioner's funeral; but we who stood around the grave realised that his death meant something fundamental had changed in our lives. It was simply this: you could cut down a score of oak trees, or plough a dozen meadows, but to us the passing of this one old man meant a change in the Suffolk landscape as profound as any that could be achieved by axe or tractor. As his coffin was lowered into the stiff Suffolk clay – which he had fought, as a farm worker, all his life – in that moment of final victory for the land, a part of the scenery as vivid and varied as any coastal marsh or heath had disappeared. The landscape had suddenly changed: it would never be the same again.

He once told me that at the end of the Second World War, after fighting in Italy, using the dead bodies of his comrades as stepping stones to scale the heights of Monte Cassino, he arrived back at Darsham station clad in his demob outfit, and walked the short distance to his village. On arriving home, the first words from his mother were, 'What do you want f'yer tea?' Within the hour, he'd eaten, summarised the horrors of war into a few clipped sentences, discarded the unaccustomed suit, and was milking the cows as if nothing had happened. I asked him what had changed while he'd been away, to which he replied, 'Not much'. He didn't set foot outside Suffolk for another fifty years.

He was right, of course; whatever might happen in the rest of the world, it seems nothing much does challenge, fundamentally, in the broad Suffolk landscape, although the details can. A house built where we'd rather not see one always annoys, a bypass carving through an undisturbed field can make you wince, even a well-meant sculpture can seem an intrusion to some. But this is only because so little in the Suffolk landscape ever shifts that, like a rearrangement of the china on the familiar kitchen shelf, the slightest change in the order of things irritates. So we support all those who make it their business to ensure that the birds, the bees, the flowers and trees are left in peace, that the rivers flow undisturbed, and the villages still cause us to sigh with romantic bliss at the sight of them. As far as the 'big picture' is concerned, the Suffolk landscape seems as secure and protected as any can be these days. But what about that part of the landscape that is not immediately obvious to the eye? – that intangible ingredient that makes this place into definitely Suffolk, and certainly not Essex or Norfolk. By forever gasping at the broadness of the skies, or the heartbreaking ripple of the breeze through the reed beds, are we perhaps dazzled by the richness of the view and unable to see where the true landscape lies? I think we are.

Those who turn to writers for an understanding of Suffolk are drawn to either Ronald Blythe's *Akenfield*, or the many books of George Ewart Evans, the best known of which might be *The Horse in the Furrow*. Blythe famously recorded the lives of the people in a village of his own creation, and moulded the experiences of the inhabitants into a unique record of the fundamental upheavals in rural life in the first half of the twentieth century. George Ewart Evans, on the other hand, used a cumbersome tape machine to record the spoken words of the villagers of east Suffolk as they recounted customs, traditions and arcane rural practices handed down by their grandparents. As Blythe remarks in his introduction, 'this book is a quest for the voice of Akenfield', while Evans collected the voices themselves. These were different approaches, but part of a shared appreciation that the true landscape of this county might be found in the hearts and minds of the people born and bred here, and that landscape as represented by field, furrow or seashore was the smallest part of the story. In fact, there's not much 'landscape' in either book: Blythe tells us that Akenfield lies amidst 'sloping heavy soil, so tough to plough', which dominates every view, while Evans hardly gives a nod to the scenery in which his storytellers live. But neither book could be described as anything other than vivid, or accused of failing to paint a detailed picture of Suffolk. Perhaps, by choosing human experience to define the county, they may have done us a far greater service than the countless artists who, armed with pencil, watercolour or oil, depict this as a place in which no people seem to live at all. How many paintings of the Aldeburgh beach boats have you seen, and how many with a fisherman at work?

I learnt more about the nature of Suffolk in the decade during which I farmed, traditionally, employing the county's native cart-horse, the Suffolk Punch, than I could ever have done by observation alone. You will never get to know this place by standing and looking, you have to be a part of it. This is not always easy. Take my early experiences of erecting a wire fence – an apparently simple task but doomed to failure in novice hands. My next-door neighbour, a farm worker all his life, spent most of the day silently watching me from beneath the peak of his flat cap, yet only as the sun was setting on my poor attempt at animal containment did he raise his eyes to say, 'I could 'ave told yer, that you hadn't started right'. Infuriating. When a man of similar pedigree came to help out on the farm, and one day failed to turn up for vital haymaking, he said to me later, 'I'd 'ave thought you'd a known I weren't a comin'.' Maddening, both of them, but defining. They were both Suffolk through and through.

In reading Blythe and Evans, it soon becomes clear that the human landscape has changed dramatically in the last half century, to the extent that similar upheavals in the physical scenery would require a natural disaster of earthquake proportions. Evans, for example, records the superstition of the Frog's Bone, extracted from the poor creature immersed in a fast-flowing stream under the light of a full moon. Once in possession of this scrap of bone, the owner could claim to have full control over the wildest of cart-horses. Imagine how criminal you would be made to feel, these days, at robbing a frog of one of its limbs. Failing the Frog's Bone, the horseman might instead settle for possession of the Horseman's Word, a single utterance unknown to outsiders and bestowed on a young lad only following ritual humiliation, with which he could exert his superiority over a Suffolk Punch by merely whispering it into the equine ear. These were Suffolk traditions, as much a part of the landscape as the intolerably beautiful bend in the River Alde at Iken, but today they are entirely gone. Only through Blythe and Evans can we hear the voices, telling the tales, singing them to us in the Suffolk accent that rises and falls, chiming like a peal of bells.

It is, perhaps, understandable that with the passing of the characters that these two writers have recorded, we turn for some kind of stability to the physical landscape and cling on to it for dear life. The men and women who remembered the endless days of pointless, under-paid stone-picking in flint-ridden fields are now well beyond our reach, but we can still stand at the edge of the fields and see pretty much the sights they saw, if they bothered to raise their heads from their drudgery. The landscape is our only remaining link with them. And to enjoy it alone, without giving a thought to the unknown figures who once populated it, is to sell yourself short. The old countryman we buried this year had one particular trick for which he will be remembered. He could march through a field of beet, swinging his hoe, topping the weeds, singling the plants, with a rhythm and a movement that a choreographer might have created. And now he's gone, and his trick has gone with him. But I shall never pass a field of beet without seeing him, chuckling or cursing as he went about his work. Not merely a figure in the landscape, but the landscape itself.

JOHN NASH

Akenfield Revisited

Ronald Blythe

The book *Akenfield* was written in 1966–7 and first published in May 1969. I was then living at Debach, a tiny parish of some eighty souls which adjoined the larger village of Charsfield. I remember walking the ancient boundaries of flat-land Debach and hollow-land Charsfield on a grey winter's day and thinking of the ritual toil which had engaged them, and thousands of villages like them, since those who settled them made the first field. All around were similar settlements with 'field' names, so I called my book *Akenfield* after the oaks which stood in the field opposite my old house. 'Acen' = Old English for 'oak'. Also because I was born in the Suffolk village of Acton. 'Actun' = 'the homestead by the oaks'. *Akenfield* is chiefly based on Charsfield, but with the surrounding countryside and myself drawn into it. My excuse for the former extension is that, like man, no village is an island, entire of itself, but has always relied on the blacksmith, wheelwright, schools, transport, butcher, and now priest of the area.

The book is more the work of a poet than a trained oral historian, a profession I had never heard of when I wrote it. My only real credentials for having written it was that I was native to its situation in nearly every way and had only to listen to hear my own world talking. Thus a thread of autobiography runs strongly through it. Having been born between the wars during the last years of the great agricultural depression, I was in a kind of natural conversation with all three generations who spoke to me in the mid-sixties, and I was able to structure their talk over farming, education, welfare, class, religion and indeed life and death in terms such as I myself was experiencing these things, although now with a writer's vision of them. I saw the two world wars as extraordinary intrusions, walling-off two successive generations from each other, and giving each of them a distinctive voice. And I was delighted as always with those who bent the rules, dodged the system and who managed to be 'different' within the rigidities which rural communities like to impose. There is no place like the countryside for the most imaginative – and blatant – nonconformity.

* * *

The most unlooked-for change of fortune during the rural sixties would have been that for agriculture thirty years on. Then it was grow all the grain you can, never mind what eccentrics calling themselves 'ecologists' said. An often brutal and ignorant rationalisation of the old field system which so upset John Clare when his village was enclosed was government-inspired and paid for. One Suffolk village, Tannington, was in the van of such change, with scarcely a tree or hedge to its name. Although cornfields had to expand to take combine harvesters, it was shocking to see centuries-old hedgerows bulldozed, the pouring on to the land of chemicals about which the average farmer understood very little, and stubble-burning as an economy. Now there is official and social condemnation of such practices, and because of the eventual withdrawal of subsidies, plus European laws, there is a feeling of insecurity among today's farmers such as most of them have only read about and would never have imagined could return.

The labour force was small enough then but is now minute. A couple of men on eight hundred acres. The 'old people', that is, those who truly belong to a village, are the least surprised. Ups and downs are in their blood, and although vague about agronomics they don't expect anything to last. But some farmers today are nerve-racked and fearful. Gone is that first fine careless confidence when the grain grew as it never had grown before. Thus a recovered respect for nature, often brought about, I sometimes think, by their children, who have been thrillingly 'ecologised' at school and university, not to mention by television. One of my hardest tasks in the nineties has been to make the villagers look at their fields, not drive through them as though nothing existed between their houses and the supermarket. An almost total lack of contact with its growing acres by the majority of people now living in the countryside has, more than anything else, brought about its increasing urbanisation. The old work ground is seen only when it becomes a playground. But the locals as well as the visitors are walking more, which is something they would have found difficult to do during the sixties when the ancient village paths petered out in seas of grain.

❊ ❊ ❊

My father had fought at Gallipoli in the Suffolk Regiment and it was while listening to Len Thompson about what to me, as a boy, was a half-glamorous, half-terrible experience, that I recognised the 'iceberg' quality in those I thought I knew pretty well. Only the tip of them showed, all the rest ran deep. A similar revelation occurred when I listened to our retired district nurse. She was the secretary of the PCC and I was a churchwarden, and we had every reason to believe that there was not much we could tell each other which was not already known. Many years after *Akenfield* I sat by her death-bed and watched the old 'authority' come and go in her dark eyes.

❊ ❊ ❊

The earlier poet of this region was Edward FitzGerald, who lies buried under rose-trees seeded from those which grow round Omar's tomb at Xaishapur in Boulge churchyard, just a mile or two from my house. How often he would have seen it, and how often I sat in what was once his lodge-cottage distributing our Flower Show prizes – mainly to now grimly competitive farm-workers who yearly cleared the board. Tramping and cycling about, I frequently found myself haunted by FitzGerald. Many of his lanes had been obliterated by the American bomber base across which the Welsh rector and myself would take our blowy walks. The poet in *Akenfield* is James Turner, my first writer friend, who lived three miles away, and with whom over many years I explored Suffolk – a vivid, sometimes testy man whose wife moved him on and on until he reached Cornwall.

* * *

There was the question of dialect. 'Suffolk' being my first language, so to speak, I did not find it wholly impossible to write even if it is thought to be notoriously hard to get right. I sat with the wheelwright's nephew as we asked each other the meaning of words in Forby's *The Vocabulary of East Anglia*, 1830, and found that we were rarely stumped. Eventually I decided to keep to what was being said, and to a certain personal rhythm in each speaker, using a story, 'Tom-tit-Tot', from the Suffolk Folklore Society's collection to give a wonderfully accurate example of our dialect. It has always intrigued East Anglians how their speech gradually broadens out between the Stour and the Wash. This is one thing which hasn't altered much since the sixties. In fact, certain 'country' groups may be re-establishing the local speech of their grandparents.

* * *

One can compare the economics of then and now but it would need an expert to explain the real difference. The Rural Dean's annual stipend in 1969 was £1,175; in 1998 it is £15,000. The farm-worker's weekly wage then was £11.11; now it is £200 with overtime. But the long struggle against the poverty wages and grim conditions of the inter-war years continues to lie like a barely credible memory at the heart of today's prosperity and leisure. The middle-aged, let alone the aged, have to shake themselves to admit that things were so. There are various ways to describe a time, a place, a condition. One can come to them from outside and say what one saw. Or one can emerge from within a community, as so many rural writers do, and be at a particular moment its indigenous voice.

Written as the Introduction to the Penguin reprint of *Akenfield*, 1998

DAVID GENTLEMAN

The Power of Patience

Adrian Bell

I saw a fisherman mending his nets one summery, autumn day, sitting quietly absorbed among the people of the resort. So poor – he seemed to have the riches of time. Among the many amenities of enjoyment and among the people – best-clothed or hardly clothed, according to their class – this small patch of beach, of fishing-boats veiled with their nets, was like a rent in the present, revealing the past that lay behind. Or was it eternity shining through? All the restless movement of holiday-making was checked there; for me that figure was timeless. I sat down where I was, on my way somewhere for something, I forget what; I forgot everything in the mysterious joy of that moment. The battered old hat, the sand-coloured blouse-like jacket, and the corduroy trousers, all were at one with the shore and the sea. Stars danced behind him; I became aware as I watched of how the tide fused the light on a million wavelets: it was a morning firmament all around that old hat and jacket, and that absorbed, old-fashioned face, bent slightly down as the fingers moved with a peculiar airy rhythm, threading twine in and out with a sort of bodkin. A family party marched to the sea-verge in stiff coat-hanger clothes and stood staring at it. Children rushed about in flower-garden colours; people picnicked, paddled, dived, swam, played with dogs. He stood within and beyond it all, plying his patience.

No doubt but he had a power of sudden movement to some purpose when there was need. Out in his little boat, trawling, at an emergency, I have no doubt he could move powerfully, swiftly, yet with a decisive economy of action, beyond all the bright agitation of pleasure going on around him now. Craftsmen are like that. They know their moment and gather to it: they know likewise when to have patience. The power of patience: a man having that is prayer incarnate.

The man who came to kill our pig had it. Year after year I watch and assist this rite. It is beastly, I admit, but in the most ample and literal sense. It is, in fact, a sort of sacrificial art, flowering into a mellow humanity, associative and intimate. The red fact confronts one as one eats one's bacon of a morning; and one cannot get round it or beyond it or above it as long as man is man and spirit is confined in flesh. The essential 'beastliness' once faced in strident fact, leaves one, I say, with a more humble and an enlarged charity. We can't stake out much of a claim, after all, on the infinite goodness, by virtue of being man. Yet no civilised revulsion can detract from the art that the pig-killer's work really is, as precise as the toreador's in miniature, but of a more sober purpose.

When you visit the pig-killer to arrange about his visit, you find him nursing his babe in his warm cottage, while two other children play on the hearthrug. He is very fond of children: he has a dark, quick, imaginative eye; has a creative felicity in the possession of his cottage and his acre; it is a kingdom with which he has done (and she, his wife, has done), is doing, will do, wonders. Last year it was peas; now potatoes: next a venture in blackcurrants. Rich, black, fenny soil, imaginative stuff to the husbandman: not like our brick-clay land, wheat-and-bean land; and latterly, for some reason, the beans don't pod. Just wheat, then, and clovery pasture – ah, that's where our imagination strikes root. What new pastures we shall have when we are allowed to sow down the yellow clay! After twenty-five loads of black muck to the acre it ploughs up next season just as jaundiced at you...

The pig-killer has a love born of insight into the nature of material things – tubs, steel, a wheel or a hoof. Yes, and the lorry he drives for a haulage contractor. Pig-killing is only his spare-time occupation – his hobby, his pastime. A man is not in the temple precincts all hours of the day: but of an evening when flame reflections lick the threshold of his doorway, so polished it is like wet iron, and he sits with his children. The precise pointed knife, and large-armed laughing affection in his cottage home – by these his being is kindled. The lorry driving is very well – in its way. Now, and for months ahead it is sugar-beet loading, haulage and unloading. An awful swink it is, of medieval severity, throwing up great forkfuls of beet, hour after hour, day after day, without a medieval amplitude of bread and beer. 'If you've a good mate, who'll work in with you' – he meant a cheerful-hearted fellow – 'you can jog along comfortable.' To feel yourself 'jogging along comfortable' at that job certainly calls for imagination and fellowship. But for the last week he has had as mate a man fresh from the army, who has found sugar-beet carting an extremely disillusioning entry into civilian life. Better a 'desert rat' than a drowned and mud-bespattered rat. A most doleful companion, dreary fork-propper in a week of rain. Hard work in a greatcoat in muggy autumn is the hottest form of hell. 'It's not often I'm fed up, but last night when I got home I said to my wife, "I'm fed up." "For you to say you're fed up – you must be fed up," she said.' I, too, believed him.

We were motoring to my home on the day of the yearly pig-killing. A remark I made about poultry produced a highly technical disquisition on Rhode Island Reds, of which, he told me, with an occasional glance backward to see that his big scalding-tub was still securely roped, there are several varieties. An awkward thing is a tub to tie to the back of a car. My house was silent, save for a bubbling copper and a purring cat. Nora had taken the family for a walk up the road to see a neighbour. Martin had protested, 'But I'd like to see the pig killed.' Yes, it is strange, but children are like that – children as imaginative and tender-hearted as my pig-killer himself. Anthea, with a last look at the live pig, had agreed that, 'The only time you really feel a little bit fond of a pig is the day it is going to be killed.'

I was never more pleased with my premises than on this day. I thought I had a good pig-house, stable and back yard. My friend saw in them the ideal slaughterhouse. Everything to hand: capacious copper, brick flooring with central swill-down drain. 'I wish I had a little place like this; I could kill three pigs of an afternoon, comfortable.' A neighbour, Jake, was here to help – a man of the freemasonry of the local arts of sustenance; a man, give him but the ground he trod on, so be it was his own native ground, who could conjure from it corn, milk, mutton, bacon, and maintain a neatness in the process; making as a secondary and unconscious creation a picture to please the eye, because he understood the inner structure of this life. A man to survive civilisations.

Now the gait of this man is deliberate, and his contemplation of such a thing as a length of hoop-iron so still and concentrated, it is of a piece with the patience of that fisherman in the sun beside the sea.

To fetch a pig from its sty across the yard to its place of execution would appear to be a job for two or three strong men. Actually Jake and I did very little that afternoon; the pig-killer's real allies were a small length of cord and a pulley and chain. The moment he went into the pigsty his art was at work. He dangled over the pig his piece of cord, looped at the bottom into a small noose. In no time this had the pig by the snout and upper jaw, and with one or two little shakes of the head the pig trotted as docile as a poodle on a lead, to the spot directly under the pulley. The cord was fixed: he was raised a little ... Without knowing that he was dying, he was dead. This all took place in the quietest manner possible, with the utmost economy of effort and gesture.

Now he was hoisted into the tub, and our moment of haste was at hand. We trotted, Jake and I, to and fro with buckets of water from the copper. The pig-killer held some of the water suspended in a bowl over the pig, spilled a little out over him, watched, waited, spilled a little more. It was like an oblation or act of augury, while Jake and I trotted to and fro in our folk-dance of the pails. What the man was really at was testing the heat of the water. Our job was to deliver the stuff boiling; his job to apply it at just the right temperature. 'In bacon factories they have a thermometer: I tell by just feeling.'

A pig-killer is very particular about there being plenty of boiling water. If the householder fails him in that respect, he will not come again. He cools it himself to just the right degree. Too hot, it cooks the bristles on, instead of scalding them off. Now that the mysterious current of life is switched off, no message of pain can be transmitted from the thousand nerve-endings of the skin. The frame of the pig is in a twinkling as a civilization that is extinct.

While they worked, scraping and shaving the pig, they talked, these two, of the qualities of things. Of the making of a hoop for a tub, how one edge of the hoop-iron must be long and patiently dinged on the anvil to flatten and spread it to fit the expanding curve of the tub. Of the wood of tubs. 'Russian oak,' said Jake. 'There's nothing else can stand the strain – there's never a knot in it bigger than a nut.' Of sharpening steels – better have the old one reburred than buy a new today. Of how the pig scrapes. Not so well as he looked as though he might. Every pig 'scrapes' differently. This one is hard work. About the hide of a black pig there is a sort of gluey quality: the Essex pigs' hides have a sort of 'mealiness'. Hard work, but each man is searching for words, too, to describe pigs' hides they have scraped, pork they have eaten, casks they have 'happened on' and bought and sawn asunder.

In an hour the pig is hanging up as immaculate as one in a butcher's shop. The family return: the yard is swept, swilled, clean and tidy. (Only a week later my man is to dig up something out of the vegetable garden that I had buried hurriedly by torchlight insufficiently deep.) Tea all together in the kitchen. The pig-killer kindles again to talk of his children, and to talk of ours. He cuts some of the pig's 'fry' to take home, and Jake cuts himself some – a snippet of this and that – liver, 'skirt', sweetbreads. In abatement of his fee the man asks for a small piece of belly pork to go with his dumplings next week. Indeed, yes, for I think of the labour of the beet-loading.

'How do people manage these days?' 'How we should do I don't know if my wife weren't such a manager. Ah, she's a wonderful manager. She was in service as a girl. How chaps get on that marry these girls out of shops –'

There is something triumphant in being able to manage. Those dumplings next week, with strips of belly pork; the ploughing of his black acre. 'Those Rhodes of yours, yes, of course, they would be slow in making flesh, from that sort of cockerel.'

We stopped on the way back to his house, and dropped the tub at a farm where he was to kill a pig the next week. Cows were in a byre being milked. I could hear the voices of the farmer and farmer's wife, discussing with my friend where and when the pig should be killed. 'Well, how far off is your copper?' I heard him ask. All-important, that. 'My cowman didn't turn up till a quarter to eight this morning,' I heard the farmer say.

'I went to cut Mr Grote's pig up for him on Sunday morning, and found him with fifteen cows to milk because his cowman hadn't turned up that morning. I sat down and milked three there and then, and helped him get the milk off –'

Snatches of conversation floated out to me through the cowshed door in the rustling quiet of the farmyard at night. Dark forms of cattle peered at me, breathing heavily. Presently he returned, his arrangements concluded, and we rolled the tub into the shelter of a barn and left it there among mangolds and calves and meal and trusses of hay.

From *The Flower and the Wheel*, Bodley Head, 1949

DAVID GENTLEMAN

Food and Farming in East Suffolk

Caroline Cranbrook

The past sixty years have seen changes in agriculture and food supply as great as any that occurred during the nineteenth-century agricultural revolution. Food has never been more abundant or cheaper. For example, the price of wheat, corrected for inflation, has fallen over the years, as has the amount of money spent on food. In 1948, when the Aldeburgh Festival started, wheat was the equivalent of £286 per tonne and the average household spent 25% of its income on food. In 1970 it was £150 a tonne and food spend about 17% of income. In 2000 it had fallen to £121.31 a tonne. In 2008, the situation has started to change and the price has risen to £170 per tonne. Spending on food has declined to 8.8% of income, but this percentage will rise, reflecting world-wide food shortages. The wheat figures are typical of many other commodities. It is only this year, 2008, that rising production costs and food shortages are pushing up prices, both for producers and consumers.

In 1948 food was still rationed. The war and food scarcity were a recent memory. For the next thirty years, government policy was designed to maximise food production. Farmers were encouraged to drain their land, plough heaths and meadows, grub up orchards, cut down hedges, enlarge farms, fields, flocks and herds, invest in new machinery and buildings and use new techniques and crop protection chemicals to produce more food. In the 1950s, these changes were only just beginning. Most farms still had mixed livestock and there was more grassland, grazed by Suffolk Red Poll cattle and Suffolk sheep. Even in the 1960s, there were many people employed on the land and they still had strong links to the past, as described so vividly in Ronald Blythe's *Akenfield* and George Ewart Evans' books. Most farmers would have worked with horses, the magnificent Suffolk Punches, and the oral knowledge of farming and the countryside was alive in their memories. Outside the cities, much food was locally produced and bought in small shops, at weekly markets and from itinerant traders. People understood where there food came from, were skilled in choosing it and they knew how to cook. The supermarkets, which so dominate our lives today, were only just starting.

In 1972, when the first *Aldeburgh Anthology* was published, changes just beginning in the 1950s were now well established. Farms were bigger and more mechanised, large-scale, indoor production of pigs and chickens had been introduced, livestock were vanishing from the fields, the first crops of oilseed rape were being harvested and the direct connection between local food and local shops was starting to disappear. The increasing scale of production was much influenced by the supermarkets, which introduced efficiencies of distribution, drove up standards and demanded uniform products in order to provide food, consistent in quality and appearance.

By the end of the twentieth century, the trend to large-scale farming and the demands of the supermarkets had changed the whole system of food production, distribution, retailing and, indeed, eating. The success of convenience foods meant many were now second-generation microwave cooks. But at the same time there were two new developments: first, a growing realisation of the need to repair damage to the environment caused by intensification; and second, rising concerns about the provenance of food. Government policies now encouraged farmers to become actively involved in conservation, replanting hedges and woodland, reviving ponds and protecting or creating areas of wildlife value. Likewise, consumers, who had become accustomed to packaged, convenience foods, were starting to look for locally produced, fresh food, partly to support farmers and the environment, partly from anxiety resulting from the continual health scares in the media and partly from a genuine worry that they knew so little, if anything, about the origins of the food they were eating.

The world of *Akenfield* and George Ewart Evans has disappeared, together with oral traditions handed down from generation to generation over hundreds, even thousands of years. But in East Suffolk a thriving local food economy has survived alongside our mainstream agriculture. We still have a network of small market towns and villages, surrounded by a mix of arable fields and a treasured landscape of heaths, marshes, saltings and river valleys with their meadows, woods and grassy lanes. We also have increasing numbers of small food producers and a lot of small shops. The main reason for this is that there is no superstore in any of the small market towns – a consequence of Suffolk Coastal District's planning policy. I have been studying the local 'food web' since 1997 and have found that as the result of the absence of a superstore, independent retailing continues to flourish, as do the small producers who supply them. Between Southwold, Woodbridge, Stradbroke and Debenham we have nearly 100 small shops selling food, including 19 butchers and 13 farm shops. Contrary to national trends, new ones are opening all the time.

Small shops are an essential link in the local food chain. Nearly all food businesses start on a small scale, and it is impossible to start a small food business without small outlets. The independent shops are the vital seedbed for new products and an outlet for traditional local foods. They provide consumers with a choice that is different from the supermarket – the choice to buy local, fresh, seasonal, heritage foods which have travelled a short distance from farm to plate.

In East Suffolk there has also been an encouraging return to beef and sheep farming, organic food production and free-range chickens and pigs, providing the area with a high reputation for the quality of its meat. We have an astonishing range of local products, both traditional and new – cheeses, ice creams, yoghurts and milk, fresh and smoked fish, hams, sausages and bacons in huge variety, asparagus and strawberries, herbs and chillis, flours and cereals, cakes, bread and Suffolk rusks, jams, jellies and chutneys, fruit and vegetables, juices, beers and wines – the list is long – and growing. We even have our own Aldeburgh food and drink festival, celebrating the whole area as a food destination.

The local food network has a much wider significance. It provides employment and many other benefits for people living in isolated rural areas and it also underpins the surrounding countryside. There is a strong connection between the excellent local meat on sale throughout the area and the landscape where the animals are reared.

Consumers are increasingly concerned about where their food comes from and they are worried about food miles – the distances travelled by food. So they are turning to local food to provide some of the answers. This demand creates a virtuous circle: the increase in East Suffolk food producers and food outlets is directly related to the rising demand for local produce, which in turn supports the vitality of our market towns and villages.

The supermarkets' dominance of the food chain has provided many benefits but it has come at a cost. Agriculture has become more efficient but more industrialised. Where an area is saturated with superstores, small independent food businesses, whether farming, processing or retailing, struggle to survive. Market towns become ghost towns as the edge-of-town superstores draw shoppers away from the High Street.

Supermarkets have become disproportionately powerful in relation to their suppliers and in relation to planners. They appear to be in an unassailable position. But the situation is changing rapidly. The era of inexpensive, readily available food is unlikely to last much longer since it depends so much on cheap oil and international inequality in the costs of labour and land. For several years the world has produced less food than is consumed and reserves are rapidly declining. In 2008 food shortages appeared worldwide. The future of the global food chain looks increasingly insecure.

Perhaps we should see the successful East Suffolk food chain not as an example of an outdated system of food supply, but as a possible template for the future. The global food chain, on which the supermarkets depend, is under increasing pressure – from the effects of climate change, from population increase and migration, from water shortage, from political unrest and from depletion of natural resources, particularly oil and minerals. The combination of all these factors will impinge on the global systems of supply and the format of the large supermarkets – they all depend on availability of cheap, easily obtainable oil.

Re-localisation of much of our food sources will probably be essential. In Suffolk we have seen how this can work on a modest scale. Let us hope that this model can be refined and expanded to ensure that the nation does not go hungry.

DAVID GENTLEMAN

Snape and the Malt House

George Ewart Evans

When the Festival Council decided to make the Malt House, part of the former maltings at Snape, a permanent site for major events of the Festival, it at first seemed a sharp break with the policy of keeping the main part of the Aldeburgh Festival to the town from which its name derives. In fact, this decision was a logical extension of the Festival's development up to the present time, a growing out that is natural and appropriate to Snape's many historical links with Aldeburgh.

The association began in very early times as the two places were closely joined by road and estuary. The road which runs past Snape Church undoubtedly follows the course of a Roman *strata via*, the road linking Stratford St Andrew with an Aldeburgh that extended much farther east than the present sea-eroded town. Just beside this road, a few hundred yards on the Aldeburgh side of Snape church, there is also a reminder of Snape's early connection with the sea and the Saxons who first attacked the coastal settlements even before the going away of the Romans. This is the remains of a barrow, the survivor of a group of at least six that straddled the highway at this point. Near it a barrow containing a Saxon ship was excavated in 1862; and this – owing to the primitive technique of excavating and recording then used – has proved a tantalising curtain-raiser to the discovery in 1939 of the more famous ship-grave at Sutton Hoo. The boat, the grave of a seventh-century local chieftain, was clinker built like the Sutton Hoo boat but it was smaller, 20 ft or so shorter in length; and unlike the one at Sutton Hoo it had been robbed long before its complete excavation [see p.235].

After the Norman Conquest we have fuller evidence of the link between the two places. About the year 1155 a Norman, William Martel, joined with his wife and son in making a gift of the manors of Snape and Aldeburgh to the Benedictine house of St John at Colchester. Their purpose was to found a priory at Snape which was to be subject to the Colchester foundation. The priory was small with a total income of about £56, but this appears to have been augmented later on by the prior's ownership of wrecks along the foreshore between Thorpeness and Orford. After many ups and downs Snape Priory found itself one of the numerous small East Anglian religious houses that Wolsey suppressed in 1527–8 to enable him set up his great college at Ipswich. Nikolaus Pevsner writes that there are no remains of the priory. This is substantially true, but recently some interesting carved stones have been taken from Abbey Farm, the site of the priory, and housed in the nave of Snape church. There is, too, a local tradition that a house called Stone Cottage, near the Crown Inn, was built with stones from the priory remains.

The village of Snape is essentially what the geographers call a settlement at a nodal point – the lowest bridgeable place on the River Alde. This in itself has tied the village indissolubly to Aldeburgh, because formerly most of Aldeburgh's traffic to the south passed over Snape bridge. It was its link with the important borough of Orford and it was one of the main – and shorter – routes to Ipswich. Both Aldeburgh and Orford recognised their obligation to contribute towards the upkeep of Snape bridge; and there are records dating from the thirteenth century of sums of money given for its repair. Until recently the bridge was a very narrow, hump-backed structure, built during the early nineteenth century: the present bridge replaced it in 1959. In addition to the road, a very old track called the Sailors' Path crossed the river here. Its course was across the heathlands to the south of the Aldeburgh–Snape road, continuing on the south side of the bridge over the heaths to Orford.

Edward Clodd, the historian of Aldeburgh, states that according to an 'early seventeenth-century writer the lord of the manor of Snape-cum-Aldeburgh had the appointment of a burgess to Parliament'; and he infers that it was like Orford a pocket-borough from which, presumably, both Snape and Aldeburgh enjoyed some of the cosy benefits associated with this form of representation. Yet the Malt House itself and the buildings of which it is a part are the most appropriate symbol of this long association between the Borough and its outlying village. Newson Garrett who founded Snape Maltings was also founder of the Aldeburgh branch of a most remarkable family – the Garretts who at Leiston built up one of the biggest farm machinery factories in Britain from a modest establishment that was 'little more than a roadside smithy'. Newson Garrett was a man of outstanding enterprise and energy: ship-owner, grain transporter, Lloyd's agent, mayor of Aldeburgh, he yet found time to devote to a large and talented family that included Elizabeth Garrett Anderson, the first woman doctor, and Millicent Fawcett, the feminist and pioneer in education [see p.86].

Garrett built Snape Maltings in the mid-nineteenth century, and a contemporary account records that every year he shipped to the port of London 200,000 quarters of barley and 16,000 quarters of malt in vessels of from 60 to 90 tons burthen. The vessels came to the wharfs on each side of Snape bridge: they were chiefly sprit-sail barges which continued to navigate the difficult upper reaches of the estuary and the river until the inter-war years. Since 1965–6 the maltings at Snape have ceased to operate but most of the buildings have been taken over by a grain-storage firm which has renewed the tradition by deepening the channel of the river and, in November 1965, bringing up the first of a number of barges (all fitted with engines now) which transport grain to London and Rotterdam. For many years much of the grain and malt from Snape was also carried by rail along a small branch line which left the London–Yarmouth line near Burnt House, Farnham. This line was closed a few years ago [1960].

It is worth noting that Garrett's enterprise at Snape, like many others elsewhere, grew out of the concentration of small, village malthouses at a convenient embarking place. The Snape enterprise must have been well in advance of its time as it embodied the latest improvements on the previous rough-and-ready methods of malting. These improvements were chiefly concerned with the preservation of the correct temperature at various stages of the malting process, and also with economy of labour in handling the grain. For these reasons the new Maltings were built very high. Undoubtedly it was the height of the building and a realisation of its acoustical possibilities that first attracted the Festival

A maltster in the 1890s

Council to consider the Malt House as a centre from which to reach a wider public than it has hitherto been able to accommodate.

The site, moreover, can well symbolise a new link with the Festival's hinterland: the wider Suffolk background and the arable farming that is the region's most typical and traditional work. A quarter of a mile or so across the river from the Malt House is the Crown Inn; it was in a field adjoining this – so the older generation in Snape maintains – that the first field of sugar-beet grown in Suffolk was sown and harvested. The field belonged to Ted Pryke, landlord of the Crown, and he brought Dutchmen over to tend the crop. Older Snape inhabitants remember these Dutchmen 'singling' or thinning out the young beet plants with short hoes, getting down on their knees the better to do the work, their knees protected with thick cloth pads. This happened about 1911; and although the claim may stand for the first sugar-beet grown here in this century, it must be recorded that a sugar-beet factory was set up in Lavenham in 1869, closing four years later because local farmers grew insufficient beet to keep it going.

A short distance away from the Malt House, on the same side of the river and not far from Dunningworth Hall, there is another link with the farming history of the county. Here is a field which was the site of 'Dunnifer' (Dunningworth) Horse Fair. This was held on 11 August; and the date (1 August under the old Julian calendar) suggests a medieval

Lammas fair. For Lammas Day was the occasion when the animals were first allowed to graze the meadows that had been cut for hay. The custom is remembered in East Anglia as Lammas Shack to distinguish it from the freedom to feed on the corn stubble, called Michaelmas Shack in Norfolk. 'Dunnifer' Horse Fair continued until at least the middle of the last [nineteenth] century and included in its latter years a race on horseback from the Crown, across the common to Priory Road. Afterwards it petered out as an August amusement fair in Snape Street.

Therefore, it can fairly be said that the Malt House has a central place in Suffolk history, both ancient and more recent; and the move to embrace Snape can only bring about a deepening and a strengthening of the Festival's indigenous character. Nor could another spot have been chosen that so much enshrines the atmosphere or ambience of the Aldeburgh Festival. For the Malt House is within a stone's throw of the river; and from its east side there is a remarkably fine view of the heath, marshland and estuary which – along with the grey, silvernecked Aldeburgh sea – are the Festival's continuing undersong, the inspiration it grew from and still draws upon for much of its artistic sustenance.

Reprinted from the Festival programme book, 1966

Building Snape
Edwin Heathcote

It is hard to imagine now that when Snape Maltings was conceived in the mid-1960s the idea of re-using a historic industrial structure was a radical proposal. We have become so familiar with the notion of the transformation of a manufacturing to a cultural industry and of the conversion of hulking rusted behemoths into artistic attractions that we have become inured to quite how strange the idea may have seemed. The late 1960s was the apex of heroic Modernism, concrete blocks were seen as the solution to every problem, demolition and rebuilding the only answer to any question. Yet it was also the time when the results of these experiments had begun to be questioned. Snape Maltings' construction coincided with that of the meccas of the last Brutalist concrete, London's Elephant and Castle, Boston's City Hall and Washington DC's J. Edgar Hoover Building. The year after Snape Maltings was completed, the Ronan Point Tower block in East London, its architectural contemporary, partially collapsed. It was the end of the utopian Modernist dream. Barely a single fine concert hall had emerged during the Modernist period, each experiment was plagued by problems with acoustics, with site, with aesthetics. The references remained the halls of the nineteenth century or earlier.

So the decision by the clients and architects Ove Arup to convert the nineteenth-century maltings into a music venue was both eccentric and prescient. This was, remember, the firm that was then in the middle of what Arup engineer Derek Sugden called 'the agony of the Sydney Opera House'. But at the same time there was both a historical logic to the move and an echo of an international zeitgeist. Logic because it had long been acknowledged that it was the industrial buildings of the Victorian era which had been the true harbingers of Modernist architecture and culturally on-the-button because industrial architecture and the scale of its found-space was about to become the key driver in contemporary cultural design. Nikolaus Pevsner had highlighted the lineage of Modernism through its industrial forebears as long ago as 1936 in his *Pioneers of the Modern Movement* and British critic J.M. Richards had elaborated on the theme in his 1958 book *The Functional Tradition in Early Industrial Buildings*, with wonderfully evocative photography by Eric de Maré. This was a moment when the utopian idealism and zeal of the early modernist movement began to fade as some of its inadequacies and over-simplifications began to be realised. In its re-use and adaptation, Snape Maltings was to prove one of the most prescient of architectural interventions at a moment when British architecture was beginning to digest the Modernism which it had never properly come to terms with. What emerged proved hugely influential.

The choice of Snape Maltings, an un-selfconscious set of nineteenth-century (and a few

later) structures, was not only physically handy for founders Britten and Pears but a deliberate statement of architectural intent. If the Sydney Opera House is the proto-icon, the forerunner of every megalomaniac arts project in which every city from Bilbao to Beijing attempts to re-brand itself through design for the arts, then Snape Maltings is a pioneer in the re-use of good solid historic buildings with their own peculiar history and atmosphere, in which the feel is engrained in the very walls, ready-made. It is part of the lineage and history of Donald Judd's decommissioned military structures in the desert in Marfa, the Palais de Tokyo in Paris and of the astonishing spaces at Tate Modern and the Baltic, grand public volumes of a scale which would never have been possible had the architects had to justify building these structures from scratch.

As the forerunner of the anti-icon alone it deserves a special place in architectural history, particularly at a point now where an *ennui* is beginning to set in about the value of such over-branded architecture. But its prescience alone would not have assured it such stature and success. Snape Maltings is among the most successful and atmospheric venues because it suits its purpose so well and because it was adapted so skilfully.

The range of buildings on site, their differing scale and accidentally picturesque layout lent themselves perfectly to the new functions. The centre revolved around a brooding and impressive 832-seat concert hall, adapted with a new, self-effacing roof structure. The darkness, the rawness, the solidity and the history of the materials that formed the space lend a remarkable intensity and atmosphere which has proved impossible to reproduce. It also chimes with the harsher Brutalist ideas which were then dominant in British architecture in which materiality, texture and a peculiar earthiness and rigour replaced the whiteness, transparency and ethereality of earlier Modernism. The space was realised with minimal architectural intervention. Britten was himself, according to Sugden, distrustful of acousticians, dismissing their whole field as a 'pseudo-science'. Consequently, the composer left the work to the Arup engineer and the result has remained an enigmatic marvel.

Alongside the concert hall, separated by a perfectly appropriate courtyard, is the Britten–Pears Building which provides rehearsal facilities as well as a 114-seat Recital Room, another surprisingly intense and effective space. In 2000 architects Penoyre & Prasad added further facilities including the long restaurant which reveals the breathtaking expanse of the long, low horizon, as close as Britain gets to its own great plains.

These key facilities are now supplemented by an ambitious expansion into a neighbouring set of long-abandoned structures. This encompasses a large new studio to accommodate an audience of up to 340 and the renovation of a kiln structure, retaining the whole of its double-height space to provide accommodation for chamber music and groups and up to 80 seats. These, together with a number of new rehearsal spaces and facilities, are knitted together around a courtyard and foyer in an attempt to create an artistic hub. Snape is a long way from anywhere, it demands an effort to get there but repays it with silence and its own extraordinary atmosphere and intensity. The idea behind the new works is to draw those artists in and keep them here, to allow the place to continue to inspire them as it has inspired audiences and musicians for four decades.

The architects for the new music campus are Haworth Tompkins. They could hardly be better qualified. Haworth Tompkins made an indelible impression on the London theatre scene with a series of hugely successful interventions beginning with their renovation of the genteel Royal Court in Sloane Square. Rather than a plush velvet and gilt stucco refit they opted for a stripping hack of extraneous layers, dragging the backstage functional aesthetic into the foyer to create a series of spaces which are simultaneously tough and vulnerable, which reveal their scars but also their soul. They went on to create some of the most memorable theatrical spaces in London, including two temporary spaces for the Almeida Theatre and a fine reworking of arguably London's most successful theatrical performance space, the Young Vic. This grittily urban instillation was almost lost to a new building but Haworth Tompkins instead retained the original space and wove around existing fabric to create a hard-wearing, unselfconscious, almost industrial set of spaces with sparkles of humanity never far from view, from the superb new bar to the retained Art Nouveau tiles of the butcher's shop which still provides the heart of the complex.

What Arup managed so successfully and so presciently in the Summer of Love, that particular blend of self-effacement and grit, of allowing these wonderful buildings to speak for themselves and maintain their organic and rooted relationship with this powerful landscape, could so easily have been lost. Haworth Tompkins, I am sure, are capable of maintaining the balance and thoughtfully enhancing the complex. Industrial and agricultural buildings have been inhabited by cultural facilities for so long now that they can seem like parasites gnawing away at a world of which they have no understanding, no comprehension. Most have become the cultural equivalent of garden centres, places to spend a Sunday, stuck halfway between the twee world of heritage and the catch-all platitudes of regeneration. Snape has an intensity, a relevance and a difference which has ensured it has maintained its own highly specific identity and fostered its own culture. It uses the landscape to inspire, the buildings to hear. The buildings of agriculture which once processed the fruits of the earth now allow the land to filter back into high culture. It is a profound and uplifting place which, as I walked around the dark, dank spaces which will provide the new facilities, continues to inspire and to haunt the memory and the imagination.

Reprinted from the Festival programme book, 2007, with architectural sketches by Steve Tompkins of Haworth Tompkins

Iken

Ian McMillan

In R.H. Dove's book, *Church Bells in Britain*,
Iken is down as a four-bell tower. I had to walk
past a barking animal, through a field of stones,
to discover that the roof had gone, that they
were digging for Saxon evidence, that services
were held in ten feet near the table, boarded off.
Services were held monthly, tightly, by the ruff,
gripped to stop them blowing over the fields, held
to stop them rushing past the empty wall-space,
flying like ladies' scarves and hats, over into
the water near an old boat called Robin. Ropes
of the bells were tied high above a wheelbarrow
and they flapped in the wind which shuddered
even the Saxon evidence in pre-bag jugs below
the grass. As the ropes moved, twitching tails,

stray notes, blown from the Maltings, a mile away
across the water, soaked up into the bell-mouths
of the four bells, humming a little, to make sounds
which were carried away from me and the wild hound,
across marshland to a resort where they were no doubt
appalled by the general hubbub and noise of the tide.

From McMillan's *Handbook of Suffolk Churches*

Framlingham
Mark Mitchels

The sweet season, that bud and bloom forth brings,
With green hath clad the hill and also the vale.

So wrote Henry Howard, Earl of Surrey, for whom Framlingham was home – and final resting place. To us the castle, church and town seen from across the delicious richness of the Mere recreate the poet's vision of an English idyll. But castles were once places of danger. Uncertainty and violence were never far away, and Framlingham's story combines both triumph and despair.

The Domesday Book provides a glimpse of Framlingham in Anglo Saxon times: 'Aelmer, a thane, held Framlingham. Now Roger Bigod holds it.' Roger's son Hugh supported King Stephen, who rewarded him with the title Earl of Norfolk. His first castle in 1140 was probably more timber than anything else, consisting of a keep surrounded by a stockade. Bigods could never live at peace with their king, and after an unsuccessful rebellion Hugh was obliged to surrender Framlingham to Henry II in 1157.

The castle that dominates Framlingham today was built in the 1180s by Hugh's son Roger, who set about incorporating all the latest ideas in castle design he had learnt from the crusades. A Keep was no longer considered necessary; instead there was a curtain wall, which included towers, all linked by a battlement walkway. Ingeniously, the towers were denied a back wall, and used a wooden platform to cross them: should the castle wall be invaded, the attacker could not move easily from tower to tower. The slits in the wall indicate the different requirements of the crossbow and the longbow. Wooden shutters gave some level of protection, being tilted just enough to loose off an arrow or bolt. All the evidence for these is still there. A drawbridge and portcullis were more traditional hazards but none the less effective. Inside the great court were the many buildings required to house Bigods and their retainers, not to mention soldiers and animals – a natural pairing one suspects! The Chapel built into the east wall was beside the Great Hall, where the lord and his retinue entertained or plotted, with no clear line between the two. The well was in use only thirty years ago.

Roger Bigod was one of the barons who forced King John to sign Magna Carta in 1215, which resulted in John besieging Framlingham Castle. John had been his guest just two years earlier, and had not wasted his time either, as he knew enough about Framlingham for it to surrender in two days! There were 58 soldiers, which would seem to have been the regular size of garrison size at this time. Within a century the Bigods were ready to show defiance of authority once more. Legend claims that Edward I shouted at another Roger

Bigod, 'By God, sir Earl, you shall go to Flanders or hang!' to which the vassal retorted: 'By God, O king, I will neither go nor hang!' and history shows he did neither.

But time had run out for the Bigods when they failed to provide a male heir. In 1307 Edward I took back all the family estates when Roger died and passed them to his own friends and family. In time the lordship of Framlingham came to the Mowbray family who, as Dukes of Norfolk, dominated East Anglia, and so played their part in the Wars of the Roses. They lived at Framlingham and enjoyed its parkland and the hunting it provided. They added a bridge across the ditch, so giving direct access to the deer park, which avoided the delay of passing through the town. The remains of that bridge can still be seen today.

John, 4th Duke of Norfolk, was at Framlingham when he died in his early twenties. Sir John Paston wrote on 17 January 1476: 'It so happened that whereas my lord of Norfolk was yesterday in good health, this night about midnight he died.' Within a generation the castle had new owners, who wasted no time adding their crest to those already over the gate. The Howards had arrived. The first Howard died at Bosworth fighting for Richard III, but his son, although denied the dukedom, remained Earl of Surrey, and redeemed his family titles by defeating the Scots at Flodden in 1513. His war helm still gazes down from the chancel walls in St Michael's church. And that is where the next part of the story is told.

The church of St Michael stands between the Market Place and the Castle, which is as it should be. The chancel arch dates from the twelfth century, and since that time benefactors have left their mark. The tower was built in the fifteenth century and still has the full peal of eight bells. One of them has the sweet inscription: 'Gabriel now sings sweetly in this chamber'. From this period comes the fabulous hammer beam roof which cunningly conceals its construction behind timber fan vaulting. It is a wonder which in other churches would draw pilgrims from afar. But Framlingham has more, much more, to delight the eye.

The Howards once buried their dead at Thetford Priory. Following the Dissolution Thomas, the 3rd Duke, determined to remove the family mausoleum to Framlingham. He caused to be created a wide chancel, bathed in light where his ancestors could rest in peace. He was a man of stupendous ambition, and sought to rule the crown itself. His daughter Mary married Henry Fitzroy, the illegitimate son of the king, and for a moment he could dream the impossible. But in 1536 Fitzroy died at the age of just seventeen. Howard moved the young man's tomb from Thetford to Framlingham, where in time it would be joined by others, including his own.

The last years of Henry VIII were dangerous for everyone, especially Thomas Howard. Both he and his son were arrested in the final year and condemned to death. Henry, Earl of Surrey, courtier and poet, suffered death by the axe on 19 January 1547. The king died that very night, so Thomas Howard was spared. In the church Surrey's brilliant alabaster tomb (which dates from 1614) provides at first glance no evidence of his fall: he rests beside his wife in gorgeous robes, and his sons and daughters kneel around him. Only the detached coronet, strangely abandoned, betokens the manner of his death.

Places like Framlingham cannot have rushed to embrace Protestantism. They reluctantly painted over their wall paintings (one still survives) and struggled to use the new forms of service, but in their hearts the Old Religion remained. Suddenly, in 1553, Mary, daughter of good Queen Catherine of Aragon, was riding through the town and into the castle, where she was proclaimed rightful heir to the throne. Thousands joined her and the Protestant cause was lost in days. She processed to St Michael's Church, set up her

JOHN NASH

crucifix and bid them sing Te Deum. What joy there must have been that day! How did they see her reign in retrospect?

Within a year Thomas, the ambitious 3rd Duke of Norfolk, died, and his tomb offers a glimpse of all that would be lost, for he was buried according to the old Catholic rites in what has been described as 'one of the finest monuments of the Early Renaissance in England'. Around him in their shell niches are the Apostles, praying for his soul and offering him peace at last. His son, also Thomas, married the daughter of the Earl of Arundel and from that time the Howards fade from Suffolk, but a monument in St Michael's Church gives a sense of the authority they once commanded. Treason was never far from their name, and in 1572 Thomas was executed for plotting to marry Mary Queen of Scots. Two of his wives sleep side by side in Framlingham, and the gossips say the space between them was reserved for the Scottish queen, had he married her!

And then it was all over. By 1635 the castle had been sold to a lawyer, Sir Robert Hitcham, who left it to Pembroke College, Cambridge, with orders for its demolition. But the walls proved too much of a challenge, so the executors turned to Hitcham's other instruction and built an almshouse for the poor. In 1708 Pembroke College gave to St Michael's the exquisite Thamar organ of 1674, which in parts may be even earlier. In the course of time it has attracted recitals by the most eminent musicians and, of course, continues to accompany weekly worship.

By the beginning of the eighteenth century the castle had lost all the buildings which had stood within its courtyard, and instead there was a new Poorhouse: 'Our poor people now lead idle expensive and extravagant lives without anybody to inspect them'. Only in 1839 did the poor forsake the castle ruins which then hid behind forests of ivy for almost a century. *White's Directory* of 1844 brings us into the present age with a vision of the castle we recognise and appreciate: 'Though now a mere shell, it has, when viewed from a distance, the appearance of being entire, its outer walls being nearly all in their pristine proportions.'

Framlingham represents all that is best in Suffolk. The market place is pretty and welcoming, and other wonderful buildings in the town provide ample evidence that from earliest times they have served the community and moved with the times and fashions. Framlingham is one of East Anglia's great secrets and those who love it can – on the whole – be relied upon to keep the knowledge to themselves.

Blythburgh

Ronald Blythe

Like those at Lavenham and Long Melford, this beautiful parish church was built mainly in the fifteenth century in that wave of strenuous piety and unfounded religious optimism with which the Middle Ages closed. It stands mid-way between these two great wool churches in date and although a lesser structure than either, it is yet so marvellous a work of art, and has so much extraordinary invention in wood and stone, that it holds a particular respect in a county where fine churches are the rule and not the exception.

Churches such as this were the result of lavish mercantile endowments added to an unquestionable conviction that Heaven was beautiful as well as good. They dominated the short, dark lives of medieval people and their carved glory was in a sense a foretaste of what was to come. As the nineteenth century's popular conception of Paradise was a gentle landscape of water-meadows and flowers, so must the builders of Blythburgh have imagined it as a colourful Gothic church, vast, and loud with music.

The wealth of Blythburgh came from the sea. It was a port and it possessed a great herring industry. When the Reformation came to the town, it did so with singular irony. It not only tore down the prosperous Augustinian Priory which was the very heart of the place, but sweeping away fasts with so much else, it absolved the inhabitants from the obligation to eat fish at least twice a week. The same new freedom applied to the rest of the country. The result was that the Blythburgh fisheries languished, the comfortable little port crumbled away for lack of proper use, the River Blyth itself silted up and dissolution in every sense of the word approached until only the splendid church was left to hint of better times.

The first glimpse is of a stark high tower and a frozen, lacey greyness. A curtain of pierced stone quatrefoils is poised along the entire length of the nave and, recessed above this ornament, are the clerestory windows. The long arcade is assured, every downward tracery pencil-fine, and the repetitive detail is brilliantly controlled, so that, though it recurs again and again, it is never once mechanical. Each buttress carries the elegant M of the Virgin's monograph in black flints. Above the window, instead of the customary cross, there is a superb Christ in Majesty and by the porch, a holy-water stoup, the biggest in Suffolk.

Blythburgh is all suggestion, all evocation. It is a Job of a place that has sustained every hazard before coming to its present tranquility. A thunderbolt wrecked the west end in 1577 and the scarred font still shows the force with which the tower crashed through the roof. This font is immensely impressive. It rises from a high, stepped platform and the whole thing seen against the dessicated, rose-coloured floor is like a great gaunt cup. The

floor was crunched into its coarse mosaics by
the restless hooves of horses, belonging to the
Parliament-men, which were stabled in the
church – perhaps during the attentions of
William Dowsing the iconoclast.

JOHN NASH

After Dowsing had left and the windows
had been reduced to a heap of gaudy splinters
glinting in the common ditch, a long period
of intense neglect prevailed. The east winds
howled through the broken gaps and rain
beat down steadily through the painted roof
and poured off the angels' wings. And to
finish matters, a few years after the formal
desecration of the church, Blythburgh itself was destroyed in a great fire in 1676. Now
nothing was left, no sign that the place had ever been anything more than a village. A
network of rather meaningless lanes might puzzle the visitor. They were once busy streets
where such men as wealthy John Hopton lived, and William Chilson, who left his godson
a book called *Vanquites Cronackles*.

Blythburgh Church has outlasted all these vicissitudes, emerging phoenix-like from the
flames which took so much else. Its texture and quality is like one of those vivid, lustrated
bricks which have been for a long time in the sea. It is blanched by the East Anglian
climate. Inside, it is pale and as though drenched in centuries of fine, marine light. The roof
is a dull white stencilled over with crimson and green flowers. Seraphs bear down from a
great height, hugging against their breasts the heraldic claims of local knights. Each of
their wings is said to be made from a single board. Carved and gilded curls spring from
their temples. The roof is spattered with shot from the guns of the Puritans in their attempt
to shoot down the angels. The scene is grotesque to imagine – the horses tethered to
the piers, the stupid faces of the men, sweaty, perhaps, from so much window-smashing,
looking up the barrels of their nearly perpendicular guns. And above them, the same
sweetly-bland countenances that we see now. One fancies a brutal, pot-shotting mirth
and an outlandish noise from the rag-tag usually recruited to carry out orders of this
kind. But the angels won. They inhabit their pallid Eden much the same as they did 500
years ago.

There are many things to see, the wonderful woodwork, the moralising pew-ends, the
signature a boy cut in a choir-stall, 'Dirck Lowerson von Stockholm Anno 1665 Ag 12' –
Scandinavians and Dutchmen came to Blythburgh in the seventeenth century to assist in
draining the marshes. They brought their families and the children were taught to read and
write in the church. We may take it that Dirck showed great promise in both subjects – the
superb clerestory of eighteen closely-set windows, Sir John Hopton's marble tomb chest,
the two priests' doorways, each sheltered by a flying buttress, the bracket with the word
M.A.R.I.A. jutting out from a pillar, suggesting the Altar of the Salutation, and an ancient
timepiece called Jack-of-the-clock which was once connected with the tower clock and
gave the hour for Divine Service.

There is much more, of course, and, not least, the most remarkable acoustics.

Blythburgh was the first church outside Aldeburgh to be used for Festival concerts. In
June 1956 the Purcell Singers, with Peter Pears, gave a programme here which included

works by Palestrina, Priaulx Rainier, Bach and Thomas Tomkins. The concert opened with Purcell's *Magnificat in G Minor*. But the most dramatic role which this lovely building has assumed in recent years was that of an opera-house for a brilliantly re-staged performance of Mozart's *Idomeneo* after the burning-down of the Maltings.

Staring about one in Blythburgh brings to mind the words of David Gascoyne:

Tenebral treasure and immortal flower
And flower of immortal Death!
O silent white extent
Of skyless sky, the wingless flight
And the long flawless cry
Of aspiration endlessly!

Reprinted from the Festival programme book, 1956

Local churches
became festival
venues

The Storm, Blythburgh, 1577

Anne Beresford

Sky darkening
and then the wind
from far off
far over the sea
sweeping waves, sand and pebbles
against the cliffs
on leathern wings.

And we heard it coming
had no fear
being in God's house.
Louder it came
shrieking among us
licking us with fire
swift and terrible
as the great beams tumbled.

Two men died that day.
Later we found a huge handprint
blackened on the North door.

A Modern Architecture for Suffolk?

Alan Powers

The phrase 'Critical Regionalism' entered the discussion of architecture in the 1980s, but the idea that modern architecture should reflect local character is an older one. The historian and theorist Kenneth Frampton offers three ways in which this can happen: through the inspiration of 'such things as the range and quality of the local light'; through learning from local materials and construction methods; or finally by means of a sensitive adaptation to a particular landscape. We are reminded of Peter Grimes' explanation of what binds him to the Borough:

> By familiar fields,
> Marsh and sand,
> Ordinary streets,
> Prevailing wind.

All three possibilities are amply available in Suffolk, especially along the coast, to the east of the Ipswich-to-Lowestoft road, now the A12, which divides the clay soils to the west from the Sandlands or Sandlings towards the sea, with their slow rise and fall, their broad tidal rivers fringed by river walls and reclaimed pasture, and their ancient oak woods. Soil, water and light seem to work together to create its character. In his autobiographical essay 'The Other Side of the Alde', first published in *A Tribute to Benjamin Britten on his Fiftieth Birthday* [see p.93], Kenneth Clark, who spent much of his childhood at Sudbourne Hall near Orford, wrote of the way that the intense light of Aldeburgh, the result of the sun reflected off sea and river together, made him feel more intelligent than he did in other places. After listing in his *Shell Guide to Suffolk* several poets who took inspiration from the place, Norman Scarfe elegantly states the undeniable: 'In that less familiar and accessible world of the ear, one hears Mr Britten's immediate response to Suffolk.' It is the physical setting for several works by Britten that have a specific location in which ordinariness is often significant, while others such as *Curlew River* describe a landscape that is typical of the east coast from the Thames to the Wash, not an immediately welcoming or warm one, nor dramatically sublime, but apt for melancholy as well as illumination. It can be foolish to look for close parallels between different art forms, but nonetheless tempting to make comparisons between Britten's music and the buildings of his contemporaries that similarly seem to respond to the Suffolk landscape and light.

The idea that an architect should be closely associated with a particular territory has come and gone in the course of the past 150 years, enjoying strong support in the Arts and Crafts period, and then being challenged by the idea that for philosophical as much as commercial reasons, architecture should aim for universal character regardless of place. This was exemplified in certain phases of the Modern Movement, although rejected by many of its followers who developed critical regionalism in practice long before Frampton established it in theory. For these, any landscape will serve, but once selected, it requires patient study before its essence can be transmuted into form that can be localised without resort to kitsch or cliché.

Aldringham had its own Arts and Crafts hero, Cecil Herbert Lay, while Walberswick had Frank Jennings, the father of film director Humphrey Jennings, one of Benjamin Britten's contemporaries in left-wing documentary production in the 1930s [see p.108]. Between Crabbe Street and Crag Path, Aldeburgh has a row of houses by an almost unknown but estimable Arts and Crafts designer, Thomas Stevens Lee, including the corner house with its rather aggressive flintwork, and 2 Crabbe Street, where Britten and Pears lived between 1947 and 1957. Edwardian and 1920s prosperity scattered other houses in the upper and lower parts of the town, including several by Oliver Hill and Horace Field. Thorpeness was Modern in its use of concrete blocks, but in other ways delightfully defies the laws of architectural correctness, as a holiday village ought.

The Modern Movement grew out of the Arts and Crafts, although it was a long and devious evolution and there are no major examples in Suffolk of the first fruits of the new style, abundant though these tended to be at the seaside. After 1920, women could qualify as architects (unlike Agnes and Rhoda Garrett) and go into practice, and Hilda Mason (1880–1955) built a concrete version of a perpendicular church at St Andrew, Felixstowe in 1930, a strange hybrid. Her own flat-roofed house at Woodbridge, overlooking Martlesham Creek, was less constrained by convention. Arthur Welford, the future father-in-law of Beth Britten, converted Hudson's Mill on the crest of the hill in Snape in 1937–8 for the young composer, creating a typically 1930s run of curved steel windows for the first-floor bedroom, with views over the Alde valley.

Apart from these works, which were not of national significance, Suffolk, like many other counties, effectively missed out on Modern architecture before the war. In the years since 1945 it has acquired a scattering of distinguished works by nationally known practices, among which Norman Foster's Willis Faber Dumas offices in Ipswich (1975, which he designed with Michael Hopkins) take precedence for showmanship and anticipation of future trends in construction methods and office planning. There is a scattering of post-war Modern houses across the county, including a cluster in the Stour Valley by Edward Cullinan at Nayland and Aldington & Craig at Higham St Mary. In West Suffolk, Philip Dowson built a much-published house, Long Wall, near Long Melford, and also worked on the conversion of Snape Maltings. Modern houses by the coast tended to be holiday houses, even if their owners retired to them later on. In the mid-1960s, Jack Pritchard, the creator of Isokon furniture and patron in the 1930s of Wells Coates, Marcel Breuer and Walter Gropius, built a discreet single-storey house in Angel Lane, Blythburgh, designed by his daughter, Jennifer Jones. In the mysterious backlands of the plateau above Aldeburgh High Street H.T. Cadbury-Brown and his wife Betty, who ran a small but prestigious architectural practice in London, built a weekend house that is similarly hidden in a large garden. He was drawn to Aldeburgh because of a family connection running back through two generations, and acquired the site after the abandonment of an opera house he had planned there for the Festival. An earlier scheme for an opera house beside Aldeburgh Parish Church was abandoned because the site was too small, and the second one, whose format was influenced by Britten's discovery of Noh plays, failed because insufficient funds were raised, and it would have had too few seats to be viable. The Cadbury-Brown house, with its lovely effects of light falling through skylights and well-placed windows onto white walls and tiled floors, is architecturally a more successful use for the site, and is the only post-war building in Aldeburgh to be listed.

While Modernism is generally seen as the natural home of every free-thinking architect of the 1930s, this was not entirely the case. Raymond Erith (1904–73) lived and ran his practice in Dedham, just across the Stour from Suffolk, and among the classicists of his generation was the one whom Modernists respected for his invention and originality. Suffolk contains only minor works by him, but his unexecuted design for offices, warehouse and factory in Ipswich in 1948 would have been, had it been built, a model for reinterpreting the early nineteenth-century warehouse style for modern uses. Erith built a series of small houses in East Bergholt, many of them now sadly altered, which are models for modest domestic grandeur, and a village hall that dignified a cheap structure with well-scaled detailing. Best seen from Iken beach or from a boat, his Georgian refronting of the late Victorian Blackheath House on the north bank of the Alde has exactly the right scale for the sweep of water and sky. Blackheath is now home to distinguished Modern architects Sir Michael Hopkins and his wife Patty, who admit a growing admiration for the quality of Erith's work there, which now encases a restructured interior of Palladian purity.

On a spectrum between tradition and Modernism, we might place the Lowestoft practice of Tayler & Green next in line after Erith. Both partners trained, as Erith did a few years earlier, at the Architectural Association in London, and began their practice with a Modern-style studio in Highgate. The war changed their lives, however, and for family and professional reasons they spent the war in Lowestoft, where their office remained. Herbert Tayler (1913–2000) was a designer of immense talent, if not genius, who came closer than any of his contemporaries to creating a critical regionalism that gives a sense of belonging both in time and place – the time being the period 1947–73, and the place largely the rural villages of the Loddon District in Norfolk, divided from Suffolk by the Waveney, where almost every village has one or more of Tayler & Green's terraces of council houses with shallow-pitched pantile roofs, decorated brick gable ends, and variegated colours. They knew Britten because David Green (1913–98) had been a school friend of his. Both were opera buffs, and planned a conversion of the Jubilee Hall in Aldeburgh into a small opera house in 1950, which was probably over-ambitious for its time. But a special kind of ordinariness was their forte, in which the more dogmatic aspects of Modernism such as the flat roof were made secondary to practicality, popular taste, and a feeling for place.

John Penn (1921–2007) grew up on the Suffolk coast at Bawdsey, and returned after formative professional experiences in America in the office of Richard Neutra. The clean lines and simple plan forms of post-war American Modernism, close in spirit to the purest forms of classicism, are reflected in Penn's series of small but consequential houses up and down the coastal strip. The Lodge, Hasketon, the first of the series, established the principle of a symmetrical, usually square, plan form rising from a plinth like a Greek temple from its stylobate. His houses lie low in the landscape, answering the broad horizons, and one needs to know where to find them in villages such as Rendham, Orford, Westleton and Shingle Street. As Penn wrote, 'these houses resemble little temples, whose altars have been replaced by hearths, focal to all the designs'. At the time of his death early in 2007, Penn's work was undergoing a process of rediscovery, with an exhibition of photographs of his houses held in Margaret Howell's fashionable London store near the Wigmore Hall.

When it came to buildings commissioned by Britten and Pears or by the Festival, architects generally came from further afield, although another of Cadbury-Brown's small jobs was to create a simple music room for Britten above a stable building at the Red House in 1957, when they first moved there. In 1964, they commissioned Peter Collymore to design the more ambitious library, on the site of a former cow shed, as a room for chamber music and entertaining as well as books. Collymore is not a well-known architect, but is the author of a standard monograph on the Anglo-Swedish architect Ralph Erskine (designer of the Byker Wall housing in Newcastle and Clare Hall in Cambridge), which gives a clue to his lively and sensitive approach to materials, structure and light, making the room perfect in its way. In 1993, it was enlarged to fulfil its institutional function by Robert Wilson and Malcolm Ness without detracting from its quality. Amusement was created in the national press when Britten's garden shed at Horham, to which he used to retreat in later life for absolute peace and privacy, was listed (quite properly) as a building of historic if not architectural interest. On the subject of libraries, mention should be made of the branch library in Victoria Road, Aldeburgh, seen by almost every visitor as they enter the town on the road from Snape. It represents a period of high quality local authority design in Britain fostered as part of the public service culture of the post-war period. Its ingenious roof and tall windows attract attention, and inside it is always cheerful and bright.

The architectural history of Snape Maltings, including its conversion to a concert hall in 1967, deserves a more extended discussion than it can receive here [see p.205], but the manner of the conversion by Arup Associates, led by Derek Sugden, won praise not only for the quality of the acoustic but for its response to the style of the original buildings. Sugden is an engineer, and at the start of the project, he declared to a colleague, 'I think we'll keep the architects out of this if we can.' He was right. The conversion responds to the unselfconscious quality of the original buildings. The cane seating, locally made although inspired by Bayreuth, brilliantly hinges at the cultural intersection between country Georgian and the Bauhaus, and conveys the quality of the whole scheme in microcosm. At the Maltings, one has faith that Modern architecture can be simple and inevitable, in tune with its surroundings and revealing of human love and skill in its making.

In Suffolk as elsewhere, it is hard to find new buildings or conversions that strike the right note with so little apparent effort, when planners so often seem to favour complication. Like perfect pitch, this kind of attunement is born rather than made, but for some reason it is harder for most people to recognise it in architecture than in music. Sadly, if you have eyes to see, you don't have to look far in Aldeburgh in 2008 to find proof.

Castles in the Sand: Summers in Thorpeness

William Taylor

Around 1910, a coastal hamlet called Thorpe, about a mile and a half north of Aldeburgh, became Thorpeness, a Seaside Resort for the discerning holidaymaker, described by its architect, in *à la mode* terms, as a 'Garden Village by the sea.'[1] The acquisition of its slightly aspirational suffix, which distinguished it at the time from the sixteen other mere 'Thorpe's in England, certainly marked a turning point in the fortunes of this string of fishermen's cottages along the Suffolk coast. But the change of name also heralded the arrival of a twentieth-century institution: the middle class 'buckets and spades' summer holiday.

It was a Scottish architect (and sometime playwright) called Glencairn Stuart Ogilvie who saw the hamlet's potential as a sort of upmarket Butlins, before its time. He purchased the entire estate, established a company ('Seaside Bungalows Ltd.') and laid out his new model village, footpath by footpath, adapting its natural features to his fantasy formulations. He dammed and sluiced, designed and dug, planted and planned his way towards the creation of his own 'Garden Village'. With a range of customised bungalows, a Country Club, a village store-cum-post office, a new pub, a rebuilt church and an assortment of designated recreational zones (tennis courts, croquet lawns, a bowling green, a rounders ground, a cricket pitch – with plans for a golf course, not to mention the boating lake), Ogilvie was busy putting the 'resort' into the seaside holiday experience.

Visitors to Thorpeness are still easily distracted by the village's bizarre architectural and landscaping features. The one-time Water Tower – known familiarly as the 'House in the Clouds' – appears like a totem on all the postcards and the Meare, or boating lake, with its mock Norman keep and Swallows and Amazon fantasy follies, is also unique, if uniquely weird, even a little sinister. The prize for architectural pastiche is reserved, however, for the Elizabethan style cottages that surround the 'Country Club' – what Ogilvie called the *Kursaal*, a German word for 'Cure Hall' or place of healthy amusement – now a collection of privately leased apartments. These black and white weather-boarded and half-timbered dwellings look as though they have been transported by lorry straight up the A12 from Chigwell in Essex. They are essence of suburbia.

The fact is that much of Thorpeness, to the *Aga*-ed out metropolitan sensibility, is a bit vulgar. Quaintly rustic, it is not. For the committed Thorpeness resident this is partly, however, the point. The village mocks the studied charm and rather more elegant whimsy

---

1. Background material on the history of Thorpeness is drawn from W.H. Parkes, *Guide to Thorpeness* (original 1912, republished 2001 by Meare Publications).

of Aldeburgh. They may have the Moot Hall down the road but we, at least, have Wendy's House on Peter Pan's island in the middle of a shallow ditch of a boating lake referred to locally as the Spanish Main.

One suspects that, when it comes down to it, what the dissenters actually dislike about Maggi Hambling's Scallop sculpture, positioned as it is over at the Aldeburgh end of the beach, is that it draws attention to itself a little bit too self-consciously. It's just a little bit too, well, you know, Thorpeness.

❊ ❊ ❊

But all this is to miss the point of Thorpeness. These accidental follies and architectural peculiarities came about only because of a natural feature of the village that is both delightful and rare indeed along the Suffolk Coast. Although Ogilvie may have brought the Seaside Resort into being, the raw material was already there. And the raw material is still pretty much there. The point of Thorpeness is the beach and the sand.

Whereas shingle is pretty much the order of the day elsewhere along the coast, Thorpeness still offers a temporary reprieve. There is actually work here for the bucket and spade to do. You can build castles with moats and trenches running down to the water, which, unlike Ogilvy's fantasy keeps, will thankfully be gone by morning. Having pursued a summer romance with a girl staying with her family in the Country Club, you can sign your names to some wildly extravagant covenant in complete confidence that it will be revoked by the turning tide.

The cliffs rise at the north end of the village and then crumble at their base into the dunes, with their scrub and fauna. Here lies the possibility of hidden treasure: rusty bits of boat, coloured rope, driftwood, fossils, even starfish. This is where you can occasionally find amber after a spring storm and where you can also take shelter from the wind, barbequing your sausages to a frazzle. This is also where, as a teenager in the early '80s, I had my first cigarette and, later that summer, my first snog.

The 'Ness' of the Thorpeness is, in fact, a spit of sand, which runs out into the sea a few hundred yards north of the village and at low tide forms a sand-bank that my brother and I would swim out to, much to my mother's alarm. She would stand on the beach and wave us back in. We would cheerily wave back and continue to pretend that we had been

shipwrecked or, if we were prepared to face the consequences when we returned to shore, were drowning. Later, as we sat in a warm bath, between her telling us to hurry up and clean the sand from between our toes, she would warn us darkly about things called 'currents' that could sweep us away forever. Her fears were palpable but also to my child's mind, somewhat inexplicable. What could be lovelier than rolling around on the wet sand?

✳ ✳ ✳

It was my arrival in the world that caused my family, in fact, to discover Thorpeness in the first place. Following their marriage in the late 1950s my parents had always spent two weeks every summer at the same hotel in the same town on the East coast of Sutherland in Scotland – Dornoch. First with my brother's birth and then with mine in 1965 these holidays became, however, logistically impossible. My father, a barrister, heard about Thorpeness through a colleague at his chambers, and my mother persuaded him to give it a try. He was initially very reluctant, grumbling that it wasn't Dornoch all the way down to the cottage that they had rented in the village from the Estate, for a trial week, in 1967.

What was it about Thorpeness that won him over? The golf course in the village will have helped. But my mother says it was also the purple heather that flourished across the Suffolk heathlands; it was the Scotch pines that clustered around the fields like elders discussing the sermon after kirk on the Sabbath; it was the view of the River Alde and its wide estuary channel (as seen from Aldeburgh golf course) as it snaked its way from Snape towards the sea; it was the golden yellow gorse that lit up the dunes in the early evening beyond the perimeter fence of the seaside cottage where we were staying. It all reminded him of his beloved Scotland.

Within two years my parents had decided that they wanted their own seaside bungalow in Thorpeness and my father began negotiations with Captain Ogilvie (Glencairn Stuart's nephew) over the purchase of some land. The Estate was selling a few development plots, very selectively, up on the cliff at the north end of the village. They wanted to encourage the right sort of people – families who were prepared to invest in Project Resort. Negotiations were conducted much as though a job interview, or for membership of a club. It probably helped my father's cause that he was a Scot. They played a round of golf together. Wives were introduced. My brother and I were fielded as exhibit A and B. In the end a plot of land, a third of an acre, became ours, in September 1968, for five thousand pounds. My parents built a bungalow with views of the sea and a short drop to the dunes. It was ready for occupation the following summer.

We went down to Thorpeness for two weeks in 1969. For the first week we rented our usual cottage from the Estate while my mother fitted and kitted out the new bungalow, receiving sofas from Habitat and a delivery of curtains from Peter Jones. I have vivid memories of playing with my father on the beach, making castles, indeed entire walled cities, in the sand. There is Super 8 cine evidence to prove it – though, to be honest, I'm not quite sure which came first, the memories or the film. I also have a photograph of me sitting on his shoulders as he pointed out to sea, probably to distract me from some more pressing complaint.

We moved into our state-of-the-art holiday house in September 1969 and spent a week together there, commuting between the sea and the hosepipe in the back garden. My parents named the bungalow after a small village in Scotland, just outside Dornoch, the site of a salmon leap they loved. We now had our very own slice of Seaside Resort.

Returning to Surrey at the end of the two weeks, my father resumed his more prosaic commute between Guildford and Waterloo. Not, however, for very long. At the end of October, barely two months later, returning home one evening on the train from London, he died of a heart attack. He may have brokered the deal but was never himself to set foot into the land of the 1970s family holiday-by-the-sea.

* * *

Records show that the family holiday taken in Britain, rather than abroad, peaked at 40 million between the early to mid-1970s. Most of these were taken at the seaside and a fair proportion of them, it seemed – certainly from my perspective as young boy – were taken in Thorpeness. The village was full of noisy and boisterous families having jolly holiday fun and there was, of course – thanks to the Ogilvie Estate – lots of it to be had. There was the annual competitive Regatta on the Meare, followed by an evening of floats and fireworks, as well as a series of knock-out tennis tournaments at the Country Club, which also hosted General Knowledge quiz nights, Housey Housey (a.k.a. Bingo) evenings and, the social highlight of the week, Community Dancing on Saturday night.

The thought of these dances still brings me out in a cold sweat. My brother and I would head up to the Country Club in our jackets and our neckerchiefs, accompanied by our mother. We would order a Purple Passion at the bar (lemonade and blackcurrant juice) and then try and cadge some spare chairs at the end of a bustling table. As families flung themselves ever more hysterically around the dance hall, Stripping the Willow or chasing down the Dashing White Sergeant, we would sit there rigid, nursing our drinks, looking on with fixed grins. I loved these dances and hated them in equal measure. I felt exposed and awkward and anxious without being able quite to work out why.

Inevitably I took up golf and the pro at Thorpeness, a man called Willie Cattell, showed a kindly interest in me. He would take me out with his dog looking for lost balls and tell me golfing stories. I also used to wander down to the Meare and spend afternoons talking to Albert, the boat-keeper, who would give me little jobs to do, mooring up the kayaks and swilling out the punts.

On one occasion the local parson took me out for a drive around the local villages in his vintage car. He said he was sorry to hear about my father. He said that sometimes you had to let go of the things you loved the most. I had no idea what he was talking about. I was fascinated, however, by the fact that he only had one hand – the other, I seem to remember, had been lost in an industrial accident and had been replaced by a human-sized action-man fist, which seemed to be made of bakelite, at least something hard. I remember Mr Cowley preaching on the text – 'And if thy hand offend thee, cut it off' – and demonstrating the point all too vividly by flinging off his prosthetic member into the midst of his horrified holiday congregation, as though he were tossing a fish into a pool of penguins. The adults sat bolt upright in their pews, unable to move, as the children scrabbled around the aisles and fought to retrieve his errant limb for him.

Sometime in the 1980s, I stopped spending my summers in Thorpeness. I moved on. I discovered student inter-railing and then cheap flights to find foreign sand. Captain Ogilvie had died by then and the estate began offloading its assets to pay for death duties. St

Mary's Church, only ever open in the summer, was sold for flats. It was around that time that the Country Club also discontinued its dances and Bingo nights and tufts of grass sprung up around the tennis courts, as though the dunes were reclaiming their own. The old wartime pillbox on Thorpeness cliff, which my brother and I had taken turns to defend from the other, was helped onto the beach by a crane, courtesy of Suffolk Coastal Health and Safety, joining the flotsam and jetsam along the sands.

As increasing numbers sought the assurance of sun abroad, Thorpeness seemed to take a turn away from Seaside Resort towards Retirement Village.

* * *

But something has changed over the last ten years. The buckets and spades have returned, along with the dances and the Bingo. Maybe it's global warming and a concern about carbon emissions, or maybe it is a more basic rediscovery of the pleasures of wet sand between your toes, but Thorpeness seems to be rediscovering its vocation as a resort of choice for the discerning holidaymaking family. The Country Club has found an excellent new patron in Mr Heald and is open again for business. Down at the Meare, they've even taken a bucket of disinfectant to Wendy's House and the boating lake is as strangely popular as ever.

My mother, meanwhile, is selling up after forty years. Nothing, I suppose, lasts forever. I guess sometimes you have to let go of the things you love the most. You can build your castle on the beach, but no matter how well trenched your moats with drainage systems, no matter how well castellated your keep with pebbles and shells, no matter how well defended your walls with shingle and driftwood, by morning it will all be gone.

But that's the thing about sand and sea. That's also the beauty of the Seaside Holiday. That's Thorpeness.

Frontier County

Patrick Dillon

At Shotley Spit, where the Orwell flows into Harwich Harbour, the river narrows suddenly alongside a steep, sandy beach. It's a peaceful spot, except on race days. There is nothing marked on the chart, and the nearest buoys are called Pepys and College, but to folklore this is Bloody Point. King Alfred's navy is said to have fought a fleet of Viking raiders here until the shallow waters were churned red by the fighting, and the wreckage of longships was strewn all along the shore.

The skyline above Bloody Point is topped by the mast of HMS *Ganges,* Shotley's shorebound training ship. My father climbed it in 1943 as a young naval recruit – sail was long gone, but the Royal Navy still believed in the character-building properties of thin rope and dizzying height. Years later, walking round the ramparts of Framlingham Castle, I discovered he suffered so badly from vertigo that he couldn't even let go of the handrail. But duty had called. Somehow the demands of war had propelled him to the top of Shotley mast and given him the courage to open his eyes to the North Sea.

Alfred's sailors weren't the last to drown in these waters; my father wasn't the first young man to stare east at a green horizon full of enemies. The Suffolk coast has been a frontier for centuries, and for many of them a contested one, its sandy waters offering too easy a highway to Angles and Vikings, Dutch, Germans and Russians. For two thousand years and more, young men like my father have scanned that horizon, shivering at mastheads or on castle battlements, peering into North Sea fog for the dragon-prows of longships, or man-of-wars' topsails, for snub-nosed landing-craft, or more recently, since war became technical and moved indoors, for the blips on a screen signalling aircraft. And today, the watchtowers they left behind can still be found all over the county, pillboxes choked in nettles and castles perched on dunes, reminding us that this peaceful coast happens also to be England's eastern frontier.

King Alfred's fleet left no mark at Bloody Point. Of the ships which have defended this shore, nothing remains – not of HMS *Conqueror,* built at Harwich and battered at Trafalgar, not of the bravely-named Harwich Force which sailed out of the Orwell on its way to the battle of Heligoland Bight, or of HMS *Setter,* foundered after a collision off the Sunk. Nothing, indeed, remains of the only North Sea invasion of recent centuries that actually succeeded. King James II had been Lord High Admiral and knew these waters well, but he still refused to believe that his nephew, William of Orange, might transport an army of Dutch veterans, mercenaries and English radicals across them to challenge his Catholic regime. It was on 4 November 1688 that the Earl of Dartmouth's fleet, anchored behind the Gunfleet sand, saw Dutch sails on the horizon. The weather was as bad as only the North Sea in autumn can conjure up, a south-easterly gale blowing 'so very hard that we were forced to strike all our yards and topmasts, and ride with two cables and a half out'.

Dartmouth knew that half of his officers supported the Prince of Orange; nonetheless he would have made a fight of it if only the 'Protestant Wind' had backed enough to let him weather the sandbank. Instead he had to watch the Dutch fleet sail past into the Channel, and endure the withering letter which Samuel Pepys, secretary of the Navy, despatched to him afterwards: 'I have nothing to say to your Lordship saving that since it has so unhappily fallen out, that the Dutch are at this hour peaceably putting on shore their whole land force and baggage, consequently their men of war will now be at an entire liberty to attack *you*.' Six weeks after the Dutch landed, William of Orange marched into London and James was escorted down the Thames to Rochester. James's failure of nerve in the Revolution of 1688 was uncharacteristic, for as Lord High Admiral he had won a reputation for bravery. In 1672 three flagships were destroyed under him when he fought the Dutch at Sole Bay, within sight of the Southwold cliffs.

Whatever wreckage survives of those naval encounters is hidden beneath the North Sea. On dry land, though, Suffolk's history as a frontier province has left relics enough – towers of flint, brick or concrete, gates draped in rusting barbed wire, walls which are neither church nor manor house. These are things special to a coast; things which belong not to the peaceful farmland around them, but to faraway conflicts of which these enigmatic fragments are the last surviving signs.

To the Romans, this was the Saxon shore, north-eastern frontier of an empire that stretched into Asia. They built their fortress at Gariannonum – Burgh Castle – with walls three metres thick. It safeguarded the province until its cavalry garrison rode away to fight civil wars in Gaul. After that, ramparts crumbling, it did nothing to deter the invaders who sailed across the North Sea to claim their 'East Anglia'. They were the ancestors of Raedwald, whose burial ship, alone of the North Sea fleets, has survived – or rather its ghost, etched dimly into the sand at Sutton Hoo.

Angles were the first successful invaders, but others, still more feared, followed them across the North Sea. Ramsholt's Saxon tower – or a predecessor of it – is said to have been a lookout for Viking longships, and two battles at least were fought on the Blackwater, at Maldon. Much later, Henry II built his castle at Orford to prevent Hugh Bigod of Framlingham from summoning mercenaries from Germany. When it was built, around 1165, Orford was the easternmost point of a Plantaganet Empire, which reached as far as the Pyrenees. From its battlements, soldiers in chainmail rusted by sea wind stared out at the North Sea horizon, just as my father would, and maybe saw the same things there – the unknown, a place beyond England, death. Orford was still on the coast, then. The North Sea's scouring tides hadn't yet deposited the shingle spit on which, centuries later, shivering in wooden huts, Robert Watson-Watt and his team of scientists would develop radar to scour the same horizon for a new enemy.

Like Orford, most coastal fortifications have something rudimentary about them, perhaps because of the knowledge of how quickly these early-warning stations might be overrun. The Martello Towers built in a chain from Aldeburgh to Seaford, Suffolk to Sussex, were thrown up in brick, a hasty cordon against Napoleon's revolution. Today, converted to rental lets and holiday homes, they still provide good landmarks for the river mouths. Each had one gun on it, and rockets to signal where invasion had struck. A few stayed in service for years, gradually accreting the debris of new wars and new technologies. Garrison Point at the mouth of the Medway is the oddest of all, a brick cone topped with a barnacle-like encrustation of rusting catwalks and concrete gun platforms.

The Napoleonic wars over, it was for this coast that Erskine Childers feared when he wrote *The Riddle of the Sands* as a warning against the battleships which a newly-wealthy Germany, industrialised and aggressive, had launched in Baltic ports. They only put to sea once, but the gunfire off Jutland is said to have been heard in Aldeburgh. Harwich became home to a large naval squadron, but its steel leviathans were already too unwieldy for the North Sea. Without radar, radio or GPS, a North Sea fog made them as blind as any Viking longship, and the Navy lists are full of ships lost not to German guns, but to gale, grounding or collision.

Technology kept changing, though, and so did war. Yarmouth was the first town in Britain to be bombed from the air, when a Zeppelin attacked it on 19 January 1915. In June 1917 the town was attacked again, but this time the Zeppelin was shot down. A fragment of its steel skeleton, twisted by fire, still hangs in the porch of Theberton church. 'The bomber will always get through' was the mantra of between-wars planners. To protect London, helpless up the Thames Estuary, the Ministry of Defence perched concrete castles on every sandbank off the coast – the Roughs Tower can still be seen from Felixstowe on clear days. Fighter squadrons were stationed inland. Douglas Bader flew his first missions from Martlesham Heath, while the Spitfire's seaplane ancestor, the Supermarine S5, was tested from the sheds at Harwich. On the south coast, the Ministry of Defence constructed huge parabolic reflectors in an effort to catch the sound of an aircraft engine being fired across the water in France.

Radar was more promising technology, although more complex. Its principles were already established by the time war approached. The challenge for Robert Watson-Watt and his team of researchers at Orford was to turn it into a usable system of defence. The scientists worked until last orders at the Crown and Castle, tackling the problems of range-finding, of low-flying aircraft, of airbourne radar sets. In 1936 they moved to Bawdsey Manor, where spindly masts rose up above the shoreline, and the technicians spent hours peering into hooded screens, trying to entrap the ghosts of the planes from Martlesham which droned endlessly up and down the coast. On the day Churchill visited, the machines refused to work. He heard the planes, then saw them, but the screens stayed blank. Fortunately, a successful test the following day convinced him that radar still had a future.

It was in the summer before the war began that archaeologists further up the Deben found the ghost of a longship in the sand at Sutton Hoo, and the sword and helmet which proved how feeble a barrier the North Sea could be, how smooth a highway to a determined enemy. Against a later invasion threat, the MOD littered the coastal plain with tiny concrete pillboxes. Most of them are still there, as Orford Castle is, and the Martello Towers, nestling in weeds and smelling of urine. Their walls, closely examined, still carry the boardmarks of the timber planks nailed together by some work party on a hot summer afternoon in 1940. Fragments of concrete left behind by a global conflict, they never had any other purpose to serve, and exist now only to house the ghosts of bored 18-year-olds who stare out through the castellated eyeslits at imaginary Panzers.

By the time they were built, physical fortifications no longer provided much protection for the east coast. But its last and greatest struggle has left perhaps the most momentous relics of all. Bentwaters was off-limits when I was a child, known only from the barbed wire in Rendlesham Forest, and the sound of American voices in the Woodbridge Co-op. We didn't know what went on behind the MOD signs, although sometimes we heard the thunder of jet engines overhead and once, on the news, saw a group of protesters carrying slogans against cruise missiles. Years later I met an electrician from Alabama who had been stationed at Bentwaters. For him, the Cold War had meant only homesickness relieved by station dances and imported hamburgers. It wasn't until Aldeburgh Music adopted Bentwaters for its *Faster than Sound* events in 2006 that I could visit it myself, and finally understood the enormous scale of that conflict.

Bentwaters' roadways stretched as far as we could see, and the sky seemed endless. The hangars which dotted the plain looked like the lairs of extinct dinosaurs. Everything in sight – control towers, feeder roads, bomb stores – had been positioned with a cold purpose we could no longer read. We went into one of the hangars. The warm June evening didn't reach inside. It smelled of wet concrete, and its blast doors were rusting. There was nothing in it but a black stain on the floor, but that was enough, just for a moment, to summon up the ghost of a technician with an oilcan, and the silver gleam of the aeroplane above him. Like every child of my age, back in the seventies, I had nightmares of nuclear war. There, in that chilly hanger, I finally tracked that terror to its source.

The aeroplane is gone, scrapped like King Alfred's ships and Dartmouth's fleet. But the hangar itself will be too expensive to demolish. Like Orford, like the Martello Towers and pillboxes, it will stay there forever, weeds growing through the floor, admired by tourists who no longer remember why the Russians wanted to kill us, or why the Americans cared about life in Saxmundham. There are no more Nazis to assault the pillboxes, or German Dreadnoughts to bombard Harwich. There is no Napoleon across the sea from the Martello Towers, or Angevin empire stretching behind Orford; there are no barbarians to attack the forts of the Saxon shore. The reasons for conflicts don't last. But their debris does, flotsam from storms which have long died down, to litter the beaches of Britain's eastern frontier. All over comfortable Suffolk it reaches out to nudge us with the uncomfortable reminder that peace rarely lasts, and that here, on the shore of the North Sea, we are living on an edge. Like dinosaurs' footprints, proving that monsters really can exist, these castles and bomb stores still hold the dank chill of a time of fear.

After the concert we were the last car to leave the airfield. There was a row of cones to keep us on the perimeter road, but they were easy enough to dodge. So, still chasing monsters, or the ghosts of those watchers in ships and on battlements, we turned right. And just for a moment, with the Suffolk sky spread out before us, we were accelerating along the runway, racing faster and faster as we tracked the concrete ribbon down which the B52s once thundered, before lifting into the air to face east.

Lethality and Vulnerability
Louise K. Wilson

Notes about spending time on Orford Ness

Extraordinary sounds travel freely around the empty military buildings on Orford Ness. The wind animates this Cold War site, producing noises like oddly tuned musical or percussive instruments. The flute-like harmonics on top of the Bomb Ballistic building hit me first – a breathy presence in the steel railings of the external staircase that provides a soundtrack to a landscape that encourages just standing and staring. Elsewhere, in a small building called the Control Room (built in the mid-1950s as the control centre for Laboratory 1, where Britain's first operational atomic bomb Blue Danube was vibration-tested), the wind intermittently enters the building through discrete wall holes to produce symphonic 'voices'.

These sounds can be magical but also relentless. Angus Wainwright, the archaeologist who extensively surveyed the Ness when the National Trust took over the site in 1993, recalls how 'in the evening it was really nice to just sit and stare and listen, and suddenly you'd just start hearing the birds and interesting little tiny noises that you wouldn't normally hear because you're crunching on the shingle. After a while you're aware that all you're hearing is your footsteps in the shingle going crunch crunch crunch and the wind and the seagulls. It's a kind of monotonous soundscape and it was good to be aware of the quietness and just these little noises.'

In the absence of heavy machinery and monitoring equipment, some of the ex-AWRE Orfordness (Atomic Weapon Research Establishment) laboratory or test cell spaces have become incredibly reverberant. The animals, especially birds which now seasonally occupy these buildings, broadcast their presence: pigeons and doves audibly nest in the air conditioning ducts, but are sometimes trapped, especially juvenile ones that have walked the wrong way. When you approach Lab 3, there is an auditory 'explosion' of pigeons flying out, leaving a feather or two in their wake from the metal grille that separates dark 'oven' interior from exterior. A few white downy feathers on the grimy floor of Lab 5 are the sole traces of a duck that had become ensnared in the razor wire ('its wings all outstretched like a First World War victim': Wainwright). But mainly these bird and other animal traces are more life-affirming. Hares create trails over the sides of shingle-topped buildings constructed to test weapon parts, for example.

Sounds voyage far on the wind here but there are also curious smells that carry some distance from their source – explicitly the pungent and sweet-smelling odour (like the perfume put into cheap bleach) that emanates from the AWRE Magazine Building. This was where bombs were stored before removal to the labs for testing, then latterly used for storage of explosives. It is hard to know if this actually dates from the clean-up of Orford Ness or from some nefarious chemical process that has taken place in a building that looks as though something has been burnt in it.

Airborne Trials

Things have had a habit of arriving on the Ness, whether intentionally fired or dropped decades ago or more recently released and left to travel at the whim of the tides or air currents. Wainwright remembers the arrival one day of 30–40 bottles on the same stretch of beach, sent from a school in Holland, due east. Balloons also touch down en masse. 'I think they're all from fairs and for some reason they must blow across the country and descend when they get to Orford Ness and end up inside the buildings – sometimes drifting round in the eddies.' He recalls the shock of first encountering a 'Mr Blobby' balloon (a regular intruder) floating around like some live being in a little dark room off Lab 3.

The unique landscape of unusual and rare flora on the vegetated shingle spit with its variety of habitats is supplemented by plants that are human introductions at moments in its twentieth-century occupation – like the clumps of daffodils outside certain buildings, the one or two decorative hawthorns down the 'street' and the domestic variety of red valerian near Black Beacon.

Wind blows vegetation inside the labs, this rots down and forms a fertile habitat for various plants. When Lab 2 (the primary centrifuge building) was cleaned out for contamination, a cluster of elder bushes was removed as well. A photograph shows these tenacious bushes valiantly occupying the centrifuge pit, giving the impression of 'something you might see in a zoo which may have interesting tropical animals in it' (Wainwright).

The austerity of the weather across this simple landscape can be as wearing as the footsteps on shingle soundtrack. Grant Lohoar, National Trust Property Manager (for Orford Ness and Dunwich Heath) describes the effects of the force and constant sound of the wind: 'By the time you reach April you're walking at a permanent 75 degrees.' The relentless wind sets in motion some of the remaining fixtures inside buildings that have long since been stripped of their more valuable metal assets. Amongst the dereliction of Lab 5, one of the pagoda buildings, a ceiling fan intermittently revolves with the action of the wind. A spooky presence indeed when first seen in the corner of your eye.

An Acoustic Memory

The Official Secrets Act has ensured that the Ness's Cold War secrets are, for the most part, still concealed from public scrutiny. Lohoar has spoken of how 60–70% of what is now known to the National Trust guardians about the history of AWRE Orfordness has been garnered through oral testimony from ex-employees. Leaving aside the truths and untruths of unconfirmed technological detail, there are other memories that can be more easily shared: of how the landscape sounded different, that fog horns were once in operation, klaxons sounded, and how the bird life was not as vibrant as it is now, how some of the AWRE workers would go swimming at lunchtime (and once one continued to conduct his airborne trial in Black Beacon, wearing swimming gear), and so on.

RONA LEE

Ex-AWRE employee Jim Drane recalled an incident that occurred when he was working in Lab 1 during one of the 1000-hour trials in the early 1960s. There was a defective camera in the lab, apparently, and Drane volunteered to correct it. He went in on his own and as he approached the two vibrating units (working four and a half shake so they were in opposite frequency) the noise was quite horrendous. But when he reached the camera which was dead centre, he suddenly realised there was no noise. He took his earpiece off and as he described it 'it was virtually absolute silence. The noise was canceling itself out, dead centre, something I knew in theory should happen but something I've never experienced before.' Mr Drane couldn't remember the name of the weapon being tested: 'There were so many of them – I can't remember all the names now even though they were massive things and only when we got the American ones – design – that we were going down to football-sized virtually, very small...'. This story of 'aural epiphany' was subsequently 'quoted' by composer Yannis Kyriakides with the sine wave sweep that travels under the voices in his commissioned piece U for A Record of Fear.

A Record of Fear (2005) was part of 'Contemporary Art in Historic Places', a collaboration between the National Trust, English Heritage and Commissions East, supported by Arts Council England.

311

Winter Sun, East Suffolk

Michael Hamburger

Rarer, briefer the rays
More preciously shine,
More widely through the stripped
Bulk of deciduous trees.
And the conifers, black,
Come into their own
As memorials of night
Outlasting glints on leaves,
Whether, cypress, straight up they're urged
Or sideways, yew, must amass.

Before clash of clouds, thunder,
Downpour, darkening,
Quickly a robin dips
To the table strewn with seed,
No vegetarian, snatches
One protein mite from pheasants
That staidly can feast, supreme;
At risk, because fearless, innately
Knows all he needs to know
For so little a life's fulfilment.

This morning with ultramarine
To scarlet the eastern sky warned
Shepherds who long have lain
Where hopes and fears are void,
Their weather-wise ways defunct.
Shifted by sundown, reversed
Against black above, matt greys,
Wisps of bleakness, brightness
More amply those lucent hues fade
Foretelling confusion to come.

8   LAND, RIVER
    AND MARSH

'Beneath a dazzling sky
The sea rolls silken-white,
Calm morning hours drift on
To scented dusk and melting night . . .'

Chorus in *Death in Venice*
Act 1, Scene 7

Beneath
a dazzling sky

To the Sea

Roger Deakin

JOHN NASH

It was late September, just over two years after the rainstorm in the moat when I had first conceived my amphibious journey, and eighteen months after my first swims on the Scilly Isles. I had been at my desk all summer writing up my log and often swimming in the moat, which helped clear my mind, rendering the impressions and recollections of my swimming journey more lucid. The more I wrote, the more I missed my adventures and longed to make one more swim across the county, beginning in my moat and ending in the sea.

I rose early in the autumn half-light, crossed the wet lawn in my nightshirt, and swam several lengths of the moat, mist rising off it from six inches above the surface. I wore goggles and plunged my face underwater at each stroke so that the clusters of duckweed looming up looked like the models of molecules built by Crick and Watson in their Cambridge laboratory in the early sixties. It was a cold, grey dawn, and the icy water jolted me awake, then settled me into an aquatic frame of mind for the journey ahead. I had drawn a sort of leyline across the map of Suffolk, beginning in my moat and joining up all the swimmable water on the way in a 'subterranean stream' to the sea twenty-five miles to the east at Walberswick. This was to be my route, a kind of homage to John Cheever and 'The Swimmer'. Instead of walking or running like Ned Merrill in the story (or Burt Lancaster in the film), I would bicycle, in the hope of doing the trip in a single day under my own steam,

After breakfast, I pedalled off down our village green in a dense fog. In spite of a promising weather forecast, here I was with both bike lamps on at half-past eight wondering what on earth I was doing. My route lay along a procession of some of the most beautiful churches in Suffolk – Mellis, Yaxley, Eye, Horham, Stradbroke, Laxfield, Ubbeston, Huntingfield, Walpole, Bramfield, Blythburgh (which is probably the finest, anywhere), and finally the wonderful ruins of Walberswick. If the mist would only clear, their flint towers would stand out on the horizon like milestones all the way to the sea.

I soon reached Eye, where I leant the bike beside the Abbey bridge over the River Dove and clambered down the bank to the pool almost directly below the brick arch, hidden from the road by the parapet, where the girls from the old Eye Grammar School used to come to bathe. Two frayed and much-knolled ropes still dangled from a tall Scots pine. I was mentally preparing myself for a ritual dip when a pair of loudly disputing kingfishers shot past me straight through the bridge. They shocked me into going in, and going in soon shocked me into coming straight out again into the relative warmth of the mist, now penetrated by sunbeams and beginning to lift as I went up Dragon Hill on the long haul to Stradbroke. My course passed through Horham, where Benjamin Britten used to retreat from the endless visitors at Aldeburgh and compose at his cottage. Always a keen bather, he had a plastic swimming tank in the garden.

By the time I reached Stradbroke five miles on, I was looking forward to the warmth of the village swimming pool. Here was a place that has had the good sense to build its health centre, indoor pool and village hall next door to each other as if to confirm that swimming can seriously improve your health and social life. Inside, twenty Suffolk women in grey rinses and black one-piece costumes were having a fine time doing water aerobics, like a bingo audience. I swam lengths in a lane down one side of the little twenty-metre pool, in water at eighty-two degrees, with two other local swimmers, and was struck by the easy informality of the place. This is where the citizenry of Stradbroke come to relax, take their exercise, exchange gossip, and linger in the privacy of steam under the hot shower. The infants learn to swim here almost from birth, and the older children are taught to roll like the Esquimaux in the brightly coloured kayaks that hang upright round the walls like chrysalids.

It was mid-morning when I came out of the pool and the sun had chased the mist away. I passed an old man in a ditch, clearing it with a sickle in the proper way, and there was home-made jam set out for sale on a little table at the roadside. At Laxfield they were selling apples outside the allotments and there was late-flowering yarrow and buttercups in the verges. From the Low House pub below the graveyard, I followed the infant River Blyth along a winding back lane down the Vale of Ubbeston for three miles, through a tunnel of ancient hornbeam, hazel, field maple and oak, bombarded as I rode by falling acorns, conkers, crab apples and, at one point, walnuts. This stretch of country is so hilly that you cycle over the crest of the dizzy eminence and you're level with the church tower just peeping over the next. The tractors were all out seizing the day, attacking the pale stubble with huge ten-farrow ploughs, painting the rounded hillsides brown against the perfect blue sky.

By one o'clock I had gone through the village of Heveningham, and was speeding down Cock's Hill past venerable stag-headed parkland oaks when I at last beheld Heveningham Hall, sunlit in Palladian splendour on its grassy hillside, with an endless lake twinkling and flashing in the sun below. I made my way through the grounds along a footpath and found a quiet spot by the western shore to leave my things. There was nobody about, and the owners, who had given me permission to swim, were away. Hauling on the wetsuit, I had a moment's doubt about the wisdom of swimming nearly a mile-and-a-half of lake alone. But the weather was ideal. Nobody had been available at such short notice, and in the wetsuit I would he unlikely to get cold or cramped.

I swam straight for the middle, heading for a wooded island. It felt fine. The water was green and clear. I wore goggles and gazed into the translucent sunlit mist of millions of microscopic creatures and algae, with here and there a patch of slender ribbon weed reaching up for the ceiling of the lake like an Indian rope trick. I soon fell into the trance of rhythm, the fish-like feeling that can take you a long way before you've noticed it. You lean into the water and feel its even gentleness lifting you as you steal through the surface. The secret is to respect it but never fear it, so you can relax and sense the molecules moving around you as you swim.

By the standards of the A12, no doubt my journey would have seen absurd. But it was always an entirely serious enterprise, if at times surrealist, and I felt enriched by my long swim.

I turned off down a timeless sandy avenue of oaks, potholed by rabbits, to a distant farmhouse on a promontory jutting into the wide Blyth marshes. It was four-thirty. I had arrived just in time to catch the high tide and swim off a hundred-foot wooden jetty built out from the headland over the water a few years ago for the filming of Peter Greenaway's *Drowning by Numbers*. There was no need for the wetsuit because the brackish tide was warmed by the huge solar collector of black mud it had flowed over, all the way from Walberswick harbour, as it rose. I lowered myself off the jetty into a foot and a half of estuary water and propelled myself over the bed of delicate, smooth mud, out into the deeper waters of a maze of submerged drainage channels. Rows of gnarled wooden stakes, on which the unwary swimmer might impale himself, marked these channels, many of them just beneath the surface, so I embarked on a kind of maze swim which took me all the way back to my very first day's swimming on Bryher. But the water was astonishingly warm and delicious, and so was the sensual healing of the silky mud.

Afterwards at the house, my friend Meg filled watering cans from the hot tap in the kitchen, and I stood in the back yard holding them one by one above my head, sluicing off the mud in a glorious hot shower. Tim came out of his workshop and joined us for tea outside the back door. There was now just time to bike on down to Walberswick across the heath before sunset.

I cycled by the woods where George Orwell made love to Eleanor Jaques, his neighbour when he lived at Southwold, and into the village past the ruined church where he used to sit and read. I passed the house of Freddy the fisherman ('The Sole Plaice for Some Fin Special'). It was a quarter past six, and the sun, which already shared the sky with the blushing new moon, was beginning to go down. I hurried out over the little wooden bridge where they hold the annual crabbing contest in summer, and printed faint tyre-tracks across the last two hundred yards of cracked saltpan desert mud on Walberswick marsh. Scaling the sand dunes, I ran down the deserted beach, flung off my clothes and waded into the surf.

I felt the sweetness of tired limbs and fell headlong into the waves, striking towards the horizon that appeared intermittently beyond the breakers. I had left my rucksack and clothes beside a beautiful pebble starfish on the beach, another echo of the Scilly Maze. Perhaps I had at last swum my way through it. When I reached the relative calm of unbroken swell, I looked back towards the shore. A crimson mist lay over the sea as a red-hot sun dropped over the pantiled roofs behind the sand dunes. The sea-fret shaded to a deep purple along the curve of the bay where Dunwich should have been, and obscured the giant puffball of Sizewell B. One of the beauties of this flat land of Suffolk is that when you're swimming off the shore and the waves come up, it subsides from view and you could be miles out in the North Sea. An orange sickle of new moon hung above the chimneys in a deep mauve sky. Autumn bonfires glowed in the mist and floated white smoke-rings above it. The beach shone in the gathering dusk as the tide fell and the sea grew less perturbed. I turned and swam on into the quiet waves.

A Sad Splendour?

Richard Mabey

On hot summer nights, when the River Blyth is low, the grey mullet swim up from the rivermouth and into the freshwater reaches below Wenhaston. Their backs ripple the surface of the dark water like swirls of oil. Their story could be a Suffolk creation myth. They haunt the estuaries, browsing the bottoms, creatures so wholly of the marsh that they don't feed like other fish, but suck up the silt, spit out the sand, and digest the rest, mud and mudworm alike. They ferry the mudflats inland.

The whole landscape of the Suffolk coast seems to share their easy passing between salt and sand, and the strange alchemy of their feeding. Between Southwold in the north and Bawdsey in the south, and stretching inland some eight miles, is a swath of wild country in which heath and reedbed and marsh and saltflat are interbraided, mutually entangled, like nowhere else in England. The whole area is called the Sandlings because it lies on a baulk of fine sand left here after the glaciers retreated twelve thousand years ago. But it might just as reasonably be called the Mudlings, so thoroughly have Suffolk's erratic but indomitable rivers cut and pasted their way through the whole region. The reed-swamp of Walberswick's Westwood Marshes, in the flood-plain of the relict Dunwich River, lies at the foot of what feels like a hill of heathland, and you can have the disorientating experience of standing in the broom and hearing a bittern's boom echo up from depths. Four miles south, the straightened Minsmere River cuts a vein of otteriness from the buckthorn bushes at the sea's edge to the arable fields of Middleton. At Aldeburgh the 'Curlew River', as mud-laden as a mullet, silted up its estuary in the sixteenth century and now, joined with the Ore, flows out to sea by Orfordness. The curlews themselves, of course, relish the flooded sandflats that grew in consequence between Snape and Iken, and throng there in winter in their hundreds.

It's this tangle of expansive and contrary rivers that has saved the Suffolk littoral. There's never been the slightest possibility of building a coast road across their soggy flood-plains, and in the whole 25 miles of the Sandlings coast there are only half a dozen roads which go as far as the shore. This sense of isolation, heightened by the empty, desert-like quality of the heaths and marshes, has thrown a veil of melancholy over the region's natural life and landscapes – at least in many writers' eyes. The mournful curlew's cry, the blasted heath, the fallen flood … We slip so easily into seeing it as a lost coast, forever slipping into metaphorical desolation, as Dunwich itself slips literally into the sea.

I'm afraid that Suffolk's poet laureate George Crabbe must take part of the blame for this sad and distorting cast. Crabbe was a good botanist and gave vivid accounts of the hermit vegetation of the Aldeburgh coast. His 'blue bugloss' which 'paints the sterile soil', his 'slimy' mallows, common and marsh, are still there. Yet there is something in the way he details their meagre proportions and miserly habits which echoes his misanthropic portraits of the people of Aldeburgh. As his contemporary John Clare remarked, Crabbe 'writes about the peasantry as much like the Magistrate as the Poet – he is determined to show you their worst side'. E. M. Forster was more generous, and felt that Crabbe had ambivalent feelings about the local landscape: 'The idea of regeneration, so congenial to Wordsworth and the Lake District, does not appeal to this son of the estuary... Dull, harsh, stony, wiry, soft, slimy – what disobliging epithets, and yet he is in love with the scene.' In a famous passage, Crabbe has the despairing Peter Grimes perceive the whole ebullient ensemble of Suffolk's coastal wildlife – eels, crabs, bitterns, 'the tuneless cry of fishing gull or clanging golden-eye' – as a prospect which 'Oppress'd the soul with misery, grief and fear.' Elsewhere Crabbe writes of the 'sad splendour' of the coastal landscape.

This desolate and dystopic view became fashionable, and at times it seemed mandatory to view the 'sterile' coast and its natural life through a Claude Glass labelled 'forlorn'. Most recently W.G. Sebald, in his bleak odyssey, *The Rings of Saturn* (1998), used the landscape as a register of his own despair. Even Dunwich Heath in full bloom reduced him to disorientated panic. He was 'numbed by this crazed flowering ... The low, leaden sky; the sickly violet hue of the heath clouding the eye, the silence ... all this became oppressive [he uses the same word as Crabbe] and unnerving.'

We all see nature hued according to our own emotions, and perhaps do not try hard enough to see it simply as it is. When I first became acquainted with the Sandlings, it never occurred to me that one could view the region's airy openness and tumult of water-birds as melancholy: they seemed more like inspiriting signs of survival to me. I'd fetched up at Crabbe's Aldeburgh as a young man armed with a flower-book – unaware, I must confess, that the poet had even existed, let alone been about the same business. Between concerts at the Festival I tramped the shore, writing the plants I found in the flyleaf of my book. I listed more than a hundred, including many of the classic species of this shore that Crabbe knew, like yellow-horned poppy and henbane and wall-pepper. But also many new arrivals that he could not have known, and whose luxuriance might have confounded him. Tree-lupin, naturalised from the easy-going coasts of California; giant hogweed from the Caucasus, terrorising the roadsides towards Thorpeness; and the now celebrated self-sown, prostrate apple tree whose early fruits dangle just inches above the shingle [see p.36]. And still thriving was the sea-pea, a lineal descendant of the colony whose presence was noted here in 1555, in Suffolk's very first natural history record. Its peas had sustained the population of Aldeburgh during a famine, and 'its supposed sudden growth was very generally regarded by them as a miraculous interposition of Providence'.

A few years later I bought a tiny cottage at Wenhaston, just inland from Blythburgh. On my first night there in May, I lay in bed with the window open, listening to nightingales. One sang from the little heath of gorse and bell-heather above the house – as pure a patch of east Suffolk as you could imagine. The other in the churchyard of St Peter, where there is an exuberant sixteenth-century painting of the Last Judgement (which Pevsner describes, in a rather Crabbed way, as 'distressingly rustic'). I thought of the local painters listening to them, and of Keats' phrase 'The voice I heard this passing night was heard/ In ancient days...'.

Might the nightingale be east Suffolk's totem bird? It's a species that is reaching this country in ever-declining numbers, and the concentrations in the scrub and woodland between Walberswick and Dunwich may be the highest in England. Here, for the moment at least, they seem indomitable. One perishing May night in the cold spring of 2004, when the temperature was only three degrees above freezing, I heard one in the heart of a rhododendron bush on Westleton Heath, its notes as clear as ice.

Close-by, but on a much hotter dusk, I once listened to a nightingale singing a duet with a nightjar. The nightjar lay silhouetted along the branch of a dead oak, turning its head slightly as it poured out it dry, reeling song. Six feet below it a nightingale whistled from the thick entanglement of a blackthorn. They sung on, pipe and drone, deep into the night. Nightjars abound on the Sandlings' heaths, where their charred brown plumage and parched rattle seem like embodiments of the landscape. I first heard – and saw – them at Walberswick, in glow-worm time, when a pair circled me so inquisitively close that I could see their moth-catching gapes and the white spots on their arched wings. Down in the south, they have moved into the open spaces left after the 1987 storm laid Rendlesham Forest's intruding conifers flat.

The Sandlings' birds have a habit of exploiting change. The avocet returned as a British breeding bird when the coastal marshes were deliberately flooded during the Second World War. This exquisite pied wader had bred in Suffolk up to the mid-nineteenth century, though never commonly. When the grazing marshes were turned back in to wetlands as part of the coastal defences in 1940, avocets returned too, and colonised both Minsmere and Havergate Island.

Perhaps the marsh harrier has the most ancient local provenance. The sixteenth-century angels that soar in the roof of Blythburgh Church have had eventful lives: shot up by Cromwell's soldiers, repaired, attacked by woodworm. But look at their wings closely – at their slight uptilt, at their long span and fingered tips – and it seems inconceivable that the carvers had not watched harriers quartering the reedbeds outside the church.

But for me, the essence of the Sandlings is not this or that species. It's a particular accent in the landscape, a kind of repeated shading-off of one kind of habitat into another. It happens as fluently as the merging of watercolour paints, and creates exceptional moments. The sudden, comic rise of Dingle Hill's bushy tump in the vast flatness of Walberswick's reedbeds. The long track from Waldringfield that meanders into the very heart of the Deben estuary just inches above high-water, and then simply stops – at which point you are as close as you can ever be to the great flocks of redshank and grey plover and oystercatcher that are the internationally important treasures of the Suffolk estuaries. Or the many places – both sides of the Blyth estuary, at the back of Minsmere, on the slope that is rather grandiosely called Iken Cliff – where you can have that quintessential glimpse, a peek through east Suffolk's indigenous kaleidoscope, of the shimmer of open water through a blaze of chrome-yellow gorse.

Yet in this intimate landscape there's an interpenetration between the wild and human worlds, too. Sitting in the bar of the Harbour Inn at Southwold one winter lunchtime, I watched four short-eared owls quartering the Town Marsh, their wings like spinakers scooping up the wind. Now, from the same perch, you can watch the more delicate gavottes of little egrets, newcomers to Britain. Things change, and not always for the worse. Marsh harriers glide alongside the traffic where the A1095 road passes through the newly created Hen Reedbeds. I've seen a bittern cross the road here – and heard another booming through the mist at Snape Maltings, during the interval of Haydn's *Creation*. The 4,000 cranky oaks of Staverton, near Butley, have grown up over the past four centuries partly on the remains of a medieval deer park. Defying conventional wisdom, the aged pollards survived the 1987 storm, whilst the young striplings in the conifer forests around them were totally destroyed.

Down in these southern reaches the landscape flattens out, becomes less imbricated, passes through the vast, overgrazed levels of Sudbourne Marshes to reach a kind of vanishing point at Orfordness. The extraordinary ridges of shingle here, built up like the rings in a tree-trunk, were, like so many beautiful places stereotyped as 'wasteland', commandeered by the military. Now the place is at liberty again, and barn owls roost in the derelict watchtowers. Orfordness is the *reductio ad absurdum* of the Sandlings paradox: a stone spit which, while much of the rest of the land is succumbing to water, is inexorably growing.

Climate change is adding to the turbulence of this mutable shore. The sea level is rising and storms becoming more frequent. Tidal surges are repeatedly breaching the defences all along the coast. In itself, this is nothing new. Julian Tennyson (the poet's great-grandson) wrote in his incomparable study *Suffolk Scene* (1939) of the effects of the 1938 storm-surge on Iken Marsh: 'I found it a brown, filthy, stagnant, stinking swamp, a muddy morass of leering oily pools, at the back of which sprawled ancient trees on the edge of the wood, gaunt and misshapen and hideously naked.' Iken Marsh recovered, and prospers, though not quite as it was. The Sandlings are a dynamic landscape, not a museum set. Over the great stretches of ecological history it was the upheavals of weather that shaped the landscape, laid down the labyrinthine marshes and washed up the swells, and created that thrilling local disjunction of sea-water lapping at the foot of gorse bush. We can't keep the sea out, but we can learn from our region's history that shifting water will make new indigenous prospects further inland, if we give it the chance.

And they will be graced by a new, or restored, totem. In the Middle Ages the 8-foot wing-spanned fish-eating white-tailed eagle soared over east Suffolk. It is known now as the sea eagle, but throughout East Anglia it was called the fen eagle. Now there are dreams of reintroducing it to the wild coastal heaths and fens between Walberswick and Dunwich. With luck, it will knit together sea and land as naturally – and as splendidly – as the grey mullet.

JASON GATHORNE-HARDY

18 **Butley Creek** *(top)*
Slaughden Quay *(bottom)*
Nick Sinclair

January 24 08.57
January 29 12.54
February 8 08.58
February 9 07.52

February 21 10.40
February 29 07.00
March 3 08.59
March 21 16.57

May 11 17.50
July 24 14.54
August 28 06.00
October 17 18.52

October 26 09.57
October 28 17.54
October 29 07.51
November 3 15.00

19 'At the same time the same dull views to see'
(preceding page)
Images from the Aldeburgh Music webcam, 2004/5. Courtesy of Lavinia Greenlaw

20 Lighthouse at Orfordness
(above)
Kirsten Lavers

Birds: The Suffolk Trinity

Neil Bartlett

It is a truth universally ignored that there are just not enough experiences in modern life that can stop the heart with a shock of pure, undiluted joy. The more our culture deluges us with promises of short-cuts to pleasure – buy this, and you'll feel that – the more we forget what the real thing feels like. Well, if anyone ever asks me what it is that makes me dream of making the long drive back to Snape, the simplest answer would probably be just that one word; it's a place where I can more or less guarantee that I will feel joy.

Being invited to spend six weeks at The Maltings to create a production of *The Rake's Progress* in the early summer of 2006 gave me one of the happiest experiences of my career. It was daunting – because I'd never directed a professional opera before – but working here turned out to be like having the best kind of affair. Every morning, I woke up knowing that once again my new love (Stravinsky's score) was going to demand more of me than I quite knew how to give, but that it was, in return, going to be unfailingly passionate, gratifyingly exhausting, alarmingly dirty in all the right places and supremely technically adroit in the rest. And every morning, quite apart from the thrill of being invited to spend all day every day in the company of exciting young voices, I had a guilty secret to keep me going. It wasn't just the music that was keeping me in a near-permanent state of arousal, you see; it was the birds.

Let me explain. I was the kind of suburban child who lived mostly in his books – one of those little boys whose fantasies were largely fuelled by his bedroom library. In pride of place on my particular shelf was a treasured copy of a gloomy Edwardian masterpiece of ornithological illustration known simply as *Thorburn's Birds*, so called after the painter who made it his life's work to catalogue every single bird ever seen (or shot) on these shores. By the time I was ten, I knew every one of the coloured plates more or less by heart. My favourites – inevitably – were those which featured the talismanic rarities which you knew you would never see, but whose mere existence gave you a little kick of excitement every time you turned to their particular page. Their names alone hinted at the existence of another world entirely from the mundane one of starlings and sparrows and suburbia. So when I was offered the job at Snape, Stravinsky aside, I have to admit that my very first thoughts were of the birds I might see – beautiful, never-seen birds. Before I'd ever heard of Tom Rakewell, this particular bit of Suffolk was already lodged in my imagination as the last-known British refuge of a glamorous trinity of particularly legendary specimens: the Avocet, the Marsh Harrier, and the near-mythical Bittern. As elaborate and crowded schedules for all the different kinds of rehearsals were drawn up by my new colleagues (what *was* a 'Stage and Orchestra', exactly, and why did everyone seem to assume I already knew?) I secretly started to worry about when I was going to have time to sneak off and pace the marshes. Excitedly, I packed my binoculars – and my copy of Thorburn – next to my score.

When I got here, I was shocked to hear these magic names being dropped as casually as those of Stravinsky, Britten, Pears. Birds I had only ever thought of in hushed tones were mentioned, in reply to my questions, as familiarly as if they were, well, familiar – 'Oh yes,' I was told, 'we see avocets all the time'. I assumed this was just part of the rather grand proprietorial-ness that often seems to go with the classical music business – the assumption that the enjoyment of the most refined things in life is, if not actually commonplace, certainly reliably *frequent*; but I was wrong – wonderfully wrong. What I hadn't understood was that – like the flawlessly generous acoustic of the concert hall, like the carefully chosen Festival programme itself – the mudflats and reed-beds beyond The Maltings' lawns offer up their rarities with supreme casualness. When I was a child, the very word 'avocet' shimmered with an aristocratic halo; the illustration in my Thorburn was an icon of impossibility. But here, on my very first day, a mere ten minutes' walk across a perfectly ordinary field from the rehearsal room door, here were a pair – a *pair*! – of the beauties, close enough to watch without binoculars, pottering about as ordinarily as a pair of mallards. They behaved as casually...well, as casually (it seemed to me) as the extraordinary people I was working with sung Stravinsky at ten o'clock in the morning.

Then, when I got back to the canteen just in time to grab a bite to eat before returning to rehearsals (to hear Anne Truelove's show-stopping Act 2 aria sung through for the first time), an unmistakeable silhouette hanging low over the reeds right outside the window – a great flung glove, suspended lazily in the air – stopped me mid-forkful. It was a harrier – my first – and my colleagues must have wondered who on earth this idiot was, transfixed over a baked potato by the glimpse of a bird. As it turned out, there was nothing special at all about this sighting either; a pair of harriers was nesting in the reedbed immediately below the canteen windows that summer, and so I was to see them every day of rehearsals. Every day, I couldn't quite believe it – couldn't quite believe that such beauty and rarity could be as common as eating. As much part of the place as... as the sound of Stravinsky's incomparably rare and beautiful orchestration in the opera's final, heart-dissolving chorus.

On our one day off before the final week of work, I drove up to Minsmere. This is reputedly the best place in the country to spot the elusive third member of the Suffolk Trinity, the bittern – with the proviso that even there, the bird more often than not disdains to be seen. Minsmere is the Walsingham of birdwatching; for the devotee, the experience is as much about faith and homage as the actually likelihood of spotting the Virgin Mary – or, in this case, a squat, brown, eel-eating heron. I paid my entrance fee and walked quietly to the first hide. Opening the door, the sight of a bevy of hairy, telescope-festooned men made my heart sink; here were the real experts, the ones who talked in Latin names and could tell one kind of little brown warbler from another. They made me feel exactly the same way I had felt the first time I was ever tried to follow the Stravinsky score whilst listening to my CD of the Rake: a hopeless amateur.

After an hour of gazing at an empty patch of reedbed, one by one, they left. And then, a casual ten minutes later, the impossible happened: in a flash of burnt-orange wings whose spread and magnificence that Thorburn had left me entirely unprepared for, a bittern flew out of the reeds. He landed; he posed briefly for my astonished benefit, then stalked haughtily back into the reeds and dissolved. At which point, I started breathing again – and, I think, finally began to understand something of what I was learning in this extraordinary place. A bittern's wings, you see, blaze with exactly the same magnificence as the fanfare of trumpets that opens Stravinsky's opera. They announce, with summary majesty, that yes, this is happening; beauty is about to happen, right here, right now.

The rest of the day was equally miraculous. At Minsmere, in Festival-time, avocets are as common as woodpigeons; one mudflat was a bickering, fluttering, aristocratic dazzle of birds. Then as the long day ended in sunset, I watched the reed-beds being quartered by no less than seven harriers; dark-winged, languorous, unforgettable.

The business of birdwatching, like rarity-collecting in the concert-hall, can of course be a dubious one. At its worst it can be the symptom of a peculiarly English and rather desperate sentimentality, two parts nostalgia to one part trainspotting. But when you lose all the list-ticking, and keep the essential encounter, it is true that the flash of a rare bird's wings can be (almost) as pleasurable as hearing the first twenty bars of *The Rake's Progress*. Only at Snape, however, could the two pleasures be so closely associated. And perhaps only at Snape could I have understood quite so vividly that in both of those moments, pleasure is not just an inadequate word, but also an inaccurate one. Like I said, the proper term is *joy*.

JASON GATHORNE-HARDY

Four Suffolk Recipes from Field, River, Heath and Sea
Jason Gathorne-Hardy

Jason Gathorne-Hardy, who founded Alde Valley Food Adventures in 2005 to celebrate food, farming, landscape and the arts in the Alde Valley and East Suffolk, has collected four recipes from local chefs using a range of fresh, seasonal farmed and wild foods that can be found in the Suffolk countryside.

FOOD FROM THE FIELD
Recipe from Peter Harrison, chef and restaurateur.

Lamb with Butternut Squash and Puffball Salad

The landscape of Suffolk grades from heavy clay topland in the middle of the county through loamy meadowland to acidic water meadows and sandy heathland by the coast. With appropriate care, all these lands can support the rich production of cereals, root crops, vegetables and livestock. Indeed they have done so for centuries. The intervening fabric of hedgerows, woodland, green lanes and rivers, within which the more productive land sits, can also yield an abundance of wild produce, including wild meats and many seasonal fruits, shoots and more elusive funghi. The Alde Valley Lamb flock at Great Glemham provides new season lamb reared on grass, mothers' milk and crushed barley mixed with molasses. The fresh lamb is traditionally hung and sold at Salters Butchers in Aldeburgh.

Using a sharp knife cut 2 boned middle loins of local or Alde Valley Lamb lengthways, but not all the way through – leave a couple of centimetres uncut so you can later fan the loin out into a butterfly shape. Open the split loin out and rub in 2 cloves of crushed garlic together with mixed herbs and spices (1 teaspoon of paprika, 2 teaspoons of dried oregano, 1 teaspoon of ground fenugreek and 1 teaspoon of dried cumin). Use a meat tenderiser or the palm of your hand to do this. Then drizzle some olive oil over the lamb and place it cut side down onto a very hot chargrill pan for about 2 minutes each side. The lamb can be served with butternut squash from one of the Valley's market gardens, and wild puffball (making this an early summer or early autumn dish, when warm wet weather will bring out the puffballs).

Peel, de-seed and quarter the butternut squash from north to south. Cut each quarter into 3cm-thick slices and place on a baking tray. Drizzle some Suffolk rapeseed oil over the squash, and season with salt and pepper. Roast in a hot oven (220c) until soft, but still holding its shape (approx 15 mins). Put the squash to one side and reserve all the roasting juices for later. Puffballs are always mysterious guests in the countryside, coming and going according to the season and weather. If you can find a good specimen of this East Anglian equivalent to the white truffle (ripe ones sound like a tight drum when flicked with the finger) slice the puffball into 1–2cm thick slices and place on a hot chargrill pan for a few seconds on each side. Now return to the lamb. Serve with 200gm Thorpeness salad leaves tossed in the roasting juices and a splash of balsamic vinegar. Thinly slice the seasoned lamb and place it on the plate, with alternate layers of the roasted squash, salad leaves and grilled puffball. Finish by sprinkling the salad with toasted pumpkin seeds.

FOOD FROM THE RIVER
Recipe from Kenneth Jamieson, chef at the farm café, Marlesford.

Wild Duck Breast with Wild Plum Sauce

One of the defining characteristics of the Alde Valley and East Suffolk is the River Alde itself. Through its steady passage over time, it has given form to the landscape, moulding and draining the inland valleys before emptying into the broad estuary at Snape. The weir at the Maltings has curtailed the tidal movements, which used to carry estuarine fish as far as Langham Bridge, but there is still an abundance of wild foods to be found alongside the river, both inland and downstream. Vegetables come in the varied forms of nettles, water mint, wild garlic, jack-by-the-hedge, samphire, sea spinach and wild kale. Wild meats include pike, eel, grey mullet and, when in season, wild duck and geese. An interesting winter dish is wild duck breast with wild plum sauce [made from bullaces].

The duck can be sourced from Campsea Ashe Market or any one of the Valley's excellent game-licensed butchers. Preheat an oven to 200C or Gas Mark 7. Score the fat of 4 duck breasts and rub with sea salt. Preheat a large frying pan. Add the duck breasts skin side down over a medium heat for about seven minutes, until most of the fat is rendered from under the skin. Turn the breasts over to seal and then put on a rack in the preheated oven for 15 to 20 minutes. Pour the fat from the pan, saving it for other recipes, and wipe clean. Add the juice of one orange and 4 tablespoons of redcurrant jelly. Add 5oz of de-stoned wild plums (blue plums are best, with green flesh) and $1/2$ teaspoon of white wine vinegar to season. Let the sauce mix simmer until it thickens and becomes syrupy. Take the duck out of the oven to rest for a few minutes, then slice, pour over the sauce and serve.

FOOD FROM THE HEATH
Recipe from Andy Blackburn, chef and owner of The Bell Hotel, Saxmundham.

Gorse Flower Pannacotta

There is a Suffolk saying that when the gorse is in flower, 'tis the season for courting. As the heathland gorse bush erupts into bright yellow flowers pretty much all year round, come rain, wind, sleet, snow or sunshine, there is always scope for romance! A well-kept secret of the gorse bush is the extraordinary flavour of its yolk-yellow flowers.

To extract their fragrance, pick 400gm of flowers, spread on a tray and dry at room temperature for a day. Pour two pints of double cream into a saucepan and then add the dried gorse flowers together with the thinly paired rind of a quarter lemon. Bring to the boil and reduce by a quarter. Remove from the heat and leave the mixture to infuse for 2 hours. Strain off the flowerheads, then stir 150gm of icing sugar into the cream infusion. Meanwhile, soak three gelatine leaves in 200ml of cold milk until soft, then remove the leaves from the milk. Heat the milk gently and then return the gelatine leaves to dissolve. Do not reboil. Add the milk and gelatine mixture to the hot cream and gorse-flower infusion, and stir together. Pour the mixture, still warm, into small dariole moulds and allow to set, preferably for 12 hours. To remove from the moulds, run under hot water for 30 seconds and tip out into serving dish. Serve the pannacotta with langues de chat brushed with local honey or a homemade banana cake.

FOOD FROM THE SEA
Recipe from Claire Bruce-Clayton of Lawson's Delicatessen, Aldeburgh.

Aldeburgh Whiting with Sea Kale

Wild sea kale grows on the shingle beaches between Aldeburgh and Bawdsey, often in long drifts along the strand lines. It is a delicious, iron-rich vegetable with the qualities of a robust, storm resistant broccoli. It also grows well as a garden vegetable, either in the open, with other brassicas, or forced under pots. To prepare home-grown sea kale for cooking, it is best to treat it simply. Trim away the tough split ends from the stalks, cut into lengths the width of your hand and wash thoroughly. Blanch in boiling salted water, as you would sprouting broccoli, for 5–8 minutes depending on thickness. When a knife pierces the sea kale easily, drain and toss with a little oil and a squeeze of lemon.

Sea kale makes a wonderful accompaniment to fish. Talk to the inshore fishermen on the coast of Suffolk and you may here fascinating stories about their ancient trade. The underwater landscape has just as many features as onshore Suffolk: craggy gulleys, broad muddy shoals and shallow sandbanks. And just as the deer, rabbits and birds on land have their habitual tracks, feeding areas and breeding grounds, so to do the fish, crab, lobsters and shellfish at sea. For a simple dish that marries the iron-rich shoots of home-grown sea kale with a freshly caught harvest from the sea, try serving it with fillets of cod or whiting. Take thick fillets of either fish, season with a little salt and ground black pepper, score the skin with a sharp knife and then fry, skin side down, in a very hot, lightly oiled pan until a good crisp brown crust forms. Turn the fillets over and finish cooking skin side up in a hot oven for 6 – 8 minutes. Serve with the sea kale, lemon and oil.

I asked my dear grandmother Fidelity Cranbrook if she could think of a recipe that she had served to Ben and Peter during the great early years of the Festival. After some discussion, she concluded that they would have liked 'something straightforward, nothing too fanciful, nothing too spicy'. We agreed that a recipe using fresh white fish from Aldeburgh beach might have been spot on, made into a pie or served with white sauce or vegetables. I think this recipe for whiting or cod with served with sea kale would have done the trick – something straightforward, nothing too fanciful, nothing too spicy. This is therefore my nomination as a recipe for Ben and Peter, in memory of the two great men.

The River Alde

Julian Tennyson

What shall I tell you of the Alde? I know it all so well, every bend, every landmark, every marsh, every creek; I know every fisherman that sails it, every wildfowler that shoots it. I could tell you exactly how to find those few strips of mud that are the only ones in the whole river which will not swallow you alive in less than a minute; I could tell you where to look for redshanks' and plovers' nests, which are the best saltings for snipe, how to get to the teals' favourite ponds at high tide, how to approach the heronry and where you will be most likely to see the oyster-catchers feeding. I could tell you all this and a thousand other things until I had no space left for anything else. Most of my early life was bound up with the Alde; I spent my days and nights walking by it, swimming in it, sailing on it, sleeping on it, shooting in its saltings, poaching in its marshes. My life then was just one grand adventure on that river; I could find my way blindfold across the marshes, or row a punt in pitch darkness from the top of the narrowest creek to the moorings at Slaughden Quay. I have written many stories and diaries of it; but to write a sober description of it is impossible.

When I think of the Alde I can see the whole shape of it from Snape Bridge to the bar at Shingle Street. It is an eccentric shape, rather like a snake in the act of turning round to bite its own tail. Before reaching Slaughden Quay it runs almost spirally; then it suddenly changes its name, twists right round, nearly doubling on its tracks, and straightens out beside the coast. But it can never keep straight for long; it winds broadly through the marshes, takes in a long island, sends off another river through Butley, and finally, getting nearer and nearer to the sea, washes over the bar into Hollesley Bay. The loveliest part of the whole river is at Iken, where the church and rectory stand lonely on a little wooded hill at the head of the bay that curves sharply back beneath bracken and oak trees and steep, sandy cliffs. There is something very restful about this place, very old and very friendly; there is no church in England which gives you in quite the same way such a feeling of security and changelessness. Behind it are fields, woods and heaths stretching down to Orford, to the right of it are the marshes and the distant sea. A huge expanse of river lies before you when you lean over the graveyard wall; the long, dark pine wood of Blackheath and the bay in the corner where widgeon gather in thousands on winter nights, seem at least two miles off; but wait till low tide and you will see the whole river fall away until it becomes a flat, shining ocean of mud with the channel a thin thread through the middle of it. Whimbrel, curlew, redshank, dunlin, shelduck, mallard, all the birds of the river come up to feed around Iken flats, and their din sets the tame duck quacking raucously in the decoy at the back of the marshes. The noise of birds is all that you will hear at Iken, except when the east wind drives across the marsh and lashes at the thatch of the church. When I was a child I decided that here was the place for me to be buried. I have not altered my mind. Everyone wants to lie in his own country: this is mine. I shall feel safe if I have the scream of the birds and the moan of the wind and the lapping of the water all round me, and the lonely woods and marshes that I know so well. How can anyone say what he will feel when he is dead? What I mean is that I shall feel secure in dying.

From *Suffolk Scene*, 1939, reprinted by Alastair Press, 1987

Home Reach

Ian Tait

Look north, a Cotman scene, a period piece;
Martello fort, the white sea mill, the tumbled town,
And in the trees the square church tower.

The cluttered masts around the quay
Are hollow steel but pierce the sky
Just as the old pine used to do.

Look south; it has a different feel.
The open sea's down there and that uncertain bar
That sailors fear.

While high above the Ness
The early warning masts
Hint at wars unthinkable.

Salt Water

Andrew Motion

The village of Orford, five miles south of Aldeburgh on the Suffolk coast, survived for centuries as a fishing port; now it is separated from the sea by the river Alde, and by a strip of land known as the Ness. The Ness is ten miles long, stretching from Slaughden to North Wear Point. It is overlooked by a twelfth-century castle, and is also known as the Spit and the Island. During the First World War, the Armament Experiment Flight of the Central Flying School was stationed on the Ness, which became a site for parachute testing and, later, a firing and bombing range. In the late 1930s Orford Research Programme was founded, and the Ness became a Listening Post and a centre for experimental work on radar. It was later taken over by the Atomic Weapons Research Establishment, and laboratories were built in which the triggers for nuclear bombs were tested; these were closed down in 1971. The Ness was then cleared by the Explosive Ordnance Disposal Unit. It was sold to the National Trust in 1993. In the reign of King Henry II, when the village still faced the sea, a local historian recorded the capture of the Orford Merman. This Merman was kept in the castle, where whether he would or could not, he would not talk, although oft-times hung up by his feet and harshly tortured. Eventually he was released into the harbour.

In the late eleven-fifties
when the river and the sea
were still in one another's arms
and lived in harmony

there came a summer day so hot
the sea seemed hardly wet,
and the fishermen remained at home
until the sun had set,

had set and rustled up a breeze
and high tide at the full,
so just like that their sails were out
beyond the harbour wall.

A mile offshore, before the shape
of home had slipped away,
they hushed, and cast their clever nets
like grain into the bay.
One hour passed. Another hour.

The house lights on the land
began to jitter and go out,
the darkness to expand,

and silence in a steady flood
rushed round them silkily,
and even filtered through their nets
to calm the rocking sea.

No iron-filing shoal of fish
criss-crossed the rock-strewn floor,
no oyster winked, no battling crab
stuck out an angry claw,

the clear-cut worlds which make the world
lost all their difference,
the sea was sky, deep down was high,
and nonsense seemed like sense.

Enough like sense, at least, to mean
that in the red-eyed dawn,
with courses set and sails poised
to catch the first wind home,

it seemed the sort of miracle
that no one thought was rare
for one of them to haul on board
his streaming net and there

to find a merman large as life –
a merman! – half death-pale,
half silver as a new-made coin
and fretted like chain-mail.

❋ ❋ ❋

For a million years one life simply turns into the next –
the spider hangs between driftwood and sea holly,
the sparrow hawk balances exactly over a shrew,
the hare sits bolt upright and urgent, all ears:
there is no reason why any of this should change.

But a new thought arrives and the island is invaded –
a radio mast stands up and starts cleaning its whiskers,
a field of mirrors learns to see clear beyond the Alps,
a set of ordinary headphones discovers the gift of tongues:
there is no reason why any of this should change.

Work goes ahead smoothly but no one breathes a word –
a slim needle is sensibly embarrassed by the red,
a pressure gauge puffs out its cheeks but is always steady,
a bird-walk of mathematics knows just where it is going:
there is no reason why any of this should change.

❊ ❊ ❊

Not rare? Not like a miracle?
No, not until he spoke,
when feebly as a rotten thread
the spell that held them broke

and every clear-cut bit of world
snapped back into its place:
the sea was sea, the sky was sky,
the merman's face his face,

which slid between its salty lips
an eel-dance of a tongue,
a tongue which could not fix or shape
the words it splashed among.

This made the fishermen afraid;
it told them they had caught
a devil deaf to every law
their own religion taught,

or else, perhaps, a different god
they could not understand
but had to honour and obey
when they returned to land.

❊ ❊ ❊

To create an explosion is the point of all this,
an explosion neither too soon nor too late,
an explosion precisely where it needs to be,
over the head of an enemy.

Not yet.

Scientists arrive to test triggers for the explosion,
triggers which must boil like hell and also be frozen,
triggers which must shake themselves silly and still work,
still know how to create a vacuum.

Not yet.

Weird laboratories spring up for these triggers,
Chinese pagoda-roofs which will protect the triggers
and which in the case of an accident with the triggers
will collapse and bury everything.

Not yet.

But it turns out that the vacuum cannot wait to be born,
the vacuum feeds itself on the very idea of discovery,
the vacuum wants to swallow the whole village and show
the explosion might as well already be over.
Not yet.

* * *

They made their choice; they froze their hearts;
they bound the merman's wrists
and wound him tightly in their net
with clumsy turns and twists;

then swerved towards the shore again,
and just as sunlight came
above the crescent harbour wall
they brought their trophy home.

Wives and children crowded round,
mouths gaping with surprise,
and gaping back the merman cried
baleful, senseless cries,

cried tears as well as sighs and sobs,
cried gulps, cried gasps, cried blood,
cried out what sounded like his soul
but never cried a word.

This made the fishermen afraid
again, it made them guess
the merman might have come to them
to put them through a test

and they, by cruelly catching him,
marooning him in pain,
and putting him on show like this
had blundered into sin.

* * *

Then the triggers are ready, they neither boil
nor freeze, they spin at any speed you please,
and are carried off like gifts in velvet boxes.

Then the bomb disposal men pick to and fro
with their heads down, each one carefully alone
and quiet, like pioneers prospecting for gold.

* * *

Then the radio masts die, their keen whispers
and high songs go, their delicate necks bow,
and voices fill up the air without being heard,

Then the field of mirrors folds too, its flat glare
shatters and shuts up, cannot recall the highest Alp
or anything except types of cloud, come to that.

Then the waves work up a big rage against roof-tiles
and breeze blocks, against doors, ventilation shafts, clocks,
and moon-faced instrument panels no one needs any more.

Then the wind gets to work. It breaks into laboratories
and clapboard sheds, it rubs out everything everyone said,
clenching its fingers round door jambs and window frames.

Then the gulls come to visit, shuffling noisily
into any old scrap-metal mess, settling on this for a nest,
and pinning their bright eyes on bare sky overhead.

And in due season flocks of beautiful shy avocets –
they also come back, white wings scissored with black,
calling their wild call as though they felt human grief.

❋ ❋ ❋

They wound a rope around his net
and dragged him through the square,
up the looming castle keep,
then down the castle stair

and down and down and down and down
through wet-root-smelling air
into a room more cave than room
and hung him there.

Not hung him up until he died,
but hung him by his tail,
his tail which shone like silver once
and crinkled like chain-mail,

then built a fire beneath his head
to see if he could learn
the language that he still refused,
plain words like scare, like burn,

and other words like agony,
like hatred, and like death,
though hour by hour not one of these
weighed down the merman's breath.

This made the fishermen afraid
once more; it made them see
that somehow they the torturers
had set their victim free.

❋ ❋ ❋

The waves think their hardest task
is to work each stone into a perfect O;
the marram thinks all it must do
is hold tight and not trouble to grow.

There's no story, never a point of view,
there's nothing here that's trustworthy or true.
Each grain of salt thinks it is able to see

333

over the highest Alp with its pure white eye;
the sea holly thinks it alone
can support the whole weight of the sky.

There's no clue, never a word in your ear;
there's nothing here that's justified or clear.

Winter storms think they will bring
the worst news anyone can bear to be told;
the east wind thinks it can certainly blow
colder than the coldest possible cold.

There's no code, never an easy cure;
there's nothing here that's definite or sure.

❋ ❋ ❋

They cut him down. They hauled him up
the whirlpool of the stair,
they dragged him past their wives and children
gawping in the square,

and silently, as though the words
they used to know before
were all dead now, they carried him
down to the shingle shore.

They slid him tail-first in the sea
and washed the bitter drops
of blood-crust from his finger ends
and salt-spit from his lips,

and all the while, still silently,
they watched the tide bring in
a brittle, dimpled, breaking flood
of silver through his skin,

then open up his glistening eyes
in which they saw their fear
rise up to greet them one last time
and fade, and disappear,

disappear while they stood back
like mourners round a grave,
and watched his life ebb out of theirs
wave by wave by wave.

JASON GATHORNE-HARDY

'At the same time the same dull views to see'
Lavinia Greenlaw

The Aldeburgh poet George Crabbe, from whose poetry came the story of Peter Grimes, knew well the ennui of a small town: 'At the same time the same dull views to see.' In descriptions of the town, the word 'dull' comes up again and again: 'This miserable, dull sea village,' sniffed Virginia Woolf. This, I want to insist, is a kind of compliment. Aldeburgh's dullness is not so much about a lack of light as a lack of life, of obvious drama, which in many ways is not a bad thing.

I find this dullness compelling and while I live in London, I look at the Aldeburgh Music webcams situated behind Snape Maltings several times a day [see plate 19]. I love these two views because nothing ever happens. Dullness translates into emptiness: the cameras rarely catch a bird, let alone a boat or passer-by, and this makes me concentrate on the absolutes – light and water. Dullness gives us the kind of light we can look into, interrupted light which creates endless gradations of tone, texture and shadow. In other words, because the view is boring, it's never boring. My eyes have become so accustomed to grey that I feel as connoisseurial about its variations as an Inuit about snow. There is the smoky ember grey of winter dusk; the trout grey of overcast summer mornings; the grubby polyester grey of the July afternoon; the industrial pre-fab grey of clouds in the autumn doldrums.

I save many of the images, which are taken hourly between dawn and dusk, and have discovered that I have about 150 spanning the last three years. They surprise me. A dawn of palest pink and blue, with the sun concentrating into a rosy laser beam, is from February. At the same time on a morning in June, the sky is heavy grey cloud reluctantly parting as if the sun were having to wear a hole in it. One April dawn is mist, with the river and sky breaking up into one another while the reed beds feather and blur. Another spring morning is full of such a total white light that I cannot meet it with my eyes – I am pushed out of the picture. One March there is snow on the reeds and the next year, a brilliant blue sky laid over with cirrus as thin as tissue paper. In December and January, the pictures at seven in the morning or five in the afternoon are inky smears. Real dullness is found mid-afternoon midsummer but is compensated for by an August dawn in which the sun spills fire.

My favourite of the two views is focused on the River Alde as it sweeps round a bend through the reedbeds. The river's flatness and slowness mean that it mirrors the sky exactly and, like a camera obscura, heightens what it reflects. It seems that the webcam lens produces a further kind of heightening or simplification. This April morning, at two minutes to eight, it translated the sunrise into a pink stripe that ran down one side of the picture like a barcode. These optical accidents draw attention to depths of colour which are really there: cobalt on an April morning, cerulean in June, parma violet in September. The reeds can appear as straw, seaweed, heather or Astroturf.

The webcams also seem to record what's in the air, like a cloud chamber detecting the movement of sub-atomic particles. One March, when there were thick white crusts of snow on the ground and a white crust of sun edging the clouds, the light travelling between them was showing up as flickers of soap-bubble iridescence. I particularly like a shot from last November, just before four in the afternoon, when the sun's angle is that of a low overhead spot and it blasts the river with light, blackening the reed beds and trees, and bouncing off a soft backcloth of thin cloud. The relatively crude mechanics of the webcam have caught some refractive quality in this light and if you look carefully you can see that the river bed is lined with a tiny strip of rainbow. There are other, more dramatic smears of colour – scarlet, green – which might be read as apparitions of meteorological disturbance, as well as times when the sun is too much for the camera and so seems to be exploding the view.

In 1940, not long after Woolf's visit, Aldeburgh was scrutinised as part of the national social research project Mass Observation: 'Considering that the town is now one of the quietest and dullest places in Britain, the degree of depression and irritation in Aldeburgh is not remarkably high.' Perhaps this has to with the light, which of course has to do with the sea, which is palpable as if just beyond the webcam frame. Edward FitzGerald, the Victorian scholar and dilettante who translated *The Rubáiyât of Omar Khayam* (and who was said to go sailing in a top hat which he tied on under his chin) declared, 'I have always said that being near the sea, and being able to catch a glimpse of it from the tops of hills and of houses, redeemed Suffolk from dullness; and, at all events, that our turnip fields, dull in themselves, were at least set round with an undeniable poetic element.'

Like an enthusiastic tourist, the webcam produces any number of bad paintings (this is watercolour country after all) but it can also capture something of what the best artists of the region are properly alert to – the ways in which water formulates light. You can see this in a painting of Aldeburgh by Mary Potter. She was a friend of Britten's, swapping houses with him after her divorce so that she moved to the sea front she depicts in *Crag Path*. This picture shows someone pushing a bicycle (which of course they couldn't ride because it was too windy) along the seafront. The sea rises like a wall and solidifies into glitter, the houses loom, staunch and gloomy, and everything else dissolves into muted uncertainty. The cyclist's reflection spills across the ground. It has been raining. It ought to look dull but it doesn't because the sun, corning from somewhere off high behind the viewer, splashes across the sea and then onto a tiny distant roof. It is a dab of weak yellow but from there it seeps all the way along the street towards us. Water is the vehicle for light and makes much of it. This is just another grey, wet English day, but it is radiant.

Occasionally something does happen. Last October was full of excitement. On the 17th, the camera caught a full moon rising over the river. I still stare at that picture – the bleary moon like a dollop of butter, melting into its own reflection, illuminating nothing beyond itself. A week later a fly landed on the webcam lens and the next day, the dawn picture was a gaseous swirl of red as if the camera had been retrained on Mars. Shortly after that the camera caught one end of a double rainbow. Sometimes all kinds of weather are happening at once and sometimes things just don't add up. How could a January day begin with a bank of peach-coloured luminous cloud when the sun is nothing more than a papery disc barely nuking it over the treetops?

Without clouds the view would be static and empty, and the only cloudless pictures I have are of a blue sky in October, another in February scribbled all over by jet trails, and a blazing white January morning. There is almost always cloud of some kind, most usually nimbostratus and stratocumulus – low level, vaguely defined and associated with drizzle. Despite this, there isn't much evidence of rain – perhaps an August shower caught as delicate white streaks against luminous greens and on some autumn days, watery smears on the screen.

This last winter with its hard bright days has brought a new kind of picture in which the sun has been hitting one webcam so square on that the midday pictures have looked like unstable overexposed 1970s holiday snaps. Such innovations are all the more exciting because despite all the nuances of light and bursts of meteorological drama, the truth is that there are many days when the view is so monotonous that I think the camera's got stuck. Sometimes it is stuck, and then I get anxious. One day, the views were replaced by the words 'Webcam Unplugged'. I felt as if someone had boarded up two windows.

Reprinted from the Festival programme book, 2006. The Aldeburgh Music webcams can be viewed on www.aldeburgh.co.uk

After Nature

W.G. Sebald

When morning sets in,
the coolness of night
moves out into the plumage
of fishes, when once more
the air's circumference
grows visible, then at times
I trust the quiet, resolve
to make a new start, an excursion
perhaps to a region of
camouflaged ornithologists.
Come, my daughter, come on, give
me your hand, we're leaving
the town, I'll show you the mill
twice each day set in motion by current,
a groaning miraculous construct
of wheels and belts
that carries water's power
right into stone,
right into trickling dust
and into the bodies of spiders.
The miller is friendly,
has clean white paws,
tells us all kinds of lore
to do with the story of flour.
A century ago here Edward Fitzgerald,
the translator of Omar Khayyam,
vanished. At an advanced age
one day he boarded his boat,
sailed off with his top hat
tied on, into the North Sea
and was never seen again.
A great enigma, my child, look,
here are eleven barrows
for the dead and in the sixth

the impress of a ship long gone
with forty oars, the grave of
Raedwald of Sutton Hoo.
Merovingian coins, Swedish
weaponry, Byzantine silver
the king took on his voyage
and his warriors even now
on this sandy strip keep their weapons
hidden in grassy bunkers
behind earthworks, barbed wire
and pine plantations, one great
arsenal as far as your eye can see,
and nothing else but this sky,
the gorse scrub now and then,
a capacious old people's home,
a prison or mental hospital,
an institution for juvenile delinquents.
In orange jackets you see
the inmates labour
lined up across the moor.
Behind that the end of the world,
the five cold houses of the place
    called Shingle Street.
Inconsolable a woman
stands at the window, a children's swing,
rusts in the wind, a lonely
spy sits in his dormobile
in the dunes, his radio's earphones
clipped on. No, here we can
write no postcards, can't even get out
of the car. Tell me, child,
is your heart heavy as
mine is, year after year
a pebble bank raised

by the waves of the sea
all the way to the North,
every stone a dead soul
and this sky so grey.
So unremittingly grey
and low
as no sky I have seen
anywhere else.
Along the horizon
freighters cross over
into another age
measured by the ticking
of geigers in the power station
at Sizewell, where slowly
they destroy the nucleus
of the metal. Whispering
madness on the heathland
of Suffolk. Is this
the promis'd end? Oh,
you are men of stones.
What's dead remains
dead. From loving
comes life. I don't know
who's telling me what, how,
where or when? Is love
nothing, then, now, or all?
Water? Fire? Good?
Evil? Life? Death?

Translation by Michael Hamburger of
section 6, Part III of W.G. Sebald's poem
'Nach der Natur', © 1999

Finale of *Peter Grimes*

Montagu Slater

Chorus
In ceaseless motion comes and goes the tide
Flowing it fills the channel broad and wide
Then back to sea with strong majestic sweep
It rolls in ebb yet terrible and deep.

After George Crabbe

Appendices

Appendix 1

Britten's Britishness: the operas viewed from abroad
Rupert Christiansen

Although Britten's very surname recalls his geographical origin, his music has never seemed narrowly nationalistic. It has in consequence always travelled well, free of the burden of mystic pastoralism which infused Vaughan Williams' work, or the sense of imperial destiny which ennobles Elgar's. So Britten was not so much British, perhaps, as Brittenish: distinctive for his pellucid setting of the English language, his clean, bright orchestral textures and rhythmic bounce and twist, as well as his use of boys' voices and gamelan-style percussive effects. A certain simplicity, honesty and directness irradiated every bar. Composing in an epoch when new 'classical' music seemed both driven and constricted by theory and intellectual pretension, he showed a Mozartian readiness to enjoy and entertain. This wasn't modernism as a salutary dose of cod liver oil, and the world lapped it up happily.

It's often forgotten that Britten's operatic career started in the US, and grew formally as much out of the American tradition of musical theatre (notably the great hit of the late 1930s, Gershwin's 'folk opera' *Porgy and Bess*, with its vivid depiction of a community) as it did out of Berg's *Wozzeck* or Mussorgsky's *Boris Godunov*. Seeds sown in the operetta *Paul Bunyan* blossomed in *Peter Grimes*, which was commissioned in America by the Koussevitsky Foundation with the intention of an American premiere. His later operas have remained solidly popular there, with campus and conservatoire groups regularly performing the chamber works and *Peter Grimes* and *Billy Budd* featuring in the repertory of the major companies and

drawing outstanding interpretations from many of North America's most distinguished singers – the first Budd was an American baritone Theodor Uppman, and two of the greatest readings of Grimes have come from Canadian tenors Jon Vickers and Ben Heppner.

In Europe, *Peter Grimes* caused an immediate post-war sensation, but a more solid basis to his reputation was the touring of *The Rape of Lucretia*, *Albert Herring* and *The Turn of the Screw* by the English Opera Group throughout the late 1940s and 1950s, under the auspices of the British Council and frequently conducted by Britten himself. Perhaps the Mediterranean countries have been somewhat slower on the uptake than the Nordic ones: Germany seems to have consistently clocked up the highest number of productions, with leftist directors presenting stagings which emphasise elements of social critique, and the Komische Oper in Berlin, Hamburg Staatsoper and Frankfurt Oper treating Britten as a staple part of their menu.

One remarkable feature of Britten's operatic reputation is that it has never gone into any serious decline, and didn't suffer from the slump that is usual after death. Apart from the intrinsic appeal of his music, the superb management of his affairs by his estate must take some credit for this. One can trace lapses and surges in the performance of a particular work – at the time of writing, *Death in Venice* is once again prominent on the circuit, while *Gloriana* remains sadly sluggish – but over the last fifty years, there can scarcely have been a week when a Britten opera wasn't being performed somewhere in the world. South America,

Australia and Japan have long been receptive to Britten; one awaits his penetration of the new opera houses that have sprung up over Eastern Asia in recent years.

Paul Bunyan

Following its first production at Columbia University, New York, in 1941, *Paul Bunyan* was swiftly forgotten, until Britten revised the score for a 1976 revival at Aldeburgh. Suddenly, America rediscovered a neglected gem. In 1977, it was produced by the junior wing of the Manhattan School of Music, and in 1984 Colin Graham staged it in St Louis. The first recording came in 1987, courtesy of the Plymouth Music Series, Minnesota, and productions have since been mounted in Cleveland, Glimmerglass, Pittsburgh, Miami, Denver, and Omaha, as well as at the New York City Opera in 1998, where Mark Lamos's staging, according to the distinguished critic Martin Bernheimer, did 'charming 1940 style things with moons and hills'. In Europe, the piece has been scarcely heard at all, though a staging at the 2007 Bregenz Festival is scheduled to move on to the Vienna Volksoper and Lucerne.

Peter Grimes

Although its commissioner the conductor Serge Koussevitsky had hailed it as the 'the greatest opera since Carmen', *Peter Grimes* got off to a poor start in the US. A version presented at the Tanglewood Festival in 1946, conducted by the young Leonard Bernstein, was described by the tight-lipped Britten as 'a very lively student performance' and its debut at the Metropolitan Opera in New York in 1948 drew mixed reviews – one of the best of which came from Virgil Thomson, who called it a 'rattling good repertory melodrama'.

But its success in London spread round Europe like wildfire: within a year of its sensational 1945 premiere at Sadler's Wells, it had been mounted in Antwerp, Stockholm, Rome, Basle and Zurich; in 1947, it reached La Scala, Milan (conducted by Tullio Serafin), as well as Copenhagen, Hamburg, Mannheim, Berlin, Graz, Brno, Budapest, and Sydney; in 1948, Brussels, Los Angeles and Paris. In 1952 it was reported that the East German Ministry of Culture had instructed amateur societies to perform the work as often as possible, as it served as anti-capitalist propaganda offering 'a harrowing but authentic picture of the degeneracy of life in Britain as portrayed by and for Englishmen.'

Interest in the opera waned markedly in the mid 1950s, although there were premieres in Tokyo in 1956 and Warsaw in 1958. The two turning points were Britten's Decca recording of the piece in 1959 - which over the ensuing five years seems to have prompted productions in Cincinatti, Rome, Montevideo, Wuppertal, Riga, Sofia, Leningrad, Oslo and Sofia – and a new production in 1967 at the Metropolitan Opera, with Jon Vickers making this first appearance in the title-role. His overwhelmingly powerful interpretation, recorded under Colin Davis, was subsequently seen at Covent Garden and La Scala as well as in San Francisco and Chicago, and since then the opera has remained standard repertory.

Peter Grimes has also enjoyed enormous popularity in German-speaking Europe. In 1980 Joachim Herz's Marxist production at Berlin's Komische Oper advertised itself as a study of the Konflict zwischen Individuum und Gesellschaft ('conflict between individual and society') by an antifascististicher Musiker ('anti-Fascist composer'). Another significant staging of this ilk appeared at the Vienna Staatsoper in 1996, when Christine Mielitz's even more radical version set the opera on a motorway, with Bob Boles played as a shop steward and Auntie's pub pulsating with neon lights, fruit machines and transvestite orgies. This line was also followed at the Komische Oper in 2003, when Katja Czellnik set the opera in what appeared to be a department store. Britten would doubtless have preferred Trevor Nunn's realistic staging, firmly set in nineteenth-century Suffolk, originally mounted for Glyndebourne but transferred in 2005 to the Salzburg Festival, where it was conducted by Simon Rattle. Since then there have been further Germanic visions of the piece in Mainz, Dresden, Hanover, Wuppertal and Cassel.

It is greatly to be regretted that Placido Domingo never undertook the title-role. He was to have sung it in a production, to be directed by John Schlesinger, announced for Los Angeles in 1998, but this never materialized – perhaps because of his reluctance to sing in English.

The Rape of Lucretia

Performed in Basle, Chicago, New York, Rome and Salzburg in the years following its Glyndebourne premiere in 1946, it then went out of fashion until it was revived by the English Opera Group for Janet Baker and Helen Watts in the early 1960s. Since then, performances have chiefly been concentrated in Germany and the US. A staging by Christopher Alden for New York City Opera in 2003 was set in 'a petit bourgeois living room' and brought out a homoerotic subtext. In Deborah Warner's 2004 production for Munich, with Sarah Connolly and Ian Bostridge, the war in the Middle East was subtly but inescapably evoked.

Albert Herring

A piece consistently popular with American music conservatories, because it offers so many opportunities for young singers, and equally appreciated in communist Eastern Europe as a satire of the bourgeoisie. Joachim Herz directed it in 1957 at the Komische Oper in a production which also visited Moscow; and in 1964, it was much appreciated in Leningrad, when it formed part of the English Opera Group's 1964 tour. In 1966, the great dramatic soprano Martha Mödl (who also sang Elizabeth in Gloriana), took the role of Lady Billows in Hamburg, repeating it a decade later at the Vienna Volksoper. The humour of *Albert Herring* may seem dated in contemporary Britain, but abroad it continues to satisfy stereotypes: in 2007 new productions were staged in Tokyo and Salzburg.

Billy Budd

This has one of the more chequered performance histories in Britten's oeuvre. Following its premiere at Covent Garden in 1951, it received two performances at Paris' Théâtre des Champs Elysées in 1952, and a new German production in Wiesbaden. In the same year, it enjoyed its US premiere when it became the first of Britten's operas to be televised, in a condensed version broadcast on NBC.

Billy Budd then languished unperformed until Britten revised the work, changing four acts into two, for a 1960 BBC broadcast, which became the basis for a new production at Covent Garden in 1964. This two-act version has since become the norm. Productions at the Florence Maggio Musicale (in Italian) and in Cologne followed. But it was with the austere yet breathtakingly spectacular production by John Dexter in Hamburg in 1972 – restaged at New York's Metropolitan Opera six years later – that the opera came into its own, and the title role became coveted by every athletic young baritone. Nevertheless, it was not until the mid 1990s that *Billy Budd* began to rival *Peter Grimes* in popularity (perhaps in part due to its burgeoning reputation among gay audiences). Francesca Zambello's 1994 production was a chief agent of this process, travelling from Geneva to Covent Garden, Los Angeles, Dallas, Seattle, Tel Aviv and Washington.

In 2001, the four-act version was resurrected at the Vienna Staatsoper, directed by Willy Decker with a set which consisted of little more than scrubbed white boards and black walls. In 2007, the two-act version was performed in Munich, Cologne, Hamburg and Frankfurt – the latter staging a landmark production by Richard Jones, which illuminatingly set the opera in a 1950s naval academy rather than on board a Napoleonic man-o'-war.

Gloriana

Despite its brilliant score, familiar Tudor subject-matter and magnificent productions by Colin Graham for English National Opera and Phyllida Lloyd for Opera North, this has always been the least performed of Britten's major operas in the UK, and remains barely known abroad. One can only hope that a great dramatic soprano like Waltraud Meier or Karita Mattila will one day take the marvellous role of Elizabeth I into her repertory and broaden its appeal.

After the initial run of performances (including a visit to Rhodesia) following its damp Coronation premiere in 1953, stagings of *Gloriana* have been exiguous. In 1956, it made its bow in the US in concert form (in Cincinatti), but then remained unheard anywhere until another concert performance, at the Royal Festival Hall took place on 22 November 1963, when it was overshadowed by the dreadful news of Kennedy's assassination.

Five years later, it received its European premiere, when Martha Mödl sang the role of Elizabeth in Münster. In the 1970s and early 1980s, Colin Graham's production toured with ENO to Munich, Vienna and New Orleans, reaching New York's Metropolitan Opera in 1984. Yet it wasn't until 2001 that an American company actually staged the piece, when Central City Opera in Colorado did the honours. This was followed by productions in Des Moines and St Louis – the latter with Christine Brewer. But *Gloriana* has yet to win the hearts of a foreign audience.

The Turn of the Screw

Instantly recognised as a masterpiece and relatively easy to stage and cast, this has proved the most consistently performed of Britten's operas since its premiere at the Teatro La Fenice, as part of the 1954 Venice Biennale, in a staging by the English Opera Group. The following year it reached the Holland Festival and Florence's Maggio Musicale, as well as receiving a student performance in Tokyo. Paris, Milan (La Scala), Berlin, Stockholm and even Montevideo followed, but it wasn't until 1961 that it received an airing in the US – students at Santa Barbara were first off the mark, followed by a professional staging in Boston. Oddly, the piece seems never to have subsequently caught on in North America to the same extent as it has in Europe and elsewhere.

In 1964 Britten conducted *The Turn of the Screw* on an English Opera Group tour which included performances in Soviet Russia. The piece returned to Leningrad in 1985, and to the Maryinsky Theatre in 2006, where it became the second Britten opera to be staged by this celebrated company (the first being a Sovietised *Peter Grimes*). The conductor was Valery Gergiev, the director David McVicar. A review in *Opera* magazine reported that 'it was sung in English (with Russian surtitles), a decision one respects even if discerning the sung text proved a struggle.'

With directors as diverse as Luc Bondy, Michael Hampe and Keith Warner attracted to its drama, this opera has never lacked for fine productions worldwide, and listing them would be otiose. A snapshot of its 2006-8 schedule shows it receiving over a hundred performances, in Bari, Biel, Cleveland, Como, Cremona, Glyndebourne, Hildesheim, Innsbruck, Kiel, Leipzig, Liege, London (ENO), Oviedo, Pavia, Phoenix, Ravenna. Sacramento, Santa Cruz and St Petersburg.

A Midsummer Night's Dream

Another instant success at its first performance in Aldeburgh in 1960, it reached the Holland Festival, La Scala, Milan, and San Francisco within months. But the key to its international success was the simultaneous production of two extraordinary stagings – one in Hamburg, directed by Gunther Rennert (greeted by 'a storm of enthusiastic applause', according to one reviewer); the other, on the hard side of the iron curtain, directed by the legendary Walter Felsenstein at the Komische Oper in Berlin – the house which has some claim to be Britten's European home.

Productions from Stockholm to Zagreb, Tel Aviv to Tokyo have ensued at a fairly unrelenting pace. Among the most successful have been Thomas Langhoff's fashionably austere 'white-box' staging for Frankfurt in 1989, with Jochen Kowalski as Oberon and the star of *The Tin Drum* David Bennent as Puck; and Robert Carsen's much-travelled 1994 Aix Festival version, which turned the whole stage into a giant bed. Grunge finally overtook this most enchanting of Britten's operas in 1999, when the *National Post* reported a production in Toronto where the stage was strewn with junk on a graffiti-covered patch of urban wasteland, ruled by a gangland boss and his moll.

The Church Parables

Like Puccini's *Il Trittico*, the trilogy of *Curlew River*, *The Burning Fiery Furnace* and *The Prodigal Son* amounts to an excessively long evening if they are performed together, and outside the UK they have always been separately staged. *Curlew River* has been the outright winner here, often paired with *Suor Angelica* or *Dido and Aeneas*.

One might suppose that its roots in Noh drama would have made *Curlew River* popular in Japan, but the records of its publisher, Faber Music, reveal that this is wishful thinking. Since its premiere in 1964, it has in fact only received four performances there – the first in 1991, and the last in 2001, in a staging mounted by the Britten–Pears School.

Owen Wingrave

By common critical consent the weakest of Britten's full-length operas, *Owen Wingrave* was staged in Santa Fe, Ghent and Hanover shortly after its 1973 stage premiere. The next production didn't emerge until 1987, when Roderick Brydon conducted the opera in Lucerne. It wasn't a great success, not least because one critic, Fritz Schaub, notorious for his dislike of Britten, reviewed it unfavourably in five different organs. A French production which toured Colmar, Strasbourg, Mulhouse, Angers, Besancon, St Quentin, and the Opera Comique in Paris in 1996–7 is the last foreign staging that the piece has received to date, although in 2009 it is scheduled for a new production in Frankfurt, to be directed by Wally Sutcliffe.

Death in Venice

Immediately after its 1973 Aldeburgh premiere, Colin Graham's production of Britten's last opera visited the the city of its inspiration for a single consecratory performance at the Teatro La Fenice (where *The Turn of the Screw* had also been born some thirty years earlier).

This dark and difficult work – one perhaps more admired than loved - has since travelled far. In 1974, Peter Pears sang Aschenbach at the Metropolitan Opera in New York, and a production by Berlin's Deutsche Oper toured the major German cities. A fairly steady stream of international performances followed, but for no discernible reason, *Death in Venice* experienced a sudden surge in popularity in the early 1990s – within three years, it was variously staged in Melbourne, Nancy, Johannesburg, Nuremberg, Berkeley, Gelsenkirchen, Liege, New York, Klagenfurt and Vienna. Philip Langridge and Anthony Rolfe Johnson often sang Aschenbach with great distinction. Britten's operas are so tightly and theatrically conceived that they have suffered relatively little from the pretensions of modern producing trends, but *Death in Venice* has been interfered with (the Britten Estate retains the right to object to any cuts or tampering with the text or ordering of scenes, but has no right to call the shots on interpretation). Yannis Kokkos' Nancy production featured a female Tadzio, for example, and in 2004, at Buenos Aires' Teatro Colon, Alfredo Arias made the homosexual theme violently overt, with a tattooed Tadzio and a shaven-headed Aschenbach resembling a psychotic convict.

Nevertheless, the opera's future looks assured. In 2007, two superb productions opened in the UK within a month of each other, and both are being widely exported. Deborah Warner's English National Opera staging will move to Brussels, New York City Opera and La Scala, Milan; Yoshi Oida's Aldeburgh staging will be seen in Bregenz, Prague and Toronto. Other productions are planned for Paris, Madrid, Hof and Vienna. In June 2008, the opera returned to Venice for the first time since 1973.

Appendix 2

Aldeburgh Festival Artistic Directors

1948–54	Benjamin Britten, Peter Pears, Eric Crozier
1955	Benjamin Britten and Peter Pears
1956–67	Benjamin Britten, Peter Pears, Imogen Holst
1968	Benjamin Britten, Peter Pears, Imogen Holst, Philip Ledger
1969–73	Benjamin Britten, Peter Pears, Imogen Holst, Philip Ledger, Colin Graham
1974–76	Benjamin Britten, Peter Pears, Imogen Holst, Philip Ledger, Colin Graham, Steuart Bedford
1977	Peter Pears, Imogen Holst, Philip Ledger, Colin Graham, Steuart Bedford
1978–82	Sir Peter Pears, Mstislav Rostropovich, Philip Ledger, Colin Graham, Steuart Bedford
	Artistic Director Emeritus – Imogen Holst
1983–85	Sir Peter Pears*, Philip Ledger, Colin Graham, Steuart Bedford, Mstislav Rostropovich, Murray Perahia*, Simon Rattle, John Shirley-Quirk, Oliver Knussen* (* = programming)
	Artistic Director Emeritus – Imogen Holst
	Composers in Residence – Witold Lutoslawki ('83), Toru Takemitsu ('84), Henri Dutilleux ('85)
1986	Steuart Bedford*, Colin Graham, Oliver Knussen*, Philip Ledger, Murray Perahia*, Simon Rattle, Mstislav Rostropovich, John Shirley-Quirk (* = programming)
	Composer in Residence – Hans Werner Henze
1987–89	Steuart Bedford, Oliver Knussen, Murray Perahia
	Composers in Residence – Lukas Foss ('87), Alfred Schnittke ('88), Leon Kirchner and Peter Lieberson ('89)
1990–92	Steuart Bedford, Oliver Knussen
	Guest Artistic Directors – Elisabeth Söderström ('90), Donald Mitchell ('91), Reinbert de Leeuw ('92)
	Composers in Residence – Elliott Carter and Alexander Goehr ('90), Harrison Birtwistle ('91), John Tavener ('92)
1993–98	Steuart Bedford, Oliver Knussen
	Festival Composers – Toru Takemitsu ('93), Late Stravinsky ('94), Magnus Lindberg ('95), Hans Werner Henze ('96), Mark-Anthony Turnage ('97), Peter Lieberson ('98)
1999–2003	Thomas Adès
2004	Thomas Adès. Guest Artistic Director – John Woolrich
2005–08	Thomas Adès. Associate Artistic Director – John Woolrich
2009–	Pierre-Laurent Aimard. Associate Artistic Director – John Woolrich

Appendix 3

Music that Belongs Here

Paul Griffiths

Paul Griffiths surveys the music and tradition of the first 60 Festivals.

Just as the idea of a place is made by things that last – watchtowers staring at the wind and the sea, a labyrinth of brick-walled lanes running from the pebbles' edge to the broad market street, a flint-faced church on an eminence – so a festival gains its character from what is stable and regular. Aldeburgh found itself quickly. The pioneer endeavour, in 1948, established not only the Festival's mid-June season but also many of its musical proclivities. On the programme were new works by young composers, Mozart chamber music, songs by Britten and Schubert, a new small-scale opera, a recital by a great pianist and a dash of Purcell – things that were all to be replicated in virtually every festival since. As if with a will of their own, the Festival's preferences and prejudices have persisted, even through the long and adventurous period since the death of Peter Pears in 1986.

Britten, of course, has featured every year from the beginning, but so, too, have Mozart, Schubert and Purcell, three of his great loves, while there have been few Festivals without something by his teacher, Frank Bridge. Beethoven, on the other hand, has never been so much an Aldeburgh composer. Nor for a long time was Stravinsky. William Alwyn, a local, and other composers of roughly Britten's generation have been among occasional presences; Tippett and Lennox Berkeley, followed later by Shostakovich. Early music, not only Purcell, has nearly always been strongly represented – though not so the early music movement. Mahler, despite the fact that few of his works fit Aldeburgh's spaces, has often been remembered, Schoenberg less often.

Of performers, the star pianist of 1948 (apart from Britten himself) was Clifford Curzon, who returned several times and began a roll continuing through Noel Mewton-Wood, Sviatoslav Richter, Alfred Brendel, Radu Lupu, Murray Perahia (for several years an artistic director), Mieczyslaw Horszowski in his extraordinary nineties, Imogen Cooper and Pierre-Laurent Aimard. Other musicians with lengthy Aldeburgh histories - apart from Britten, Pears and Imogen Holst, who were for so long the guiding spirits - have included the keyboard players Ralph Downes and George Malcolm, the cellists Mstislav Rostropovich and Steven Isserlis, the Amadeus and Borodin quartets, and such singers as Janet Baker, James Bowman, John Shirley-Quirk and Robert Tear. Those defining Aldeburgh in the early twenty-first century, alongside the artistic director Thomas Adès, include the Belcea Quartet, Anthony Marwood and a new clutch of singers around Ian Bostridge and Simon Keenlyside. Though too young to have known Britten, they have come to fit here – even if they will have to stay a while to rival Pears' record of performance at 38 consecutive Festivals, or Julian Bream's span of 41 years (1952–93).

These have been the presences (and in some cases the absences) creating the Festival. Continuity, though, is not everything. Tides shift, structures come and go. Little by little the landscape alters, even while the place remains the same.

1948–58: The first eleven Festivals

The first Aldeburgh Festival lasted a long week, nine days – and none of the first dozen extended beyond eleven. For that period of time the English Opera Group, which Britten had helped establish in 1947, would descend on the place, not only to present an opera or two (or three) but also to provide the personnel for concerts and recitals. Normally these 30 or so singers and instrumentalists would be joined by a string quartet, several distinguished solo players and choirs from the locality. Lectures, plays and poetry readings filled out the programme more than would be the case in later years. Occasionally there were grander imports: for the third Festival's opening Britten and Pears invited Bertus van Lier to present the St Matthew Passion with his soloists, choir and orchestra from Rotterdam. Most of the time, though, this was a home-team event.

Nobody batted harder than Britten and Pears. (The metaphor may be justified by a photograph in the 1953 programme book showing these gentlemen in cricket whites; among others, presumably on the same side, is Lord Harewood, the Festival's founder president.) Pears in the first few sang almost daily, and Britten appeared no less often, in his various roles as conductor, accompanist and chamber musician. Starting in 1950 Britten often directed a concert of Classical-period symphonies and concertos, usually with himself as soloist in a Mozart piano concerto. One of these concerts, in 1956, was recorded by Decca (the CD transfer includes the programme's two Haydn symphonies, the 'Farewell' and the 'Schoolmaster', as well as Mozart's A major concerto K414), who had begun making occasional recordings at Aldeburgh three years earlier.

As for Britten's own music, the usual pattern was to bring into Aldeburgh works that had recently been introduced elsewhere. Thus the first Festival included *Albert Herring* (Glyndebourne, June 1947) and *Canticle I* (London, November 1947), though exceptionally there was a preview performance of *Saint Nicolas* in advance of its official Lancing College premiere the following month. The only works destined specifically for Aldeburgh during this early period were two that could involve children – *Let's Make an Opera* (1950) and *Noye's Fludde* (1958) plus *Lachrymae* (also 1950). In 1951 Britten included nothing of his own apart from repeat performances of *Albert Herring* and *Saint Nicolas*; the next year, when for the first time there was no opera of his, he started to bring older pieces to Aldeburgh, beginning with *A Ceremony of Carols*, *Rejoice in the Lamb* and the Sinfonietta.

Right from the first other composers were also encouraged to contribute. Two were commissioned for the first Festival: Martin Shaw, then in his seventies, and the 21-year-old Arthur

Oldham, Britten's pupil. Tippett and Lennox Berkeley were also on the programme, and both returned frequently; both took part. with Britten, Oldham, Walton and Humphrey Searle, in the *Variations on Sellinger's Round* written for the 'Coronation Choral Concert' of 1953.

Soon Aldeburgh was welcoming composers of a younger generation: Richard Rodney Bennett (from 1954, when he was 18), Malcolm Williamson (1956) and Cornelius Cardew (1957). If Bennett and Williamson were asked back but Cardew never was (later in the year he was to go to Cologne as Stockhausen's pupil), that may say something about Britten's and Pears's discomfort with the avant-garde then starting to emerge. Nothing by Stockhausen was heard at the Festival until 1972, and most of his European contemporaries made their Aldeburgh debuts even later - in some cases much later: Ligeti in 1976, Xenakis in 1993. Boulez in 1997 and Nono in 2007.

Against that tendency the 1954 Festival offered a morning programme of *musique concrète*, which must have been among the earliest public presentations of electronic music in this country. The French cultural attaché, in his note, refers to his radio's 'team of musician-engineers, led by André Boulez' [sic], so it is possible that one or other of Boulez's etudes was included in the programme, anticipating his performed music's Aldeburgh debut by 43 years. Along with the tapes from Paris came Poulenc. Indeed, 1954 was quite a year. There was a Janáček centenary concert; Imogen Holst, beginning her quarter century of exploratory choral offerings, included music by the 12th-century master Pérotin; and Arda Mandikian, appearing as the Female Chorus in *Lucretia*, sang some survivals of Greek music from the second century BC. Equally striking four years later is the presence of Vilayat Khan's name on the programme - a venture into non-western music Aldeburgh has repeated rarely.

With such exotic events proving the rule, the Festival was developing as a home for British musicians, among whom it could now and then embrace senior composers of relatively advanced tastes: Searle, Roberto Gerhard, Priaulx Rainier, Matyas Seiber. Strangely little of Poulenc's music was programmed when he came in 1956 as well as 1954. Not until 1957 did Aldeburgh start looking outside the country for new music. That was when Hans Werner Henze made his first appearance on the programme. (He arrived in person two years later, with the work he had written for Pears: *Kammermusik*.)

Also in 1957 Pears and Britten closed a recital of Viennese songs with one by Gottfried von

Einem, coming after Mahler, Schoenberg and Webern, all being heard at Aldeburgh for the first time. And it was again at this tenth Festival that Aldeburgh at last heard something by Stravinsky.

1959–76: A composer at home

There were plans from the mid-1950s for a new auditorium in the town. (Almost all musical events took place in the Jubilee Hall or the Parish Church, with occasional sorties to the churches of Blythburgh, Framlingham and Orford.) When hope of that was lost, the effort went into creating an enlarged, refurbished Jubilee Hall, whose opening in 1960 took the Festival into a new epoch. Now, beginning with *A Midsummer Night's Dream* that year, Britten wrote his works most often for performance at the Festival, so that there was at least one Britten premiere nearly every year. Besides the three church parables and *Death in Venice*, the roster includes the sonata and three suites for cello, the Blake songs, *The Building of the House*, *Children's Crusade* and *Phaedra*. One could add the Cello Symphony, planned for the 1963 Festival but in the event performed elsewhere. The following year it came to Aldeburgh, like the rather few works Britten wrote to outside commissions. Older compositions, too, figured more prominently, their revival in many cases tied to a recording.

All this required some readjustment. As a major composer's centre, Aldeburgh became an international venue. It became, deep in the cold war, a bridge especially to Russian musicians. All that cello music was, of course, written for Mstislav Rostropovich, who came to the Festival for the first time in 1961 and returned often. With him came the music of Shostakovich, for which, too, Aldeburgh became a source. In 1970, most spectacularly, the composer's Fourteenth Symphony, dedicated to Britten, had its first performance outside USSR at the Festival, which saw the premieres as well as three subsequent chamber pieces. Sviatoslav Richter and the Borodin Quartet also became frequent guests during this period.

The Festival's expansion afforded room. 1960 brought extension to a long fortnight, and though after that the Festival fell back to its 1950s scale, it was abruptly lengthened to three weeks with the opening of the Maltings in 1967. More soloists came, more and larger orchestras. (Orford church was used for the first full symphonic concert, in 1961, when Britten conducted the London Symphony Orchestra in Mahler's Fourth.) Still, though, most of the music was made by regulars: the English Opera

Group, the English Chamber Orchestra (as the Aldeburgh Festival Orchestra became in 1961), the Amadeus Quartet, Bream, Malcolm and Rostropovich, and, not least, Britten and Pears.

Britten was no longer playing Mozart concertos, but he appeared several times each year up to 1972 as conductor, chamber musician and accompanist. The programme that year – when the Festival fell back to the scale it has kept, spanning three weekends and the weekdays in between – may serve as a reminder of Pears' versatility and stamina, continuing into his sixties: besides singing Quint in *The Turn of the Screw*, he took part in evenings of Schubert songs and madrigals, gave a recital with Britten, sang in Schumann's Scenes from *Faust* and delivered the first performance of a work written for him by Vagn Holmboe.

Such additions to Pears repertory had begun in 1959, with the Henze piece, and continued with works by Peter Racine Fricker, Witold Lutoslawski, David Bedford, Ronald Stevenson, Gordon Crosse and Arne Nordheim. This reflects how new music continued at the Festival, emphasising – apart from the omnipresent Britten and now frequently programmed Shostakovich - British composers with occasional others. Copland came in 1960; Lutoslawski and Kodaly were both visitors in 1965.

But many more British composers were invited, among them Berkeley, Williamson, Crosse, Birtwistle and Thea Musgrave, all of whom wrote new pieces for the English Opera Group. Birtwistle was first at Aldeburgh in 1960, for an extraordinary event that had pieces by four young composers performed and discussed, under the chairmanship of Arthur Bliss. He was back in 1965 with a choral piece and in 1968 with his EOG commission, *Punch and Judy*, after which he was banished until 1977. Aldeburgh heard more regularly from its older discoveries – Bennett, Crosse and Williamson – and from its new one, David Bedford, whose brother Steuart was taking over Britten's conducting responsibilities. As for older 20th-century composers, the Festival discovered a passion for Percy Grainger in 1968. Stravinsky, though, remained out in the cold.

1977–82: A solar system without a sun

Though Britten's physical decline had long been evident (he had not performed at the Festival since 1971), his death in December 1976 came as a shock. Just over a year earlier Shostakovich had died. The 1976 Festival had presented new works by both: Britten's *Phaedra* in its world premiere and Shostakovich's Viola Sonata for the first time in Britain. Now Aldeburgh would have to look elsewhere for the new music that had always given it vitality.

One source was Britten's bottom drawer. The practice of digging out unpublished works had begun when the composer was still alive, with the revival of his student quartet in D (1975) and long-abandoned, long-tantalising first full-length stage work, *Paul Bunyan* (1976). Cautiously, starting with *Young Apollo* in 1979, the Britten Estate began releasing other music – pieces Britten had dropped or salvage operations worked on his many early scores for the theatre and radio. Thus Britten premieres continued intermittently through to the late 1990s.

But that could not be all. Bravely Pears commissioned works for himself not only from the familiar Bedford but from composers new to Aldeburgh: Robin Holloway, Colin Matthews, John Tavener and Krzstof Meyer (presumably a Lutoslawski recommendation). However, Pears' singing career was almost at an end after a stroke in 1980, and for the last five Festivals of his life (1981–5) he performed only as a reciter (in which role Holloway and Peter Paul Nash created new works for him).

One new breeze came from close by: the founding of the Britten–Pears School provided the Festival with a store of fresh talent, deployed for the first time in a 1979 production of *Eugene Onegin*. BPS productions were to supply the Festival with opera through the 1980s, replacing the English Opera Group (by now restyled English Music Theatre). The *Onegin* was conducted by Rostropovich, who had joined the board of artistic directors and retained that position until 1991, even though he never played at the Festival again, or even appeared at all, after conducting a concert in 1981. (In 1983–5 he had his own festival at Snape over an August weekend, which later became the Snape Proms.) By contrast, Perahia was present every year from 1977 to 1989. It was respect for him, for Pears, and for Britten's memory that kept the Festival going artistically, so that even these shaken years had their moments of glory. In 1981, for instance, there wre recitals by Ileana Cotrubas, Jan DeGaetani, Martti Talvela and Radu Lupu, a Mozart concerto twofer with Perahia, the Rostropovich concert repeating Shostakovich's Fourteenth Symphony, and, among new works, George Benjamin's A Mind of Winter.

1983–97: Plural worlds

The broadening of the board in 1983 brought in not only Perahia but also Oliver Knussen (who

had had a piece done back in 1969, when he was just 17) and Simon Rattle (who had not appeared at the Festival before). Rattle came with his Birmingham orchestra to the Festival almost every year until 1991, but the artistic direction seems to have been largely in the hands of Perahia, Knussen and Steuart Bedford, especially after Pears' death in 1986.

They made a diverse triumvirate and the Festival became – like so many majestic old cinemas at that time being replaced by multiplexes – a plurality, without much overlap between its areas of interest. Perahia attracted to Aldeburgh other pianists of his own generation (Lupu, Andras Schiff) and older (Cherkassky, Horszowski, Annie Fischer), but his collaborations with the other artistic directors tailed off after Pears' demise, as did theirs with each other. Bedford was usually responsible for BPS enterprises, for accompanying singers and for an English Chamber Orchestra concert; Knussen's band was the London Sinfonietta. Both conductors programmed Britten (as did Rattle), but otherwise Knussen's main concern was new music (though he also helped redress the neglect of Stravinsky). He and Bedford were, from 1990, the sole executive artistic directors.

Knussen invited a sequence of distinguished composers-in-residence, starting with Takemitsu (1984), Dutilleux (1985) and Henze (1986), and in 1983 a composers' competition was instituted in Britten's name, with the young Mark-Anthony Turnage the first winner. Turnage was back in 1990 as one of the first composers given the chance to create a portrait concert; that was how Aldeburgh in 1995 first got to hear the name and the music of Thomas Adès. Also that year came an Elliott Carter premiere, while other composers arriving to supervise new pieces during this period ranged across the generations from Goehr and Birtwistle to Julian Anderson, Sam Hayden and Joseph Phibbs.

If new music at Aldeburgh was thriving again, another of the Festival's original purposes, to present small-scale opera, became harder to maintain in financially difficult times. The production of new opera stalled: John Tavener's *Mary of Egypt* (1992) was the first since Musgrave's *The Voice of Ariadne*, 18 years before. The Festival even had to buy in productions of *The Burning Fiery Furnace* from Kent Opera in 1989, of *Curlew River* from Japan in 1991 and of all three church parables – those central items of its legacy – from Birmingham in 1997.

1998 to present: Reintegration

An association with the Almeida Theatre, of Islington, enabled the Festival to start presenting chamber operas annually again from 1998. The next year Adès took over as artistic director, John Woolrich joining him as 'guest' in 2004 and 'associate' after that.

There might be a temptation to see Adès as a second Britten: a composer of astonishing gifts and an equally fine musician, too, at the piano or on the conductor's podium. However, Adès is not at all (yet) as prolific a composer as Britten, and Aldeburgh has been hearing only two or three pieces of his each year (in 2003 there were none). Instead he and Woolrich have revived some of the Festival's old enthusiasms (notably Janácek) and added new ones, from senior masters - Kurtag, Ligeti, Birtwistle – through the middle generation of Brian Ferneyhough and Gerald Barry (joining the established Aldeburgh residents Knussen and Colin Matthews) to Emily Hall. These composers have little in common apart from being extremely themselves. They have helped make the Festival an exciting forum for new music, one to which other composers of international renown - Salvatore Sciarrino, Poul Ruders, Mauricio Kagel – happily come for first performances.

In other respects the festival has reasserted its traditions: chamber music and song, choral music from the Renaissance to the present day, and everything seen through a lens on musical history that emphasises Purcell, Bach and Handel, Mozart and Schubert, Mahler and Shostakovich, Britten, of course, and, no less importantly, his successors. Recovering its past, Aldeburgh is also recovering its future.

Reprinted from the Festival programme book, 2007

John Woolrich and Thomas Adès. (Photograph by Nigel Luckhurst)

Notes on Contributors

Dawn Adès is Professor of Art History and Theory at the University of Essex and Director of the University of Essex Collection of Latin American art. She has published widely on Surrealism, and curated or co-curated many exhibitions, including latterly *Undercover Surrealism: Georges Bataille and Documents* (2006).

W. H. (Wystan Hugh) Auden (1907–73) was regarded by many as one of the greatest writers of the twentieth century. In the 1930s he collaborated with Britten on films for the GPO Film Unit, plays and songs, and wrote the libretto for *Paul Bunyan*.

Dame Janet Baker CH is one of the great mezzo-sopranos of the age, and is particularly associated with baroque and early Italian opera and the works of Benjamin Britten.

Richard Barber is a medieval historian, publisher, and author of many books on the Middle Ages, including lives of Henry II, the Black Prince, and of Edward III and the first Knights of the Garter. He has lived in Suffolk for the past thirty years, and has sailed off the East Coast since the 1950s.

Neil Bartlett is a theatre and (sometimes) opera director. His most recent novel, *Skin Lane*, was shortlisted for the Costa Award.

George Behrend, a self-confessed railway fanatic, worked as an assistant to Benjamin Britten from 1947–58 and was involved in the early years of the Festival, as he recounts in his memoir *An Unexpected Life*.

Adrian Bell (1901–80) was the author of many books on rural life beginning in 1930 with the publication of the first title in his trilogy *Corduroy*, *Silver Ley* and *The Cherry Tree*. He was also the compiler of the first and many subsequent *Times* crossword puzzles. *The Flower and the Wheel* was published in 1949.

Anne Beresford has published 13 books of poetry and one book of translations, among them *The Lair* (1968), *The Curving Shore* (1975), *Selected Poems* (1997), and *Hearing Things* (2002), and *Collected Poems* (2006). She lives in Suffolk.

Ronald Blythe's work includes poetry, essays, short stories, history, novels and literary criticism over a long and distinguished career. His study of Suffolk village life, *Akenfield*, is now a Penguin Modern Classic.

Ian Bostridge took part in the French song course and the English song course at the Britten–Pears School in 1989 and 1990 with Suzanne Danco, Hugues Cuénod and Ian Partridge. He has sung the Britten roles of Lysander, Flute, the Male Chorus, Captain Vere, Peter Quint and Gustav von Aschenbach; Britten's five orchestral song cycles, which he has also recorded; and most of Britten's songs for voice and piano. He performs regularly at Aldeburgh.

Alfred Brendel is known as one of the most distinguished pianists of the recent decades, and an occasional poet and essayist. He performed regularly at the Aldeburgh Festival until 2008, when he retired from the stage.

Craig Brown is the author of many humorous books, including *The Hounding of John Thomas* and *Imaginary Friends*. He is a regular columnist for the *Daily Telegraph*, *Vanity Fair*, the *Mail on Sunday* and, for the past twenty years, *Private Eye*. He lives in Aldeburgh.

James Cable was born in Aldeburgh in 1851 of a long line of lifeboatmen, and wrote a memoir of his action-packed life as coxswain, *A Lifeboatman's Days*.

Jon Canter is a comedy scriptwriter and novelist whose works include *Seeds of Greatness* (2006) and *A Short Gentleman* (2008). He has lived in

Aldeburgh since 1993 with the painter Helen Napper and their daughter.

Martin Carver is Professor of Archaeology at York and Editor of *Antiquity*. He has directed research at the Sutton Hoo archaeological site since 1983, and has just brought to light a seventh-century monastery in north-east Scotland, published as Portmahomack. Monastery of the Picts.

Rupert Christiansen is the opera critic for the *Daily Telegraph* and author of several books on the subject, including *Prima Donna* and *The Pocket Guide to Opera*.

Kenneth Clark (1903–83), one of the most distinguished art historians of his generation, was a museum director, broadcaster and author who grew up at Sudbourne Hall, 'the other side of the Alde'.

Nicholas Clark is Curator for Reader Services at The Britten–Pears Foundation. Apart from Britten his other principal research interest is 19th-century English literature, on which he has published a number of articles. He is currently writing a history of The Britten–Pears Library.

Ian Collins is an art writer and curator. His books include *A Broad Canvas: Art in East Anglia Since 1880* and *Making Waves: Artists in Southwold*. In 1997 he curated a 50-artist show for the 50th Aldeburgh Festival. He lives in Southwold and the Barbican.

William 'Wilkie' Collins (1824–89) was the hugely popular author of 27 novels, among them *The Woman in White* and *The Moonstone*, as well as numerous short stories and plays.

Aaron Copland (1900–90) was a prolific American composer, pianist and conductor, whose music achieved a balance between modernism and American folk styles.

George Crabbe (1754–1832), poet, naturalist and clergyman, was the Suffolk-born author of *The Village* and *The Borough*, and the creator of the story of *Peter Grimes*.

Caroline Cranbrook is married to the 5th Earl of Cranbrook. She has lived and farmed at Great Glemham in the Alde Valley since 1970. Her main interest is the rural economy and she has undertaken landmark research in East Suffolk, publishing *Food Webs* (1998) and *The Real Choice* (2006) for the CPRE.

Gathorne Cranbrook (5th Earl of Cranbrook) was brought up in the warm family atmosphere of Great Glemham. The circle of friends included Ben Britten and Eric Crozier, who borrowed the names of Gay, Juliet, Sophie, Tina, Hugh, Jonny and Sam Gathorne-Hardy for characters in *The Little Sweep* (*Let's Make an Opera*).

Kevin Crossley-Holland published his *Selected Poems* in 2001 and, with Norman Ackroyd, *Moored Man: Poems of North Norfolk* in 2006. He has translated *Boewulf* and many of the shorter Anglo-Saxon poems and is a Carnegie Medal-winning author for children. He wrote the libretto for Nicola LeFanu's *The Wildman*, premiered at the Aldeburgh Festival in 1995.

Eric Crozier (1914–94), theatre director and librettist, was co-founder and first artistic director of the Aldeburgh Festival with Britten and Pears, with whom he had a long and fruitful friendship and collaboration.

Jan Dalley is the Arts Editor of the *Financial Times*. She is the author of a biography of Diana Mosley (1999) and a study of the myth of the Black Hole of Calcutta (2006), as well as numerous articles and reviews. She has three children and lives in London.

Roger Deakin (1943–2006) was a writer, naturalist and documentary film-maker based in a moated grange in north Suffolk, and author of *Waterlog* and *Wildwood*.

Peter Dickinson, the composer and pianist, is emeritus professor, University of Keele and University of London. He has written or edited several books about twentieth-century music, including *Copland Connotations* (2002), *The Music of Lennox Berkeley* (2003), *CageTalk* (2006) and *Lord Berners* (2008).

Patrick Dillon is a writer and architect. He has written histories of the eighteenth-century Gin Craze and of the Glorious Revolution and is now completing a children's history of the British Isles. As an architect with Haworth Tompkins he has spent the past three years on the redevelopment of Snape Maltings, including the new buildings for Aldeburgh Music.

James Dodds left school early to train as a shipwright, rebuilding Thames barges before studying painting at the Royal College of Art. One his first exhibitions was at the 1984 Aldeburgh Festival, followed by several more Festival exhibitions, and his work is sold internationally.

Laurence Edwards studied traditional metal casting in India after graduating from the Royal College of Art. In 1990 he settled in Suffolk, establishing a foundry and studios at Butley, near Orford. His award-winning work is exhibited in the UK and Europe.

George Ewart Evans was born in South Wales in 1909 and died in 1988. After a career in teaching he and his family moved to Blaxhall in Suffolk. He became an oral historian; he wrote eleven books, and did numerous programmes for the BBC.

Matthew Evans, the son of George Ewart Evans, was born in 1941. He worked at Faber & Faber and was made a Life Peer in 2000.

James Fenton has been a journalist, critic, poet and academic. He was Professor of Poetry at Oxford from 1994–9 and received the Queen's Gold Medal for Poetry in 2007.

Edward Morgan Forster (1879–1970) was an acclaimed novelist and essayist, and wrote the libretto for *Billy Budd* (based on Melville's novel) for Britten in 1951.

Matthew Fort's food writing career began in 1986 when he began a column about food in the *Financial Times Saturday Review*. In 1989 he became Food & Drink Editor of the *Guardian*, a position he still holds. Since then he has written for a wide variety of British, American and French publications.

Bettina Furnée is an artist who uses language. Her project 'If Ever You're in the Area' took place at two art venues and coastal sites in East Anglia during 2005–06, in collaboration with writers Simon Frazer and Tony Mitton.

Jason Gathorne-Hardy (Lord Medway) was born near Ulu Gombak in Malaysia and grew up at Great Glemham in Suffolk. He works as an artist, farmer and food promoter. He is the founder of Alde Valley Food Adventures, Alde Valley Lamb and Patron of the Bario Food Festival in the Kelabit Highlands of Central Borneo.

David Gentleman is an artist, illustrator and designer who studied at the Royal College of Art under Edward Bawden and John Nash. He married the daughter of George Ewart Evans and illustrated several of his father-in-law's books.

Lamorna Good is a painter who lives in part of the house in Aldeburgh built by the first Marquess of Salisbury. She is writing a book about the house. She is also organising a survey and a 24-hour record of Aldeburgh in 2009 on behalf of the Aldeburgh and District Local History Society.

Lavinia Greenlaw is a poet and novelist, and Professor of Creative Writing at the University of East Anglia. Her last book of poems was *Minsk* (2003) and she published her first non-fiction, *The Importance of Music to Girls*, in

2007. She has collaborated with a number of composers, writing song texts and libretti. She lives in London.

Joyce Grenfell (1910–79) was an actress, comedienne and writer of inimitable songs for the stage. She was a regular visitor and sometime performer at the Aldeburgh Festival.

Paul Griffiths was a Hesse Student at the 1970 festival and began writing music criticism professionally the following year. He has published many books on music, as well as three novels and various librettos.

Christopher Grogan is Director of Collections and Heritage for the Britten–Pears Foundation. He is the editor of *Imogen Holst: A Life in Music* (Boydell Press, 2007) and is currently managing a major project to develop a web-based thematic catalogue for the works of Benjamin Britten.

Kathleen Hale (1898–2000) was an artist, ilustrator and author of children's books, best remembered for her series about Orlando the Marmalade Cat, who visited Owlbarrow.

Maggi Hambling studied at the East Anglian School of Painting under Cedric Morris from 1960, was the first Artist in Residence at the National Gallery, and is widely known for her portraits and sculptures such as *Memorial to Oscar Wilde* and *Scallop*.

Michael Hamburger (1924–2007) settled in Suffolk after an academic career in England and America. He won many awards for his translations from Baudelaire, Celan and Hölderlin, among others. His acclaimed critical study *The Truth of Poetry* was published in 1968. His *Collected Poems* (1995), drawing on some 20 earlier books, was followed by five more; the last, *Circling the Square*, was published in 2007, the year of his death.

Lord Harewood is an acknowledged expert on opera, known to aficionados throughout the world for his definitive work as Editor of *Kobbé's Complete Opera Book*. He was Artistic Director of Edinburgh Festival (1961-65), Director of the Leeds Festival (1958-74) and Managing Director of English National Opera (1972-85) and of Opera North (1978-81).

Edwin Heathcote is an architect and writer living and working in London. He is the architecture and design critic of the *Financial Times* and has written about a dozen books on cities, buildings and things.

Paul Heiney is a TV and radio presenter who has farmed with horses for ten years in Suffolk, where he lives with his wife Libby Purves. He is the author of several books including *Last Man Across the Atlantic*, about his participation in the single-handed transatlantic race in 2005.

Hans Werner Henze is a German composer well known for his left-wing political convictions. He has lived in Italy since 1953, and made several visits to the Aldeburgh Festival over the decades.

Susan Hill was brought up in Scarborough and became a noted and prolific writer of novels, short stories and non-fiction. She acknowledges a strong debt to the influence of Benjamin Britten.

Imogen Holst (1907–84), only child of Gustav Holst, was a composer and conductor who became close friends with and music assistant to Benjamin Britten. She was joint Artistic Director of the Aldeburgh Festival from 1956 to 1977.

Steven Isserlis is one of the world's leading cellists. In addition to his impressive performance history he has a prolific discography and is the author of two children's books, *Why Beethoven Threw the Stew* and *Why Handel Waggled His Wig*.

Paul Kildea is a conductor and author. He has written extensively on twentieth-century music and culture, including two acclaimed books on Benjamin Britten for Oxford University Press.

Michael Laskey has lived in Suffolk for thirty years. He co-founded the Aldeburgh Poetry Festival in 1989 and directed it through its first decade. He has published four collections – *Thinking of Happiness*, *The Tightrope Wedding* and *Permission to Breathe* and most recently *The Man Alone: New & Selected Poems* (2008).

Kirsten Lavers lives in Cambridge where she is engaged in a variety of projects as artist and photographer.

Alun Lewis (1915–44) was a soldier and poet, born in Wales and killed in Burma in 1944, also known for a volume of short stories, *The Last Inspection* (1942).

Simon Loftus attended the first performance of Britten's *Noye's Fludde* in1958, spent two consecutive Aldeburgh Festivals as a Hesse Student and is now a member of the Council of Aldeburgh Music. He has lived and worked in Suffolk all his life.

Herbert Lomas was a regular critic for Alan Ross's *London Magazine* for thirty years and is a long-term critic for *Ambit*. *The Vale of Todmorden* (2003) is the most recent of his ten books of poetry, and he has received Guinness,

Arvon and Cholmondely awards. He lives in Aldeburgh.

Richard Mabey is the prize-winning author of some 30 books on the relation between landscape, nature and culture, including *Flora Britannica*, *Whistling in the Dark*, *Nature Cure* and *Beechcombings: the Narratives of Trees*. He writes regularly for the *Guardian*, *Times* and *Granta*, is Patron of the John Clare Society and lives in the Suffolk–Norfolk border country.

Christopher Matthew is the author of *Now We Are Sixty*, *Now We Are Sixty (and a Bit)* and *When We Were Fifty*, and the creator of Simon Crisp, the hapless hero of *Diary of a Somebody*. He was last heard on Radio 4 going off in all directions with Alan Coren in *Freedom Pass*. He lives in Suffolk and London.

Colin Matthews is a composer whose music has been played worldwide since the early 1970s. He worked closely with Benjamin Britten and Imogen Holst, and is now chairman of the Britten Estate, a trustee of the Britten–Pears Foundation and has close links with the Aldeburgh Festival and the Britten–Pears Young Artist Programme.

Ian McMillan is a poet, journalist and broadcaster who hosts *The Verb* on BBC Radio 3.

Tim Miller was born and brought up in East Suffolk. He lives at Shingle Street and in London, where he was Senior Tutor in Film and Fellow of the Royal College of Art. He is a screenwriter (*The Warrior*, *Far North*) and works with the director Asif Kapadia.

Donald Mitchell CBE was Britten's publisher from 1965 and has long been internationally recognised as a leading authority on both Britten and Mahler. He is author of *Benjamin Britten: Pictures from a Life* (with John Evans), *Britten and Auden in the Thirties*, and the *Cambridge Opera Handbook on Death in Venice*.

Mark Mitchels taught at Woodbridge School for many years, where he was Head of Cultural Studies. With his wife Elizabeth he has written a number of successful books about East Anglia. He is well known as a lecturer speaking on subjects from Elizabethan theatre to the lost city of Dunwich.

Blake Morrison is a poet, author and Professor of Creative and Life Writing at Goldsmiths, University of London.

Andrew Motion is a poet, novelist and biographer, and currently Britain's Poet Laureate. He also holds the Chair of Creative

Writing at Royal Holloway and Bedford College, University of London.

Graham Murrell taught at and later headed the Photography department at St Martin's School of Art from 1967–2001, since when he has exhibited widely. His work on 'Silence' was shown at Snape Maltings Concert Hall in 2008.

John Nash (1893–1997) was the younger brother of Paul Nash, and also served as a war artist in the First World War. Thereafter he mainly painted landscapes, and settled with his wife in a house on the Suffolk-Essex border which he bequeathed to Ronald Blythe.

Sidney Nolan (1917–92) was one of Australia's best-known painters and printmakers, most famous for his iconic series on Ned Kelly in the Australian outback. He became a close friend of Britten and Pears in the 1960s.

Mark Padmore was born in London and grew up in Canterbury. His Aldeburgh connections include two opera courses at the Britten–Pears School – *Don Giovanni* with Suzanne Danco and *Falstaff* with Renato Capecchi – and the John Passion residency. He is a frequent visitor to the Aldeburgh Festival.

John Piper (1903–92) was a prolific painter and print-maker, designer of sets for theatre and opera, and of stained windows for Coventry Cathedral and the church in Aldeburgh. He enjoyed a long and fruitful friendship with Britten.

Andrew Plant is a pianist and musicologist. He is Assistant Director of Music at St George's School, Windsor Castle, and appears frequently as an accompanist to established artists and rising young singers. He has contributed to several scholarly publications and until recently was Curator for Exhibitions at the Britten–Pears Foundation.

Katrina Porteous is a poet based on the Northumberland coast. In 2002 she was Writer-in-Residence at the Aldeburgh Poetry Festival and wrote *Longshore Drift* for BBC Radio 3's *The Verb*. Katrina's other publications include *The Lost Music* and *The Blue Lonnen*.

Mary Potter (1900–81) studied at the Slade and became a celebrated painter and a close friend of Britten and Pears, who built up a significant collection her work at the Red House.

Neil Powell is a poet and author of several biographies, *George Crabbe: An English Life* (2004) and *Amis & Son: Two Literary Generations* (2008) among them. He lives in Suffolk.

Alan Powers is Professor of Architecture and Cultural History at the University of Greenwich, Chairman of the Twentieth-Century Society and a specialist in mid-twentieth-century art and design. He has published widely on architecture and design, and organised exhibitions on the work of Tayler & Green and H. T. Cadbury-Brown, among others. He has visited East Suffolk every summer of his life.

David Ramsbotham was appointed HM Chief Inspector of Prisons in 1995 after a 41-year career in the army, from which he retired in the rank of General. From 2004 to 2007 he chaired the Koestler Arts Trust, dedicated to bringing arts to offenders. He was appointed a crossbench member of the House of Lords in 2005.

Simon Read is an artist who 29 years ago solved a living/studio problem by buying a barge in Holland and sailing it over to the Suffolk Coast. This was to be the start of an enquiry into the tension between land and sea that has developed and informed his work ever since.

Norman Scarfe, a native of Suffolk, is a historian who has taught at Leicester University and written frequently on aspects of Suffolk history for Aldeburgh Festival programme books. He has attended every Festival except the first, prevented by sitting his Finals at Oxford.

W.G. (Winfred Georg) Sebald (1944-2001) was a German writer and academic who held the chair of European Literature at the University of East Anglia, until his untimely death in an accident at the age of 57.

William Servaes (1921–99) moved to Suffolk in 1967 with his wife Pat and five children, from a Royal Naval background. Britten appointed him General Manager of the Festival in 1971, and he played an integral part in the creation of the Britten–Pears School for Advanced Musical Studies, until his retirement in 1980.

Tom Service writes about music for the *Guardian* and is a regular contributor to the *BBC Music Magazine*, *Opera* and *Tempo*. He has presented *Music Matters* on BBC Radio 3 since 2003.

Nick Sinclair is a photographer who settled in Aldeburgh in 2003. He has had exhibitions of portraits at the National Portrait Gallery in 1994 and 1998. Recent projects on the landscape and the environment include *Water, Ice, Vapour* at the Winchester Gallery, 2008.

Montagu Slater (1902–56) was a poet, novelist and playwright involved, with Britten and Auden, in many of the John Grierson documentaries such as *Coal Face* and chosen by Britten to be the librettist for his opera *Peter Grimes*.

Frances Spalding CBE is an art historian and biographer. Her books include *British Art since 1900*, a centenary history of the Tate and lives of Roger Fry, Vanessa Bell, John Minton, Duncan Grant and Gwen Raverat. Her biography of John and Myfanwy Piper will be published by Oxford University Press in 2009.

Derek Sugden, structural engineer and acoustician, has been involved in the creation and conservation of auditoria throughout the UK, including Snape Maltings, the Theatre Royal, Glasgow, the Bridgewater Hall, Manchester and the opera houses at Buxton and Glyndebourne. He is a founder partner of Arup Associates and founder principal of Arup Acoustics and has attended the Aldeburgh Festival almost every year since 1957.

Elizabeth Sweeting was General Manager of the Aldeburgh Festival from 1948 to 1955, then became General Manager of the Oxford Playhouse for twenty years. Following this she went to Adelaide as Director of the Arts Council of South Australia. In 1971 she was awarded the MBE for services to the arts.

Ian Tait, as a GP in Aldeburgh from 1959 to 1990, was medical adviser to Benjamin Britten and Peter Pears. Sailing on the Alde has been an important part of his life. Two small volumes of his poems, *River Songs* and *Wave Watch*, reflect his feelings for the river and the Suffolk coast.

William Taylor is an Anglican priest. His book about the changing face of the East End of London, *This Bright Field*, was published by Methuen in 2000.

Julian Tennyson (1915–45) was, with Adrian Bell, George Ewart Evans and Ronald Blythe, one of the great writers about rural Suffolk life in the twentieth century. He was killed in Burma at the age of 29.

Marion Thorpe CBE is the daughter of Erwin Stein, publisher and close friend of Britten, and attended virtually all world premieres of his works. Before her marriage she played the piano parts in the first Aldeburgh Festival in *The Little Sweep* and *St Nicolas*, and remained a close friend of Britten all his life.

Anthony Thwaite OBE is author of fifteen volumes of poetry, has been a publisher and literary editor of *The Listener* and *New Statesman*, and has lectured at universities worldwide.

Steve Tompkins is senior partner, with Graham Haworth, of the award-winning Haworth Tompkins architectural practice, which is responsible for the design and conversion of the new music campus at Snape.

David Toop is a composer, author and sound curator. He has written four books including *Ocean of Sound* and *Haunted Weather*, and is in the process of completing a fifth, entitled *Ways of Hearing*. In 2000 he curated *Sonic Boom* for the Hayward Gallery, and his solo albums include *Black Chamber* and *Sound Body*.

Roger Vignoles is one of the foremost piano accompanists of our time. During the 1970s a frequent participant at the Britten–Pears School, he is now a regular visitor as teacher, giving masterclasses to young singers and pianists of the next generation.

Brian Whelan is a London-Irish artist who has had a studio in East Anglia for twenty years. What drew him to Suffolk and Norfolk were the medieval churches. He has a painting permanently hung in St Edmundsbury Cathedral as well as other holy places around Europe.

Alison Wilding RA is a leading British sculptor, twice nominated for the Turner Prize, who has had major exhibitions devoted to her work at the Serpentine, Tate and MoMA New York. *Migrant* is one of several site-specific commissions.

Louise K. Wilson is a visual artist, researcher and lecturer. Her work explores perceptual and cultural aspects of science and technology. She has undertaken many artist residencies and commissions and exhibited widely in North America and Europe. In 2006 she was awarded a NESTA Fellowship to explore the acoustics of Cold War sites.

John Woolrich is a composer. He was Guest Artistic Director of the Aldeburgh Festival in 2004 and has been Associate Artistic Director since 2005.

Jeremy Young is a location photographer based in Suffolk. He has been a regular contributor to national magazines, but currently works mainly for architectural practices. He also shoots large-format landscapes and Aldeburgh beach is a favorite location.

Acknowledgements

Any anthologist has extensive debts to acknowledge, and we have more than most, as so many of our contributors have generously waived fees for essays, poems and images both new and already published; our gratitude to them all, on behalf of Aldeburgh Music. Our thanks also to Jane Alexander for her support throughout this project and for all she does for Aldeburgh Music, Ronald Blythe for his inspiration and encouragement, David Andren, Richard Barber, Peter Clifford and Mike Webb at Boydell and Brewer, Jane Bellingham, Ian Collins, Commissions East, Marc Ernesti, Paul Fincham, Lavinia Greenlaw, Jeremy Greenwood, Jane Heath, John and Mary James, Stephen Lock, Colin Matthews, Tim Miller, Donald Mitchell, Caroline Reekie, Norman Scarfe, Alan Swerdlow and Marion Thorpe. We are grateful to Peter Silk and Sara Lewis of Silk Pearce for so generously donating the design for this book, and to Simon Loxley for its layout.

Apart from the authors themselves, particular thanks are due to the following for permission to reproduce contributions: Faber & Faber Ltd and Random House Inc. for W.H. Auden's 'The Composer'; Anthea Bell for 'The Power of Patience' by Adrian Bell, extracted from *The Flower and the Wheel*; Alfred Brendel and Faber & Faber Ltd for 'Brms'; Jon Canter and Random House for 'An Aldeburgh Boyhood', extracted from *A Short Gentleman*; Margaret Hanbury for 'The Other Side of the Alde' by Kenneth Clark; the Aaron Copland Fund for Music, Inc. for Aaron Copland's 'A Visit to Snape'; Enitharmon Press and Kevin Crossley-Holland for 'The Aldeburgh Band'; the Estate of Eric Crozier for 'Writing an Opera' and 'The Origin of the Aldeburgh Festival'; Robert Macfarlane for 'To the Sea' by Roger Deakin, and additionally Penguin Books for Deakin's 'The Crabbe Apple', extracted from *Wildwood: A Journey Through Trees*; Matthew Evans for 'Snape and the Malt House' by George Ewart Evans, and the second part of his own memoir of his father, privately published in 2003; the Provost and Scholars of King's College, Cambridge and the Society of Authors as the Literary Representatives of the Estate of E.M. Forster for 'George Crabbe' and 'Looking Back on the First Aldeburgh Festival'; Sheil Land Associates for Joyce Grenfell's 'One of my Pleasant Places', extracted from *Joyce and Ginnie: The Letters of Joyce Grenfell and Virginia Graham*; Frederick Warne & Co. for 'Owlbarrow' by Kathleen Hale, extracted from *A Slender Reputation*, and the image of Owlbarrow from *Orlando's Seaside Holiday*; Richard Hamburger for both 'Winter Sun, East Suffolk' by Michael Hamburger, and for his translation of W.G. Sebald's *After Nature*; G. and I. Holst Ltd for 'Folk-Songs' by Imogen Holst; the Estate of Frank Hussey for 'Fitz and the Sea'; Andrew Motion and United Agents for 'Salt Water'; the Random House Group for the extract from *After Nature* by W.G. Sebald; Elizabeth

Fargher for 'Call me "Imo"' by William Servaes, extracted from 'Aldeburgh Interlude: My Decade as a Festival Manager 1971–1980', an unpublished memoir; Beris Hudson for 'News from Aldeburgh' by Elizabeth Sweeting; the Tennyson Estate for extracts from Julian Tennyson's *Suffolk Scene*; Margaret Young and John Blatchly for 'A Curious Sort of Tail' by Giles Scroggins.

As for illustrations, we are indebted to Ronald Blythe for the drawings by John Nash; the Brandt Estate; the Trustees of the British Museum for figs 6 and 8 and the Suffolk County Council Archaeological Service for figs 2, 3 and 10 in Martin Carver's 'Ancestral Airs'; James Dodds and the Jardine Press; Laurence Edwards; Jason Gathorne-Hardy; David Gentleman; Maggi Hambling; Diana Hughes and the Aldeburgh Museum for photographs of the flood and coastal erosion; Kirsten Lavers; Clarissa Lewis for John Piper's *Clymping Beach*, his Aldeburgh Parish Church window and 'Loxford'; Griselda Lewis for the first Aldeburgh Festival poster; Nigel Luckhurst; Lady Nolan for Sidney Nolan's *The Initiation*; Graham Murrell; Julia Pipe for photographs of Snape maltsters; Steve Tompkins; Nick Sinclair; Alison Wilding; Louise K. Wilson and Jeremy Young.

The Britten–Pears Foundation has been enormously supportive and we are grateful for its permission to reprint writings by Benjamin Britten and Peter Pears. The staff at the Britten–Pears Library, Nicholas Clark, Kevin Gosling, Christopher Grogan and Andrew Plant, could not have been more helpful in answering queries and in supplying the photographs on pp. 123, 139, 145, 156, 168, 173, 200, 232.

Aldeburgh Music Development Plan

This £16 million development project securing the future of Snape Maltings Concert Hall and developing new rehearsal, performances and ancillary spaces was conceived and realised from 2003 to 2009 with the support of the following, amongst many others.

The Executive Group, who spearheaded the successful fundraising, brilliantly led by Dennis Stevenson with William Kendall, Trevor Pickett, Simon Robey and Robert Swannell.

The fundraising staff headed up by Julia Ransome with Victoria Dickie and supported by Nicola Anderson, Kerstin Davey, Duke Dobing and Kate Lloyd. Our campaign Aldeburgh Ambassadors and Artistic Patrons.

The professional team that realised the project led by architects Haworth Tompkins with Applied Solutions, Arup Acoustics, Charcoalblue, Clarke and Simpson, Davis Langdon, Fenn Wright, Ernest Griffiths, Haymills, Linklaters, Prettys, Price & Myers all overseen by Sharon Goddard, whose determination and attention to detail made such a difference. Simon Burrage and Eversheds for so generously donating legal services.

The trustees of Aldeburgh Music and the Aldeburgh Music Endowment Fund, not mentioned above: Stephen Barter, Michael Flint, Tim Ingram, Simon Loftus, June de Moller, Trevor Phillips, Richard Wyatt, Sarah Zins.

All of the Aldeburgh Music staff not mentioned above, especially those who supported the development day-to-day: Terry Comer, David Edwards and Harry Young.

Andrea Stark and Arts Council England, and the Gooderham family.

Dennis and Charlotte Stevenson whose contribution to Aldeburgh Music has been immeasurable and to whom we all owe a deep debt of gratitude.

And the many, many very generous donors, too numerous to list here, who helped make Britten and Pears' dream a reality.

Index of Names and Places